Contents 3

Oceania, Oceans and Poles   Topographic maps

New Zealand _____ 69
Pacific Ocean _____ 70
Arctic Ocean   Antarctica ____ 71

topographic map of the Poles

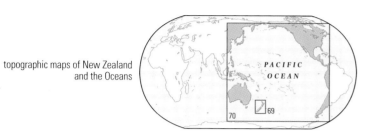

topographic maps of New Zealand and the Oceans

Africa   Thematic maps

Physical _____ 72
Political _____ 73
Seychelles   Mauritius _____ 73
Climate   Ecosystems _____ 74
Economy   Population _____ 75

Africa   Topographic maps

Northern Africa _____ 76–77
Southern Africa _____ 78
East Africa _____ 79

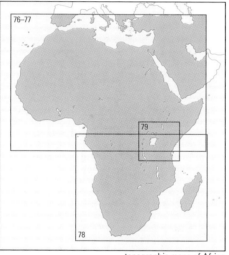

topographic maps of Africa

South America   Topographic map

South America _____ 90–91

South America   Thematic maps

Political _____ 91
Climate   Ecosystems _____ 92
Economy   Population _____ 93

topographic map of South America

North America   Thematic maps

Physical _____ 80
Political _____ 81
Climate   Ecosystems _____ 82
Economy   Population _____ 83

North America   Topographic maps

Canada _____ 84–85
United States of America _____ 86–87
Mexico, Central America,
and the Caribbean _____ 88–89

topographic maps of North America

Datasets _____ 94–101
Flags _____ 102–103

How to use the Index ____ 104
Index _____ 105–120

Equatorial scale 1: 95 000 000 (main map

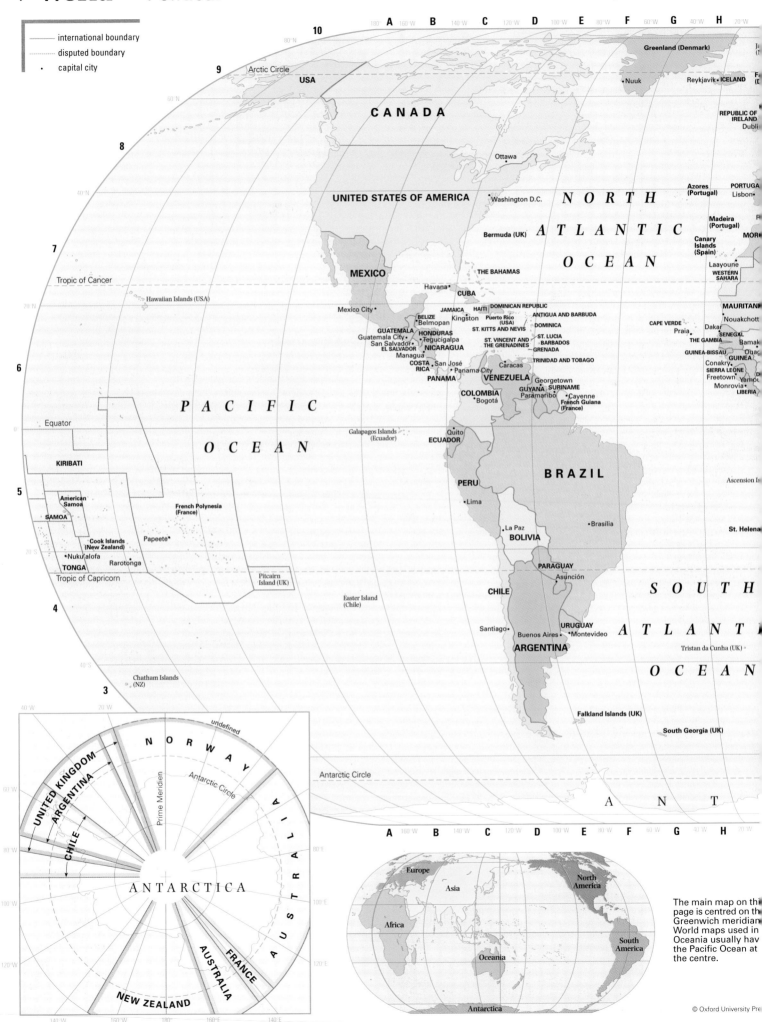

international boundary
disputed boundary
• capital city

10
9 Arctic Circle
8
7 Tropic of Cancer
6
Equator
5
Tropic of Capricorn
4
3

80°N
60°N
40°N
20°N
0
20°S
40°S

A 160°W B 140°W C 120°W D 100°W E 80°W F 60°W G 40°W H 20°W

Greenland (Denmark)

USA
Nuuk Reykjavik • ICELAND

CANADA

Ottawa

UNITED STATES OF AMERICA   • Washington D.C.

Azores
(Portugal)   PORTUGAL
Lisbon•
PORTUGA
(D

NORTH

Madeira
(Portugal)
MOR
Canary
Islands
(Spain)

Bermuda (UK)

ATLANTIC

MEXICO
Havana   CUBA
OCEAN
Laayoune
WESTERN
SAHARA

Mexico City•
Hawaiian Islands (USA)

JAMAICA HAITI DOMINICAN REPUBLIC
BELIZE   Kingston Puerto Rico ANTIGUA AND BARBUDA
Belmopan   (USA)
GUATEMALA   HONDURAS ST. KITTS AND NEVIS DOMINICA
Guatemala City•Tegucigalpa   ST. LUCIA
San Salvador• NICARAGUA   ST. VINCENT AND BARBADOS
EL SALVADOR   THE GRENADINES GRENADA
Managua
COSTA San José TRINIDAD AND TOBAGO
RICA •Panama City
PANAMA Caracas
VENEZUELA Georgetown
COLOMBIA GUYANA SURINAME
Bogotá Paramaribo Cayenne
French Guiana
(France)

MAURITANIA
Nouakchott

CAPE VERDE Dakar SENEGAL
Praia• THE GAMBIA Bamak
GUINEA-BISSAU Ouag
GUINEA
Conakry SIERRA LEONE
Freetown Yamo
Monrovia LIBERIA

PACIFIC
OCEAN

KIRIBATI

American
Samoa
SAMOA
Cook Islands
Nuku'alofa (New Zealand)
TONGA Rarotonga

French Polynesia
(France)

Papeete •

Pitcairn
Island (UK)

Galapagos Islands
(Ecuador)
Quito• ECUADOR

PERU
•Lima

La Paz• •Brasília
BOLIVIA

PARAGUAY
Asunción•

CHILE

Santiago• URUGUAY
Buenos Aires• •Montevideo
ARGENTINA

BRAZIL

Ascension Island

St. Helena

Tristan da Cunha (UK)

SOUTH

ATLANTI

OCEAN

Easter Island
(Chile)

Chatham Islands
(NZ)

Falkland Islands (UK)

South Georgia (UK)

Antarctic Circle

A N T

A 160°W B 140°W C 120°W D 100°W E 80°W F 60°W G 40°W H 20°W

UNITED KINGDOM
ARGENTINA
CHILE

NORWAY
undefined
Antarctic Circle
Prime Meridien

ANTARCTICA

AUSTRALIA

FRANCE
AUSTRALIA
NEW ZEALAND

40°W 20°W 80°E
60°W
80°W
100°W 100°E
120°W 120°E
140°W 160°W 180° 160°E 140°E

Europe
Asia North
America

Africa

Oceania South
America

Antarctica

The main map on thi
page is centred on th
Greenwich meridian
World maps used in
Oceania usually hav
the Pacific Ocean at
the centre.

© Oxford University Pre

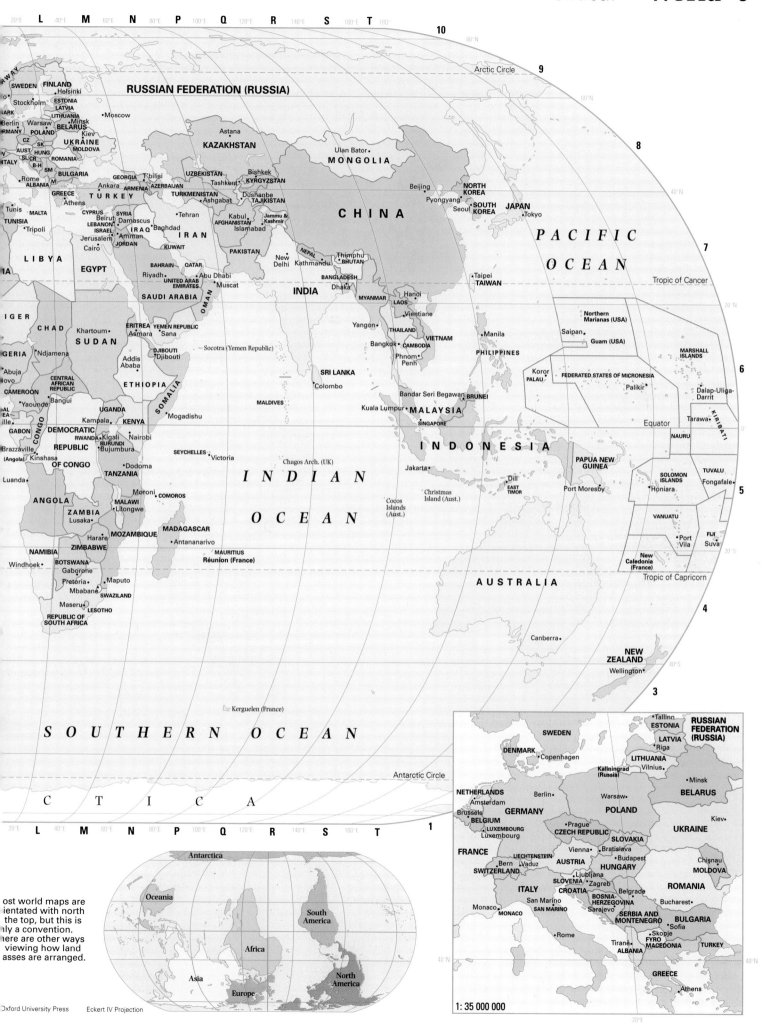

L 20°E 40°E M 60°E N 80°E P 100°E Q 120°E R 140°E S 160°E T 180°

10

9 Arctic Circle 80°N

8 60°N

7

Tropic of Cancer

6

Equator

5

4

Tropic of Capricorn

3

1

RUSSIAN FEDERATION (RUSSIA)

SWEDEN FINLAND
Helsinki
Stockholm
ESTONIA
LATVIA
LITHUANIA
Minsk
BELARUS
Berlin
Warsaw
POLAND
UKRAINE
MOLDOVA
CZ SK
AUST HUNG
ROMANIA
SL-CR
B-H
SM
BULGARIA
ALBANIA
Rome
GREECE
Athens
Moscow

KAZAKHSTAN
Astana

MONGOLIA
Ulan Bator

CHINA
Beijing
NORTH KOREA
Pyongyang
SOUTH KOREA
Seoul
JAPAN
Tokyo

UZBEKISTAN
Bishkek
KYRGYZSTAN
Tashkent
TURKMENISTAN
Ashgabat
Dushanbe
TAJIKISTAN
GEORGIA T'bilisi
Ankara ARMENIA
AZERBAIJAN
TURKEY
CYPRUS
Beirut
LEBANON
SYRIA Damascus
ISRAEL
Jerusalem
JORDAN Amman
IRAQ Baghdad
IRAN
Tehran
Kabul
AFGHANISTAN
Islamabad
Jammu & Kashmir
PAKISTAN
New Delhi
NEPAL
Kathmandu
BHUTAN
Thimphu
KUWAIT
BAHRAIN QATAR
Riyadh
Abu Dhabi
UNITED ARAB EMIRATES
Muscat
OMAN
SAUDI ARABIA
Cairo
EGYPT
LIBYA
TUNISIA
Tunis
Tripoli
MALTA

PACIFIC OCEAN

BANGLADESH
Dhaka
INDIA
MYANMAR
Hanoi
LAOS
Vientiane
Yangon
THAILAND
Bangkok
VIETNAM
CAMBODIA
Phnom Penh
Taipei
TAIWAN
Manila
PHILIPPINES
Northern Marianas (USA)
Saipan
Guam (USA)
MARSHALL ISLANDS
Dalap-Uliga-Darrit
KIRIBATI
Tarawa

NIGER
CHAD
Khartoum
ERITREA
Asmara
YEMEN REPUBLIC
Sana
Socotra (Yemen Republic)
SUDAN
Ndjamena
NIGERIA
Abuja
CENTRAL AFRICAN REPUBLIC
Bangui
CAMEROON
Yaoundé
DJIBOUTI
Djibouti
Addis Ababa
ETHIOPIA
SOMALIA
Mogadishu
SRI LANKA
Colombo
MALDIVES
Chagos Arch. (UK)
Bandar Seri Begawan BRUNEI
Kuala Lumpur
MALAYSIA
SINGAPORE
INDONESIA
Jakarta
FEDERATED STATES OF MICRONESIA
Koror PALAU
Palikir
NAURU

GABON
CONGO
Brazzaville
Kinshasa
DEMOCRATIC REPUBLIC OF CONGO
Luanda
ANGOLA
(Angola)
UGANDA
Kampala
KENYA
Nairobi
RWANDA Kigali
BURUNDI Bujumbura
TANZANIA
Dodoma
SEYCHELLES
Victoria
COMOROS
Moroni
MALAWI
Lilongwe
ZAMBIA
Lusaka
MOZAMBIQUE
MADAGASCAR
Antananarivo
ZIMBABWE
Harare
NAMIBIA
Windhoek
BOTSWANA
Gaborone
Pretoria
Maputo
Mbabane
SWAZILAND
Maseru LESOTHO
REPUBLIC OF SOUTH AFRICA
MAURITIUS
Réunion (France)

INDIAN OCEAN

Dili
EAST TIMOR
Christmas Island (Aust.)
Cocos Islands (Aust.)
PAPUA NEW GUINEA
Port Moresby
SOLOMON ISLANDS
Honiara
TUVALU
Fongafale
VANUATU
Port Vila
FIJI
Suva
New Caledonia (France)
AUSTRALIA
Canberra
NEW ZEALAND
Wellington

SOUTHERN OCEAN
Kerguelen (France)

Antarctic Circle

C T I C A

20°E L 40°E M 60°E N 80°E P 100°E Q 120°E R 140°E S 160°E T

NORWAY
SWEDEN
Stockholm
DENMARK
GERMANY
ITALY

40°N

Most world maps are orientated with north at the top, but this is only a convention. There are other ways of viewing how land masses are arranged.

Oxford University Press

Eckert IV Projection

Antarctica
Oceania
Africa
Asia
Europe
South America
North America

80°N
60°N
40°N

SWEDEN
DENMARK
Copenhagen
NETHERLANDS
Amsterdam
Berlin
GERMANY
Brussels
BELGIUM
LUXEMBOURG
Luxembourg
FRANCE
LIECHTENSTEIN
Bern
Vaduz
SWITZERLAND
ITALY
Monaco
MONACO
San Marino
SAN MARINO
Rome

ESTONIA
Tallinn
LATVIA
Riga
RUSSIAN FEDERATION (RUSSIA)
LITHUANIA
Vilnius
Kaliningrad (Russia)
Minsk
BELARUS
Warsaw
POLAND
Prague
CZECH REPUBLIC
SLOVAKIA
Vienna
Bratislava
AUSTRIA
Budapest
HUNGARY
SLOVENIA
Ljubljana
Zagreb
CROATIA
Belgrade
BOSNIA-HERZEGOVINA
Sarajevo
SERBIA AND MONTENEGRO
Tirané
ALBANIA
FYRO MACEDONIA
Skopje
GREECE
Athens
Kiev
UKRAINE
Chișinău
MOLDOVA
ROMANIA
Bucharest
BULGARIA
Sofia
TURKEY

1: 35 000 000

Equatorial scale 1: 95 000 00

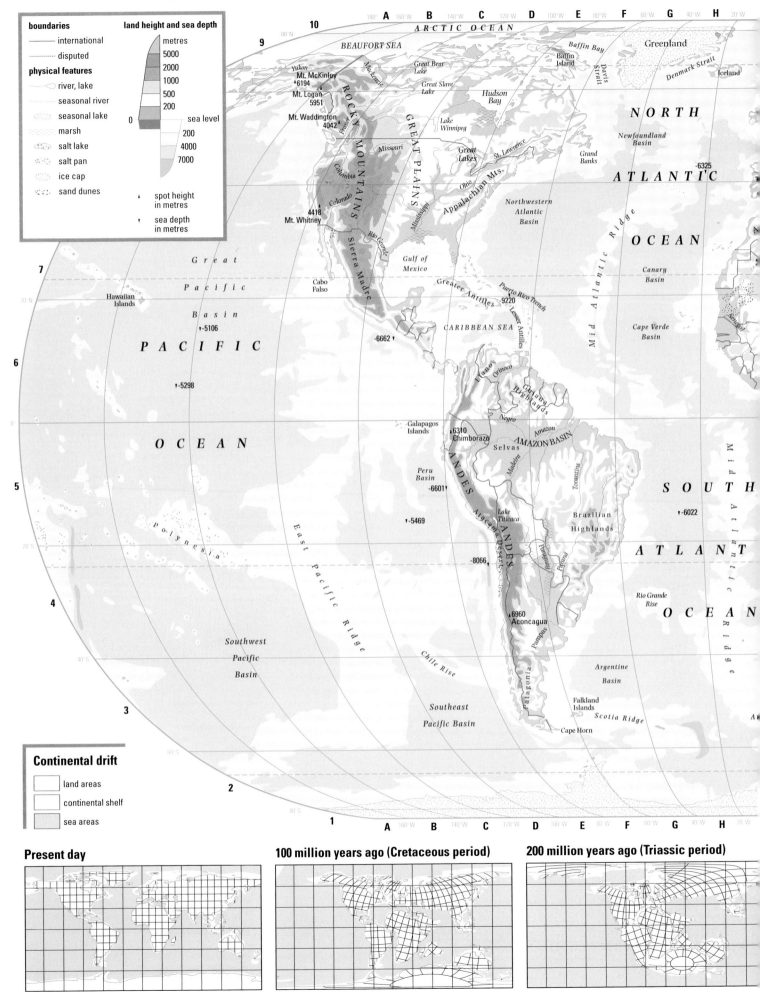

boundaries
———— international
·········· disputed

physical features
⌐◦ river, lake
———— seasonal river
⬭ seasonal lake
≈≈≈ marsh
⬭ salt lake
⋯ salt pan
⬭ ice cap
⋯ sand dunes

land height and sea depth
metres
5000
2000
1000
500
200
0 — sea level
200
4000
7000

▲ spot height in metres
▼ sea depth in metres

Continental drift
▢ land areas
▢ continental shelf
▨ sea areas

ARCTIC OCEAN
BEAUFORT SEA
Greenland
Baffin Bay
Baffin Island
Davis Strait
Denmark Strait
Iceland

Yukon
Mt. McKinley ▲6194
Mt. Logan 5951
Mt. Waddington ▲4042
Mackenzie
Great Bear Lake
Great Slave Lake
Hudson Bay
Lake Winnipeg
ROCKY MOUNTAINS
GREAT PLAINS
Missouri
Columbia
Colorado
4418 Mt. Whitney
Rio Grande
Sierra Madre
Great Lakes
St. Lawrence
Ohio
Mississippi
Appalachian Mts.

NORTH
Newfoundland Basin
Grand Banks
-6325
ATLANTIC
OCEAN

Great
Pacific
Basin
Hawaiian Islands
▼-5106
▼-5298
PACIFIC
OCEAN

Cabo Falso
Gulf of Mexico
Greater Antilles
-9220 Puerto Rico Trench
Lesser Antilles
CARIBBEAN SEA
-6662
Northwestern Atlantic Basin

Mid Atlantic Ridge
Canary Basin
Cape Verde Basin

Galapagos Islands
Llanos
Orinoco
Negro
Guiana Highlands
Amazon
AMAZON BASIN
Selvas
▲6310 Chimborazo
ANDES
Peru Basin
-6601▼
Madeira
Tocantins
Brazilian Highlands

SOUTH

-5469▼
Lake Titicaca
Atacama Desert
-8066▼
▲6960 Aconcagua
Pampas
Paraná
Paraguay
▼-6022
ATLANT
OCEAN
Rio Grande Rise

Polynesia

East Pacific Ridge

Southwest Pacific Basin

Chile Rise

Patagonia
Argentine Basin
Falkland Islands
Scotia Ridge
Cape Horn

Southeast Pacific Basin

Mid Atlantic Ridge

Present day

100 million years ago (Cretaceous period)

200 million years ago (Triassic period)

© Oxford University Pre

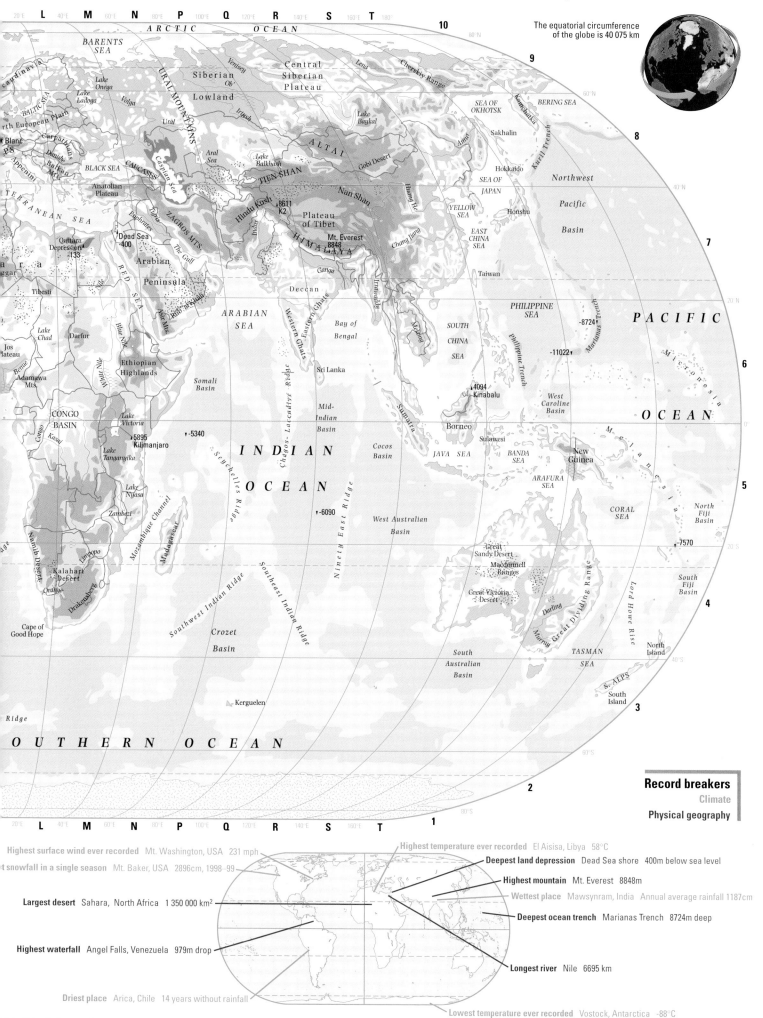

The equatorial circumference of the globe is 40 075 km

ARCTIC OCEAN

BARENTS SEA

Scandinavia
Lake Onega
Lake Ladoga
Baltic Sea
North European Plain
Blanc
Carpathians
Danube
Balkan Mts
Apennini
MEDITERRANEAN SEA
BLACK SEA
CAUCASUS
Anatolian Plateau
Sahara
Hoggar
Tibesti

Volga
Ural
URAL MOUNTAINS
Siberian Lowland
Ob
Yenisey
Irtysh
Aral Sea
Caspian Sea
ZAGROS MTS.
Euphrates
Tigris
Dead Sea -400
Qattara Depression -133
Arabian Peninsula
RED SEA
Asir Mts.
Rub' al Khali
The Gulf

Central Siberian Plateau
Lake Balkhash
ALTAI
TIEN SHAN
Hindu Kush
8611 K2
Plateau of Tibet
Nan Shan
Mt. Everest 8848
HIMALAYA
Indus
Ganga
Deccan
Western Ghats
Eastern Ghats

Lena
Chersky Range
Lake Baykal
Gobi Desert
Huang He
Chang Jiang
Amur
Taiwan

SEA OF OKHOTSK
Kamchatka
BERING SEA
Sakhalin
Hokkaido
Kuril Trench
SEA OF JAPAN
Honshu
EAST CHINA SEA
YELLOW SEA

Northwest Pacific Basin

Jos Plateau
Lake Chad
Darfur
Benue
Adamawa Mts.
CONGO BASIN
Congo
Kasai
White Nile
Blue Nile
Ethiopian Highlands
Somali Basin
Lake Victoria
-5895 Kilimanjaro
Lake Tanganyika
Lake Nyasa
Zambezi
Mozambique Channel
Madagascar
Namib Desert
Kalahari Desert
Orange
Limpopo
Drakensberg
Cape of Good Hope
Ridge

ARABIAN SEA
Chagos-Laccadive Ridge
Sri Lanka
Mid-Indian Basin
Bay of Bengal
Irrawaddy
Mekong
Sumatra
-5340
Seychelles Ridge
INDIAN OCEAN
Ninety East Ridge
-6090
West Australian Basin
Cocos Basin
JAVA SEA

SOUTH CHINA SEA
PHILIPPINE SEA
Philippine Trench
-8724
-11022
4094 Kinabalu
Borneo
Sulawesi
West Caroline Basin
BANDA SEA
New Guinea
ARAFURA SEA
Marianas Trench

PACIFIC OCEAN
Micronesia
Melanesia
North Fiji Basin
-7570
South Fiji Basin
CORAL SEA
Lord Howe Rise

Great Sandy Desert
Macdonnell Ranges
Great Victoria Desert
South Australian Basin
Darling
Murray
Great Dividing Range
TASMAN SEA
S. ALPS
South Island
North Island

Southwest Indian Ridge
Southeast Indian Ridge
Crozet Basin
Kerguelen

SOUTHERN OCEAN

Record breakers

Climate

Physical geography

Highest surface wind ever recorded Mt. Washington, USA 231 mph

snowfall in a single season Mt. Baker, USA 2896cm, 1998–99

Highest temperature ever recorded El Aisisa, Libya 58°C

Deepest land depression Dead Sea shore 400m below sea level

Highest mountain Mt. Everest 8848m

Wettest place Mawsynram, India Annual average rainfall 1187cm

Largest desert Sahara, North Africa 1 350 000 km²

Deepest ocean trench Marianas Trench 8724m deep

Highest waterfall Angel Falls, Venezuela 979m drop

Longest river Nile 6695 km

Driest place Arica, Chile 14 years without rainfall

Lowest temperature ever recorded Vostock, Antarctica -88°C

Oxford University Press   Eckert IV Projection

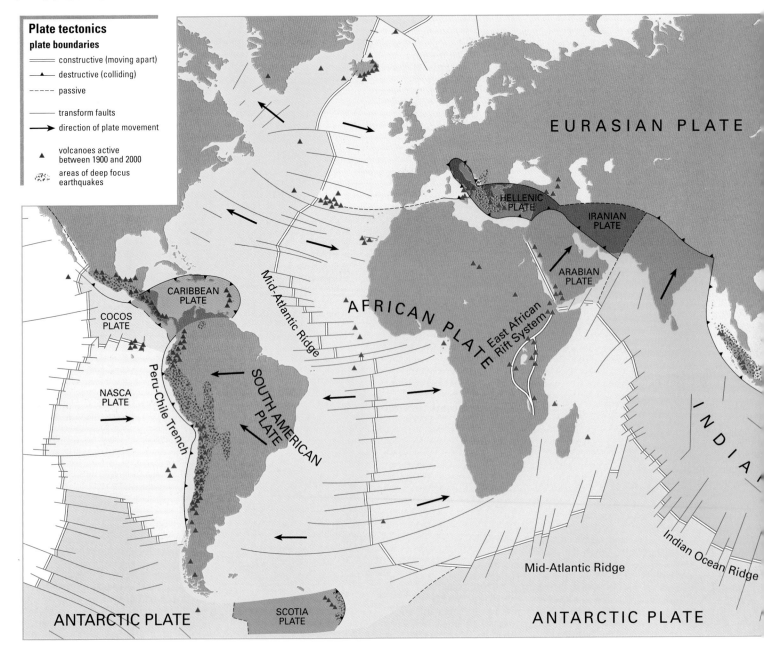

Plate tectonics
plate boundaries

	constructive (moving apart)
	destructive (colliding)
	passive
	transform faults
→	direction of plate movement
▲	volcanoes active between 1900 and 2000
	areas of deep focus earthquakes

EURASIAN PLATE

HELLENIC PLATE

IRANIAN PLATE

ARABIAN PLATE

CARIBBEAN PLATE

COCOS PLATE

Mid-Atlantic Ridge

AFRICAN PLATE

East African Rift System

NASCA PLATE

Peru-Chile Trench

SOUTH AMERICAN PLATE

INDIA

ANTARCTIC PLATE

SCOTIA PLATE

Mid-Atlantic Ridge

ANTARCTIC PLATE

Indian Ocean Ridge

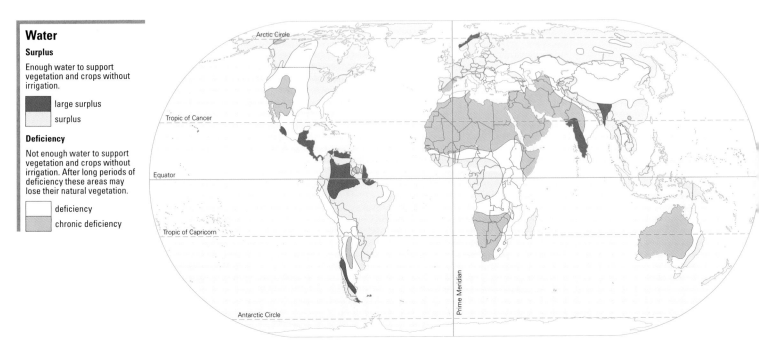

Water

Surplus

Enough water to support vegetation and crops without irrigation.

| | large surplus |
| | surplus |

Deficiency

Not enough water to support vegetation and crops without irrigation. After long periods of deficiency these areas may lose their natural vegetation.

| | deficiency |
| | chronic deficiency |

Arctic Circle

Tropic of Cancer

Equator

Tropic of Capricorn

Antarctic Circle

Prime Meridian

NORTH AMERICAN PLATE

NORTH AMERICAN PLATE

Aleutian Trench

EURASIAN PLATE

JUAN DE FUCA PLATE

Japanese Trench

AFRICAN PLATE

PHILIPPINE PLATE

Marianas Trench

CARIBBEAN PLATE

COCOS PLATE

Mid Atlantic Ridge

PACIFIC PLATE

NASCA PLATE

Peru-Chile Trench

SOUTH AMERICAN PLATE

LATE

Tonga Trench

ANTARCTIC PLATE

SCOTIA PLATE

Gall Projection

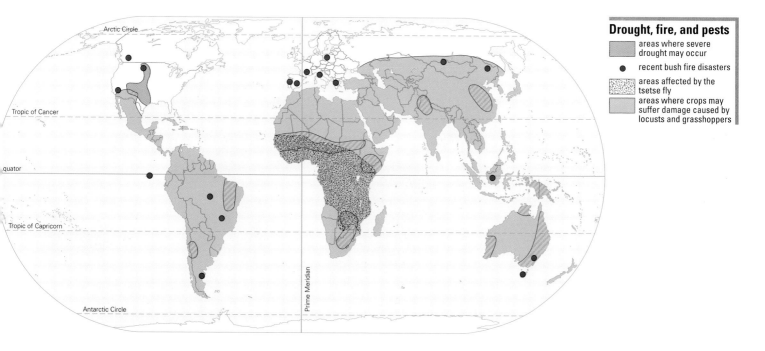

Drought, fire, and pests

- areas where severe drought may occur
- ● recent bush fire disasters
- areas affected by the tsetse fly
- areas where crops may suffer damage caused by locusts and grasshoppers

Arctic Circle

Tropic of Cancer

Equator

Tropic of Capricorn

Antarctic Circle

Prime Meridian

Scale 1: 240 000 000

January temperature

actual surface temperature

°Celsius

32
24
16
8
0
−8
−16
−24
−32
−40

→ warm sea current
→ cold sea current

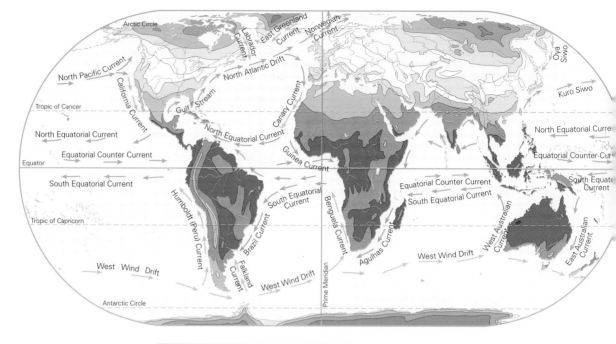

July temperature

actual surface temperature

°Celsius

32
24
16
8
0
−8
−16
−24
−32
−40

→ warm sea current
→ cold sea current

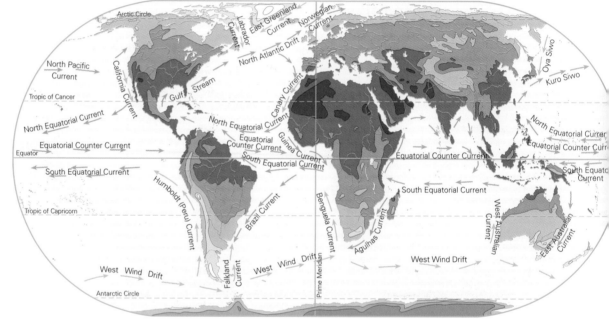

Temperature in 2050

predicted annual mean temperature increase

°Celsius

4.5
4.0
3.5
3.0
2.5
2.0
1.5
1.0

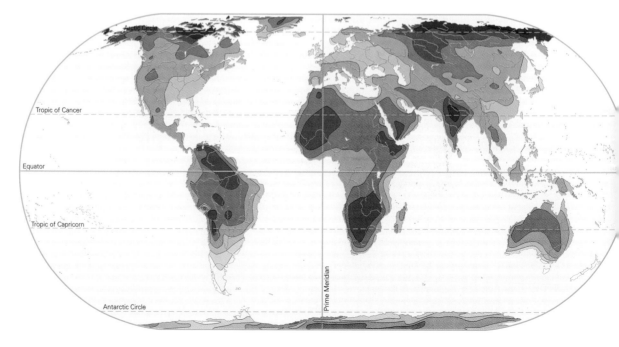

© Oxford University Press

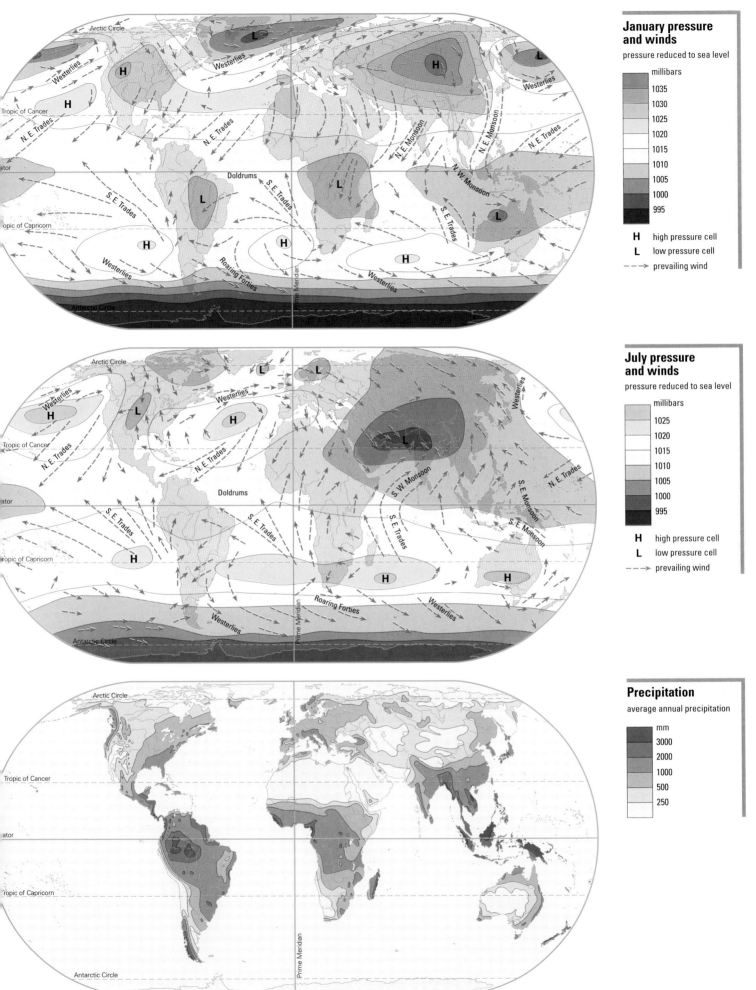

January pressure and winds

pressure reduced to sea level

millibars

1035
1030
1025
1020
1015
1010
1005
1000
995

H high pressure cell
L low pressure cell
- - - → prevailing wind

July pressure and winds

pressure reduced to sea level

millibars

1025
1020
1015
1010
1005
1000
995

H high pressure cell
L low pressure cell
- - - → prevailing wind

Precipitation

average annual precipitation

mm

3000
2000
1000
500
250

Equatorial scale 1: 105 000 000

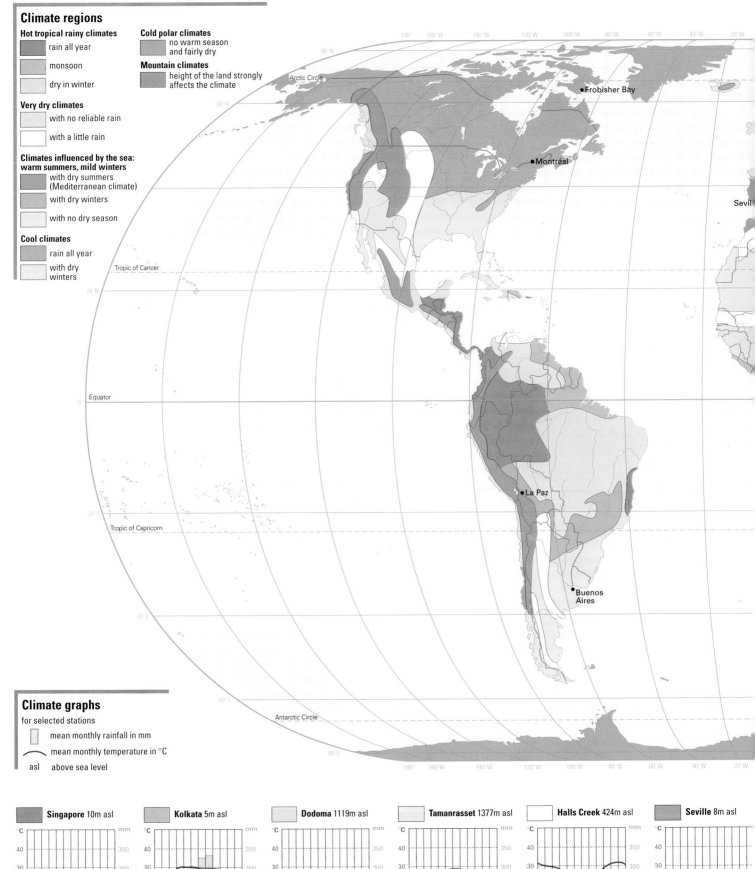

Climate regions

Hot tropical rainy climates
- rain all year
- monsoon
- dry in winter

Very dry climates
- with no reliable rain
- with a little rain

Climates influenced by the sea: warm summers, mild winters
- with dry summers (Mediterranean climate)
- with dry winters
- with no dry season

Cool climates
- rain all year
- with dry winters

Cold polar climates
- no warm season and fairly dry

Mountain climates
- height of the land strongly affects the climate

Climate graphs

for selected stations
- mean monthly rainfall in mm
- mean monthly temperature in °C

asl   above sea level

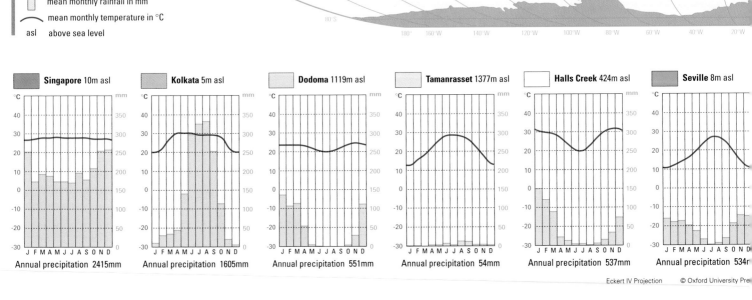

Singapore 10m asl	Kolkata 5m asl	Dodoma 1119m asl	Tamanrasset 1377m asl	Halls Creek 424m asl	Seville 8m asl
Annual precipitation 2415mm	Annual precipitation 1605mm	Annual precipitation 551mm	Annual precipitation 54mm	Annual precipitation 537mm	Annual precipitation 534mm

Eckert IV Projection   © Oxford University Press

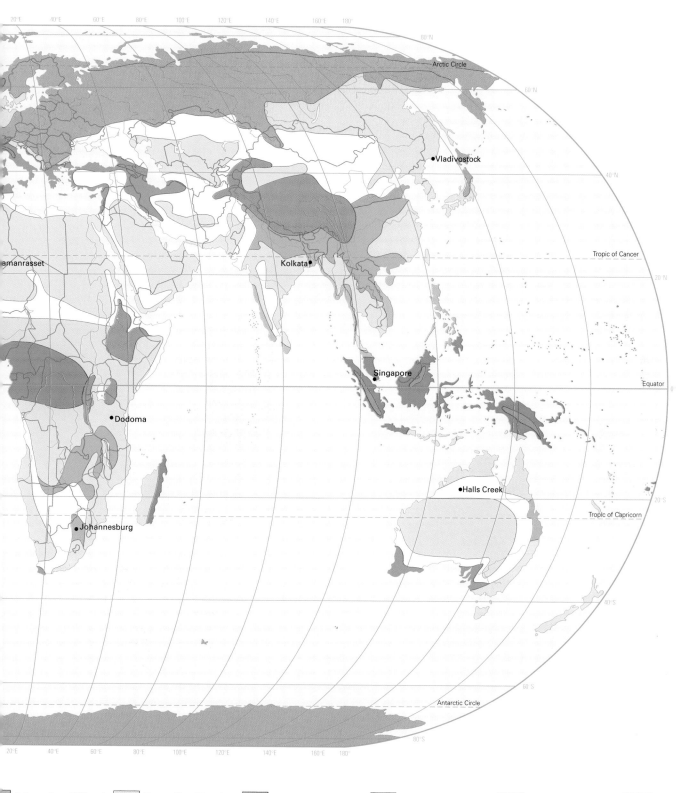

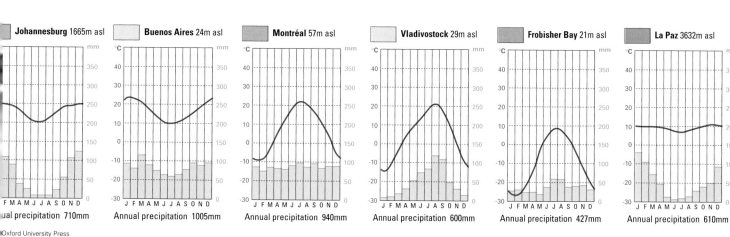

| Johannesburg 1665m asl | Buenos Aires 24m asl | Montréal 57m asl | Vladivostock 29m asl | Frobisher Bay 21m asl | La Paz 3632m asl |

Annual precipitation 710mm

Annual precipitation 1005mm

Annual precipitation 940mm

Annual precipitation 600mm

Annual precipitation 427mm

Annual precipitation 610mm

Climate data

Averages are for 1961–1990

Denver 1626m   climate station and its height above sea level

Temperature (°C)   high   average daily maximum temperature
                mean   average monthly temperature
                low   average daily minimum temperature

Rainfall (mm)   average monthly precipitation

Denver 1626m

	Jan	Feb	Mar	Apr	May	Jun	Jul	Aug	Sep	Oct	Nov	Dec	YEAR
high	6.2	8.1	11.2	16.6	21.6	27.4	31.2	29.9	24.9	19.1	11.4	6.9	17.9
mean	-1.3	0.8	3.9	9.0	14.0	19.4	23.1	21.9	16.8	10.8	3.9	-0.6	10.1
low	-8.8	-6.6	-3.4	1.4	6.4	11.3	14.8	13.8	8.7	2.4	-3.7	-8.1	2.4
Rainfall (mm)	13	15	33	43	61	46	49	38	32	25	22	16	393

Georgetown 2m

	Jan	Feb	Mar	Apr	May	Jun	Jul	Aug	Sep	Oct	Nov	Dec	YEAR
high	28.6	28.9	29.2	29.5	29.4	29.2	29.6	30.2	30.8	30.8	30.2	29.1	29.6
mean	26.1	26.4	26.7	27.0	26.8	26.5	26.6	27.0	27.5	27.6	27.2	26.4	26.8
low	23.6	23.9	24.2	24.4	24.3	23.8	23.5	23.8	24.2	24.4	24.2	23.8	24.0
Rainfall (mm)	185	89	111	141	286	328	268	201	98	107	186	262	2262

Guangzhou 42m

	Jan	Feb	Mar	Apr	May	Jun	Jul	Aug	Sep	Oct	Nov	Dec	YEAR
high	18.3	18.4	21.6	25.5	29.4	31.3	32.7	32.6	31.4	28.6	24.4	20.5	26.2
mean	13.3	14.3	17.7	21.9	25.6	27.3	28.5	28.3	27.1	24.0	19.4	15.0	21.9
low	5.0	6.6	10.7	16.1	20.7	23.5	25.7	25.2	22.6	17.6	11.9	6.5	16.0
Rainfall (mm)	43	65	85	182	284	258	228	221	172	79	42	24	1683

Havana 50m

	Jan	Feb	Mar	Apr	May	Jun	Jul	Aug	Sep	Oct	Nov	Dec	YEAR
high	25.8	26.1	27.6	28.6	29.8	30.5	31.3	31.6	31.0	29.2	27.7	26.5	28.8
mean	22.2	22.4	23.7	24.8	26.1	26.9	27.6	27.8	27.4	26.2	24.5	23.0	25.2
low	18.6	18.6	19.7	20.9	22.4	23.4	23.8	24.1	23.8	23.0	21.3	19.5	21.6
Rainfall (mm)	64	69	46	54	98	182	106	100	144	181	88	58	1190

Juliaca 3827m

	Jan	Feb	Mar	Apr	May	Jun	Jul	Aug	Sep	Oct	Nov	Dec	YEAR
high	16.7	16.7	16.5	16.8	16.6	16.0	16.0	17.0	17.6	18.6	18.8	17.7	17.1
mean	10.2	10.1	9.9	8.7	6.4	4.5	4.3	5.8	8.1	9.5	10.2	10.4	8.2
low	3.6	3.5	3.2	0.6	-3.8	-7.0	-7.5	-5.4	-1.4	0.3	1.5	3.0	-0.8
Rainfall (mm)	133	109	99	43	10	3	2	6	22	41	55	86	609

Khartoum 380m

	Jan	Feb	Mar	Apr	May	Jun	Jul	Aug	Sep	Oct	Nov	Dec	YEAR
high	30.8	33.0	36.8	40.1	41.9	41.3	38.4	37.3	39.1	39.3	35.2	31.8	37.1
mean	23.2	25.0	28.7	31.9	34.5	34.3	32.1	31.5	32.5	32.4	28.1	24.5	29.9
low	15.6	17.0	20.5	23.6	27.1	27.3	25.9	25.3	26.0	25.5	21.0	17.1	22.7
Rainfall (mm)	0	0	0	0.5	4	5	46	75	25	5	1	0	161

Lhasa 3650m

	Jan	Feb	Mar	Apr	May	Jun	Jul	Aug	Sep	Oct	Nov	Dec	YEAR
high	6.9	9.0	12.1	15.6	19.3	22.7	22.1	21.1	19.7	16.3	11.2	7.7	15.3
mean	-2.1	1.1	4.6	8.1	11.9	15.5	15.3	14.5	12.8	8.1	2.2	-1.7	7.5
low	-10.1	-6.8	-3.0	0.9	5.0	9.3	10.1	9.4	7.5	1.3	-4.9	-9.0	0.8
Rainfall (mm)	1	1	2	5	27	72	119	123	58	10	2	1	421

Libreville 15m

	Jan	Feb	Mar	Apr	May	Jun	Jul	Aug	Sep	Oct	Nov	Dec	YEAR
high	29.5	30.0	30.2	30.1	29.4	27.6	26.4	26.8	27.5	28.0	28.4	29.0	28.6
mean	26.8	27.0	27.1	26.6	26.7	25.4	24.3	24.3	25.4	25.7	25.9	26.2	26.0
low	24.1	24.0	23.9	23.1	24.0	23.2	22.1	21.8	23.4	23.4	23.4	23.4	23.3
Rainfall (mm)	250	243	363	339	247	54	7	14	104	427	490	303	2841

Limón 3m

	Jan	Feb	Mar	Apr	May	Jun	Jul	Aug	Sep	Oct	Nov	Dec	YEAR
high	27.9	28.6	29.6	29.6	28.5	27.5	27.7	27.7	27.2	27.0	27.1	27.7	28.0
mean	24.0	24.3	25.0	25.8	26.1	25.9	25.2	25.6	25.7	25.4	25.1	24.3	25.2
low	20.3	20.3	20.9	21.6	22.2	22.3	22.1	22.1	22.2	21.9	21.6	20.9	21.5
Rainfall (mm)	319	201	193	287	281	276	408	289	163	198	367	402	3384

Malatya 849m

	Jan	Feb	Mar	Apr	May	Jun	Jul	Aug	Sep	Oct	Nov	Dec	YEAR
high	2.9	5.3	11.1	18.2	23.5	29.2	33.8	33.4	28.9	20.9	11.8	5.7	18.7
mean	-0.4	1.5	6.9	13.0	17.8	22.9	27.0	26.5	22.0	14.8	7.6	2.4	13.5
low	-3.2	-1.7	2.4	7.7	11.8	16.1	19.8	19.4	15.2	9.5	3.7	-0.3	8.4
Rainfall (mm)	42	36	60	61	50	22	3	2	6	40	47	42	411

Manaus 84m

	Jan	Feb	Mar	Apr	May	Jun	Jul	Aug	Sep	Oct	Nov	Dec	YEAR
high	30.5	30.4	30.6	30.7	30.8	31.0	31.3	32.6	32.9	32.8	32.1	31.3	31.4
mean	26.1	26.0	26.1	26.3	26.3	26.4	26.5	27.0	27.5	27.6	27.3	26.7	26.7
low	23.1	23.1	23.2	23.3	23.3	23.0	22.7	23.0	23.5	23.7	23.7	23.5	23.3
Rainfall (mm)	260	288	314	300	256	114	88	58	83	126	183	217	2287

Meekatharra 518m

	Jan	Feb	Mar	Apr	May	Jun	Jul	Aug	Sep	Oct	Nov	Dec
high	38.1	36.5	34.5	29.2	23.6	19.7	18.9	21.0	25.4	29.4	33.1	36.5
mean	31.2	30.1	28.0	23.2	17.8	14.3	13.2	14.8	18.4	22.2	25.9	29.3
low	24.3	23.7	21.5	17.1	11.9	8.9	7.5	8.5	11.4	15.0	18.6	22.1
Rainfall (mm)	26	30	22	17	27	36	25	12	6	7	14	11

Montréal 57m

	Jan	Feb	Mar	Apr	May	Jun	Jul	Aug	Sep	Oct	Nov	Dec
high	-5.7	-4.4	1.6	10.6	18.5	23.6	26.1	24.8	19.9	13.3	5.4	-3.0
mean	-10.3	-8.8	-2.4	5.7	12.9	18.0	20.8	19.4	14.5	8.3	1.6	-6.9
low	-14.6	-13.5	-6.7	0.8	7.4	12.9	15.6	14.3	9.6	4.1	-1.5	-10.8
Rainfall (mm)	63.3	56.4	67.6	74.8	68.3	82.5	85.6	100.3	86.5	75.4	93.4	85.6

Ndola 1270m

	Jan	Feb	Mar	Apr	May	Jun	Jul	Aug	Sep	Oct	Nov	Dec
high	26.6	26.9	27.4	27.5	26.6	25.1	25.2	27.5	30.5	31.5	29.4	27.0
mean	20.8	20.8	21.0	20.5	18.6	16.5	16.7	19.2	22.5	23.7	22.5	21.0
low	17.1	17.1	16.5	14.4	10.8	7.9	7.8	10.2	13.6	16.2	17.1	17.2
Rainfall (mm)	293	249	170	46	4	1	0	0	3	32	130	306

Nuuk 70m

	Jan	Feb	Mar	Apr	May	Jun	Jul	Aug	Sep	Oct	Nov	Dec
high	-4.4	-4.5	-4.8	-0.8	3.5	7.7	10.6	9.9	6.3	1.7	-1.0	-3.3
mean	-7.4	-7.8	-8.0	-3.9	0.6	3.9	6.5	6.1	3.5	-0.6	-3.6	-6.2
low	-10.1	-10.6	-10.6	-6.1	-1.5	1.3	3.8	3.8	1.6	-2.5	-5.8	-8.7
Rainfall (mm)	39	47	50	46	55	62	82	89	88	70	74	64

Paris 65m

	Jan	Feb	Mar	Apr	May	Jun	Jul	Aug	Sep	Oct	Nov	Dec
high	6.0	7.6	10.8	14.4	18.2	21.5	24.0	23.8	20.8	16.0	10.1	6.8
mean	3.4	4.2	6.6	9.5	13.2	16.4	18.4	18.0	15.3	11.4	6.7	4.2
low	0.9	1.3	2.9	5.0	8.3	11.2	12.9	12.7	10.6	7.7	3.8	1.7
Rainfall (mm)	54	46	54	47	63	58	84	52	54	56	56	56

Qiqihar 148m

	Jan	Feb	Mar	Apr	May	Jun	Jul	Aug	Sep	Oct	Nov	Dec
high	-12.7	-7.8	2.3	12.9	21.0	26.2	27.8	26.1	20.1	11.1	-1.3	-10.4
mean	-19.2	-14.8	-4.5	6.1	14.4	20.3	22.8	20.9	14.0	4.8	-7.1	-16.2
low	-24.5	-20.9	-11.0	-0.9	7.3	14.2	17.9	16.2	8.5	-0.7	-12.0	-21.2
Rainfall (mm)	1	2	5	15	31	64	138	94	45	19	4	3

Rabat Sale 75m

	Jan	Feb	Mar	Apr	May	Jun	Jul	Aug	Sep	Oct	Nov	Dec
high	17.2	17.7	19.2	20.0	22.1	24.1	26.8	27.1	26.4	24.0	20.6	17.7
mean	12.6	13.1	14.2	15.2	17.4	19.8	22.2	22.4	21.5	19.0	15.9	13.2
low	8.0	8.6	9.2	10.4	12.7	15.4	17.6	17.7	16.7	14.1	11.1	8.7
Rainfall (mm)	77	74	61	62	25	7	1	1	6	44	97	101

Sittwe 5m

	Jan	Feb	Mar	Apr	May	Jun	Jul	Aug	Sep	Oct	Nov	Dec
high	28.0	29.4	31.4	34.1	31.5	29.5	28.9	28.9	30.1	31.1	30.3	28.5
mean	21.4	22.7	24.8	28.9	28.3	27.1	26.8	26.7	27.4	27.6	25.7	22.6
low	14.7	15.9	18.2	23.6	25.1	24.6	24.7	24.5	24.6	24.0	21.0	16.6
Rainfall (mm)	11	8	5	44	268	1091	1155	1025	537	289	105	17

Stockholm 52m

	Jan	Feb	Mar	Apr	May	Jun	Jul	Aug	Sep	Oct	Nov	Dec
high	-0.7	-0.6	3.0	8.6	15.7	20.7	21.9	20.4	15.1	9.9	4.5	1.1
mean	-2.8	-3.0	0.1	4.6	10.7	15.6	17.2	16.2	11.9	7.5	2.6	-1.0
low	-5.0	-5.3	-2.7	1.1	6.3	11.3	13.4	12.7	9.0	5.3	0.7	-3.2
Rainfall (mm)	39	27	26	30	30	45	72	66	55	50	53	46

Tehran 1191m

	Jan	Feb	Mar	Apr	May	Jun	Jul	Aug	Sep	Oct	Nov	Dec
high	7.2	9.9	15.4	21.9	28.0	34.1	36.8	35.4	31.5	24.0	16.5	9.8
mean	3.0	5.3	10.3	16.4	22.1	27.5	30.4	29.2	25.3	18.5	11.6	5.6
low	-1.1	0.7	5.2	10.9	16.1	20.9	24.0	23.0	19.2	12.9	6.7	1.3
Rainfall (mm)	37	34	37	28	15	3	3	1	1	14	21	36

Wellington 8m

	Jan	Feb	Mar	Apr	May	Jun	Jul	Aug	Sep	Oct	Nov	Dec
high	21.3	21.1	19.8	17.3	14.8	12.8	12.0	12.7	14.2	15.9	17.8	19.6
mean	17.8	17.7	16.6	14.3	11.9	10.1	9.2	9.8	11.2	12.8	14.5	16.4
low	14.4	14.3	13.5	11.3	9.1	7.3	6.4	6.9	8.3	9.7	11.3	13.2
Rainfall (mm)	67	48	76	87	99	113	111	106	82	81	74	74

Tropical revolving storms

▨ temperature 27°C and over at mean sea level

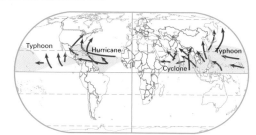

August–September
Maximum frequency in
northern hemisphere

January–March
Maximum frequency in
southern hemisphere

Hurricane Floyd, Florida
Winds in this hurricane reached 225km per hour and caused 40 deaths.
US NOAA satellite image, 15 September, 1999.

Drought and flood

▨ areas where severe drought may occur

── major river flood plains susceptible to flooding

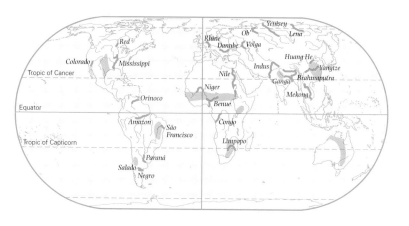

Dust storms, South West Africa
Dust streaming from SW African coastal
deserts into the Atlantic Ocean.
NASA SeaWiFS image, 6 June, 2000.

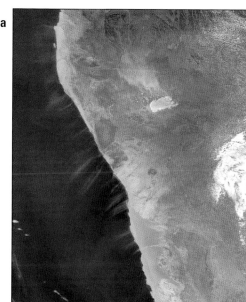

El Niño

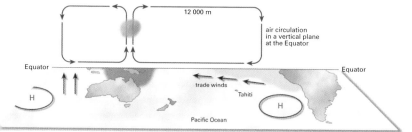

Normal year
The Humboldt current carries cold water north along the coast of Peru.
High temperatures in S.E. Asia draw in the S.E. Trade Winds which
push the surface waters west. Rainfall in S.E. Asia is high. Cold water
continues to flow north along the coast of S. America and this is rich in
plankton and fish.

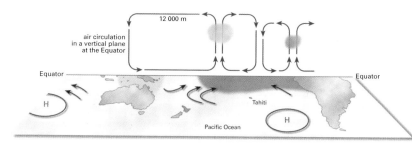

El Niño year
Weaker S.E. Trade Winds allow hot water from the western Pacific to
drift eastwards. Warm waters appear in Peru at about Christmas time.
Arid coastal areas in S. America suffer torrential rains. Coastal fish
stocks move to deeper cold water out of reach of small boats.
Drought occurs in S.E. Asia.

Equatorial scale 1: 105 000 000

Ecosystems

vegetation types are those which would occur naturally without interference by people

coniferous forest
cone bearing trees

deciduous and mixed forest
leaf shedding and coniferous trees

tropical rain forest
many species of lush, tall trees

tropical grasslands (savannah)
tall grass parkland with scattered trees

evergreen trees and shrubs
plants and small trees with leathery leaves

thorn forest
low trees and shrubs with spines or thorns

temperate grasslands
prairies, steppes, pampas, and veld

semi-desert
short grasses and drought-resistant scrub

desert
sand and stones, very little vegetation

tundra
moss and lichen, with few trees

ice
no vegetation

mountains
thin soils, steep slopes,
and high altitude
affects type of
vegetation

ice
Aerial view of Jameson Land, towards
Liverpool Land, Greenland

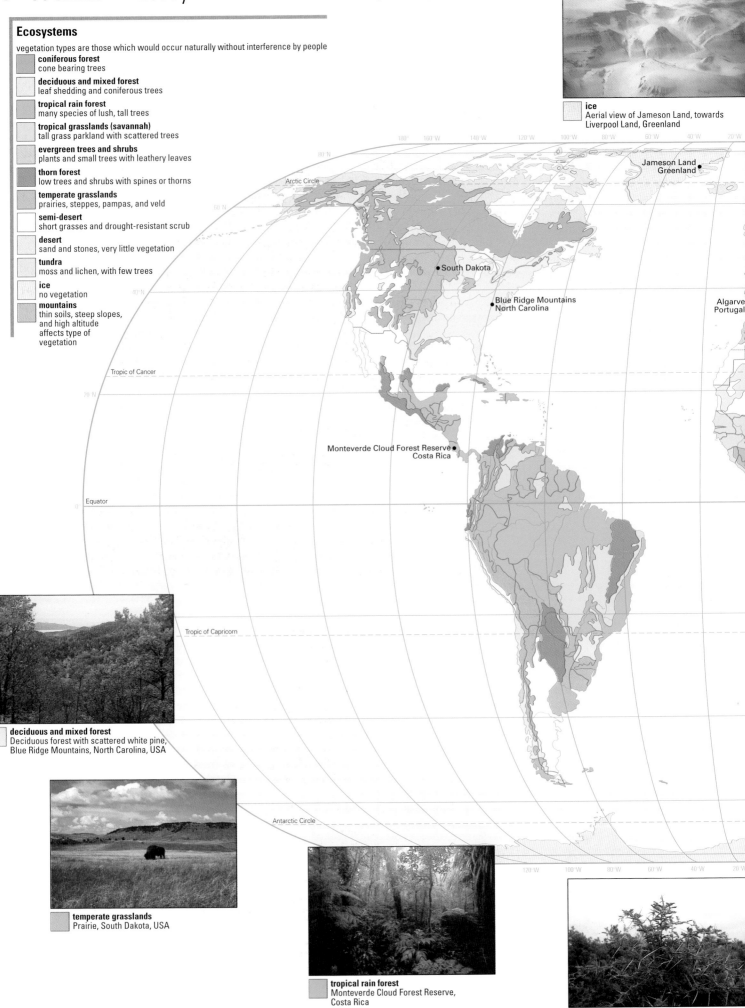

deciduous and mixed forest
Deciduous forest with scattered white pine,
Blue Ridge Mountains, North Carolina, USA

temperate grasslands
Prairie, South Dakota, USA

tropical rain forest
Monteverde Cloud Forest Reserve,
Costa Rica

thorn forest
Acacia thorns, Hwange, Zimbabwe

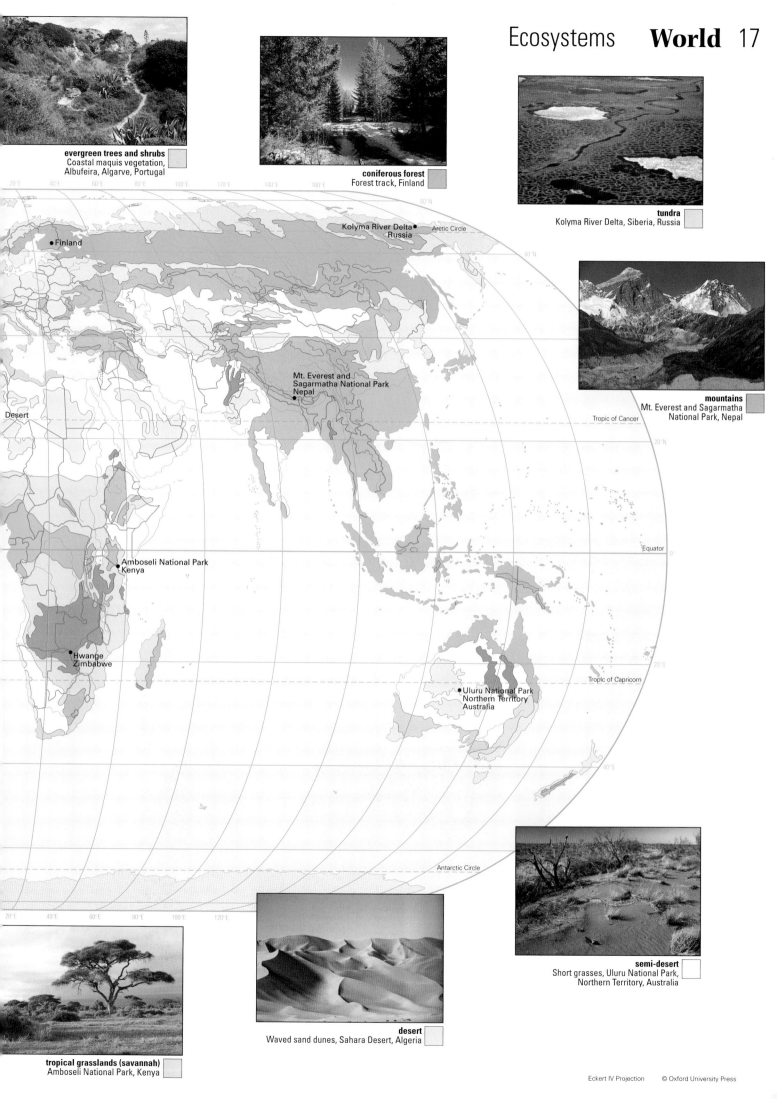

evergreen trees and shrubs
Coastal maquis vegetation,
Albufeira, Algarve, Portugal

coniferous forest
Forest track, Finland

tundra
Kolyma River Delta, Siberia, Russia

mountains
Mt. Everest and Sagarmatha
National Park, Nepal

Desert

• Finland

Kolyma River Delta •
Russia   Arctic Circle

Mt. Everest and
Sagarmatha National Park
Nepal
•

Tropic of Cancer

20°N

• Amboseli National Park
Kenya

Equator

• Hwange
Zimbabwe

20°S

• Uluru National Park
Northern Territory
Australia

Tropic of Capricorn

40°S

Antarctic Circle

semi-desert
Short grasses, Uluru National Park,
Northern Territory, Australia

desert
Waved sand dunes, Sahara Desert, Algeria

tropical grasslands (savannah)
Amboseli National Park, Kenya

Eckert IV Projection   © Oxford University Press

Population density

people per square kilometre

- over 200
- 100–200
- 50–100
- 5–50
- 1–5
- under 1

Major cities

population in millions

- ■ over 10
- ⊡ 5–10
- ☐ 1–5

Population structure, 2000

World

males | Age | females

percent of total population

Total population: 6 079 727 906
Land area: 148 940 000km²

Botswana

males | Age | females

percent of total population

Total population: 1 577 739
Land area: 581 370km²

Brazil

males | Age | females

percent of total population

Total population: 172 860 000
Land area: 8 547 403km²

Japan

males | Age | females

percent of total population

Total population: 126 550 000
Land area: 377 801km²

Italy

males | Age | females

percent of total population

Total population: 57 634 000
Land area: 301 268km²

China

males | Age | females

percent of total population

Total population: 1 261 832 000
Land area: 9 596 961km²

USA

males | Age | female

percent of total population

Total population: 275 563 00
Land area: 9 158 960km²

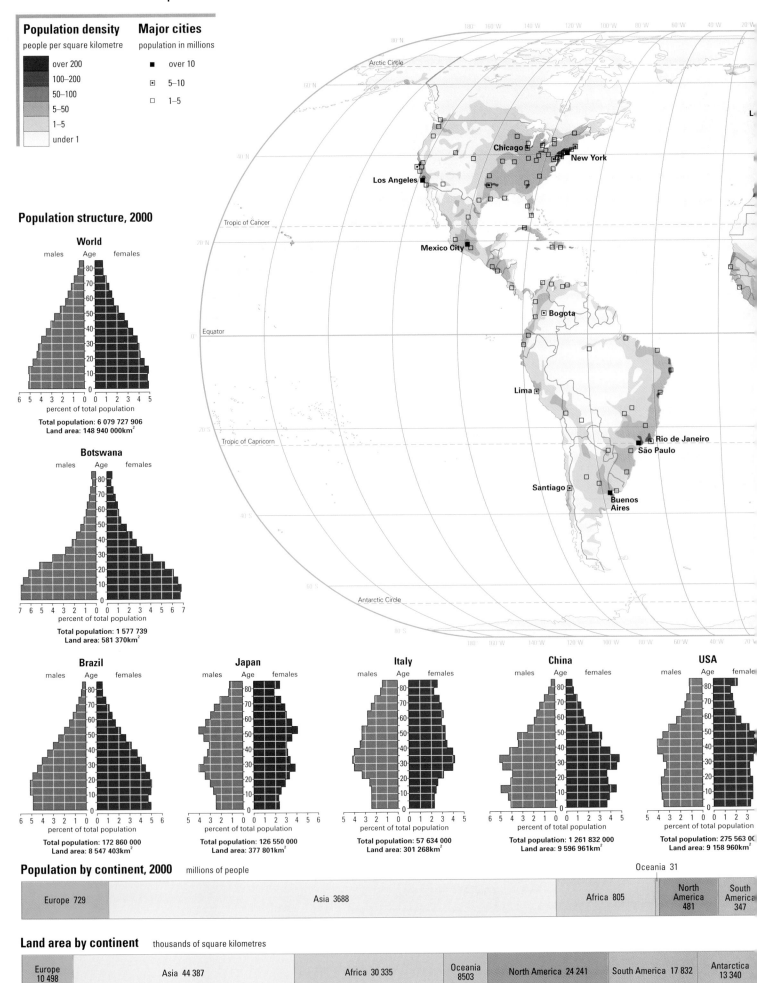

Population by continent, 2000   millions of people

Europe 729	Asia 3688	Africa 805	North America 481	South America 347	Oceania 31

Land area by continent   thousands of square kilometres

Europe 10 498	Asia 44 387	Africa 30 335	Oceania 8503	North America 24 241	South America 17 832	Antarctica 13 340

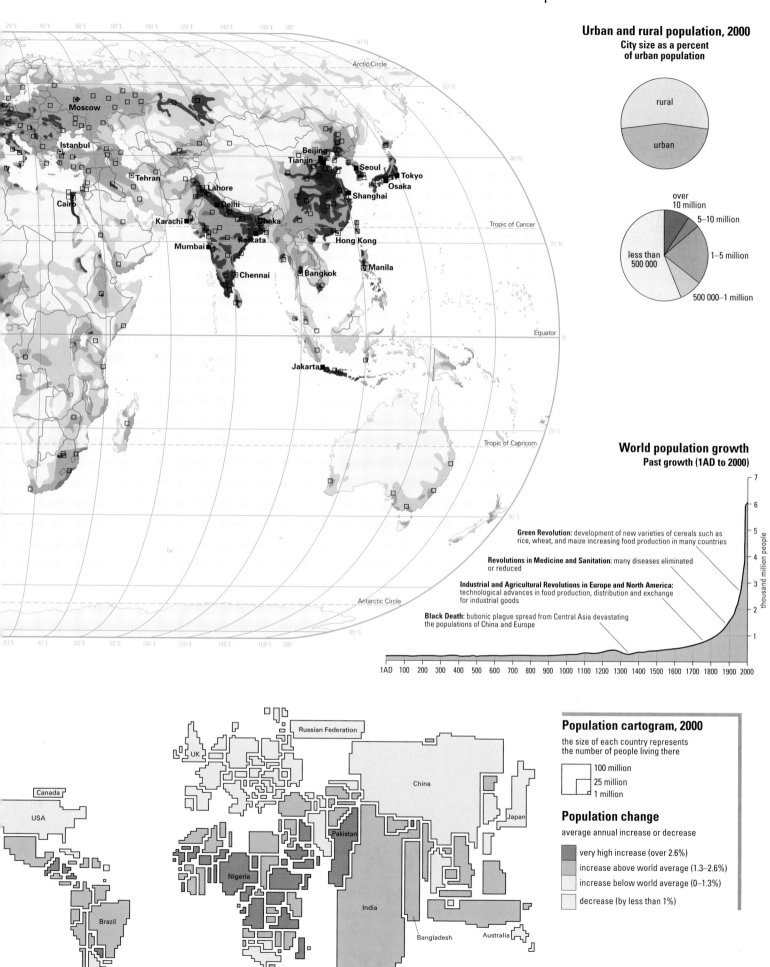

Urban and rural population, 2000
City size as a percent
of urban population

rural

urban

over
10 million

5–10 million

1–5 million

less than
500 000

500 000–1 million

World population growth
Past growth (1AD to 2000)

Green Revolution: development of new varieties of cereals such as rice, wheat, and maize increasing food production in many countries

Revolutions in Medicine and Sanitation: many diseases eliminated or reduced

Industrial and Agricultural Revolutions in Europe and North America: technological advances in food production, distribution and exchange for industrial goods

Black Death: bubonic plague spread from Central Asia devastating the populations of China and Europe

1AD 100 200 300 400 500 600 700 800 900 1000 1100 1200 1300 1400 1500 1600 1700 1800 1900 2000

thousand million people

Population cartogram, 2000

the size of each country represents
the number of people living there

100 million

25 million

1 million

Population change

average annual increase or decrease

very high increase (over 2.6%)

increase above world average (1.3–2.6%)

increase below world average (0–1.3%)

decrease (by less than 1%)

Russian Federation

UK

Canada

USA

China

Japan

Pakistan

Nigeria

India

Brazil

Bangladesh

Australia

Oxford University Press

Population change, 1990–2000

percentage population gain or loss

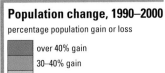

- over 40% gain
- 30–40% gain
- 20–30% gain
- 10–20% gain
- under 10% gain
- 0–10% loss

Highest population gain
Afghanistan 75.5%
Qatar 54.6%
Jordan 53.2%
French Guiana 48.9%
Marshall Islands 47.3%

Highest population loss
Kuwait -7.9%
Georgia -8%
Latvia -10%
Bulgaria -12.3%
Bosnia-Herzegovina -13.3%

Urban population, 2001

percentage of the population living in
urban areas

- over 80%
- 60–80%
- 40–60%
- 20–40%
- under 20%

Most urban
Singapore 100%
Belgium 97%
Kuwait 96%
Qatar 93%
Iceland 93%

Least urban
Uganda 15%
Nepal 12%
Burundi 9%
Bhutan 7%
Rwanda 6%

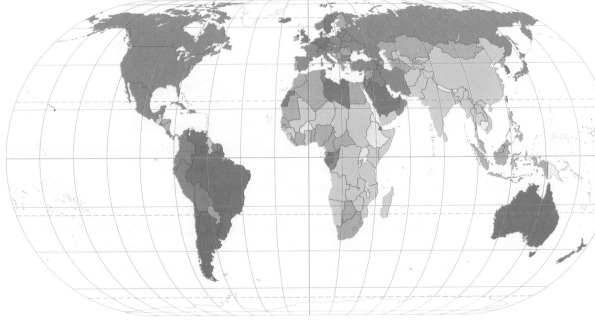

Fertility rate, 2001

average number of children
born to childbearing women

- over 6 children
- 5–5.9 children
- 4–4.9 children
- 3–3.9 children
- 2–2.9 children
- 1–1.9 children

Largest families
Niger 8.0 children
Somalia 7.2 children
Yemen 7.2 children
Congo, Dem. Rep. 6.9 children
Uganda 6.9 children

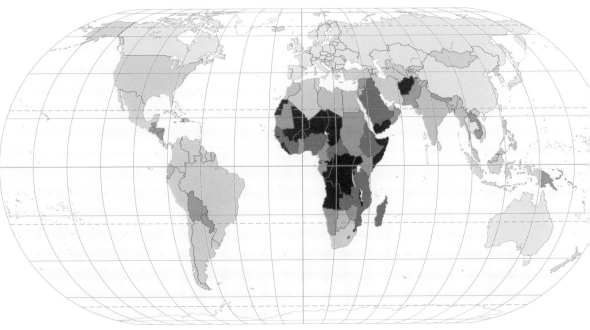

Eckert IV Projection   © Oxford University Pre

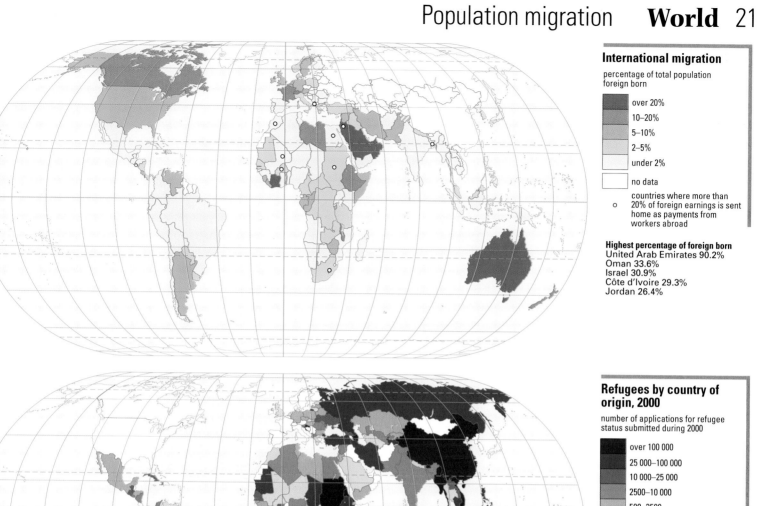

International migration

percentage of total population
foreign born

- over 20%
- 10–20%
- 5–10%
- 2–5%
- under 2%
- no data
- ○ countries where more than 20% of foreign earnings is sent home as payments from workers abroad

Highest percentage of foreign born
United Arab Emirates 90.2%
Oman 33.6%
Israel 30.9%
Côte d'Ivoire 29.3%
Jordan 26.4%

Refugees by country of origin, 2000

number of applications for refugee status submitted during 2000

- over 100 000
- 25 000–100 000
- 10 000–25 000
- 2500–10 000
- 500–2500
- under 500
- no data

Countries from which most refugees left, 2000
Burundi 568 000
Sudan 491 000
Angola 433 000
Sierra Leone 401 000
Eritrea 377 000
Vietnam 371 000
Congo, Dem. Rep. 369 000
Croatia 331 000

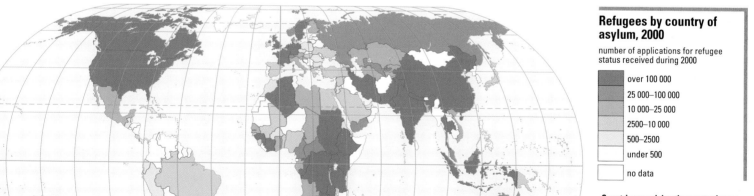

Refugees by country of asylum, 2000

number of applications for refugee status received during 2000

- over 100 000
- 25 000–100 000
- 10 000–25 000
- 2500–10 000
- 500–2500
- under 500
- no data

Countries receiving the most refugees, 2000
Pakistan 2 001 000
Iran 1 868 000
Germany 906 000
Tanzania 681 000
USA 508 000
Guinea 427 000
Sudan 415 000
Congo, Dem. Rep. 333 000

Purchasing power, 2001

Purchasing Power Parity (PPP) in US$
Based on Gross Domestic Product (GDP)
per person, adjusted for the local cost
of living

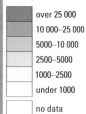

	over 25 000
	10 000–25 000
	5000–10 000
	2500–5000
	1000–2500
	under 1000
	no data

Highest purchasing power
Luxembourg $50 061
United States $34 870
Switzerland $31 320
Norway $30 440
Iceland $29 581

Lowest purchasing power
Malawi $620
Burundi $590
Congo $580
Tanzania $540
Sierra Leone $480

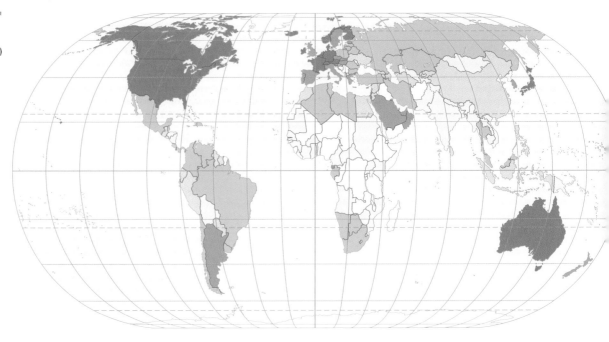

Literacy and schooling, 2000

percentage of people aged 15 and above
who can, with understanding, both read
and write a short, simple statement on
their everyday life

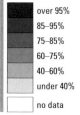

	over 95%
	85–95%
	75–85%
	60–75%
	40–60%
	under 40%
	no data

Highest literacy levels
Slovakia 100.0%
Georgia 100.0%
Estonia 99.8%
Latvia 99.8%
Poland 99.7%

Lowest literacy levels
Gambia 36.6%
Sierra Leone 36.0%
Vanuatu 34.0%
Burkina 23.9%
Niger 15.9%

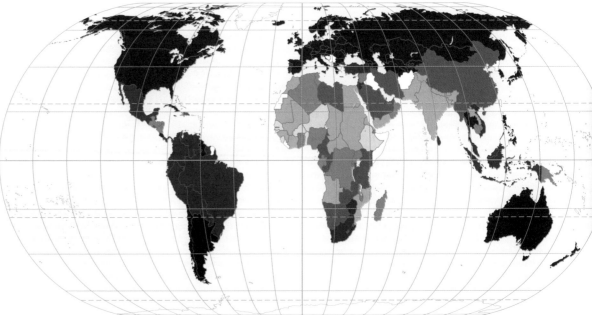

Life expectancy, 2001

average expected lifespan of babies
born in 2001

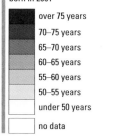

	over 75 years
	70–75 years
	65–70 years
	60–65 years
	55–60 years
	50–55 years
	under 50 years
	no data

Highest life expectancy
Japan 81 years
San Marino 80 years
Sweden 80 years
Iceland 80 years

Lowest life expectancy
Rwanda 38 years
Zimbabwe 35 years
Sierra Leone 35 years
Zambia 33 years

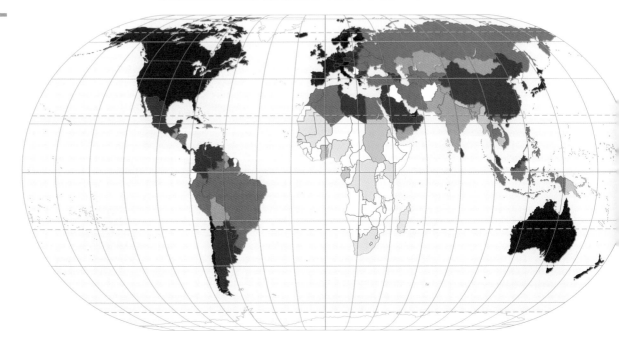

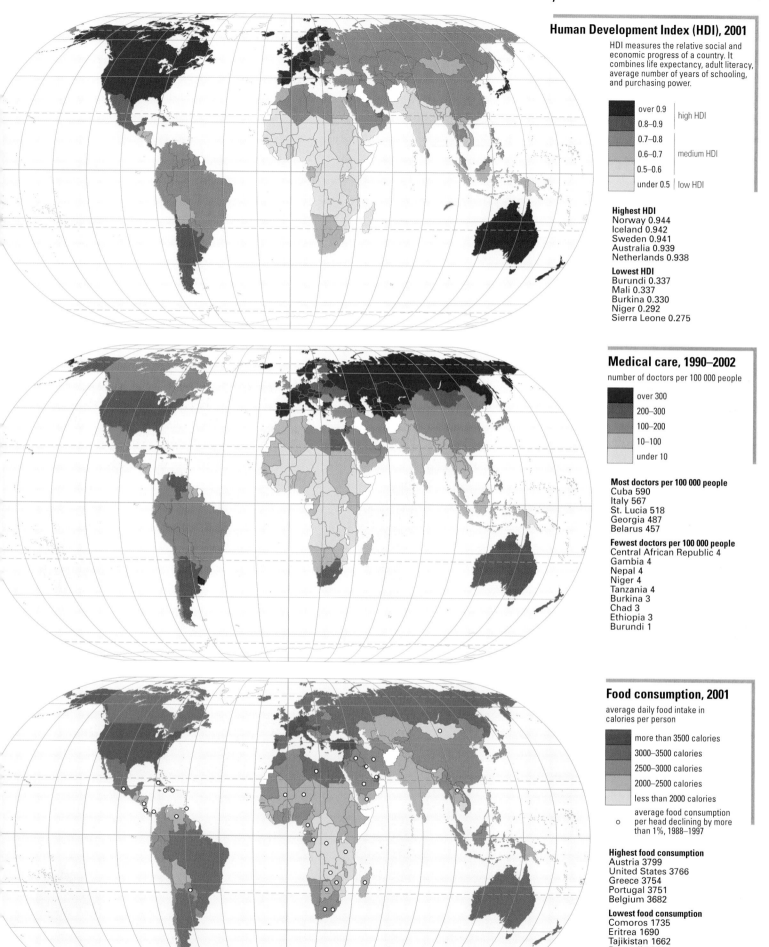

Human Development Index (HDI), 2001

HDI measures the relative social and economic progress of a country. It combines life expectancy, adult literacy, average number of years of schooling, and purchasing power.

over 0.9	high HDI
0.8–0.9	
0.7–0.8	
0.6–0.7	medium HDI
0.5–0.6	
under 0.5	low HDI

Highest HDI
Norway 0.944
Iceland 0.942
Sweden 0.941
Australia 0.939
Netherlands 0.938

Lowest HDI
Burundi 0.337
Mali 0.337
Burkina 0.330
Niger 0.292
Sierra Leone 0.275

Medical care, 1990–2002

number of doctors per 100 000 people

- over 300
- 200–300
- 100–200
- 10–100
- under 10

Most doctors per 100 000 people
Cuba 590
Italy 567
St. Lucia 518
Georgia 487
Belarus 457

Fewest doctors per 100 000 people
Central African Republic 4
Gambia 4
Nepal 4
Niger 4
Tanzania 4
Burkina 3
Chad 3
Ethiopia 3
Burundi 1

Food consumption, 2001

average daily food intake in calories per person

- more than 3500 calories
- 3000–3500 calories
- 2500–3000 calories
- 2000–2500 calories
- less than 2000 calories
- o average food consumption per head declining by more than 1%, 1988–1997

Highest food consumption
Austria 3799
United States 3766
Greece 3754
Portugal 3751
Belgium 3682

Lowest food consumption
Comoros 1735
Eritrea 1690
Tajikistan 1662
Burundi 1612
Congo, Democratic Republic 1535

Oxford University Press

Employment in agriculture

percentage of the labour force

- over 80%
- 60–80%
- 30–60%
- 10–30%
- under 10%
- no data

Highest employment in agriculture
Bhutan 94%
Nepal 94%
Burkina 92%
Burundi 92%
Rwanda 92%

Lowest employment in agriculture
Bahrain 2%
Brunei 2%
United Kingdom 2%
Kuwait 1%
Singapore 0%

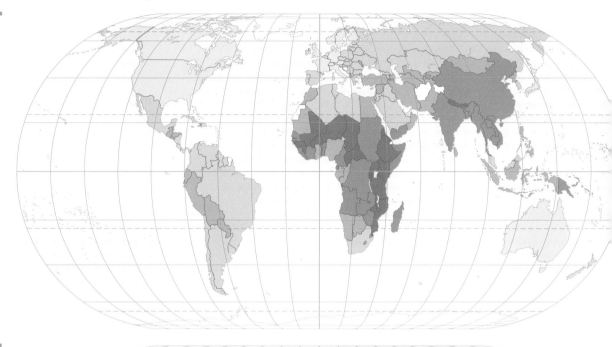

Employment in industry

percentage of the labour force

- over 80%
- 60–80%
- 30–60%
- 10–30%
- under 10%
- no data

Highest employment in industry
Bulgaria 48%
Romaina 47%
Slovenia 46%
Czech Republic 45%
Armenia 43%
Mauritius 43%

Lowest employment in industry
Bhutan 2%
Burkina 2%
Ethiopia 2%
Guinea 2%
Guinea-Bissau 2%
Mali 2%
Nepal 0%

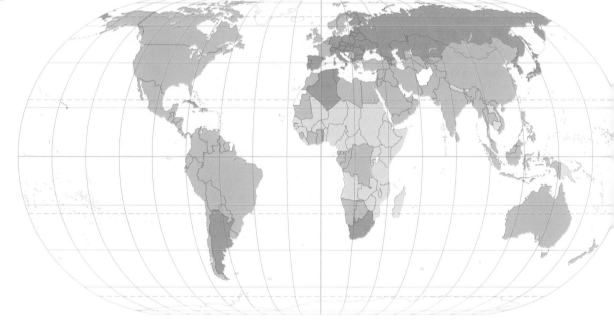

Employment in services

percentage of the labour force

- over 80%
- 60–80%
- 30–60%
- 10–30%
- under 10%
- no data

Highest employment in service
Bahamas 79%
Brunei 74%
Kuwait 74%
Sweden 74%
Canada 72%

Lowest employment in services
Burkina 6%
Nepal 6%
Niger 6%
Burundi 5%
Rwanda 5%
Bhutan 4%

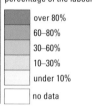

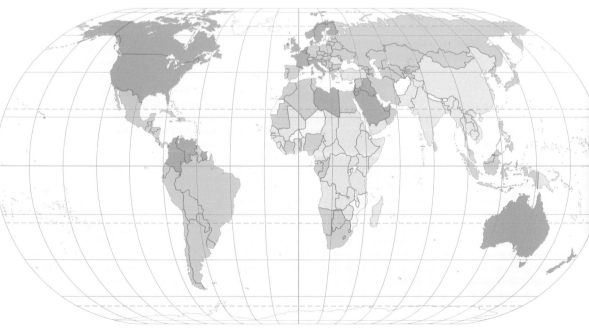

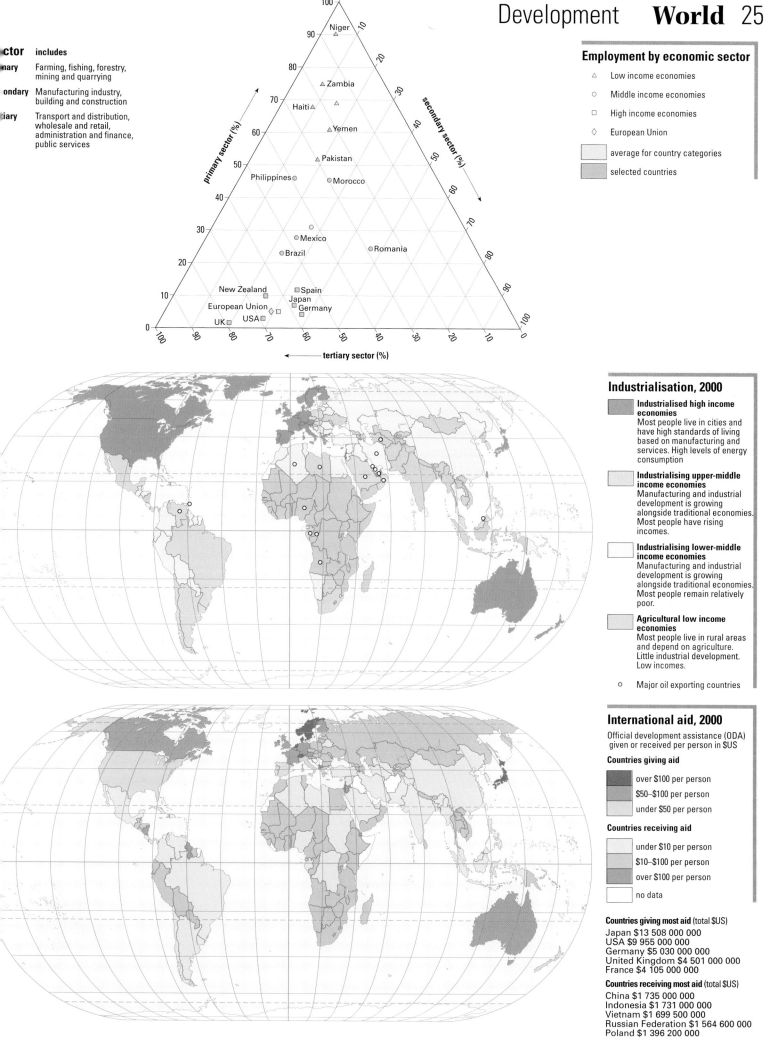

ctor   **includes**

nary   Farming, fishing, forestry, mining and quarrying

ondary   Manufacturing industry, building and construction

iary   Transport and distribution, wholesale and retail, administration and finance, public services

primary sector (%)

secondary sector (%)

tertiary sector (%)

Niger

Zambia

Haiti

Yemen

Pakistan

Philippines

Morocco

Mexico

Brazil

Romania

New Zealand

Spain

European Union

Japan

Germany

UK

USA

Employment by economic sector

△   Low income economies

○   Middle income economies

□   High income economies

◇   European Union

average for country categories

selected countries

Industrialisation, 2000

Industrialised high income economies
Most people live in cities and have high standards of living based on manufacturing and services. High levels of energy consumption

Industrialising upper-middle income economies
Manufacturing and industrial development is growing alongside traditional economies. Most people have rising incomes.

Industrialising lower-middle income economies
Manufacturing and industrial development is growing alongside traditional economies. Most people remain relatively poor.

Agricultural low income economies
Most people live in rural areas and depend on agriculture. Little industrial development. Low incomes.

○   Major oil exporting countries

International aid, 2000

Official development assistance (ODA) given or received per person in $US

Countries giving aid

over $100 per person

$50–$100 per person

under $50 per person

Countries receiving aid

under $10 per person

$10–$100 per person

over $100 per person

no data

Countries giving most aid (total $US)
Japan $13 508 000 000
USA $9 955 000 000
Germany $5 030 000 000
United Kingdom $4 501 000 000
France $4 105 000 000

Countries receiving most aid (total $US)
China $1 735 000 000
Indonesia $1 731 000 000
Vietnam $1 699 500 000
Russian Federation $1 564 600 000
Poland $1 396 200 000

Oxford University Press

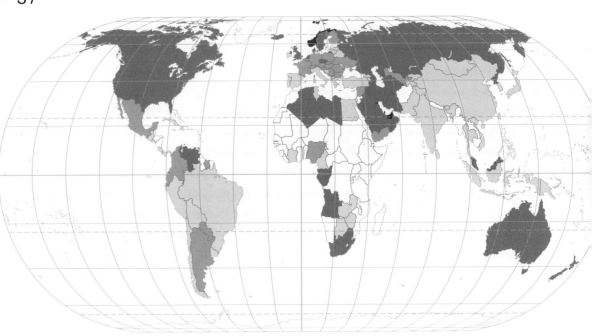

Energy production, 2000

kg oil equivalent per person

- over 25 000
- 2500–25 000
- 1000–2500
- 100–1000
- under 100
- no data

Highest energy producers
kg oil equivalent per person

Qatar 94 758
United Arab Emirates 71 971
Kuwait 65 096
Brunei 63 244
Norway 56 907
Saudi Arabia 23 974
Oman 23 293
Trinidad & Tobago 17 778
Bahrain 16 167
Libya 16 129
Canada 14 547
Gabon 14 513
Australia 12 575
Turkmenistan 11 344
Venezuela 9483

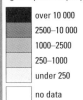

- North America
- Central and South America
- Europe
- former USSR
- Middle East
- Africa
- Asia Pacific
- Australia

Oil reserves
Proven recoverable reserves
World total: 142 100 000 000 tonnes

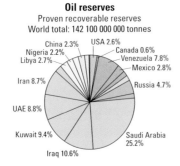

China 2.3% — USA 2.6%
Nigeria 2.2% — Canada 0.6%
Libya 2.7% — Venezuela 7.8%
— Mexico 2.8%
Iran 8.7% — Russia 4.7%
UAE 8.8%
Kuwait 9.4% — Saudi Arabia 25.2%
Iraq 10.6%

Gas reserves
Proven recoverable reserves
World total: 150 000 000 000 000 m³

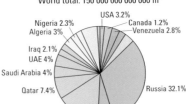

Nigeria 2.3% — USA 3.2%
Algeria 3% — Canada 1.2%
— Venezuela 2.8%
Iraq 2.1%
UAE 4%
Saudi Arabia 4%
Russia 32.1%
Qatar 7.4%
Iran 15.3%

Coal reserves
Proven recoverable reserves
World total: 984 211 000 000 tonnes

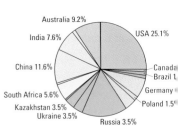

Australia 9.2% — USA 25.1%
India 7.6%
China 11.6% — Canada
— Brazil 1
South Africa 5.6% — Germany
Kazakhstan 3.5% — Poland 1.5%
Ukraine 3.5% — Russia 3.5%

Oil consumption
World total: 3 503 600 000 tonnes

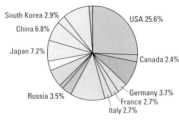

South Korea 2.9% — USA 25.6%
China 6.8%
Japan 7.2% — Canada 2.4%
Russia 3.5% — Germany 3.7%
— France 2.7%
Italy 2.7%

Gas consumption
World total: 2 404 600 000 000 m³

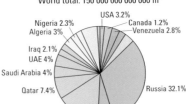

Japan 3.2% — USA 27.2%
Canada 3.2%
Russia 15.7% — UK 4%
Germany 3.3%

Coal consumption
World total: 2 186 000 000 tonnes oil equivalent

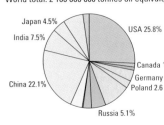

Japan 4.5% — USA 25.8%
India 7.5%
— Canada
China 22.1% — Germany
— Poland 2.6
Russia 5.1%

Energy consumption, 2000

kg oil equivalent per person

- over 10 000
- 2500–10 000
- 1000–2500
- 250–1000
- under 250
- no data

Highest energy consumers
kg oil equivalent per person

Qatar 22 177
United Arab Emirates 18 362
Bahrain 14 590
Kuwait 12 538
Iceland 11 576
Canada 10 447
Singapore 10 116

Lowest energy consumers
kg oil equivalent per person

Afghanistan 25
Burkina 24
Ethiopia 22
Cambodia 16
Chad 8

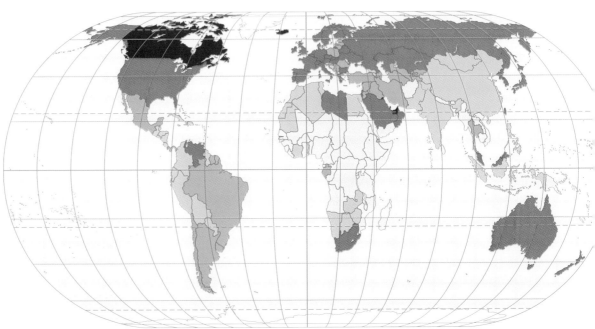

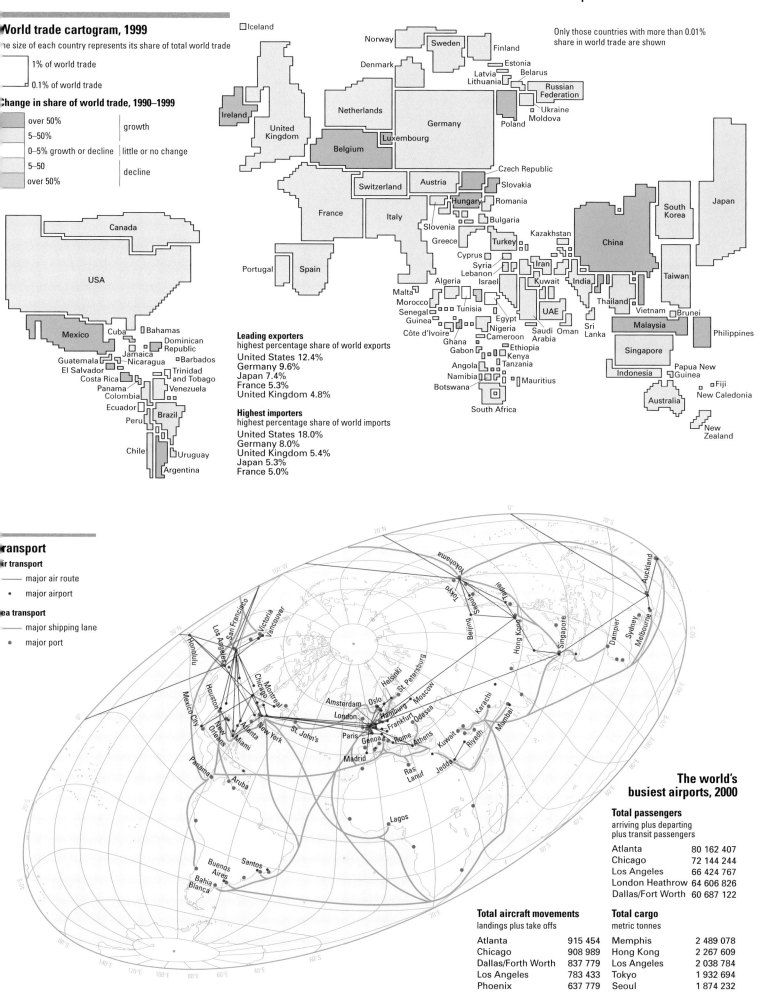

World trade cartogram, 1999

The size of each country represents its share of total world trade

- 1% of world trade
- 0.1% of world trade

Change in share of world trade, 1990–1999

over 50%	growth
5–50%	
0–5% growth or decline	little or no change
5–50	
over 50%	decline

Only those countries with more than 0.01% share in world trade are shown

Leading exporters
highest percentage share of world exports
United States 12.4%
Germany 9.6%
Japan 7.4%
France 5.3%
United Kingdom 4.8%

Highest importers
highest percentage share of world imports
United States 18.0%
Germany 8.0%
United Kingdom 5.4%
Japan 5.3%
France 5.0%

Transport

Air transport
— major air route
• major airport

Sea transport
— major shipping lane
• major port

The world's busiest airports, 2000

Total passengers
arriving plus departing plus transit passengers

Atlanta	80 162 407
Chicago	72 144 244
Los Angeles	66 424 767
London Heathrow	64 606 826
Dallas/Fort Worth	60 687 122

Total aircraft movements
landings plus take offs

Atlanta	915 454
Chicago	908 989
Dallas/Forth Worth	837 779
Los Angeles	783 433
Phoenix	637 779

Total cargo
metric tonnes

Memphis	2 489 078
Hong Kong	2 267 609
Los Angeles	2 038 784
Tokyo	1 932 694
Seoul	1 874 232

Motor vehicle Trans National Corporations (TNCs), 2000

Trans National Corporations (TNCs) are businesses with a parent company in one country and subsidiary operations in other countries. TNC foreign production accounts for about one fifth of world output.

- □ headquarters
- ○ major manufacturing plant

Corporation

- General Motors
- Toyota
- Fiat Spa
- Volkswagen

Cellphone owners, 2001

per 1000 people

- over 750
- 500–750
- 250–500
- 100–250
- 50–100
- 10–50
- under 10
- no data

Most owners
Luxembourg 920
Israel 907
Italy 883
Iceland 865
Austria 817

Least owners
Bhutan 0
Comoros 0
Eritrea 0
Guinea-Bissau 0
São Tomé & Príncipe 0

World economy

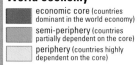

- economic core (countries dominant in the world economy)
- semi-periphery (countries partially dependent on the core)
- periphery (countries highly dependent on the core)

Global cities

Some geographers have identified a network of global cities arranged in a hierarchy according to the power they exert on the global economy. The map shows one view of this hierarchy. The position of each city in the hierarchy can change rapidly through time.

- cities dominating global financial markets
- cities dominating international and national economies
- cities dominating subnational and regional economies

City population

- 10–25 million
- 5–10 million
- 1–5 million

Source: Friedmann, 1995

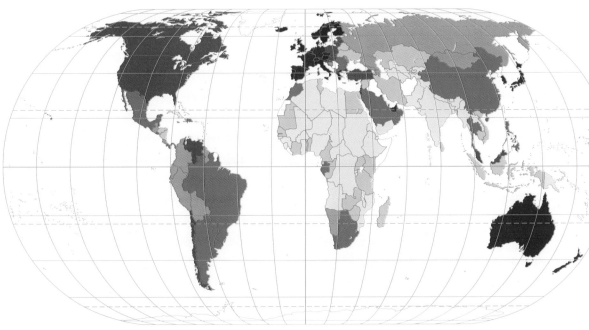

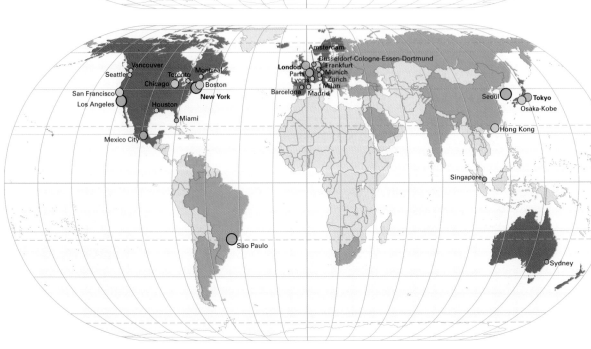

Amsterdam
Vancouver
Seattle
Dusseldorf-Cologne-Essen-Dortmund
London
Frankfurt
Toronto
Montreal
Munich
Paris
Chicago
Boston
Zurich
Lyons
Milan
San Francisco
New York
Barcelona
Madrid
Seoul
Tokyo
Los Angeles
Houston
Osaka-Kobe
Miami
Hong Kong
Mexico City
Singapore
São Paulo
Sydney

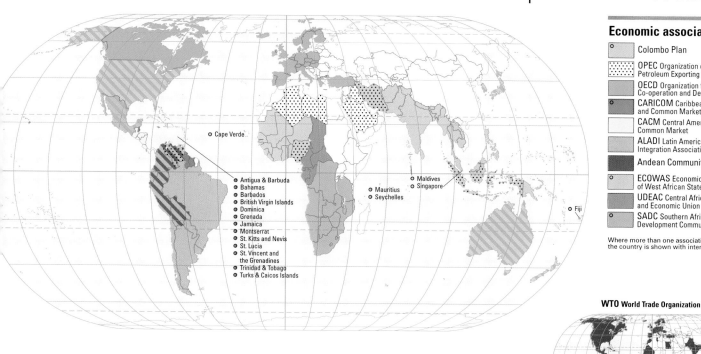

Economic associations

- Colombo Plan
- OPEC Organization of Petroleum Exporting Countries
- OECD Organization for Economic Co-operation and Development
- CARICOM Caribbean Community and Common Market
- CACM Central American Common Market
- ALADI Latin American Integration Association
- Andean Community
- ECOWAS Economic Community of West African States
- UDEAC Central African Customs and Economic Union
- SADC Southern African Development Community

Where more than one association is involved, the country is shown with interlocking shading.

Cape Verde

- Antigua & Barbuda
- Bahamas
- Barbados
- British Virgin Islands
- Dominica
- Grenada
- Jamaica
- Montserrat
- St. Kitts and Nevis
- St. Lucia
- St. Vincent and the Grenadines
- Trinidad & Tobago
- Turks & Caicos Islands

- Mauritius
- Seychelles

- Maldives
- Singapore

- Fiji

WTO World Trade Organization

WTO World Trade Organization

- Antigua & Barbuda
- Azerbaijan[†]
- Bahamas
- Bahrain
- Barbados
- Brunei
- Burundi
- Cyprus
- Dominica
- Fiji
- Grenada
- Israel
- Jamaica
- Kiribati
- Kuwait
- Laos[†]
- Liechtenstein
- Luxembourg
- Maldives
- Malta
- Mauritius
- Qatar
- St. Kitts and Nevis
- St. Lucia
- St. Vincent and the Grenadines
- Samoa
- Seychelles
- Singapore
- Solomon Islands
- Somalia[†]
- Sudan[†]
- Tajikistan[†]
- Trinidad & Tobago
- Turkmenistan[†]
- Vanuatu

[†]observer status

Commonwealth of Nations

Commonwealth of Nations

UNCTAD

United Nations Conference on Trade and Development

Almost all nations (191) are now members, Western Sahara is the only non-member.

EU

European Union

For members see page 37.

United Nations

The following countries are **non-members**

Northern Marianas
Switzerland[†]
Taiwan
Vatican City[†]
Western Sahara

[†] observer status

Headquarters of selected World Organizations

Brussels:
The European Union
North Atlantic Treaty Organization (NATO)

The Hague:
International Court of Justice

New York:
United Nations

Paris:
United National Education, Scientific and Cultural Organization (UNESCO)
Organization for Economic Co-operation and Development (OECD)

Rome:
Food and Agricultural Organization of the United Nations (FAO)

Geneva:
World Health Organization (WHO)
World Trade Organization (WTO)

Washington:
Organization of American States (OAS)

Addis Ababa:
Organization of African Unity (OAU)

Cairo:
Arab League

Singapore:
Asia Pacific Economic Co-operation (APEC)

Strasbourg:
Council of Europe
European Parliament

- Andorra
- Cyprus
- Liechtenstein
- Luxemburg
- Malta
- San Marino

- Cape Verde
- São Tomé & Príncipe

- Bahrain

- Cook Islands
- Fiji
- Kiribati
- Marshall Islands
- Federated States of Micronesia
- Nauru
- Niue
- Palau
- Samoa
- Solomon Islands
- Tonga
- Tuvalu
- Vanuatu

- Antigua & Barbuda
- Bahamas
- Barbados
- Dominica
- Grenada
- Jamaica
- St. Kitts and Nevis
- St. Lucia
- St. Vincent and the Grenadines
- Trinidad & Tobago

- Burundi
- Comoros
- Mauritius
- Rwanda
- Seychelles

- Brunei
- Singapore

International organizations

- South Pacific Forum
- ASEAN Association of South East Asian Nations
- OAS Organization of American States
- Arab League
- OAU Organization of African Unity
- NATO North Atlantic Treaty Organization
- Council of Europe
- APEC Asia Pacific Economic Co-operation
- CIS Commonwealth of Independent States

Where more than one organization is involved, the country is shown with interlocking shading.

Desertification and tropical deforestation

existing areas of desert

areas with a high risk of desertification

areas with a moderate risk of desertification

existing areas of tropical rain forest

former areas of tropical rain forest

Countries losing greatest areas of forest
('000 hectares) 1990 – 2000

Brazil	2309
Indonesia	1312
Sudan	959
Zambia	851
Mexico	631
Congo Dem. Rep.	532
Myanmar	517

Scale 1: 240 000 000

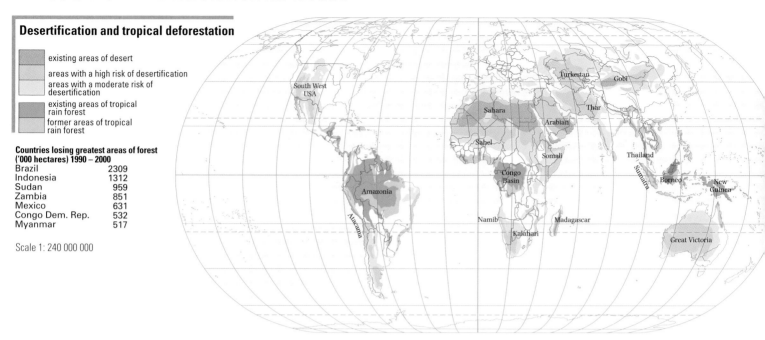

Acid rain

Sulphur and nitrogen emissions
Oxides of sulphur and nitrogen produced by burning fossil fuel react with rain to form dilute sulphuric and nitric acids

areas with high levels of fossil fuel burning

• cities where sulphur dioxide emissions are recorded and exceed World Health Organization recommended levels

Areas of acid rain deposition
Annual mean values of pH in precipitation

—— pH less than 4.2 (most acidic)

—— pH 4.2–4.6

—— pH 4.6–5.0

⊂⊃ other areas where acid rain is becoming a problem

Lower pH values are more acidic. 'Clean' rain water is slightly acidic with a pH of 5.6. The pH scale is logarithmic, so that a value of 4.6 is ten times as acidic as normal rain.

Scale 1: 190 000 000

Global warming

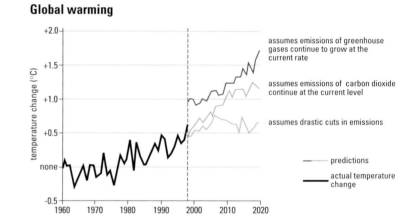

assumes emissions of greenhouse gases continue to grow at the current rate

assumes emissions of carbon dioxide continue at the current level

assumes drastic cuts in emissions

—— predictions

—— actual temperature change

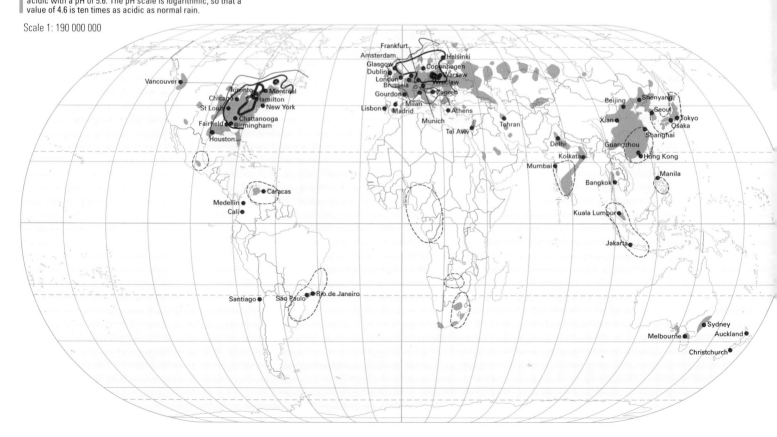

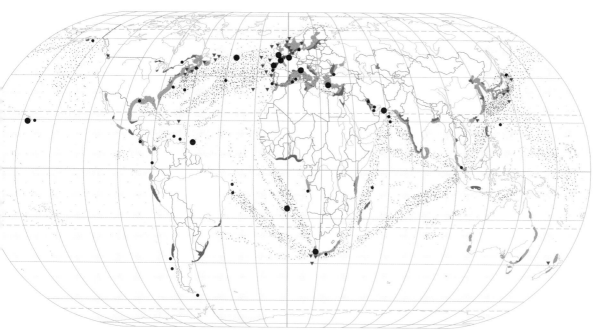

Sea pollution

Major oil spills

- ● over 100 000 tonnes
- • under 100 000 tonnes
- ∴∴ frequent oil slicks from shipping

Other sea pollution

- ◖ severe pollution
- ◖ moderate pollution
- ▼ deep sea dump sites

Major oil spills ('000 tonnes)

1977	*Ekofisk* well blow-out, North Sea	270
1979	*Ixtoc 1* well blow-out, Gulf of Mexico	600
1979	Collision of *Atlantic Empress* and *Aegean Captain*, off Tobago, Caribbean	370
1983	*Nowruz* well blow-out, The Gulf	600
1989	*Exxon Valdez* spills oil off the coast of Alaska	250
1991	Release of oil by Iraqi troops, *Sea Island* terminal, The Gulf	799
2002	*Prestige* oil tanker sinks off the coast of Spain	77

Phytoplankton in the Mediterranean Sea

Phytoplankton are micro-organisms that thrive in shallow, polluted sea areas. In this false colour satellite image red, orange, and yellow show the highest densities of phytoplankton. Green and blue show the lowest densities.

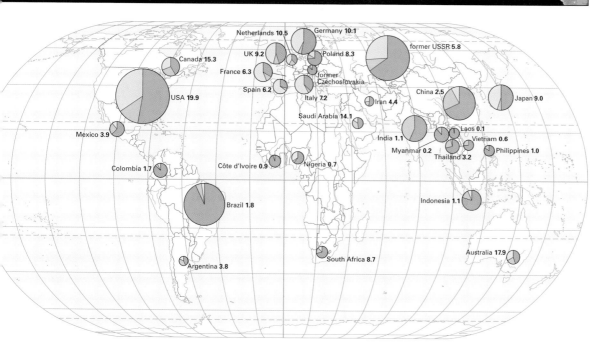

Greenhouse gases

Highest total emissions by country
thousand tonnes of carbon

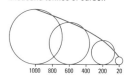

1000	800	600	400	200	20

Types of gas

- carbon dioxide
- methane
- chlorofluorocarbons (CFC's)

15.3 per capita carbon dioxide emissions for selected countries (metric tons)

Scale 1: 125 000 000 (main map

Selected tourist destinations

The locations shown represent a limited
selection of important tourism sites.

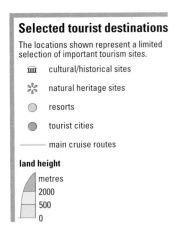

🏛 cultural/historical sites

🌼 natural heritage sites

⬤ resorts

⬤ tourist cities

—— main cruise routes

land height

metres
2000
500
0

Top tourist destinations, 2001

	arrivals (000's)	% change 2000–2001
France	76 500	1.2
Spain	49 500	3.4
USA	45 500	-10.6
Italy	39 000	-5.3
China	33 200	6.2
United Kingdom	23 400	-7.4
Russian Federation	21 200	0.0
Mexico	19 800	-4.0
Canada	19 700	-0.1
Austria	18 200	1.1

Market share, 2001

percent of all international tourist arrivals

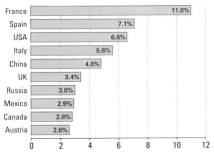

France	11.0%
Spain	7.1%
USA	6.6%
Italy	5.6%
China	4.8%
UK	3.4%
Russia	3.0%
Mexico	2.9%
Canada	2.8%
Austria	2.6%

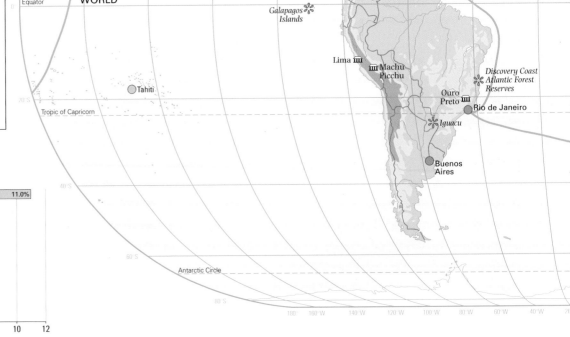

Earnings from tourism, 2000

tourist receipts in million $US

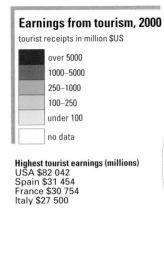

	over 5000
	1000–5000
	250–1000
	100–250
	under 100
	no data

Highest tourist earnings (millions)
USA $82 042
Spain $31 454
France $30 754
Italy $27 500

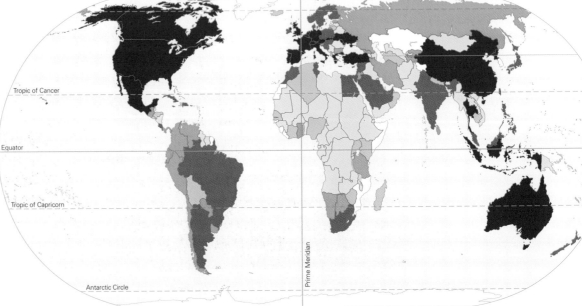

Eckert IV Projection   © Oxford University Pr

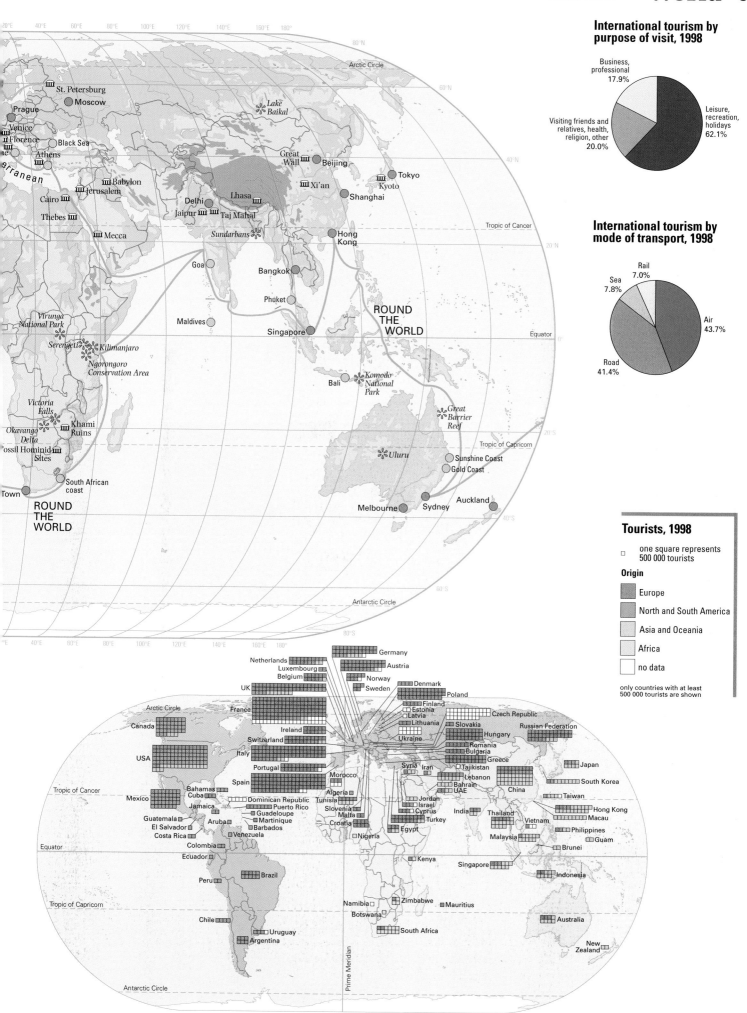

International tourism by purpose of visit, 1998

Business, professional
17.9%

Leisure, recreation, holidays
62.1%

Visiting friends and relatives, health, religion, other
20.0%

International tourism by mode of transport, 1998

Rail 7.0%

Sea 7.8%

Air 43.7%

Road 41.4%

Tourists, 1998

□ one square represents 500 000 tourists

Origin

- Europe
- North and South America
- Asia and Oceania
- Africa
- no data

only countries with at least 500 000 tourists are shown

St. Petersburg
Moscow
Prague
Lake Baikal
Venice
Florence
Black Sea
Athens
erranean
Babylon
Jerusalem
Cairo
Thebes
Mecca
Delhi
Lhasa
Jaipur
Taj Mahal
Sundarbans
Great Wall
Beijing
Xi'an
Tokyo
Kyoto
Shanghai
Goa
Bangkok
Phuket
Hong Kong
Maldives
Singapore
ROUND THE WORLD
Virunga National Park
Serengeti
Kilimanjaro
Ngorongoro Conservation Area
Bali
Komodo National Park
Great Barrier Reef
Victoria Falls
Khami Ruins
Okavango Delta
ossil Hominid Sites
Uluru
Sunshine Coast
Gold Coast
Town
South African coast
ROUND THE WORLD
Melbourne
Sydney
Auckland

Germany
Netherlands
Luxembourg
Belgium
UK
Austria
Norway
Sweden
Denmark
Poland
France
Finland
Estonia
Latvia
Lithuania
Czech Republic
Ireland
Slovakia
Russian Federation
Switzerland
Ukraine
Hungary
Italy
Romania
Bulgaria
Greece
Canada
Portugal
Syria
Iran
Japan
USA
Spain
Morocco
Tajikistan
South Korea
Lebanon
Bahrain
UAE
China
Bahamas
Mexico
Cuba
Algeria
Tunisia
Jordan
Israel
Cyprus
Taiwan
Jamaica
Dominican Republic
Puerto Rico
Slovenia
Malta
Turkey
India
Thailand
Hong Kong
Macau
Guatemala
Guadeloupe
Martinique
Croatia
Vietnam
El Salvador
Aruba
Barbados
Egypt
Philippines
Costa Rica
Venezuela
Nigeria
Malaysia
Guam
Colombia
Brunei
Ecuador
Kenya
Singapore
Indonesia
Peru
Brazil
Namibia
Zimbabwe
Mauritius
Botswana
Chile
Uruguay
South Africa
Australia
Argentina
New Zealand

Time zones, 2003

Minus numbers show hours behind
Greenwich Mean Time (GMT).
Plus numbers show hours ahead of GMT.

- even numbers of hours difference from GMT
- odd numbers of hours difference from GMT
- half an hour difference from adjacent zone
- less than half an hour difference from adjacent zone

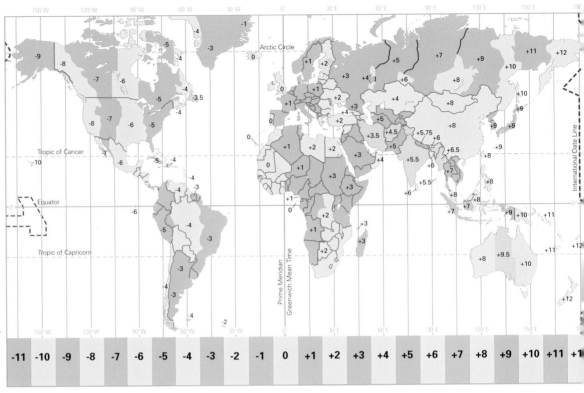

Longitude is measured from the **prime meridian** which passes through Greenwich. There are 24 standard time zones, each of 15° of longitude. The edges of these time zones usually follow international boundaries.

The **international date line** marks the point where one calendar day ends and another begins. A traveller crossing from east to west moves forward one day. Crossing from west to east the calendar goes back one day.

| -11 | -10 | -9 | -8 | -7 | -6 | -5 | -4 | -3 | -2 | -1 | 0 | +1 | +2 | +3 | +4 | +5 | +6 | +7 | +8 | +9 | +10 | +11 | +1 |

Distance

Flight distance between cities in kilometres
to convert kilometres to miles multiply by 0.62

Beijing

19 307	**Buenos Aires**										
1983	18 484	**Hong Kong**									
11 710	8088	10 732	**Johannesburg**								
8145	11 161	9645	9071	**London**							
10 081	9871	11 678	16 676	8774	**Los Angeles**						
12 468	7468	14 162	14 585	8936	2484	**Mexico City**					
4774	14 952	4306	8274	7193	14 033	15 678	**Mumbai**				
11 000	8548	12 984	12 841	5580	3951	3371	12 565	**New York**			
8226	11 097	9613	8732	338	9032	9210	7032	5839	**Paris**		
4468	15 904	2661	8860	10 871	14 146	16 630	3919	15 533	10 758	**Singapore**	
8949	11 800	7374	11 040	16 992	12 073	12 969	9839	15 989	16 962	6300	**Sydney**
2113	18 388	2903	13 547	9581	8823	11 355	6758	10 871	9726	5322	7823	**Tokyo**

The Earth rotates from west to east

The Earth rotates on its axis once in every 24 hours.

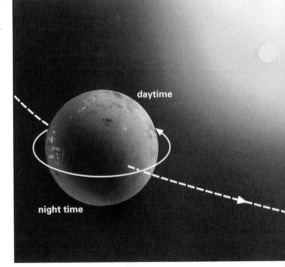

daytime

night time

Flying time

Typical flight times by air between cities in hours and minutes
ooo means there is no direct flight available, early 2002

Beijing

ooo	**Buenos Aires**										
3.00	ooo	**Hong Kong**									
ooo	ooo	13.00	**Johannesburg**								
10.25	14.50	13.30	10.50	**London**							
13.30	16.40	14.50	ooo	13.00	**Los Angeles**						
ooo	13.10	ooo	ooo	11.05	4.15	**Mexico City**					
ooo	ooo	7.45	20.15	10.30	ooo	ooo	**Mumbai**				
25.20	13.25	19.25	16.25	7.20	6.00	6.00	20.05	**New York**			
10.20	13.50	12.45	10.55	1.10	12.30	12.20	12.10	7.40	**Paris**		
6.15	ooo	4.05	10.30	14.40	18.45	ooo	6.30	22.05	14.15	**Singapore**	
12.55	16.35	8.50	14.30	22.45	14.35	ooo	14.40	21.45	22.25	8.55	**Sydney**
3.35	ooo	4.55	ooo	12.40	10.40	15.50	12.35	15.55	12.50	7.05	10.00	**Tokyo**

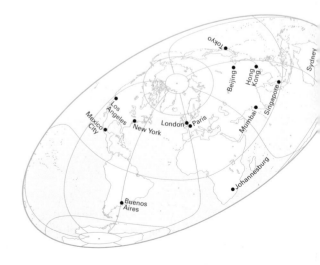

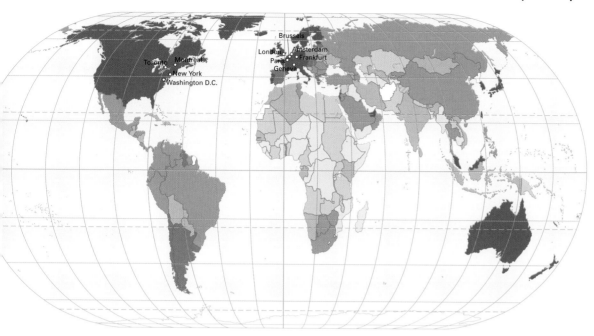

Toronto, Montreal, New York, Washington D.C., Brussels, London, Paris, Geneva, Amsterdam, Frankfurt

Internet users, 2002

per 10 000 people

over 2500
1000–2500
250–1000
100–250
25–100
under 25

○ ten most interconnected cities

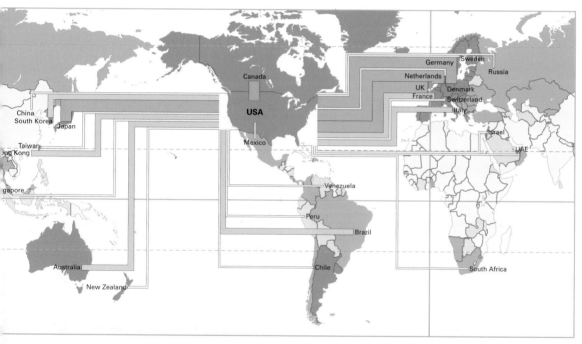

China, South Korea, Japan, Taiwan, Hong Kong, Singapore, Australia, New Zealand, Canada, USA, Mexico, Venezuela, Peru, Brazil, Chile, Germany, Sweden, Netherlands, Russia, UK, France, Denmark, Switzerland, Italy, Israel, UAE, South Africa

Internet traffic, 2002

internet providers
per 10 000 people

over 100
10–100
1–10
under 1

internet bandwidth
megabits per second (Mbps)

over 5000
1000–5000
under 1000

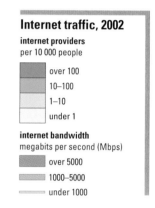

Internet traffic flow

The 'arc map' shows internet traffic between 50 countries. Arcs are coloured to show internet traffic between countries. The height of each arc is proportional to the volume of internet traffic flowing over a link, so the highest arcs represent the greatest volume of traffic.

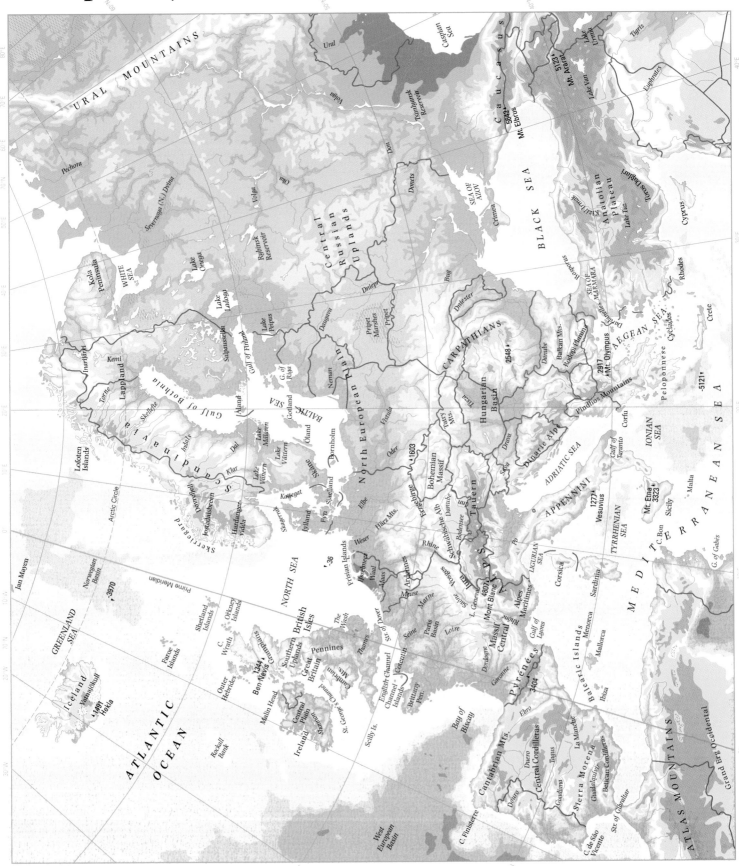

boundaries
— international
--- disputed

physical features
river, lake
seasonal river
seasonal lake
marsh
salt lake
salt pan
ice cap
sand dunes

sea ice
unnavigable
pack ice
— autumn minimum
— spring maximum

land height and sea depth

metres
5000
3000
2000
1000
500
300
200
100
0

sea level
200
3000
4000
5000
6000

spot height in metres
sea depth in metres

Scale 1:22 000 000

The European Union

date of joining

- 1957
- 1973
- 1981
- 1986
- 1990
- 1995
- 2004
- negotiating membership
- ★ headquarters

Population Growth

millions of people

550 500 450 400 350 300 250 200 150 100 50 0

1957
1973
1981
1990
1995
2004
negotiating

Political

boundaries
— international
– – – disputed

settlements
■ capital city
• other important city

The European Union

Brussels: Headquarters

Strasbourg: European Parliament

Luxembourg: European Court of Justice

Headquarters of other European and World Organisations

The Hague: International Court of Justice

Geneva: World Health Organisation (WHO)

Paris: United National Education, Scientific and Cultural Organisation (UNESCO)

Organisation for Economic Cooperation and Development (OECD)

Rome: Food and Agricultural Organisation of the United Nations (FAO)

Scale 1: 22 000 000 (main map)

Conical Orthomorphic Projection

© Oxford University Press

ICELAND — Reykjavik

ATLANTIC OCEAN

Arctic Circle

Prime Meridian

NORTH SEA

UNITED KINGDOM — Edinburgh, Manchester, Birmingham, London

REPUBLIC OF IRELAND — Dublin

NORWAY — Oslo

SWEDEN — Göteborg, Stockholm

FINLAND — Helsinki

DENMARK — Copenhagen

Hamburg, Düsseldorf, Berlin

GERMANY — Frankfurt am Main, Munich

NETHERLANDS — Amsterdam, Rotterdam

BELGIUM — Brussels

LUXEMBOURG — Luxembourg

FRANCE — Paris, Lyons, Marseilles, Bordeaux

Bern

SWITZERLAND

LIECHTENSTEIN

SPAIN — Madrid, Barcelona, Valencia, Seville, Oporto

PORTUGAL — Lisbon, Oporto

ANDORRA

Gibraltar (UK)

Ceuta (Sp.), Melilla (Sp.)

ALGERIA

TUNISIA

MEDITERRANEAN SEA

ITALY — Milan, Rome, Naples

SAN MARINO

MONACO

MALTA — Valletta

SLOVENIA — Ljubljana

CROATIA — Zagreb

AUSTRIA — Vienna

CZECH REP. — Prague

SLOVAKIA — Bratislava

HUNGARY — Budapest

POLAND — Warsaw, Łódź, Kraków

KALININGRAD (Russia)

LITHUANIA — Vilnius

LATVIA — Riga

ESTONIA — Tallinn

BALTIC SEA

BELARUS — Minsk

UKRAINE — Kiev, Kharkov, Donets'k, Odessa

MOLDOVA — Chișinău

ROMANIA — Bucharest

BULGARIA — Sofia

SERBIA AND MONTENEGRO — Belgrade

BOSNIA-HERZEGOVINA — Sarajevo

FYRO MACEDONIA — Skopje

ALBANIA — Tiranë

GREECE — Athens

RUSSIAN FEDERATION (RUSSIA) — Moscow, St. Petersburg, Nizhniy Novgorod, Volgograd, Rostov-on-Don

BLACK SEA

GEORGIA — Tbilisi

TURKEY — Ankara, Istanbul, Izmir, Adana

CYPRUS — Nicosia

SYRIA

IRAQ

JORDAN

LEBANON

ISRAEL

40°E

20°E

60°N

50°N

Arctic Circle

Prime Meridian

Scale 1: 50 000 00

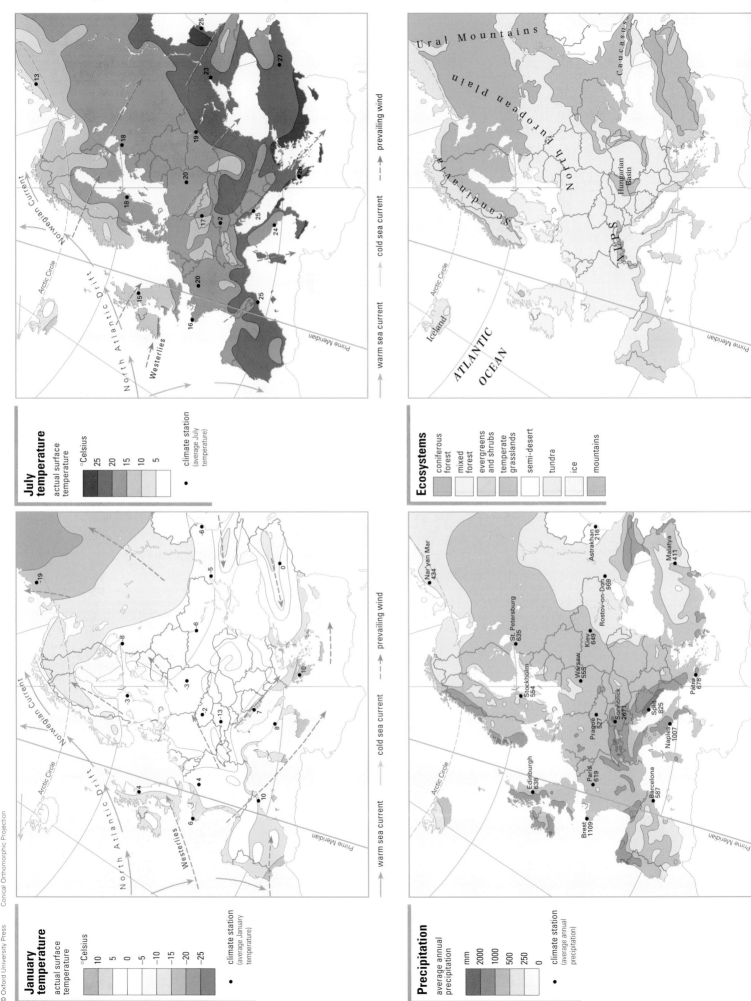

July temperature

actual surface temperature

°Celsius
25
20
15
10
5

climate station (average July temperature)

January temperature

actual surface temperature

°Celsius
10
5
0
–5
–10
–15
–20
–25

climate station (average January temperature)

Ecosystems

coniferous forest
mixed forest
evergreens and shrubs
temperate grasslands
semi-desert
tundra
ice
mountains

Precipitation

average annual precipitation

mm
2000
1000
500
250
0

climate station (average annual precipitation)

prevailing wind
cold sea current
warm sea current

© Oxford University Press

Conical Orthomorphic Projection

Scale 1: 35 000 000

Arctic Circle

Prime Meridian

St Petersburg

Moscow Basin

Donbas

London

Lower Rhine

Ruhr

Paris Basin

Po Valley

Lower Rhone

Barcelona

Naples

Bilbao

Largest urban agglomerations in Europe, 2000

An urban agglomeration is the population contained within a city plus the suburban fringe lying outside of, but adjacent to, the city boundaries.

millions of people

Paris
Istanbul
Moscow
London
Essen
St. Petersburg
Milan
Madrid
Frankfurt
Katowice
Berlin
Düsseldorf
Ankara
Athens
Cologne
Naples

Population density

people per square kilometre

over 200
100–200
10–100
1–10
under 1

Major cities

population in millions

■ over 3
□ 1–3
● 0.5–1
· 0.1–0.5

© Oxford University Press

Conical Orthomorphic Projection

Minerals

◇ iron ore
◇ manganese
◈ chromium
◇ nickel
⊟ tin
◈ lead
◈ zinc
◈ copper
◈ bauxite

Energy

▲ coal
▲ oil
△ gas
△ hydro

Livestock

sheep
cattle
pigs

Crops

wine grapes
tobacco
fruit
* sugar
cotton

Land use

rough grazing
shifting cultivation
mixed subsistence
grazing and stock rearing
mixed farming
grain farming
Mediterranean farming
dairy farming
specialized horticulture
forestry
industrial areas
unproductive land

Perm
Ufa
Samara
Kazan'
Nizhniy Novgorod
Volgograd
Rostov-na-Donu
Donets'k
Kharkiv
St Petersburg
Moscow
Kiev
Dnipropetrovsk
Odessa
Minsk
Warsaw
Bucharest
Sofia
Belgrade
Budapest
Vienna
Prague
Nuremburg
Stockholm
Hamburg
Berlin
Frankfurt am Main
Cologne
Essen
Düsseldorf
Mannheim
Stuttgart
Munich
Rome
Milan
Naples
Marseilles
Lyons
Barcelona
Paris
Lille
Rotterdam
Amsterdam
Manchester
Birmingham
London
Madrid
Lisbon
Ankara
Adana
Konya
Istanbul
Bursa
Izmir
Athens

Arctic Circle

Prime Meridian

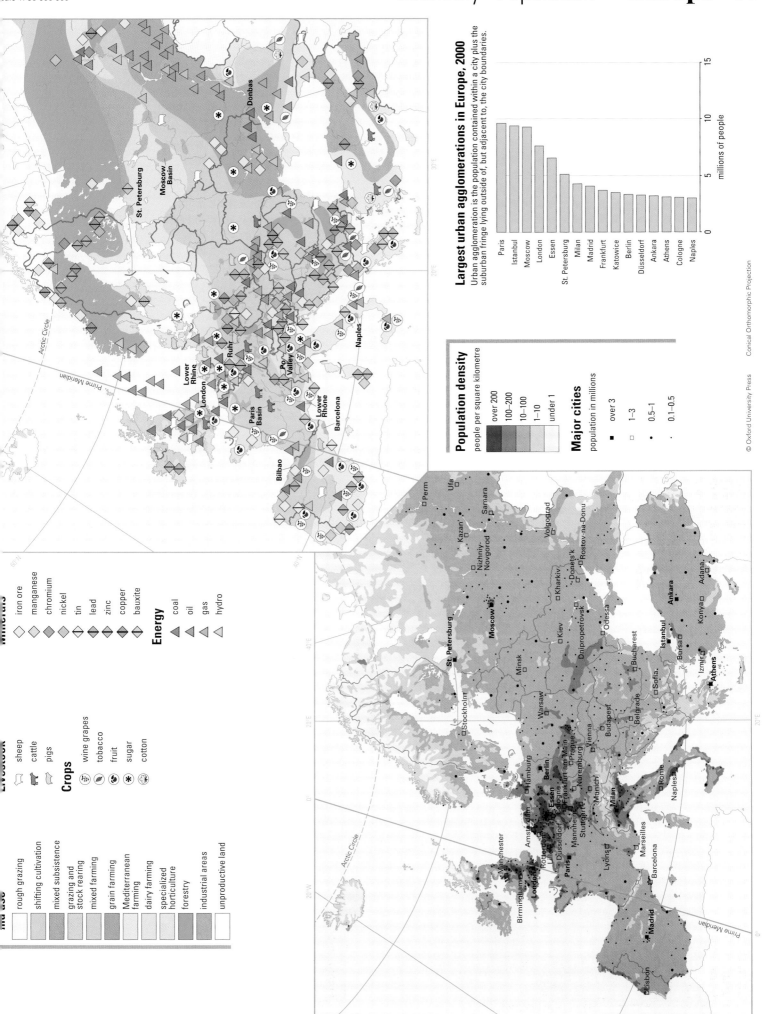

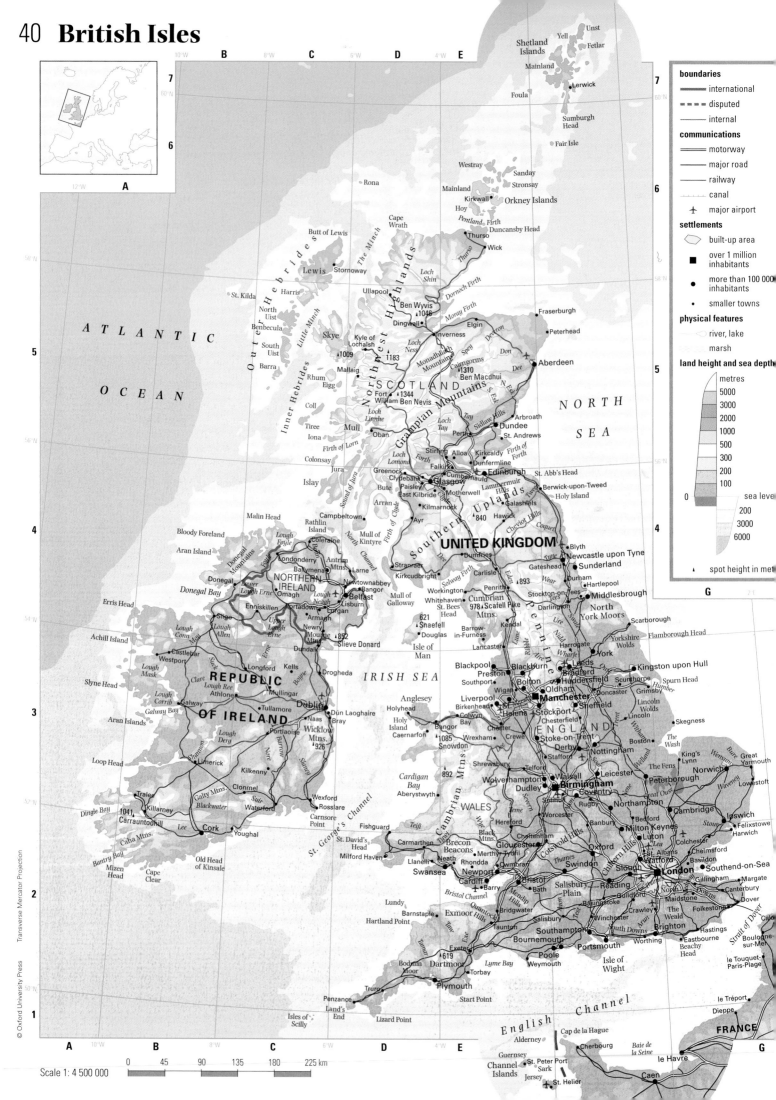

NORTH SEA

NETHERLANDS

BELGIUM

GERMANY

FRANCE

LUXEMBOURG

Amsterdam · Rotterdam · The Hague · Haarlem · Leiden · Utrecht · Groningen · Leeuwarden · Zwolle · Arnhem · Nijmegen · Eindhoven · Breda · Tilburg · 's Hertogenbosch · Dordrecht · Almere · Apeldoorn · Enschede · Deventer · Maastricht · Den Helder

Antwerpen · Brussels (Bruxelles) · Brugge · Gent · Namur · Charleroi · Liège · Mons · Leuven (Louvain) · Hasselt · Oostende · Kortrijk · Aalst

Bremen · Bremerhaven · Oldenburg · Osnabrück · Münster · Dortmund · Essen · Duisburg · Düsseldorf · Cologne (Köln) · Bonn · Mönchengladbach · Wuppertal · Mannheim · Frankfurt am Main · Wiesbaden · Mainz · Koblenz · Trier · Saarbrücken · Karlsruhe · Heidelberg · Darmstadt · Bielefeld · Paderborn

Paris · Lille · Reims · Amiens · Arras · Metz · Nancy · Strasbourg · Luxembourg

NIEDER-SACHSEN · NORDRHEIN-WESTFALEN · HESSEN · RHEINLAND-PFALZ · SAARLAND · BADEN-WÜRTTEMBERG

FRIESLAND · GRONINGEN · DRENTHE · OVERIJSSEL · GELDERLAND · NOORD-BRABANT · LIMBURG · ZEELAND · NOORD-HOLLAND · ZUID-HOLLAND · UTRECHT

VLAANDEREN · WEST-VLAANDEREN · OOST-VLAANDEREN · BRABANT · HAINAUT · NAMUR · LUXEMBOURG · LIÈGE

Waddeneilanden (West Frisian Islands) · Ostfriesische Inseln (East Frisian Islands) · Waddenzee · IJsselmeer · ARDENNES · Eifel

1 : 2 500 000

25   50   75   100   125 km

Conical Orthomorphic Projection
© Oxford University Press

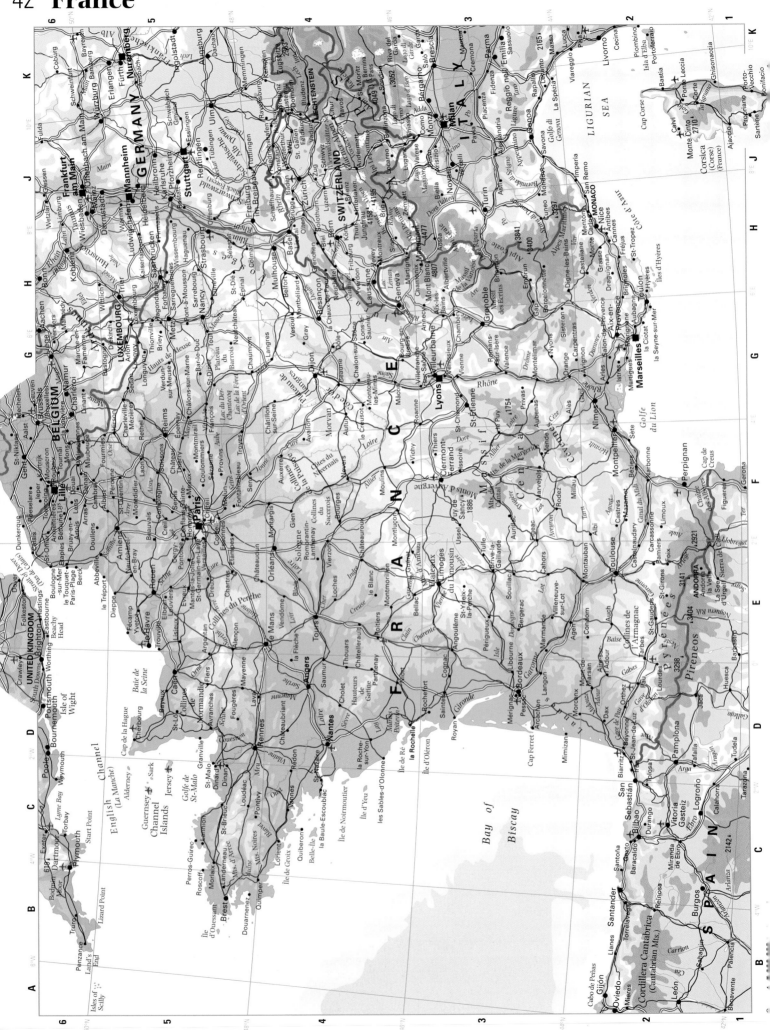

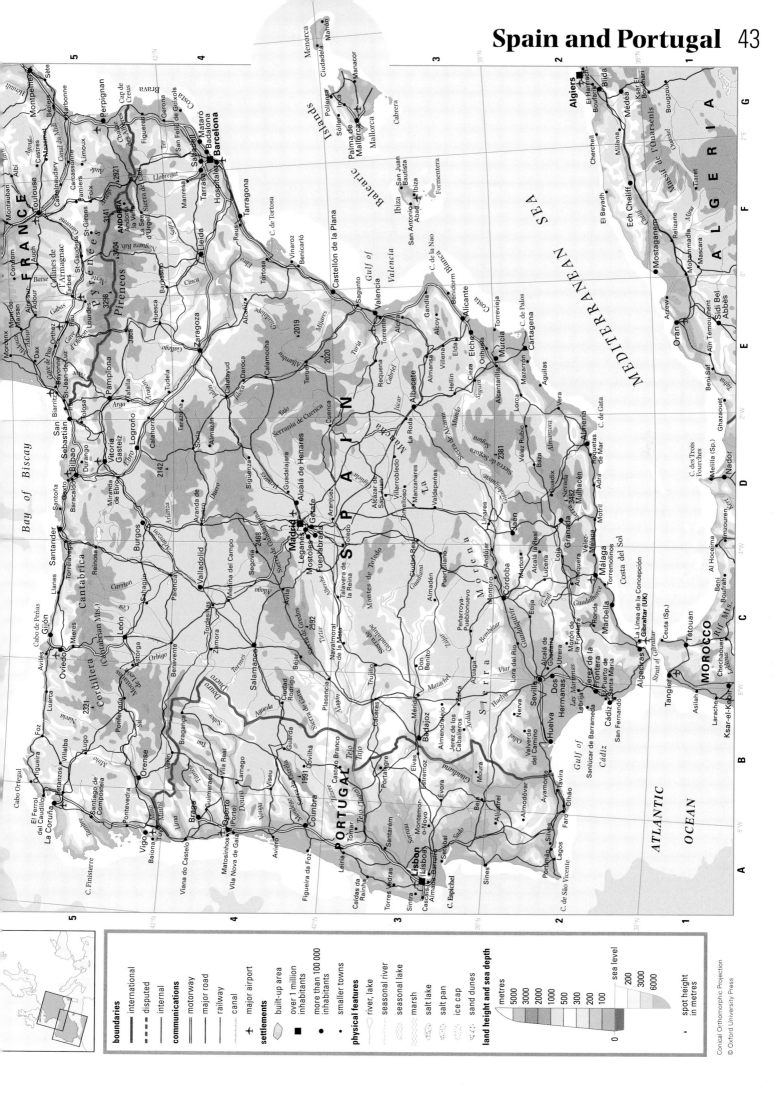

boundaries
- international
- disputed
- internal

communications
- motorway
- major road
- railway
- canal
- major airport

settlements
- built-up area
- over 1 million inhabitants
- more than 100 000 inhabitants
- smaller towns

physical features
- river, lake
- seasonal river
- seasonal lake
- marsh
- salt lake
- salt pan
- ice cap
- sand dunes

land height and sea depth

metres		
5000		
3000		
2000	sea level	
1000	200	
500	3000	
300	6000	
200		
100		
0		

spot height in metres

boundaries
— international
--- disputed
— internal

communications
— motorway
— major road
— railway
┼┼┼┼ canal
✈ major airport

settlements
⬡ built-up area
■ over 1 million inhabitants
● more than 100 000 inhabitants
· smaller towns

physical features
〰 river, lake
seasonal river
seasonal lake
marsh
salt lake
salt pan
ice cap
sand dunes

sea ice
unnavigable
pack ice
– autumn minimum
– spring maximum

land height and sea depth
metres
5000
3000
2000
1000
500
300
200
100
0 sea level
200
3000
6000

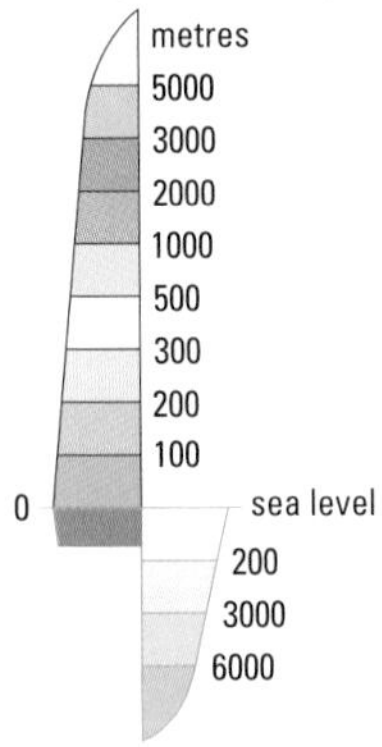

▲ spot height in metres

Scale 1: 5 000 000

0   50   100   150   200   250 km

Conical Orthomorphic Projection

© Oxford University

BALTIC SEA

LITHUANIA

BELARUS

POLAND

UKRAINE

SLOVAKIA

HUNGARY

ROMANIA

MOLDOVA

CROATIA

BOSNIA-HERZEGOVINA

SERBIA AND MONTENEGRO

BULGARIA

PUBLIC

Gulf of Gdańsk

CARPATHIANS

Meridionali

Carpatii

Dinara Planina

Major cities and towns (selection):

Kaunas, Vilnius, Orsha, Mahilyow, Kaliningrad (RUSSIA), Chernyakhovsk, Gusev, Marijampole, Maladzyechna, Barysaw, Minsk, Wejherowo, Gdynia, Sopot, Gdańsk, Elbląg, Sovetsk, Neman, Kurskiy Zaliv, Babruysk, Sozh, Słupsk, Koszalin, Tczew, Malbork, Ostróda, Olsztyn, Kętrzyn, Ełk, Suwałki, Hrodna, Lida, Slonim, Baranavichy, Slutsk, Zhlobin, Homyel', Szczecinek, Starogard Gdański, Iława, Jezioro Śniardwy, Szczytno, Łomża, Białystok, Soligorsk, Rechitsa, Wałcz, Jastrowie, Bydgoszcz, Toruń, Mława, Ostrołęka, Ostrów Mazowiecka, Bielsk Podlaski, Kobryn, Pinsk, Luninyets, Pripyat', Mazyr, Kalinkavichy, Piła, Notéc, Inowrocław, Włocławek, Ciechanów, Nowy Dwor Mazowiecki, Warsaw (Warszawa), Siedlce, Brest, Ratno, Chornobyl', Poznań, Gniezno, Konin, Płock, Pruszków, Żyrardów, Łuków, Biała Podlaska, Sarny, Ubort, Leszno, Jarocin, Kalisz, Zgierz, Łódź, Skierniewice, Piła, Radom, Lublin, Chełm, Vladimir Volynskiy, Kovel', Luts'k, Rivne, Shepetovka, Zhytomyr, Kiev, Fastov, Krotoszyn, Ostrow Wielkopolski, Pabianice, Zduńska Wola, Tomaszów Mazowiecki, Puławy, Zamość, Chervonograd, Dubno, Brody, Kremenets, Berdychiv, Bila Tserkva, Legnica, Wrocław, Brzeg, Opole, Częstochowa, Radomsko, Włoszczowa, Kielce, Starachowice, Ostrowiec Świetokrzyski, Stalowa Wola, Wałbrzych, Kłodzko, Nysa, Zabrze, Bytom, Sosnowiec, Gliwice, Myszków, Jura Krakowska, Tarnobrzeg, Przeworsk, L'viv, Zolochev, Ternopil', Khmel'nyts'kyy, Kazatin, Vinnytsya, Opava, Ostrava, Raciborz, Rybnik, Katowice, Kraków, Tarnów, Rzeszów, Przemyśl, Sambor, Drohobyč, Borislav, Stryy, Ivano-Frankivs'k, Kam''yanets'-Podil's'kyy, Mohyliv-Podil's'kyy, Zhmerynka, Olomouc, Přerov, Frýdek Místek, Bielsko-Biała, Nowy Sacz, Jasło, Krosno, Dolina, Kolomyya, Khotin, Brno, Zlín, Žilina, Ruzomberok, Martin, Poprad, Prešov, Košice, Uzhgorod, Mukachevo, Beregovo, Chernivtsi, Dorohoi, Soroca, Balta, Trenčín, Prievidza, Banská Bystrica, Zvolen, Rožňava, Uz, Sighetu Marmatiei, Borsa, Rădăuti, Botoșani, Bălti, Vienna (Wien), Schwechat, Bratislava, Nitra, Levice, Salgótarján, Miskolc, Nyíregyháza, Satu Mare, Vatra Dornei, Suceava, Pașcani, Iași, Chișinău, Eisenstadt, Wiener Neustadt, Sopron, Mosonmagyaróvár, Komárno, Esztergom, Vác, Eger, Balassagyarmat, Debrecen, Carei, Baia Mare, Bistrita, Roman, Tighina, Tiraspol', Győr, Tatabánya, Gödöllő, Gyöngyös, Karcag, Zalău, Dej, Toplita, Piatra Neamt, Buhuși, Vaslui, Cimislia, Pápa, Székesfehérvár, Veszprém, Cegléd, Szolnok, Oradea, Ciucea, Cluj-Napoca, Turda, Târgu Mureș, Bacău, Comrat, Sarata, Szombathely, Dunaújváros, Kecskemét, Salonta, Beiuș, Comănești, Onești, Bârlad, Zalaegerszeg, Nagykanizsa, Kaposvár, Kiskunfélegyháza, Kiskunhalas, Hódmezővásárhely, Brad, Alba Iulia, Sebeș, Medias, Sighișoara, Miercurea-Ciuc, Baraolt, Adjud, Tecuci, Bothrad, Szekszárd, Szeged, Makó, Arad, Lipova, Deva, Hunedoara, Sibiu, Făgăraș, Sfântu Gheorghe, Focșani, Galati, Izmayil, Pécs, Baja, Subotica, Timișoara, Lugoj, Caransebeș, Reșita, Petroșani, 2548, Râmnicu Sărat, Brăila, Tulcea, Barcs, Virovitica, Sombor, Kikinda, Zrenjanin, Vršac, Oravita, Orșova, Drobeta-Turnu-Severin, Târgu Jiu, Râmnicu Vâlcea, Câmpulung, Câmpina, Ploiești, Buzău, Urziceni, Slobozia, Constanța, Eforie, Osijek, Vinkovci, Vukovar, Novi Sad, Pančevo, Belgrade, Smederevo, Pitești, Târgoviște, Titu, Bucharest, Călărași, Oltenita, Silistra, Mangalia, Banja Luka, Doboj, Tuzla, Loznica, Valjevo, Šabac, Craiova, Slatina, Caracal, Roșiori de Vede, Alexandria, Turnu Măgurele, Giurgiu, Ruse, Dobrich, Zenica, Čačak, Titovo Užice, Kragujevac, Kruševac, Vidin, Montana, Pleven, Razgrad, Shumen, Varna, Split, Sarajevo, Kraljevo, Niš, Dunav (Danube), Iskar, Pavlikeni, Tŭrgovishte

Rivers and features: Neman, Wisła (Vistula), Odra (Odra), Warta, Noteć, Narew, Bug, Pripyat', Styr', Goryn', Sluch', Teterev, Dnepr, Desna, Dnestr, Prut, Siret, Bistrita, Moldova, Jalomita, Dunărea (Danube), Mureș, Tisza, Drava, Sava, Drina, Olt, Lacul Razim, Dobrogea

Mountains: Tatry, Nízke Tatry 2043, 2663, Beskidy Zachodnie, 1074, 1490, 1015, 1827, 1836, 2058, 2102, 2107, 1336

Conical Orthomorphic Projection

boundaries
— international
- - - disputed
— internal

communications
═══ motorway
── major road
── railway
┼┼┼┼ canal
✈ major airport

settlements
⬡ built-up area
■ over 1 million inhabitants
● more than 100 000 inhabitants
• smaller towns

physical features
〜 river, lake
--- seasonal river
seasonal lake
marsh
salt lake
salt pan
ice cap
sand dunes

sea ice
unnavigable
pack ice
 – autumn minimum
 – spring maximum

land height and sea depth
metres
5000
3000
2000
1000
500
300
200
100
0 sea level
200
3000
6000

▲ spot height in metres

Scale 1: 5 000 000
0   50   100   150   200   250 km

Malta
1: 1 000 000

Countries: HUNGARY, CROATIA, BOSNIA-HERZEGOVINA, SERBIA AND MONTENEGRO, ROMANIA, BULGARIA, MOLDOVA, UKRAINE, ALBANIA, FYRO MACEDONIA, GREECE, TURKEY

Seas: BLACK SEA, SEA OF MARMARA, AEGEAN SEA, IONIAN SEA, IONIAN SEA, MIRTOAN SEA, SEA OF CRETE, Golfo di Táranto

Budapest, Tatabánya, Pápa, Székesfehérvár, Veszprém, bathely, szeg, Balaton, Nagykanizsa, Kaposvár, Pécs, Baja, Barcs, Sombor, Virovitica, Osijek, ROATIA, Slavonski Brod, Luka, Doboj, BOSNIA-HERZEGOVINA, Tuzla, Zenica, Planina, 2107, Sarajevo, Mostar, Metković, Peljesac, Trebinje, Nikšić, Dubrovnik, Podgorica, Skadarsko ezero, Shkodër

Kecskemét, Szolnok, Karcag, Cegléd, Kiskunfélegyháza, Kiskunhalas, Hódmezovasarhely, Szekszárd, Szeged, Makó, Arad, Lipova, Subotica, Kikinda, Timişoara, Lugoj, Zrenjanin, Vršac, Oravita, Novi Sad, Reşita, Caransebeş, Pančevo, Orşova, Belgrade, Sabac, Smederevo, Valjevo, Loznica, Čačak, Kragujevac, Kraljevo, Kruševac, Titovo Užice, 1336, 2522, Novi Pazar, Kosovska Mitrovica, 2382, Peć, Priština, Prizren, 2682, Uroševac, Vranje, Kukeš, Lezhe, 2702, Tetovo, Skopje, Gostivar, Titov Veles, Štip, ALBANIA, Tiranë, FYRO MACEDONIA, Prilep, Durrës, Kavajë, Elbasan, Ohridsko ezero, Bitola, Prespansko ezero, 2379, Lushnjë, Berat, Fier, Korçë, Flórina, Vlorë, Vilosa, 2633, Korca, Gjirokastër, Kastoriá, Kozáni

Zalău, Dej, Bistrita, 2102, Roman, Oradea, Ciucea, Cluj-Napoca, Toplita, Piatra Neamţ, Buhuşi, Vaslui, Turda, Targu Mureş, Comăneşti, Bacău, Oneşti, Medias, Miercurea-Ciuc, Sighisoara, Baraolt, Adjud, Tecuci, Brad, Alba Iulia, Sebes, Sfântu Gheorghe, Focşani, Deva, Hunedoara, Sibiu, Făgăraş, Braşov, Galati, 2548, Râmnicu Sărat, Brăila, Petroşani, Meridionali, Buzău, Tulcea, Carpatii, Câmpulung, Câmpina, Ploieşti, Târgu Jiu, Râmnica Vâlcea, Târgovişte, Vrziceni, Slobozia, Drobeta-Turnu-Severin, Slatina, Titu, Bucharest, Călăraşi, Constanta, Craiova, Roşiori de Vede, Oltenita, Silistra, Eforie, Caracal, Alexandria, Giurgiu, Dunav (Danube), Mangalia, Turno Magurele, Ruse, Dobrich, Vidin, Razgrad, Pleven, Shumen, Varna, Montana, Vratsa, Lovech, Pavlikeni, Veliko Târnovo, Türgovişte, BULGARIA, Gabrovo, Stara, Sliven, Karnobat, Burgas, Pernik, Sofia, Kazanlük, Stara Zagora, Yambol, Kyustendil, 2925, Plovdiv, Dimitrovgrad, Blagoevgrad, Asenovgrad, Khaskovo, Edirne, Kirklareli, Pirin Planina, Smolyan, Svilengrad, Lüleburgaz, 2915, Arda, Rodopi Planina, Corlu, Kilyos, İstanbul, Tekirdağ, Keşan, Komotiní, Xánthi, Drama, Sérres, Kavála, Alexandroúpoli, Gelibolu, Biga, Bandirma, Canakkale, Mustafakemalpaşa, 1767, Balikesir, Edremit, Bergama, 1045, Thásos, Samothráki, Gökçeada, Limnos, Áthos 2033, Lésvos, Akhisar, Manisa, Mytilíni, Izmir, Turgutlu, Ödemiş, Nazilli, Chíos, Chíos, Torbali, Büyük Menderes, Çine, Milas, Muğla, 1215, Ródos (Rhodes), Kárpathos, Kásos

Kilkis, Edessa, Yiannitsá, Véroia, Thessaloníki, Chalkidikí, Polýgyros, Katerini, Ólympos 2917, Thermaikós Kólpos, Lárisa, Ioánnina, Tríkala, Vólos, Vóreioi Sporádes (Northern Sporades), AEGEAN SEA, Skýros, Limnos, 2128, Arta, Karpenísi, Lamía, Parnassós 2457, Évvoia (Euboea), Ákra Kafiréas, Préveza, Lefkáda, Agrínio, Leivadia, Chalkida, GREECE, Mesolóngi, Thíva, Patras, Aígio, Korinthiakós Kólpos, Kórinthos, Piraeus, Athens, Kéa, Ándros, Tínos, Sámos, Ikaría, Kérkyra (Corfu), Corfu, Iónia Nisiá (Ionian Islands), Kefalloniá, Zákynthos, Pýrgos, 2376, Trípol, Peloponnisos, Náfplio, Kýthnos, Kyklades (Cyclades), Dodekánisos (Dodecanese), Kálymnos, Gökova Körfezi, Kós, Kyparissiakós Kólpos, Kalamata, Spárti, 2407, Monemvasía, MIRTOAN SEA, Mílos, Sérifos, Sifnos, Páros, Náxos, Íos, Amorgós, Astypálaia, Anáfi, Ákra Akritas, Ákra Maléas, Neápoli, Thíra (Santorini), Ákra Taínaro, Kythira, SEA OF CRETE, Chaniá, Réthymno, Iráklion, 2456, Ágios Nikólaos, Pýrgos, Gávdos, Kríti (Crete)

Monopoli, Bari, Brindisi, Lecce, Táranto, Gallipoli, Otranto, Capo Santa Maria di Leuca, Ciró Marina, Crotone, Strait of Otranto

Oxford University Press

boundaries
—— international
--- disputed
— internal

communications
═══ motorway
—— major road
—— railway
++++ canal
✈ major airport

settlements
⬡ built-up area
■ over 1 million inhabitants
● more than 100 000 inhabitants
• smaller towns

physical features
river, lake
seasonal river
seasonal lake
marsh
salt lake
salt pan
ice cap
sand dunes

sea ice
unnavigable
pack ice
– autumn minimum
– spring maximum

land height and sea depth
metres
5000
3000
2000
1000
500
300
200
100
0 sea level
200
3000
6000

▲ spot height in metres

ICELAND
Arctic Circle
Grímsey
▲925
Ísafjördur
Siglufjördur
Húsavík
Akureyri
Vopnafjördur
Breidha Fjördur
Neskaupstadur
Stykkishólmur
Hofsjökull
Langjökull
▲2000
Vatnajökull
Faxaflói
Pjorsa
Höfn
Akranes
Hekla
Reykjavík
▲1491
Keflavík
Hafnarfjördur
Mýrdalsjökull
Vestmannaeyjar

ARCTIC OCEAN

BARENTS SEA

North Cape
Berlevåg
Hammerfest
Sørøya
Varangerhalvøya
637 ▲
Vardø
Varangerfjorden
Lopphavet
Poluostrov
Rybachiy
Vanna
Alta
1067
Pechenga
Ringvassoy
1139
Murma
Tromsø
Lakselv
Iesjavrre
Karasjok
Inarijärvi
Poluostrov
▲1144
Senja
Maanselka
Monchegorsk
Langoy
1681
Rasto
Enontekiö
Ozero Bol'shaya
Himmoya
807
Lokan
Kandalak
Narvik
Torneträsk
Porttipahdan
tekojärvi
Lofoten Is.
1901
Stora Lulevatten
Sodankylä
Ozero
Nordfold
2111
Gällivare
Pyaozero
2013
Jokkmokk
Kuolayarvi
Bodø
2021
Rovaniemi
Yli-kitka
Saltdal
Hornavan
Ozero
Mo-i-Rana
Arjeplog
Boden
Torneå
Kuusamo
Dønna
Røssvatnet
Piteälven
Övertorneå
Pudasjärvi
Mosjøen
1764
Uddjaur
Luleå
Ozero
Vega
Storuman
Piteå
Sredneye Kuy
Brønnøysund
Grane
Hailuoto
Oulu
Kiantajärvi
703
Skellefteälven
Kolvereid
Vilhelmina
Skellefteå
Oulu
järvi
Vikna
Namdalen
Hoting
Umeälven
Kajaani
Kuhmo
Folda
Lycksele
Ozero
Namsos
Tärnsjoen
Leksozero
Frøya
Dragan
FINLAND
Pielinen
Hitra Brekstad
1337
Vännäs
Kokkola
Pyhäjärvi
Iisalmi
Smøla
Stjørdal
Hammerdal
Umeå
Jakobstad
Kristiansund
Trondheim
Kallsjön
Östersund
Pulkkila
Kuopio
Joensu
Støren
Storsjön
Ornsköldsvik
Vaasa
Lappajärvi
Trollheimen
1796
Åsarna
Solleftea
Lapua
Karikko
Andalsnes
Berkåk
Härnösund
Ålesund
2286
Asarna
Ostersund
Närpes
Nässjärvi
Haukvesi
Maløy
Tynset
Linsell
Ljungan
Sundsvall
Parkano
Piutäselkä
Nordfjord
Dovrefjell
Femund
Ytterhøgdal
Kaskinen
Florø
Dombas
1755
Idre
Ljusnan
Jyväskylä
Varkhaus
2469
Österdalen
Voxnan
Bolnäs
Pori
Näsijärvi
Mikkeli
Ladozhs
Jotunheimen
Lågen
Söderhamn
Rauma
Tampere
Kouvola
Vyborg
Segnefjorden
Lillehammer
Mora
Siljan
Gävle
Pyhäjärvi
Lahti
Laedalsøyri
Voss
Hamar
Falun
Hedesunda-
Hämeenlinna
Salpausselka
Bergen
Mjøsa
Borlänge
flarddarna
Forssa
Hyvinkää
Vantaa
Kotka
1862
Avesta
Åland
Turku
Hvyinkää
Helsinki
Kronshtadt
Odda
Ludvika
Salo
Espoo
St. Petersburg
1660
Klöfta
Mariehamn
Hanko
Gulf of Finland
Haugesund
Hardangervidda
Drammen
Västerås
Uppsala
Tallinn
Kohtla-Järve
Napve
Numedal
Oslo
Mälaren
Luga
Stavanger
Telemark
Tønsberg
Eskilstuna
Stockholm
ESTONIA
RUSSIA
Sirdal
Moss
Karlstad
Örebro
Haapsalu
FEDERAT
Flekkefjord
Setesdal
Sarpsborg
Södertälje
Hiiumaa
(RUSSI
Bygland
Skien
Fredrikstad
Vänern
Katrineholm
Saaremaa
Pärnu
Tartu
Mandal
Porsgrunn
Karlskoga
Nyköping
Kuressaare
Voru
318
Arendal
Skövde
Norrköping
Fårön
Valga
Ostrov
Kristiansand
Uddevalla
Trollhättan
Linköping
Gotland
Latvia
Pskov
Skagerrak
Hjørring
Göteborg
Vättern
Västervik
Visby
Valmiera
Ozero
NORTH SEA
Mölndal
Jönköping
Ölön
Mazirbe
Gulf of Riga
Antekste
Frederikshavn
Borås
Nässjö
Riga
Limfjorden
Ålborg
Värnamo
Vetlanda
Ventspils
Jurmala
Ostrov
Ringkøbing
Viborg
Randers
Halmstad
Bolmen
Borgholm
Kuldiga
Tukums
Daugava
Rezekne
Fjord
Herning
Åsnen
Öland
Liepaja
Saldus
Jelgava
Jekabpils
Daugavpils
Nordfriesische
Århus
Helsingborg
Växjö
Kalmar
DENMARK
Vejle
Kristianstad
Karlskrona
Plunge
Siauliai
Panevezys
Inseln
Kolding
Fyn
Landskrona
Klaipeda
Venta
LITHUANIA
Esbjerg
Odense
Lund
Hanöbukten
Ukmerge
Heligoland
Sønderborg
Sjælland
Malmö
Kursky
Nyonan
Bight
Flensburg
Roskilde
Bornholm
Zaliv
Groningen
Schleswig
Naestved
(Denmark)
Gdynia
Gulf of
Kaunas
BELARUS
Rendsburg
Lolland
Nyköbing
Sassnitz
Gdansk
Kaliningrad
Cherevakhoysk
Vilnius
Bremerhaven
Neumünster
Mecklenburg
Rügen
Gdansk
KALININGRAD (RUSSIA)
Marijampole
Maladzyechna
Cuxhaven
Bay
Pomeranian
Gdańsk
Barysaw
NETHERLANDS
Kiel
Lübeck
Bay
Elblag
Lida
Bremen
Wismar
Stralsund
Kolobrzeg
POLAND
Elblag
Hamburg
Rostock
Swinoujscie
Koszalin
Malbork
Minsk
GERMANY
Schwerin
Szczecin
Tczew
Elk
Olsztyn
Hrodna

Vesterålen Is.
Saltfjellet
N O R W A Y
S W E D E N
Gulf of Bothnia
BALTIC SEA
Innherad
Namdalen
Jostedalsbreen
Filefjell
Rondane

Skagerrak
Kattegat

Scale 1: 10 000 000
0   100   200   300   400   500 km

Grid references (top)
A 20°E B 25°E C 30°E D 35°E E 40°E F 45°E G 50°E H 55°E J 60°E K

RUSSIAN FEDERATION (RUSSIA)

FINLAND

Kaskinen · Kristiinan · Pielinen · Ozero Segozerskoye · Medvezh'yegorsk · Severnaya (N.) Dvina · Vychegda · Syktyvkar · Ivdel'
Pori · Näsijärvi · Jyväskylä · Varkaus · Joensuu · Petrozavodsk · Onezhskoye Ozero (L. Onega) · Konosha · Kotlas · Kama · Krasnotur'insk · Serov
Rauma · Lahti · Mikkeli · Suonsaari · Vel'sk · Sukhona · Solikamsk · Berezniki · Nizhniy Tagil
Turku · Tampere · Imatra · Varkhaus · Tot'ma · Nikol'sk · Shar'ya · Kirov · Glazov · Kansinoye Vdkhr. · Perm
Åland · Vantaa · Kouvola · Vyborg · Vologda · Vel'sk · Vetluga · Kotel'nich · Vyatka · Votkinskoye Vdkhr. · Pervoural'sk · Yekaterinburg
Stockholm · Salo · Helsinki · Kotka · Volkhov · Cherepovets · Rybinskoye Vdkhr. · Kostroma · Uren' · Yoshkar Ola · Novocheboksarsk · Izhevsk · Krasnoufimsk · Zlatoust
Hanko · Espoo · Tallinn · Gatchina · St. Petersburg · Novgorod · Rybinsk · Yaroslavl' · Kineshma · Gor'kovskoye Vdkhr. · Kazan' · Sarapul · Neftekamsk · Miass
Hiiumaa · Tartu · Chudskoye Ozero · Chudovo · Ozero Il'men · Rybinsk · Rostov · Ivanovo · Cheboksary · Nizhnekamskoye Vdkhr. · Naberezhnyye Chelny · Zlatoust
ESTONIA · Pärnu · Pskov · Ostrov · Velikiye Luki · Tver' · Vladimir · Kovrov · Nizhniy Novgorod · Al'met'yevsk · Ufa · Magnitogorsk
Saaremaa · Riga · Gulf of Riga · Ozero Pskovskoye · Rzhev · Sergiyev Posad · Mytishchi · Murom · Arzamas · Ul'yanovsk · Dimitrovgrad · Sterlitamak · Salavat
LATVIA · Jelgava · Daugavpils · Smolensk · Moscow · Elektrostal' · Orekhovo-Zuyevo · Saransk · Samara Vdkhr. · Meleuz
Ventspils · Rēzekne · Vitsyebsk · Vyaz'ma · Obninsk · Podol'sk · Kolomna · Oka · Moksha · Penza · Novokuybyshevsk · Samara · Magnitogorsk
LITHUANIA · Šiauliai · Orsha · Kaluga · Serpukhov · Ryazan' · Tula · Zubova Polyana · Syzran' · Tol'yatti · Orenburg · Orsk
Klaipėda · Kaunas · Minsk · Barysaw · Mahilyow · Tula · Novomoskovsk · Michurinsk · Tambov · Saratov · Engel's · Ural'sk · Aktyubinsk
KALININGRAD (RUSSIA) · Vilnius · BELARUS · Babruysk · Bryansk · Orel · Yelets · Lipetsk · Balashov · Rtishchevo · Balakovo · Sol'-Iletsk · Novotroitsk
Chernyakhovsk · Hrodna · Baranavichy · Homyel' · Zheleznogorsk · Voronezh · Borisoglebsk · Kamyshin · Mikhaylovka · Vol'sk · Vol'sk

UKRAINE · L'viv · Ternopil' · Zhytomyr · Kiev · Sumy · Belgorod · Staryy Oskol · Kamyshin · Krasnyy Kut · Ural'sk
Khmel'nyts'kyy · Rivne · Korosten · Konotop · Kursk · Rossosh' · Don · Volgogradskoye Vdkhr. · KAZAKHSTAN
Ivano-Frankivs'k · Vinnytsya · Cherkasy · Poltava · Kharkiv · Kupyans'k · Kamensk-Shakhtinskiy · Volgograd · Volzhskiy · Caspian Lowlands
Chişinău · Kremenchuts'ke Vdskh. · Kremenchuk · Lozova · Slov"yans'k · Luhans'k · Shakhty · Volgodonsk · Makat
MOLDOVA · Balţi · Kirovohrad · Dnipropetrovs'k · Pavlohrad · Yenakiyeve · Novoshakhtinsk · Tsimlyanskoye Vdkhr. · Atyrau
Tiraspol' · Kryvyy Rih · Nikopol · Donets'k · Taganrog · Rostov-na-Donu · Sal'sk · Astrakhan' · Beyneu
ROMANIA · Zaporizhzhya · Melitopol' · Berdyans'k · Gulf of Taganrog · Ozero Manych-Gudilo · Elista
Odessa · Kherson · Dnipro · SEA OF AZOV · Tikhoretsk · Caspian Sea · Aktau
Bilhorod-Dnistrovs'kyy · Gulf of Karkinitskiy · Kerch' · Krasnodar · Kuban' · Stavropol' · Nevinnomyssk · Kizlyar
Bucharest · Constanţa · Yevpatoriya · Krym (Crimea) · Simferopol' · Novorossiysk · Armavir · Maykop · Cherkessk · Pyatigorsk · Prokhladnyy · Makhachkala
BULGARIA · Dobrich · Sevastopol' · BLACK SEA · Sochi · El'brus 5642 · Nal'chik · Kazbek 5047 · Groznyy · Terek · Derbent
Varna · Tuapse · CAUCASUS · Vladikavkaz 4496 · Bol. Kavkaz · Babadag · Sumqayıt
Burgas · Sokhumi · P'ot'i · K'ut'aisi · Bazar Dyuzi 4480 · Sheki · Baku
İstanbul · Zonguldak · Sinop · Bat'umi · GEORGIA · T'bilisi · Rust'avi · Mingäçevir · Baku
Üsküdar · Kocaeli · Kastamonu · Samsun · Ordu · Trabzon · Gyumri · Vanadzor · Gäncä · Nebitdag
Bursa · Sakarya · Karabük · Merzifon · Kelkit · ARMENIA · Sevana Lich · AZERBAIJAN · Krasnovodsk
Ankara · Kırıkkale · Delice · Anadolu Dağları 3931 · Kars · Yerevan · Naxçıvan · TURKMENISTAN
Eskişehir · Kütahya · Kızıl Irmak · Sivas · Erzincan · Erzurum · Ağrı · Ağrı Dağı (Mt. Ararat) 5123 · Länkäran · Astara · Ardabīl

TURKEY
İzmir · Afyon · Tuz Gölü · Kayseri 3916 · Elâziğ · Keban Baraji · Muş · Van Gölü · Van · Tabriz
Denizli 2734 · Konya · Beyşehir Gölü · Malatya · Diyarbakır · Batman · Ūrūmiyeh · Miāneh · Rasht
Muğla 2571 · Burdur Gölü · Toros Dağları · Adana · Osmaniye · Gaziantep · Mardin · Nusaybin · Cizre · Dahūk · Zanjān · Tehran
Antalya · Mersin · Tarsus · İskenderun · Şanlıurfa · Al Qāmishlī · Al Hasakah · Mosul · Arbil · Saqqez · Damāvand 5671 · Elburz Mountains
Rhodes · Fethiye · Gökdere · Antakya · Aleppo · Ar Raqqah · IRAQ · Kirkūk · Sanandaj · Hamadān · Qom
Kríti (Crete) · CYPRUS · Nicosia · Latakia · Hamāh · SYRIA · Dayr az Zawr · Mesopotamia · As Sulaymānīyah · Kermānshāh · Arāk · Kāshān
MEDITERRANEAN SEA · Larnaca · Limassol · Tartūs · Homs · Mayādin · Tikrīt · IRAN

Scale 1: 12 500 000

0 — 125 — 250 — 375 — 500 — 625 km

Lambert Azimuthal Orthomorphic Projection
Oxford University Press

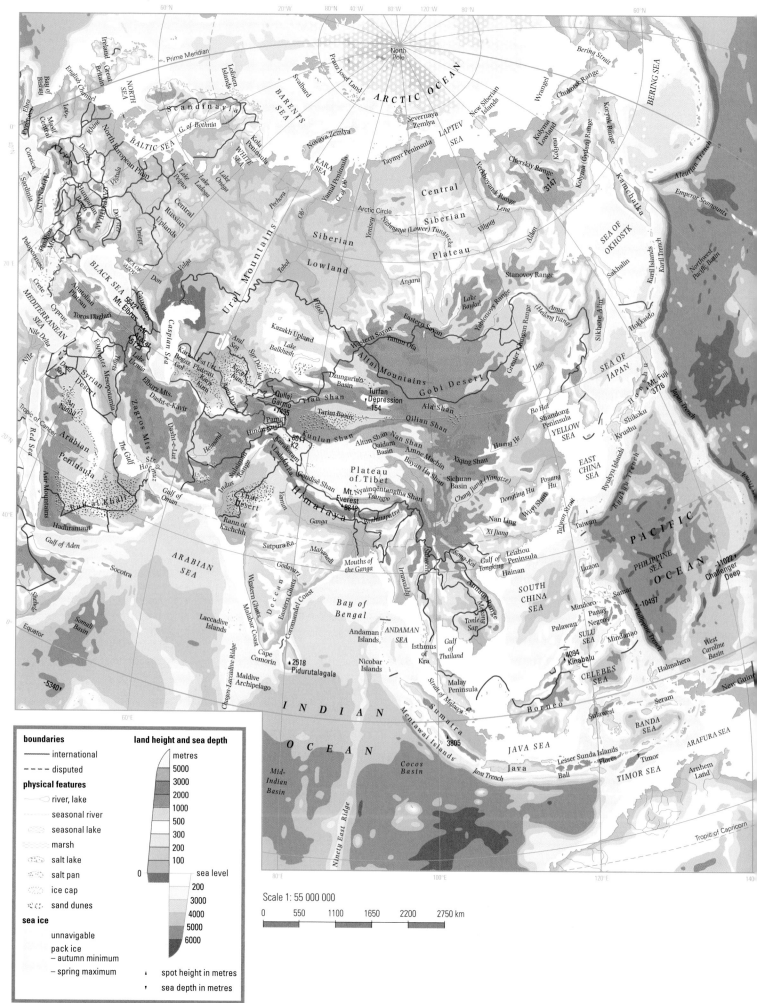

boundaries

——————	international
– – – – –	disputed

physical features

river, lake
seasonal river
seasonal lake
marsh
salt lake
salt pan
ice cap
sand dunes

sea ice

unnavigable

pack ice
– autumn minimum
– spring maximum

land height and sea depth

metres
5000
3000
2000
1000
500
300
200
100
0 — sea level
200
3000
4000
5000
6000

▲ spot height in metres
▾ sea depth in metres

Scale 1: 55 000 000

0   550   1100   1650   2200   2750 km

Zenithal equal Area Projection   © Oxford University Press

le 1: 55 000 000

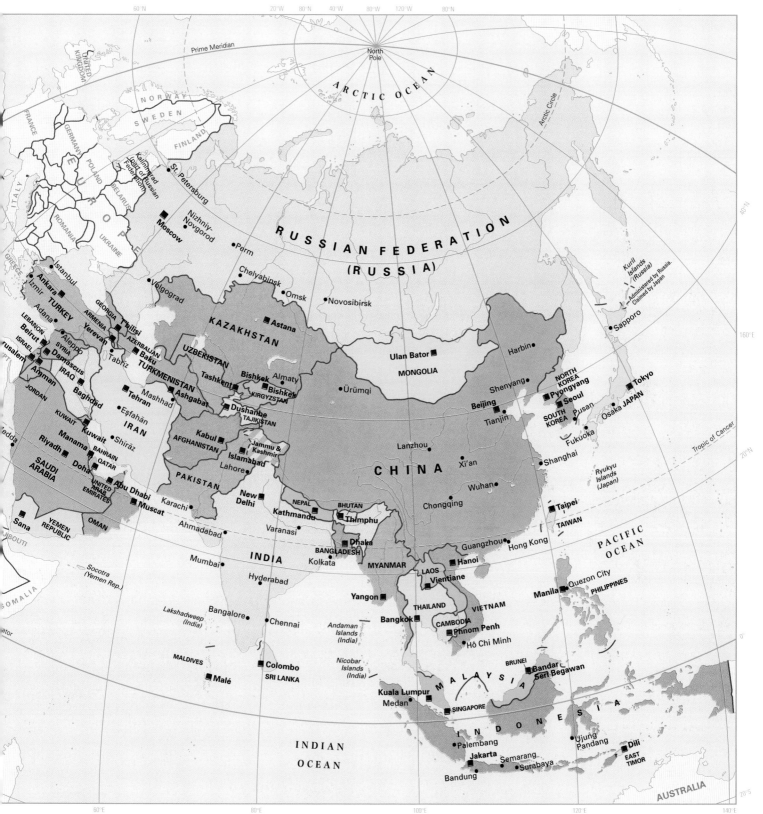

Largest urban agglomerations in Asia, 2000

Urban agglomeration is the population contained within a city plus the suburban fringe lying outside of, but adjacent to, the city boundaries.

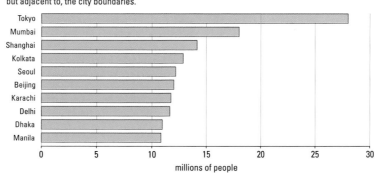

millions of people

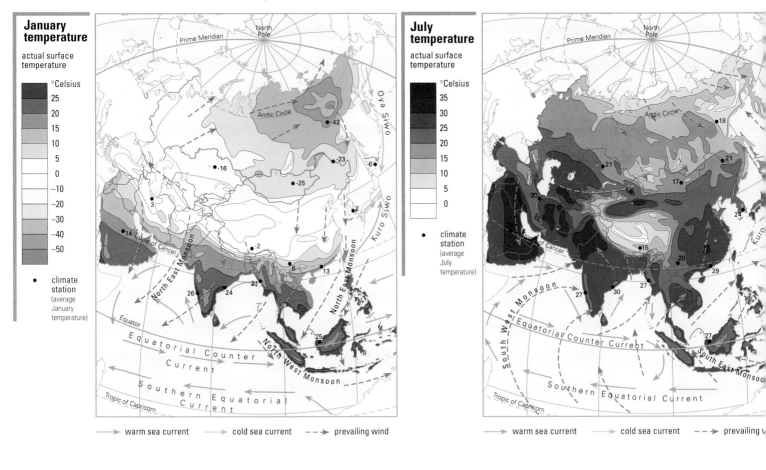

January temperature

actual surface temperature

°Celsius
- 25
- 20
- 15
- 10
- 5
- 0
- −10
- −20
- −30
- −40
- −50

● climate station (average January temperature)

Arctic Circle

-42
-23
-6
-16
-25
-2
3
14
-2
8
13
26
24
21
25

Oya Siwo
Kuro Siwo
North East Monsoon
North East Monsoon
North West Monsoon
Tropic of Cancer
Equator
Equatorial Counter Current
Southern Equatorial Current
Tropic of Capricorn

→ warm sea current   → cold sea current   --→ prevailing wind

July temperature

actual surface temperature

°Celsius
- 35
- 30
- 25
- 20
- 15
- 10
- 5
- 0

● climate station (average July temperature)

Arctic Circle

18
21
21
17
24
30
15
20
29
27
30
27
27
27

South West Monsoon
Equatorial Counter Current
Southern Equatorial Current
South East Monsoon
Tropic of Cancer
Kuro
Tropic of Capricorn

→ warm sea current   → cold sea current   --→ prevailing w

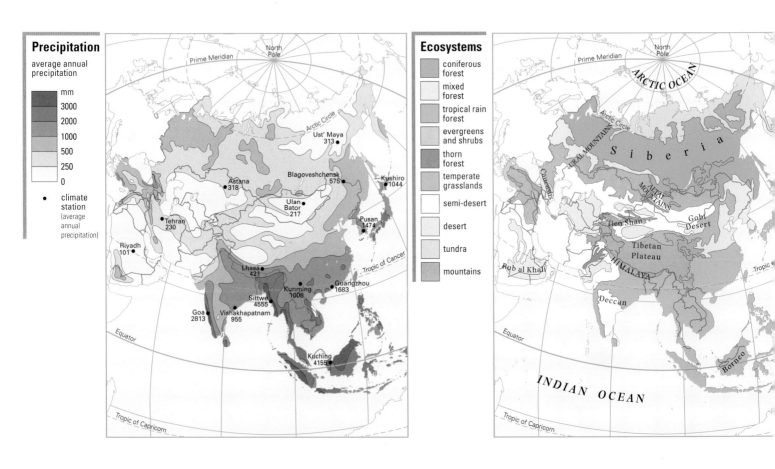

Precipitation

average annual precipitation

mm
- 3000
- 2000
- 1000
- 500
- 250
- 0

● climate station (average annual precipitation)

Ust' Maya 313
Blagoveshchensk 575
Kushiro 1044
Astana 318
Ulan Bator 217
Pusan 1474
Tehran 230
Riyadh 101
Lhasa 421
Guangzhou 1683
Kunming 1008
Sittwe 4555
Goa 2813
Vishakhapatnam 955
Kuching 4155

Arctic Circle
Tropic of Cancer
Equator
Tropic of Capricorn

Ecosystems

- coniferous forest
- mixed forest
- tropical rain forest
- evergreens and shrubs
- thorn forest
- temperate grasslands
- semi-desert
- desert
- tundra
- mountains

ARCTIC OCEAN
Siberia
URAL MOUNTAINS
ALTAI MOUNTAINS
Tien Shan
Gobi Desert
Tibetan Plateau
HIMALAYA
Caucasus
Rub al Khali
Deccan
Borneo
INDIAN OCEAN
Equator
Tropic of Cancer
Tropic of Capricorn

Zenithal Equal Area Projection   © Oxford Univer

Scale 1: 75 000 000

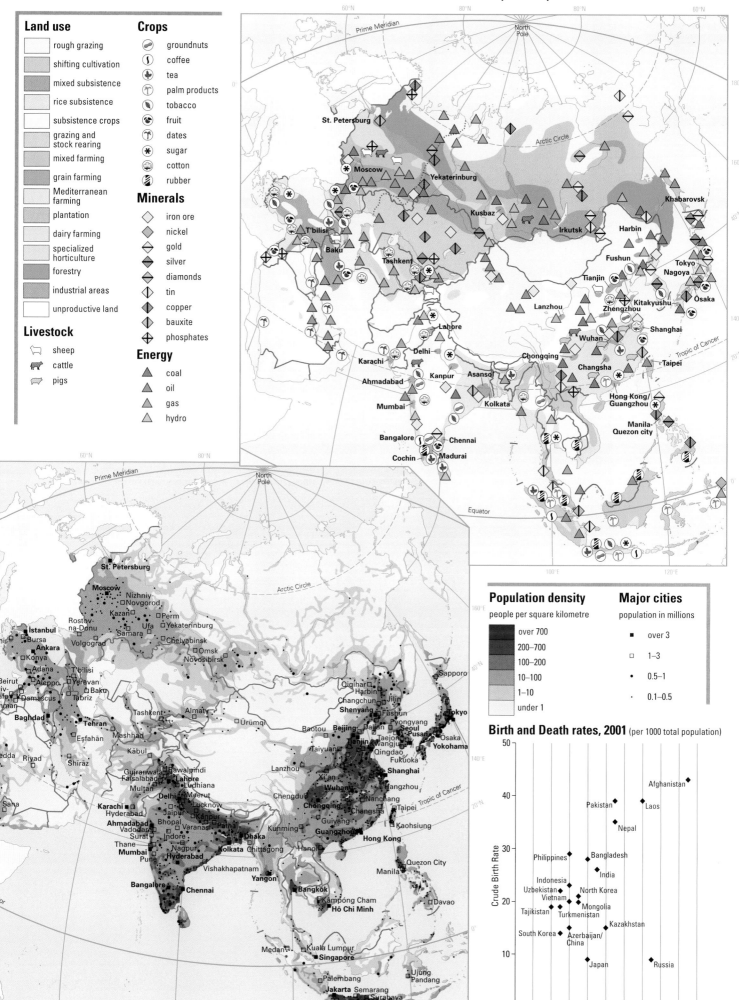

Land use

- rough grazing
- shifting cultivation
- mixed subsistence
- rice subsistence
- subsistence crops
- grazing and stock rearing
- mixed farming
- grain farming
- Mediterranean farming
- plantation
- dairy farming
- specialized horticulture
- forestry
- industrial areas
- unproductive land

Livestock

- sheep
- cattle
- pigs

Crops

- groundnuts
- coffee
- tea
- palm products
- tobacco
- fruit
- dates
- sugar
- cotton
- rubber

Minerals

- iron ore
- nickel
- gold
- silver
- diamonds
- tin
- copper
- bauxite
- phosphates

Energy

- coal
- oil
- gas
- hydro

Population density

people per square kilometre

- over 700
- 200–700
- 100–200
- 10–100
- 1–10
- under 1

Major cities

population in millions

- over 3
- 1–3
- 0.5–1
- 0.1–0.5

Birth and Death rates, 2001 (per 1000 total population)

Afghanistan
Pakistan
Laos
Nepal
Philippines
Bangladesh
India
Indonesia
Uzbekistan
North Korea
Vietnam
Mongolia
Tajikistan
Turkmenistan
Kazakhstan
South Korea
Azerbaijan/
China
Japan
Russia

Crude Birth Rate

Crude Death Rate

© Oxford University Press

Zenithal Equal Area Projection

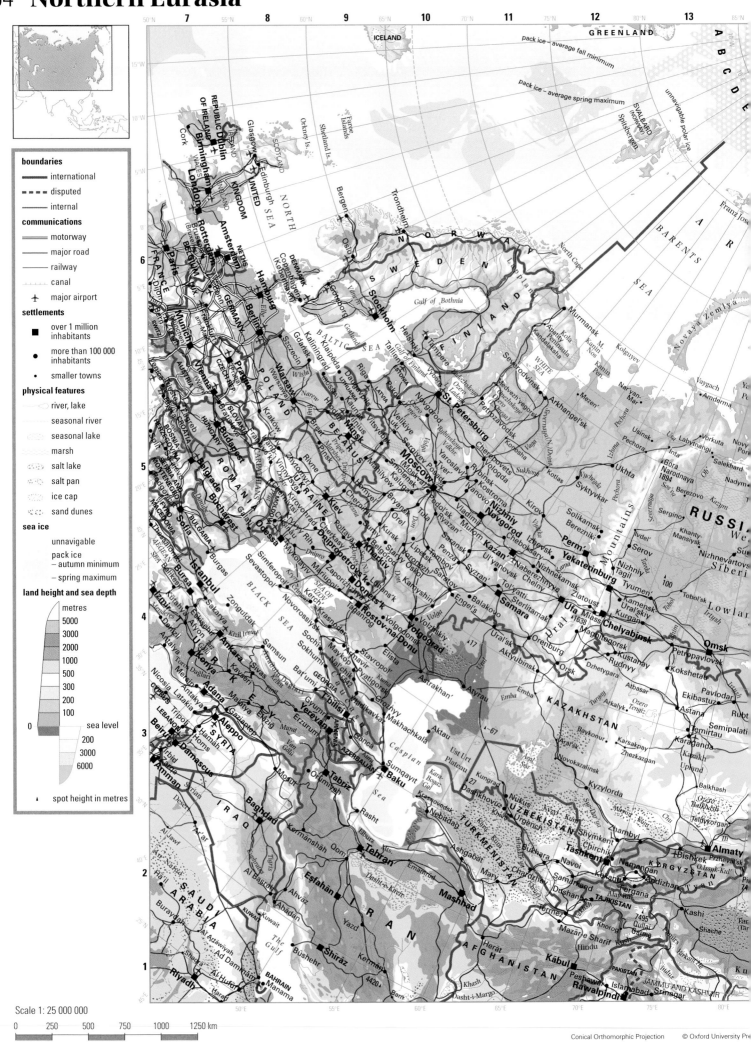

boundaries
——— international
- - - disputed
——— internal

communications
═══ motorway
——— major road
——— railway
········ canal
✈ major airport

settlements
■ over 1 million inhabitants
● more than 100 000 inhabitants
• smaller towns

physical features
river, lake
seasonal river
seasonal lake
marsh
salt lake
salt pan
ice cap
sand dunes

sea ice
unnavigable
pack ice
– autumn minimum
– spring maximum

land height and sea depth
metres
5000
3000
2000
1000
500
300
200
100
0 sea level
200
3000
6000

▲ spot height in metres

Scale 1: 25 000 000

0   250   500   750   1000   1250 km

Conical Orthomorphic Projection   © Oxford University Pre

GREENLAND

pack ice – average fall minimum
pack ice – average spring maximum
unnavigable polar ice

ICELAND

SVALBARD (NORWAY)
Spitsbergen

Franz Jose

A R C T I C

B A R E N T S   S E A

Novaya Zemlya

REPUBLIC OF IRELAND
Dublin
Cork
Birmingham
London
Cardiff
UNITED KINGDOM
Glasgow
Edinburgh
SCOTLAND
WALES
ENGLAND

Orkney Is.
Shetland Is.
Faroe Islands

N O R T H   S E A

Bergen
Trondheim
Oslo
NORWAY

North Cape
Murmansk
Kola Pen.
Kanin Nos

S W E D E N
Stockholm
Gulf of Bothnia
FINLAND
Helsinki
Tampere

WHITE SEA
Arkhangel'sk
Severodvinsk
Mezen'

FRANCE
Paris
Brussels
BELGIUM
Amsterdam
Rotterdam
NETHS.
Hamburg
GERMANY
Berlin
Munich
Vienna
AUSTRIA
Prague
CZECH REP.
POLAND
Warsaw
Gdansk
Szczecin
Wroclaw
Kraków
SLOVAKIA
Bratislava
Budapest
HUNGARY
Zagreb
CROATIA
BOSNIA
SLOVENIA
Belgrade
SERBIA
MONTENEGRO
ROMANIA
Bucharest
Sofia
BULGARIA
MACEDONIA
ALBANIA
GREECE
Athens

Copenhagen (København)
DENMARK
Kaliningrad
Klaipeda
Riga
LATVIA
LITHUANIA
Tallinn
ESTONIA
Gulf of Finland
St. Petersburg
Novgorod
Vyborg

Kostroma
Yaroslavl'
Moscow
Tver'
Ivanovo
Nizhniy Novgorod
Vladimir
Murom
Ryazan'
Tula
Kaluga
Bryansk
Orel
Lipetsk
Tambov
Penza
Saratov
Ul'yanovsk
Kazan'
Cheboksary
Naberezhnyye Chelny
Samara
Ufa
Sterlitamak

Vologda
Cherepovets
Rybinsk
Kirov
Perm'
Yekaterinburg
Nizhniy Tagil
Serov
Ivdel'

RUSSIA

Ukhta
Pechora
Vorkuta
Inta
Gora Narodnaya 1894
Salekhard
Nadym
Berezovo
Kazym
Khanty-Mansiysk
Nizhnevartovsk
Siberi
Surgut

Ural Mountains
Magnitogorsk
Chelyabinsk
Zlatoust
Miass
Kurgan
Tyumen'
Tobol'sk
Omsk
Petropavlovsk
Kokshetau

BELARUS
Minsk
UKRAINE
Kiev
L'viv
Odessa
Dnipropetrovs'k
Donets'k
Kharkiv
Zaporizhzhya
Mariupol'
Kryvyy Rih
Mykolayiv
Kherson
Luhans'k

Rostov-na-Donu
Volgograd
Astrakhan'
Stavropol'
Krasnodar
Sochi
Novorossiysk
Makhachkala
Groznyy
GEORGIA
Tbilisi
ARMENIA
Yerevan
AZERBAIJAN
Baku
Sumqayit

KAZAKHSTAN
Aktyubinsk
Orenburg
Orsk
Kustanay
Rudnyy
Atbasar
Astana
Temirtau
Karaganda
Zhezkazgan
Semipalati
Pavlodar
Ekibastuz
Balkhash

B L A C K   S E A
Istanbul
Bursa
Izmir
T U R K E Y
Ankara
Konya
Adana
Gaziantep
Kayseri
Sivas
Samsun
Trabzon
Erzurum

Nicosia
CYPRUS
SYRIA
Aleppo
Damascus
LEBANON
Beirut
Tripoli
Homs
Hama
Latakia
Antakya

C a s p i a n   S e a
TURKMENISTAN
Ashgabat
Nebitdag
Krasnovodsk
Dashkhovuz
Nukus
Urgench
UZBEKISTAN
Bukhara
Samarkand
Navoi
Tashkent
Chirchik
Shymkent
Zhambyl
KYRGYZSTAN
Bishkek
Almaty
Namangan
Andizhan
Fergana
Kokand
TAJIKISTAN
Dushanbe
Termez

ISRAEL
Amman
JORDAN
SAUDI ARABIA
Riyadh
Al Hufuf
BAHRAIN
Manama
The Gulf
Kuwait

IRAQ
Baghdad
Al Basrah
Mosul
Kirkuk

I R A N
Tehran
Tabriz
Esfahan
Shiraz
Bushehr
Mashhad
Yazd
Ahvaz
Abadan
Kermanshah
Qom
Rasht

AFGHANISTAN
Kabul
Herat
Mazar-e Sharif
Kandahar

PAKISTAN
Islamabad
Rawalpindi
Peshawar
JAMMU AND KASHMIR
Srinagar

13 12 11 10 9 8 7

A L A S K A

U

CHUKCHI SEA

C. Lisburne
Bering Strait
Norton Sd.
Nome
Arctic Circle
Uelen
Chukotsk
Gulf of
Anadyr'
Provideniya
St. Lawrence
(USA)

K L M N P Q R S T U V W X

EAST SIBERIAN SEA

Wrangel Island

Pevek
Chukotsk Range
Ayon
Ambarchik
Nizhnekolymsk
Bilibino
Markovo
Anadyr'
M. Navarin

BERING SEA

Aleutian Islands

Vise

ARCTIC OCEAN

Severnaya Zemlya

unnavigable polar ice

New Siberian Islands

LAPTEV SEA

M. Chelyuskin

Taymyr Mts.
Byrranga Mts.
Ozero Taymyr
Nordvik
Ust'-Olenek
Olenek
Tiksi
Bulun
Laptev Str.
Omoloy
Kazach'ye

Indigirka
Srednekolymsk
Kolyma
Zyryanka
Mukagir
Chukotsk Plateau
Omolon

M. Olyutorskiy
Karaginskiy

Peninsula
Khatanga
Anabar

Deputatskiy
Seymchan

Guzhiga

Shelikhov Bay
Tolstoy

Ust'-Kamchatsk
Klyuchevskaya Sopka 4750
Kamchatka

Dikson
Pyasina
Kheta

Zhigansk
Verkhoyansk
Gora Pobeda 3147

Cherskogo Range
Ust'-Nera
Susuman
Magadan

SEA OF OKHOTSK

Petropavlovsk-Kamchatskiy

Noril'sk
Gory Kamen' 2037
Putoran Mts.

Olenek

Lena
Sangar
Verkhoyansk Range
Okhotsk

pack ice - average spring maximum

Oktyabr'skiy

Kuril Islands

Igarka
Kureyka
Kotuy

Zhigansk

Yakutsk
Ust'-Maya
Ayan

Turukhansk
Yivi
Central
Siberian

Olekma
Amga
Amga
Aldan

Okha
Sakhalin
Aleksandrovsk-Sakhalinsky

Yenisey
Nizhnyaya (Lower) Tunguska
Tura

Markha 823
Mirnyy
Suntar

Sakhalin Bay

Administered by Russia.
Claimed by Japan

Belyy Yar
Podkamennaya (Stony) Tunguska
Chunya
Plateau
Lensk
Olekminsk
2481
Uda
Nikolayevsk-na-Amure

Ket'
Chulym
846
Vitim
Berkakit
Stanovoy Range
Selemdzha
Amgun'

Komsomol'sk-na-Amure
Gulf of Tartary
Terpeniya Bay
Poronaysk
Korsakov

(RUSSIA) FEDERATION

Nizhnyaya (Lower) Tunguska

Neryungri
Nagornyy
Tynda

Zeya
Svobodnyy
Bureya

Amur
Sovetskaya Gavan'

Yuzhno-Sakhalinsk

Yeniseysk
Angara
Chuna

Ust'-Ilimsk
Kirensk
Ust'-Kut

Mogocha
Skovorodino
Zeya
Belogorsk
Blagoveshchensk

Birobidzhan
Amursk
Spassk-Dal'niy

Kholmsk
Wakkanai

Achinsk
Kansk
Tayshet
Bratsk
Nizhneangarsk

2724
Bukachacha
Shilka
Sretensk
Nerchinsk

(Heilong Jiang) Amur
Jiamusi
Ussuriysk

Sikhote-Alin
Khabarovsk

Asahikawa

Krasnoyarsk
Tulun
Bratsk Vdkhr.
Ozero Baykal

Chita
Borzya

Do Hinggan Ling (Greater Khingan Range)

Nenjiang

Spassk-Dal'niy
Vladivostok
Nakhodka

Sapporo
Hakodate

Kemerovo
Cheremkhovo
Usol'ye-Sibirskoye

Manzhouli
Hailar
Argun (Ergun He)

Qiqihar
Harbin

Mudanjiang
Yanji

Chongjin
Vostochnyy

Aomori
Morioka

Novosibirsk
Prokop'yevsk
Novokuznetsk
Abakan
Sayanogorsk
Angarsk
Irkutsk
Ulan-Ude
Yablonovy Range

Chita

Jilin

NORTH KOREA

SEA OF JAPAN

Akita
Yamagata
Sendai
Fukushima
Hitachi

Biysk
Abakan
Western Sayan
Kyzyl
Hövsgöl Nuur
Sühbaatar
Selenge

Changchun
Fushun

Hamhung

JAPAN
Joetsu
Toyama

Yokohama
TOKYO
Kawasaki

4173
Tannu Ola
Uvs Nuur
Ulaangom

Ulan Bator
Kerulen
Choybalsan

Shenyang
Anshan

Pyongyang

Sinuiju

Kanazawa

Kyoto
Kobe
Nagoya
Osaka
Okayama

Altai
MONGOLIA

Hovd
Uliastay

Erenhot

NEI MONGOL ZIZHIQU
(INNER MONGOLIAN AUTONOMOUS REGION)

Chengde
Yingkou

Tangshan
Dalian

Seoul
SOUTH KOREA
Inchon
Taegu
Pusan

Hiroshima
Kita-Kyushu
Fukuoka

Dzungarian Basin
(Zungarian Basin)

Saynshand

Zhangjiakou
Hohhot

Beijing
Tianjin

Bo Hai
Yantai

Kwangju

Nagasaki

Gobi Desert

Baotou

Shijiazhuang
Zibo

Qingdao

YELLOW SEA

Kagoshima

XINJIANG UYGUR
AUTONOMOUS REGION

Hami

Ala Shan

Yinchuan

Taiyuan
Jinan

Lianyungang

EAST CHINA SEA

Turpan
-154
Turpan Depression

Anxi

NINGXIA HUIZU ZIZHIQU

Anyang

Xuzhou

Altun Shan
Qilian Shan

Xining

Lanzhou

Luoyang
Zhengzhou

Nanyang

Nanjing
Suzhou
Shanghai

Ryukyu Islands

Qaidam Pendi
(Qaidam Basin)

Golmud
Xiqing Shan

Xi'an
Wei He
Baoji

CHINA

Hefei
Wuhu

Hangzhou
Ningbo

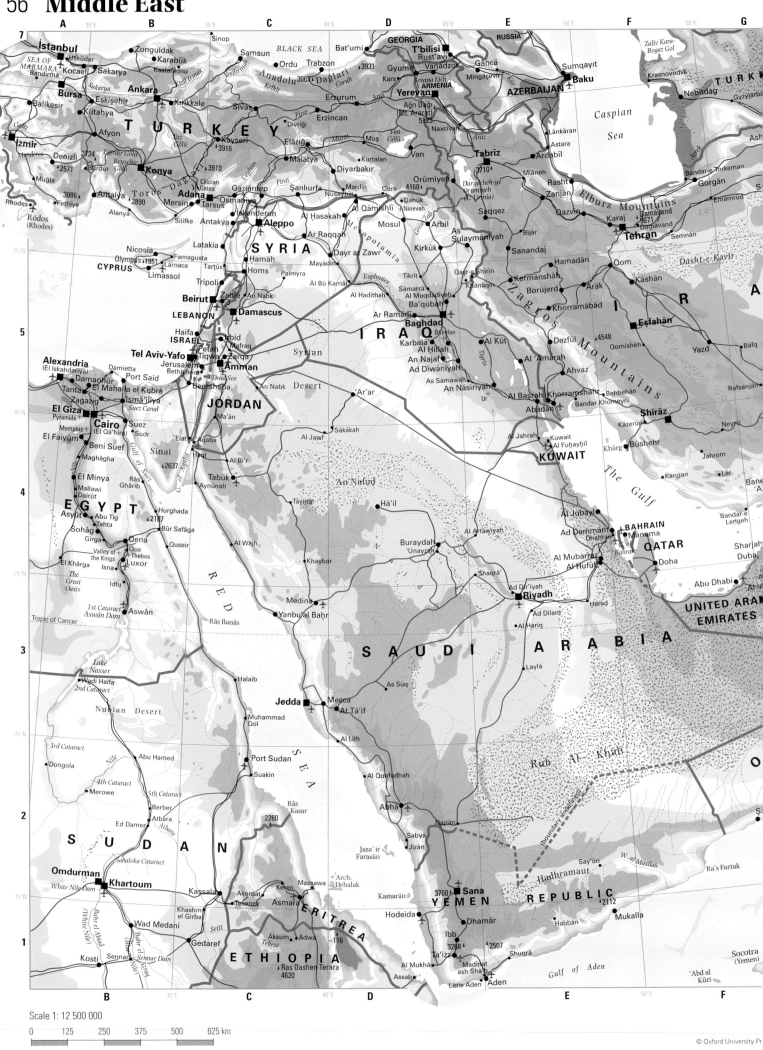

Scale 1: 12 500 000

0   125   250   375   500   625 km

© Oxford University Pr

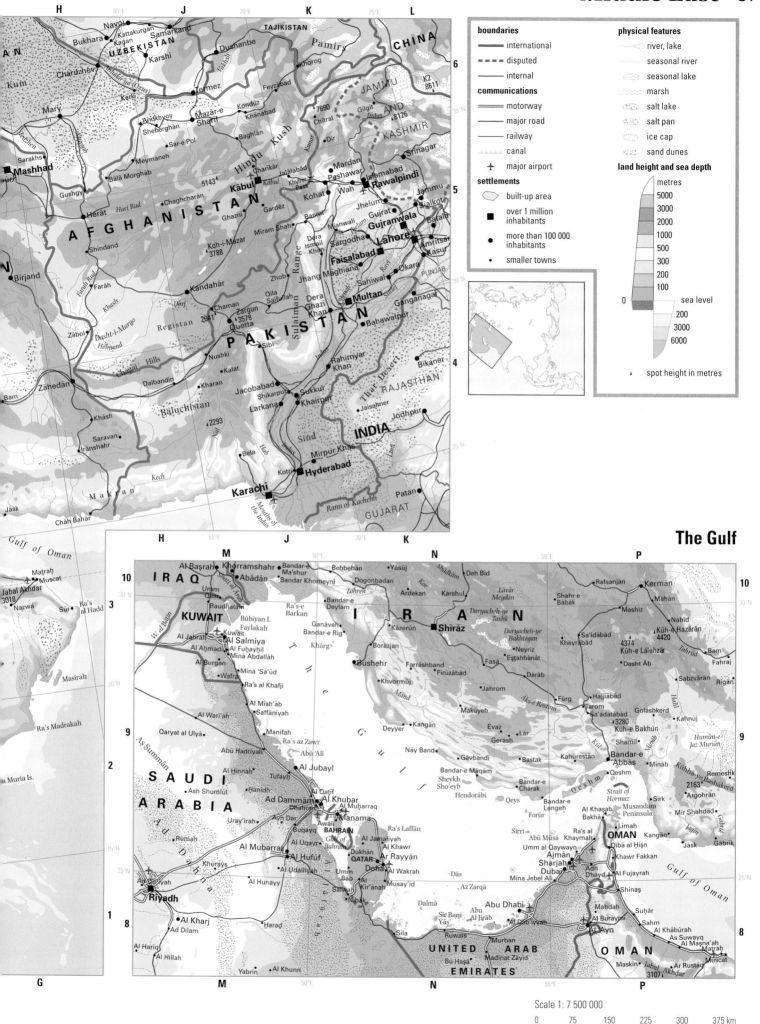

The Gulf

boundaries
——— international
- - - disputed
——— internal

communications
═══ motorway
——— major road
——— railway
┼┼┼ canal
✈ major airport

settlements
⬡ built-up area
■ over 1 million inhabitants
● more than 100 000 inhabitants
• smaller towns

physical features
river, lake
seasonal river
seasonal lake
marsh
salt lake
salt pan
ice cap
sand dunes

land height and sea depth
metres
5000
3000
2000
1000
500
300
200
100
0 sea level
200
3000
6000

▲ spot height in metres

Oxford University Press   Conical Orthomorphic Projection

Scale 1: 7 500 000

0   75   150   225   300   375 km

Main map (left)

Shan
Margat Caka
CHINA
Chibuzhang Hu
Tanggula Shan
Tangra Yumco
Zhari Namco
Ngangze Co
Siling Co
Gyaring Co
Nam Co
Nyainqêntanglha Shan
Amdo
Nagqu
Lhasa
Chibuzhang Hu
Lancang Jiang (Mekong)
Nu Jiang (Salween)
Nyingchi
Xigaze
Lhaze
Gyangze
Yarlung Zangbo (Tsangpo)
Kangto 7089
ARUNACHAL PRADESH
Sadiya
Saikhoa Ghat
Dibrugarh
Tinsukia
Putao
HIMALAYA
Mount Everest 8848
Kathmandu
NEPAL
Thimphu
BHUTAN
Darjiling
SIKKIM
Bangtok
Shiliguri
Koch Bihar
Brahmaputra
ASSAM
Naogaon
Guwahati
Dispur
Shillong
MEGHALAYA
NAGALAND
Kohima
Imphal
MANIPUR
Silchar
Chindwin
Biratnagar
Darbhanga
Purnia
Saidpur
Rangpur
Dinajpur
Rajshahi
Mymensingh
Sylhet
Agartala
TRIPURA
Patna
BIHAR
Bhagalpur
Dhanbad
Asansol
Durgapur
WEST BENGAL
Barddhaman
Jessore
Barisal
Comilla
Aizawl
MIZORAM
Mawlaik
Yeu
Falam
Shwebo
Monywa
Mandalay
Irrawaddy
Bakaro
shedpur
Medinipur
Khulna
Kolkata (Calcutta)
Kharagpur
Mouths of the Ganga
Cox's Bazar
Chittagong
Karnaphuli Reservoir
MYANMAR (BURMA)
Arakan Yoma
Sittwe
Magwe
Pakokku
Myingyan
Pye
Pegu Yoma
Irrawaddy
Cuttack
Bhubaneshwar
Puri
ORISSA
lam
Bay of Bengal
Kyaukpyu
Ramree
Cheduba
Sandoway
Bassein
Yangon
Mouths of the Irrawaddy
INDIAN OCEAN
Narcondam Island
North Andaman
Middle Andaman
Andaman Islands
South Andaman
Port Blair
ANDAMAN SEA
ANDAMAN AND NICOBAR
Little Andaman
Ten Degree Channel
Car Nicobar Island
Teressa Island
Camorta Island
Katchall Island
Nancowry Island
Sombrero Channel
Nicobar Islands
Little Nicobar
Great Nicobar

Inset map (top right) — Bangladesh region

NEPAL
Dharan Bazar
Chhukha
BHUTAN
Balipar
Biratnagar
Shiliguri
Jalpaiguri
Alipur Duar
Barpeta Road
Rowta
Nagaon
Forbesganj
Islampur
Koch Bihar
Jogighopa
Guwahati
Dispur
Saharsa
Kishanganj
Domar
Lalmanir Hat
Kurigram
Goalpara
INDIA
Purnia
Dalkhola
Saidpur
Rangpur
1412 Nokrek Peak
Khasi Hills
Shillong
Katihar
Raiganj
Dinajpur
Barengapara
Jowai
Munger
Bhagalpur
Balurghat
Ingraj Bazar
Naogaon
BANGLADESH
Chhatak
Dauki
Jaiantapur
Barharwa
Hausdiha
Jangipur
Nawabganj
Rajshahi
Sirajganj
Mymensingh
Tangail
Maulvi Bazar
Sylhet
Deoghar
Dumka
Bhairab Bazar
Khowai
Kolosib
Kulti
Murshidabad
Baharampur
Pabna
Brahman Baria
Hadraibari
Aizawl
Asansol
Jhenida
Krishnanagar
Dhaka
Faridpur
Agartala
Narayanganj
Udaipur
Tropic of Cancer
Ondal
Durgapur
Navadwip
Santipur
Bhanga
Comilla
Puruliya
Bankura
Bishnupur
Bardhaman
Chunchura
Jessore
Narail
Madaripur
Chandpur
Feni
Noakhali
Ramgarh
Lunglei
Garbeta
Arambag
Chhatpara
Khulna
Mungla
Barisal
Medinipur
Haora
Taki
Kolkata
Dakhin Shahbazpur Island
Sandwip Island
Harbang
Kharagpur
Diamond Harbour
Jaynagar
Manzilpur
Baripada
Haldia
South Hatia Island
Chittagong
Sundarbans
Rabnabad Islands
Kutubdia Island
Baleshwar
Mouths of the Ganga
Maiskhal Island
Cox's Bazar
MYANMAR (BURMA)
Bhadrakh
Bay of Bengal
Buthidaung
Maungdaw
Kyauktaw

Inset map (bottom right) — Maldives

Minicoy Island
Quilon
Tuticorin
Trivandrum
Tirunelveli
INDIA
Nagercoil
Cape Comorin
Eight Degree Channel
Ihavandiffulu Atoll
Tiladummati Atoll
Miladummadulu Atoll
Malosmadulu Atoll
Fadiffolu Atoll
MALDIVES
Kardiva Channel
Male Atoll
Male
Ari Atoll
Felidu Atoll
INDIAN OCEAN
Nilandu Atoll
Mulaku Atoll
Kolumadulu Atoll
Haddummati Atoll
One and a Half Degree Channel
Suvadiva Atoll
Equatorial Channel
Addu Atoll

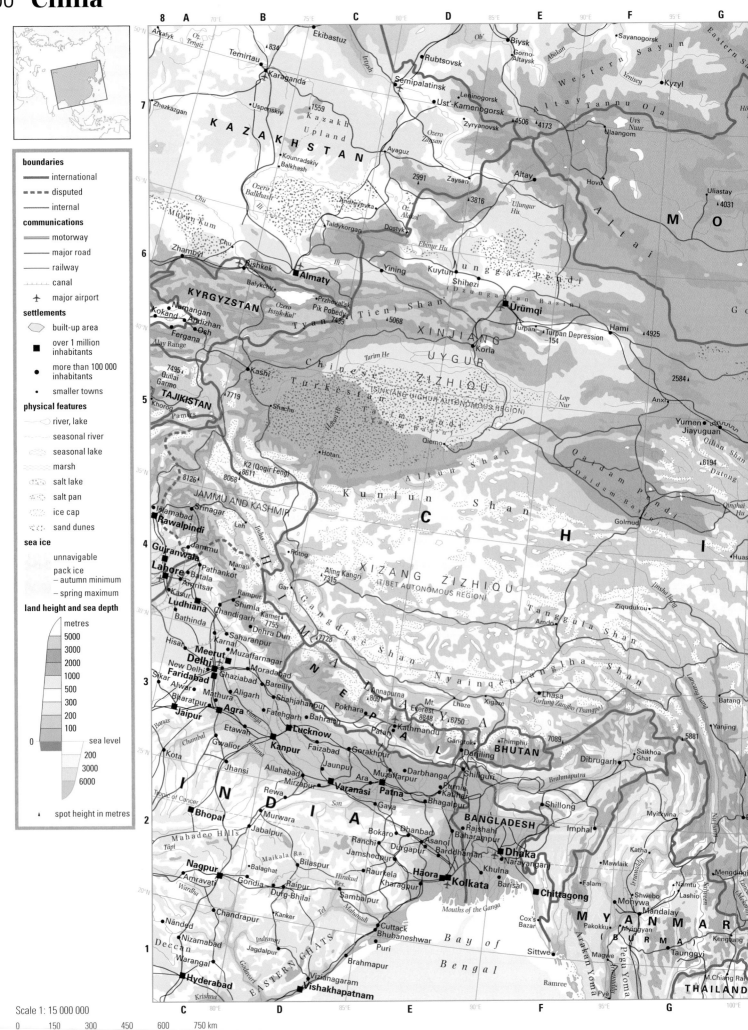

boundaries
- —— international
- - - - disputed
- —— internal

communications
- ══ motorway
- —— major road
- —— railway
- ┼┼┼ canal
- ✈ major airport

settlements
- built-up area
- ■ over 1 million inhabitants
- ● more than 100 000 inhabitants
- • smaller towns

physical features
- river, lake
- seasonal river
- seasonal lake
- marsh
- salt lake
- salt pan
- ice cap
- sand dunes

sea ice
- unnavigable
- pack ice
  - autumn minimum
  - spring maximum

land height and sea depth

metres
5000
3000
2000
1000
500
300
200
100
0 — sea level
200
3000
6000

▲ spot height in metres

Scale 1: 15 000 000

0   150   300   450   600   750 km

Conical Orthomorphic Projection

H   J   K   L   N   130°E   P   135°E   Q   140°E   R   8

RUSSIAN FEDERATION (RUSSIA)

Ozero Baykal

Usol'ye-Sibirskoye

garsk

Irkutsk

Ulan-Ude

Selenga

Khilok

Sühbaatar

Chita

Yablonovyy Range

Shilka

Mogocha

Skovorodino

Bukachacha

Sretensk

Nerchinsk

Borzya

Manzhouli

Choybalsan

Kerulen

Onon

Argun (Ergun He)

Hailar

Mangui

Mohe

Da Hinggan Ling (Greater Khingan Range)

Nenjiang

Bei'an

Svobodnyy

Belogorsk

Blagoveshchensk

Zeya

Amur (Heilong Jiang)

Zeya

Burgat

Komsomol'sk-na-Amure

Amursk

Birobidzhan

Khabarovsk

Gulf of Tartary

Sovetskaya Gavan'

50°N

7

Ulan Bator

Saynshand

Erenhot

Desert

Hegang

Jiamusi

Shuangyashan

Wusuli Jiang (Ussuri)

Sikhote-Alin

45°N

O   L   I   A

Nei

Zhonghua Jiang

1712

Qiqihar

Daqing

Harbin

Jixi

Ozero Khanka

Baicheng

Mudanjiang

Ussuriysk

Vladivostok

Nakhodka

Vostochnyy

6

MONGOL ZIZHIQU (INNER MONGOLIAN AUTONOMOUS REGION)

Jining

Hohhot

Baotou

Wuhai

2149

Shizuishan

Yinchuan

Helan Shan

Lanzhou

N

Tongchuan

Wei He

Baoji

Tianshui

Qin Ling

3767

Xi'an

Xianyang

Sanmenxia

Shan

Sichuan Pendi (Sichuan Basin)

Nanchong

Wanxian

Chengdu

Hechuan

Neijiang

qiao

Zigong

Yibin

Luzhou

Chongqing

Zunyi

Anshun

Guiyang

Duyun

nming

Nanpan Jiang

You Jiang

ou

Cai

VIETNAM

Hanoi

Hai Phong

Ninh Binh

Nam Dinh

Thanh Hoa

Gulf of Tongking

1867

Sanya

Erenhot

Changchun

Jilin

Huaide

Shuangliao

Siping

Liaoyuan

Yanji

Hunjiang

Chongjin

SEA OF JAPAN

40°N

Fuxin

Fushun

Tonghua

Chaoyang

Shenyang

Benxi

Liaoyang

Kimchaek

Zhangjiakou

Xuanhua

Jinzhou

Jinxi

Yingkou

Sinuiju

Dandong

Anshan

NORTH KOREA

Hamhung

Chengde

Qinhuangdao

Lushun

Korea Bay

Nampo

Pyongyang

Wonsan

Yalu

Hungnam

Baoting

Beijing

Tangshan

Great Wall

Datong

Huang He

Tianjin

Xinjin

Haeju

Bo Hai

Dalian

Yantai

Korea Bay

Chunchon

Kaesong

Seoul

Kangnung

Inchon

Wonju

Chongju

Taejon

JAPAN

35°N

Taiyuan

Yuci

Yangquan

Shijiazhuang

Dezhou

Weifang

Ye Xian

Zibo

Matsue

Tottori

Yonago

Daito

Fukui

Toyama

Kanazawa

Kyōto

Gifu

Xingtai

Handan

Fengfeng

Anyang

Hebi

Huang He

Jining

Tai'an

Jinan

Qingdao

YELLOW SEA

Kunsan

Chonju

Taegu

Chinju

Masan

Pusan

Pohang

Okayama

Himeji

Kōbe

Osaka

Wakayama

Changzhi

Houma

Zhengzhou

Kaifeng

Zaozhuang

Lianyungang

Kwangju

Mokp'o

Suncheon

Yosu

Hiroshima

1905

Kōchi

Shikoku

Pingdingshan

Luoyang

Shangqiu

Xuzhou

Xuchang

Zhoukou

Suzhou

Yancheng

Cheju do

Kita-Kyūshū

Shimonoseki

Ube

Fukuoka

Ōmuta

Nanyang

Luoshan

Huainan

Bengbu

Rugao

Nantong

Korea Strait

Sasebo

Nagasaki

Kumamoto

Kyūshū

Nobeoka

Miyazaki

Xiangfan

Tongling

EAST CHINA SEA

Kagoshima

Miyakonojō

Yichang

Hefei

Wuhu

Huzhou

Wuxi

Shanghai

Jiaxing

Shashi

Wuhan

Huangshi

Anqing

Hangzhou

Shaoxing

Ningbo

30°N

Jiujiang

Jingdezhen

Jinhua

Wenzhou

Dongting Hu

Changde

Yiyang

Poyang Hu

Nanchang

Shangrao

Changsha

Xiangtan

Zhuzhou

Pingxiang

Ji'an

Nanping

Ryukyu Islands (Nansei-shotō)

Okinawa

25°N

Shaoyang

Hengyang

Fuzhou

Sanming

Guilin

Liuzhou

Shaoguan

Ganzhou

Quanzhou

Xiamen

Taipei

Chilung

Hsinchu

Wuzhou

Zhangzhou

Meizhou

Chaozhou

Shantou

Taichung

Chiai

3997

TAIWAN

Taiwan Strait

Tainan

Kaohsiung

Pingtung

Tropic of Cancer

2

Nanning

Guangzhou (Canton)

Foshan

Shunde

Huizhou

Jiangmen

Shenzhen

Macao

Hong Kong

Pingxiang

Maoming

Beihai

Zhanjiang

Leizhou Bandao

Xuwen

Haikou

Hainan Dao

Qionghai

NORTH PACIFIC OCEAN

SOUTH CHINA SEA

Luzon Strait

THE PHILIPPINES

Laoag

Aparri

20°N

1

H   J   105°E   L   115°E   M   120°E   N   125°E   P   130°E

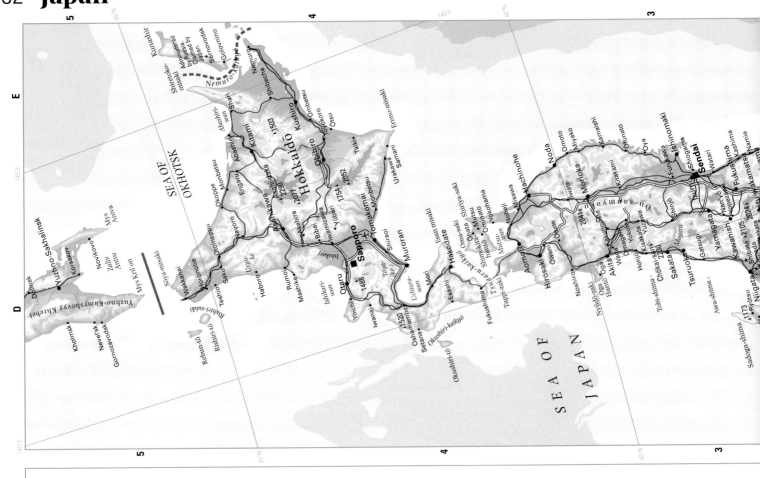

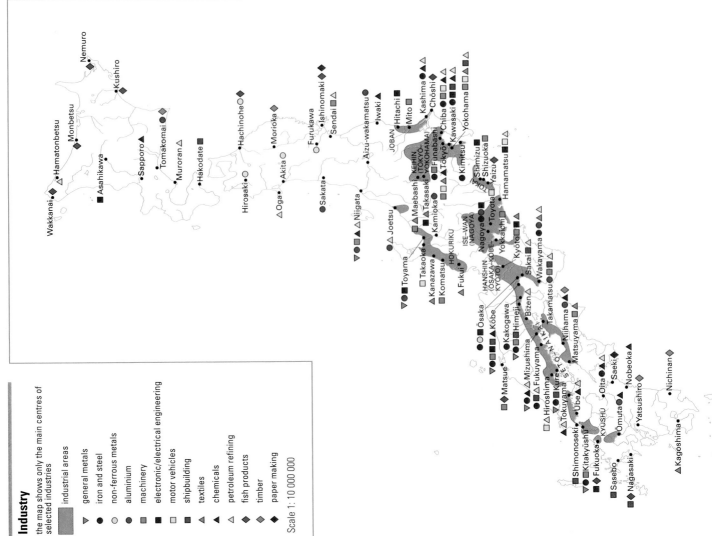

Industry

the map shows only the main centres of selected industries

industrial areas

general metals
iron and steel
non-ferrous metals
aluminium
machinery
electronic/electrical engineering
motor vehicles
shipbuilding
textiles
chemicals
petroleum refining
fish products
timber
paper making

Scale 1: 10 000 000

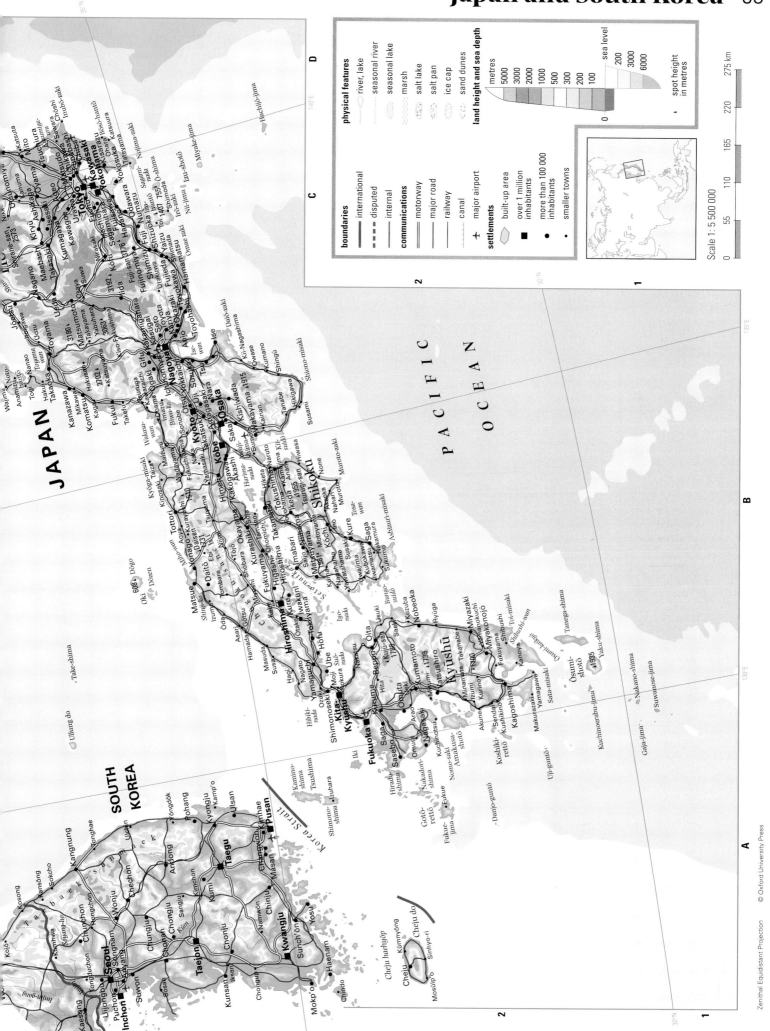

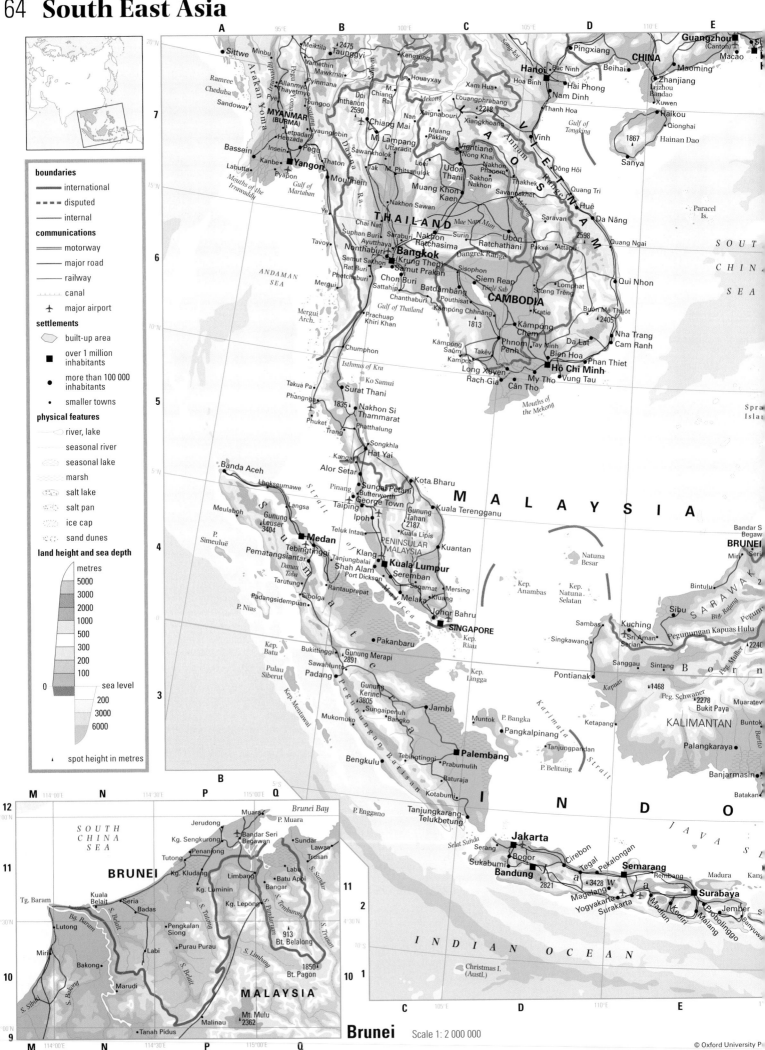

boundaries

boundaries
- ━━━ international
- ▬ ▬ ▬ disputed
- ─── internal

communications
- ═══ motorway
- ─── major road
- ─── railway
- ┈┈┈ canal
- ✈ major airport

settlements
- built-up area
- ■ over 1 million inhabitants
- ● more than 100 000 inhabitants
- • smaller towns

physical features
- river, lake
- seasonal river
- seasonal lake
- marsh
- salt lake
- salt pan
- ice cap
- sand dunes

land height and sea depth

metres
5000
3000
2000
1000
500
300
100
0   sea level
200
3000
6000

▲ spot height in metres

Brunei

Scale 1: 2 000 000

© Oxford University P

TAIWAN

Kaohsiung P'ingtung

Luzon Strait

Laoag Aparri

Tuguegarao

Mt. Pulag 2925 Ilagan

San Fernando

Dagupan Luzon

San Carlos

Tarlac Cabanatuan

Quezon City

Olongapo **Manila**

San Pablo Daet

Batangas Lucena

Calapan Naga Catanduanes

Mt. Baco 2488 Mindoro

Catarman

Calamian Group Masbate Calbayog Samar

Kalibo Roxas Cuyo Is.

Panay Ormoc Tacloban

Iloilo Cadiz Leyte

Bacolod Lapu-Lapu Dinagat

San Carlos Cebu Bohol

Negros Dumaguete Surigao Butuan

Puerto Princesa Dipolog Cagayan de Oro

Palawan 2560 Iligan

2085 Pagadian Mindanao

P. Balabac Tagum

Balabac Zamboanga Datu Piang Davao 2954

ndat Moro Gulf

alu General Santos

Sandakan Sulu Archipelago

Lahad Datu

BAH

Tawau

Tarakan

Tanjungredeb

angkulirang CELEBES SEA

Ogoamas 2207 2565 Minahassa Peninsula Manado

amarinda Kotamobagu

Donggala Gorontalo

Palu 3311 Poso Ampana

pan Teluk Tomini

rogot

Mamuju 3074 Wotu

Sulawesi Kep. Sula Pulau Peleng Kep. Banggai Pulau Taliabu

Palopo

2799 Kendari

Parepare Teluk Bone

Watampone Muna Buton

E S Baubau

Ujung Pandang 2871 BANDA SEA

THE PHILIPPINE SEA

THE PHILIPPINES

SULU SEA

INDONESIA

Kepulauan Talaud

Morotai

Galela Loloda Kau Halmahera

Ternate 1508 Waigeo

Sao-Siu Tidore

Labuha P. Bacan Maluku

Kep. Obi

SERAM SEA

Wahai

Amahai 3019 Bula

Buru Namlea Seram

Ambon Kep. Banda

Kep. Kai

Kep. Aru

Dobo

Tual Kep. Aru

Kep. Asia Kep. Mapia

P. Biak

3000 Manokwari Sarmi

Sorong Doberai Peninsula Ransiki

Teminabuan P. Yapen

Teluk Cenderawasih Jayapura

Misoöl Nabire Pegunungan Van Rees

Fakfak Bomberai Peninsula 5030 IRIAN Wamena Moake New

Kaimana Puntjak Jaya JAYA 4700 Guinea

Tembagapura Puntjak Mandala

Amamapare Tanahmerah

Mapi

Pulau Dolak

Merauke

PAPUA NEW GUINEA

Sumbawa Besar Raba

Sumbawa Sape

FLORES SEA

Flores Larantuka Lomblen P. Alor

Ruteng Maumere Endeh Pantar

Sumba Waingapu Kupang

SAWU SEA

Dili 2960 **EAST TIMOR**

Timor Kefamenanu

TIMOR SEA

ARAFURA SEA

Kep. Babar

Kep. Tanimbar Saumlaki

Kepulauan Barat Daya

Wetar

Melville I.

Bathurst I.

AUSTRALIA

MOLUCCA SEA

Maluku Kepulauan

Singapore

Singapore Scale 1: 500 000

Bukit Sekudai S. Tebrau Kong Kong S. Kong Kong Telok Sengat

85 Kempas Teberau Pelentong Tg. Juling

Sekudai S. Sekudai Larkin Mempuing Sungai Lebam

Tampoi Johor Bahru Senibong Masai

S. Danga S. Melana Telok Jawa Pasir Gudang Tanjong Langsat

Kangkar Pendas Woodlands Sembawang Pasir Puteh Tg. Buai

Sarimbun Res. Yishun Sungai Punggol P. Tanjong Surat

Kranji Res. Seletar Res. Pulau Ubin

Poyan Reservoir Bukit Panjang Ang Mo Kio Serangoon Harbour Changi Pulau Tekong

Tengeh Reservoir Bt. Gombak 138 Serangoon Changi Pt.

Bt. Timah 162 Bedok Res. Tg. Pengelih

Bukit Batok Bukit Timah MacRitchie Reservoir Paya Lebar

Tuas Jurong Clementi Toa Payoh Katong Bedok CHANGI INTERNATIONAL AIRPORT

Pasir Panjang Holland Queenstown **Singapore**

Jurong Island P. Seraya P. Pandan

P. Sakra Selat Selat Jurong

P. Busing P. Bukum Pulau Sentosa

P. Sudong P. Semakau Tg. China **SINGAPORE**

P. Pawai P. Sebarok

P. Senang Straits of Singapore

Straits of Singapore

INDONESIA

Scale 1: 15 000 000 (main map)

0 150 300 450 600 750 km

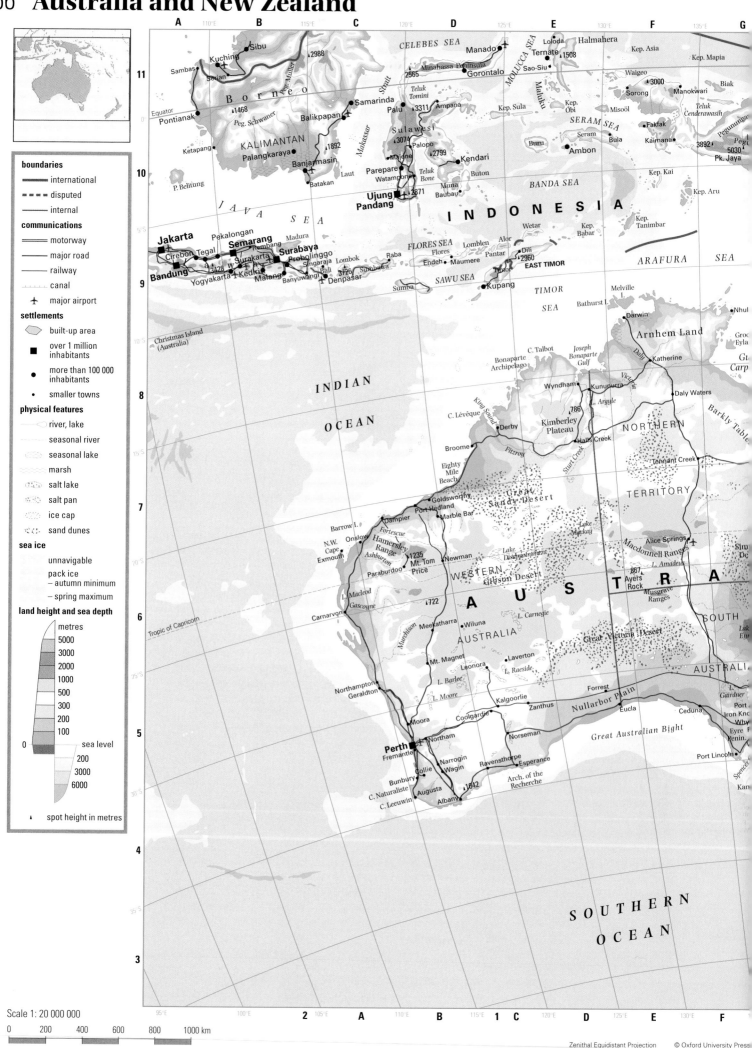

boundaries
— international
--- disputed
— internal

communications
═ motorway
— major road
— railway
⊥⊥⊥ canal
✈ major airport

settlements
⬡ built-up area
■ over 1 million inhabitants
● more than 100 000 inhabitants
• smaller towns

physical features
river, lake
seasonal river
seasonal lake
marsh
salt lake
salt pan
ice cap
sand dunes

sea ice
unnavigable
pack ice
– autumn minimum
– spring maximum

land height and sea depth
metres
5000
3000
2000
1000
500
300
200
100
0 — sea level
200
3000
6000
▲ spot height in metres

Scale 1: 20 000 000

0 200 400 600 800 1000 km

Zenithal Equidistant Projection   © Oxford University Press

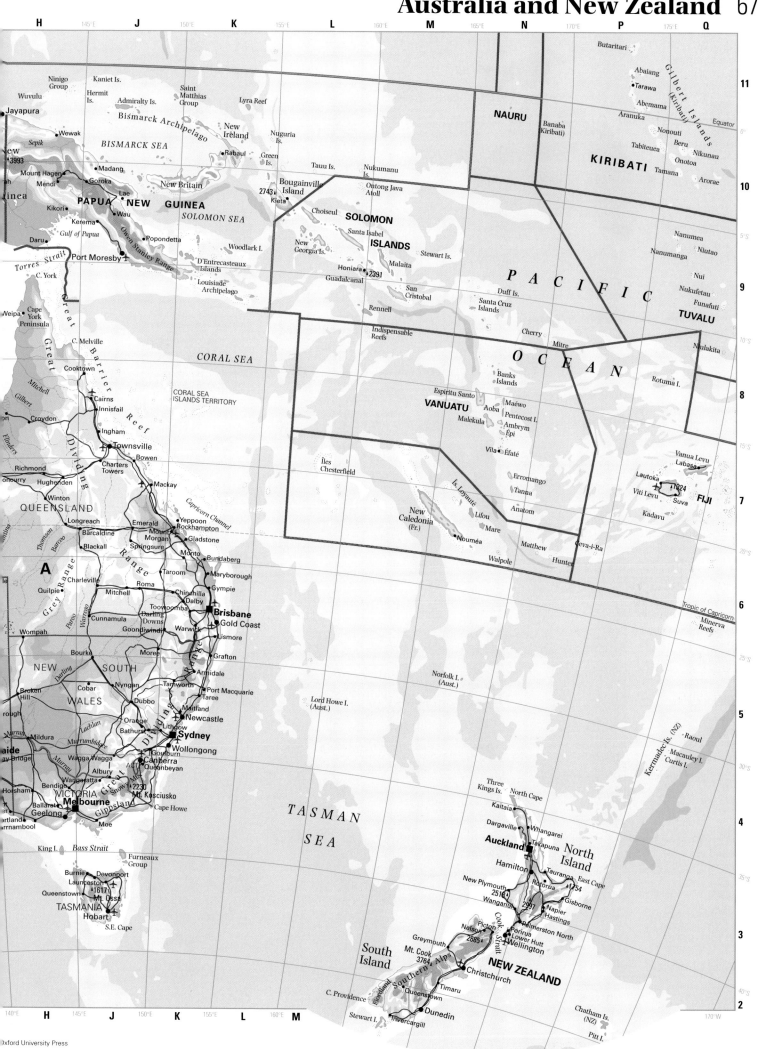

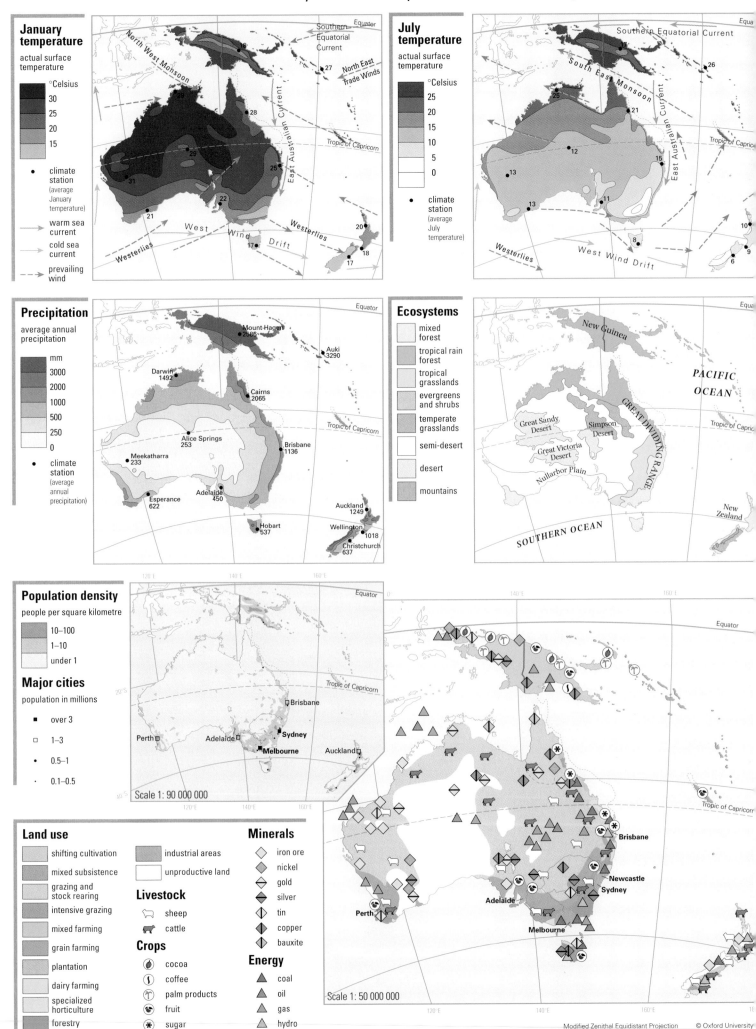

January temperature

actual surface temperature

°Celsius
30
25
20
15

● climate station
(average January temperature)

→ warm sea current
→ cold sea current
--→ prevailing wind

North West Monsoon
Southern Equatorial Current
North East Trade Winds
East Australian Current
Tropic of Capricorn
West Wind Drift
Westerlies
Equator

July temperature

actual surface temperature

°Celsius
25
20
15
10
5
0

● climate station
(average July temperature)

Southern Equatorial Current
South East Monsoon
East Australian Current
Tropic of Capric
Westerlies
West Wind Drift
Equa

Precipitation

average annual precipitation

mm
3000
2000
1000
500
250
0

● climate station
(average annual precipitation)

Mount Hagen 2586
Auki 3290
Darwin 1492
Cairns 2065
Alice Springs 253
Brisbane 1136
Meekatharra 233
Esperance 622
Adelaide 450
Hobart 537
Auckland 1249
Wellington 1018
Christchurch 637
Equator
Tropic of Capricorn

Ecosystems

mixed forest
tropical rain forest
tropical grasslands
evergreens and shrubs
temperate grasslands
semi-desert
desert
mountains

New Guinea
PACIFIC OCEAN
Great Sandy Desert
Simpson Desert
GREAT DIVIDING RANGE
Great Victoria Desert
Nullarbor Plain
Tropic of Capric
New Zealand
SOUTHERN OCEAN
Equa

Population density

people per square kilometre

10–100
1–10
under 1

Major cities

population in millions

■ over 3
□ 1–3
● 0.5–1
· 0.1–0.5

Brisbane
Perth
Adelaide
Sydney
Melbourne
Auckland
Scale 1: 90 000 000
Equator
Tropic of Capricorn

Land use

shifting cultivation
mixed subsistence
grazing and stock rearing
intensive grazing
mixed farming
grain farming
plantation
dairy farming
specialized horticulture
forestry
industrial areas
unproductive land

Livestock

🐑 sheep
🐂 cattle

Crops

ⓒ cocoa
ⓢ coffee
Ⓟ palm products
🍎 fruit
✱ sugar

Minerals

◇ iron ore
◇ nickel
◇ gold
◇ silver
◇ tin
◇ copper
◇ bauxite

Energy

▲ coal
▲ oil
▲ gas
▲ hydro

Perth
Adelaide
Melbourne
Brisbane
Newcastle
Sydney
Scale 1: 50 000 000

Modified Zenithal Equidistant Projection   © Oxford University

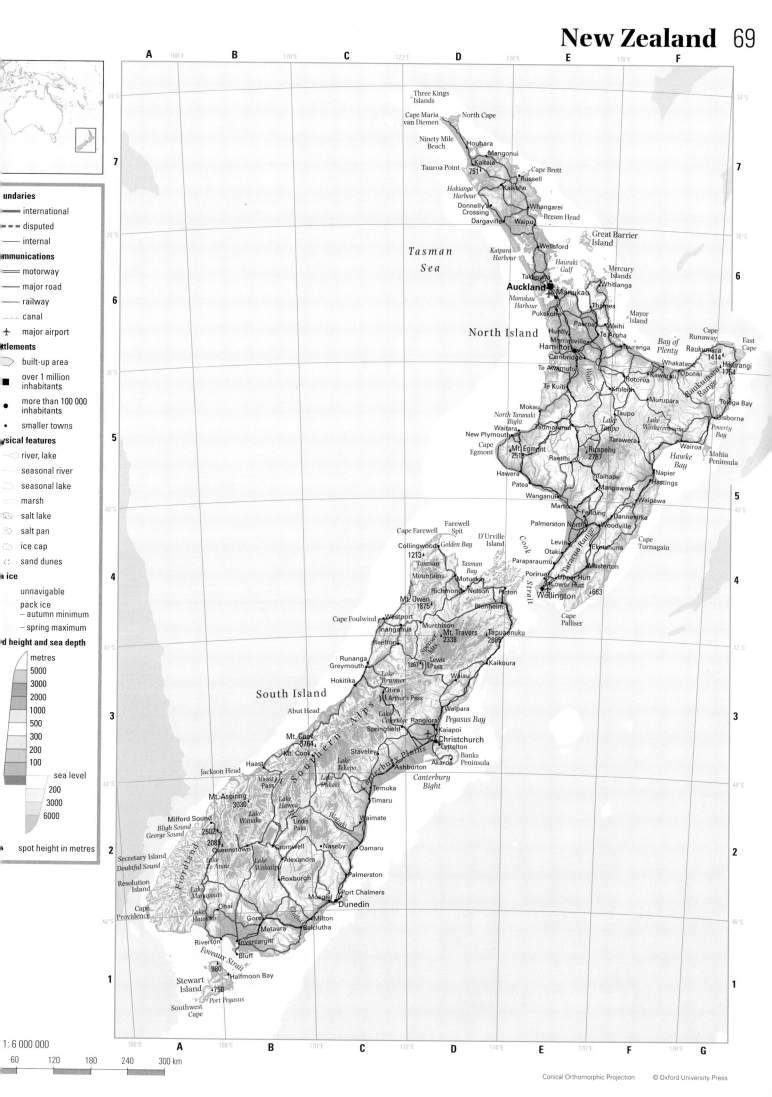

Conical Orthomorphic Projection

1 : 6 000 000

undaries
— international
- - - disputed
— internal

mmunications
═══ motorway
── major road
── railway
+++ canal
✈ major airport

tlements
▱ built-up area
■ over 1 million inhabitants
● more than 100 000 inhabitants
• smaller towns

ysical features
river, lake
seasonal river
seasonal lake
marsh
salt lake
salt pan
ice cap
sand dunes

ice
unnavigable
pack ice
– autumn minimum
– spring maximum

d height and sea depth
metres
5000
3000
2000
1000
500
300
200
100
sea level
200
3000
6000
▲ spot height in metres

60   120   180   240   300 km

Tasman Sea

North Island

Three Kings Islands
Cape Maria van Diemen
North Cape
Ninety Mile Beach
Houhara
Mangonui
Tauroa Point
Kaitaia 751
Cape Brett
Russell
Kaikohe
Hokianga Harbour
Donnelly's Crossing
Whangarei
Dargaville
Bream Head
Waipu
Kaipara Harbour
Wellsford
Great Barrier Island
Hauraki Gulf
Takapuna
Mercury Islands
Auckland Manukau
Whitianga
Manukau Harbour
Thames
Pukekohe
Mayor Island
Paeroa
Waihi
Huntly
Te Aroha
Cape Runaway
Morrinsville
Tauranga
Bay of Plenty
Raukumara 1414
East Cape
Hamilton
Whakatane
Cambridge
Kawerau
Opotiki
Hikurangi 1754
Te Awamutu
Rotorua
Murupara
Raukumara Range
Te Kuiti
Kinleith
Tolaga Bay
Mokau
Taupo
Waikato
Lake Taupo
Lake Waikaremoana
Gisborne
North Taranaki Bight
Waitara
Taumarunui
Poverty Bay
New Plymouth
Tarawera
Wairoa
Cape Egmont
Mt Egmont 2518
Ruapehu 2797
Mahia Peninsula
Raetihi
Taihape
Napier
Hawera
Mangaweka
Hastings
Hawke Bay
Patea
Wanganui
Waipawa
Marton
Feilding
Dannevirke
Palmerston North
Woodville
Cape Farewell
Farewell Spit
D'Urville Island
Cook Strait
Levin
Collingwood
Golden Bay
Otaki
Eketahuna
1213
Tasman Mountains
Tasman Bay
Paraparaumu
Tararua Range
Masterton
Motueka
Porirua
Richmond
Nelson
Upper Hutt
Mt Owen
Picton
Lower Hutt 663
1875
Cape Foulwind
Westport
Blenheim
Wellington
Inangahua
Murchison
Mt Travers 2338
Tapuaenuku 2885
Cape Palliser
Reefton
Spenser Mts
Runanga
Lewis Pass 1867
Kaikoura
Greymouth
Waiau
Hokitika
Lake Brunner
Otira
Arthur's Pass
Waipara
Pegasus Bay

South Island

Abut Head
Lake Coleridge
Rangiora
Springfield
Kaiapoi
Mt Cook 3764
Christchurch
Mt Cook
Staveley
Lyttelton
Haast
Lake Tekapo
Banks Peninsula
Akaroa
Jackson Head
Ashburton
Southern Alps
Lake Pukaki
Canterbury Plains
Haast Pass
Temuka
Canterbury Bight
Mt Aspiring 3030
Lake Hawea
Timaru
Milford Sound
Lake Wanaka
Waimate
Bligh Sound
2502
Lindis Pass
George Sound
2085
Waitaki
Queenstown
Secretary Island
Cromwell
Doubtful Sound
Lake Te Anau
Naseby
Oamaru
Alexandra
Resolution Island
Lake Manapouri
Roxburgh
Palmerston
Cape Providence
Ohai
Clutha
Mosgiel
Port Chalmers
Lake Hauroko
Gore
Dunedin
Milton
Riverton
Mataura
Balclutha
Invercargill
Bluff
Foveaux Strait
980
Halfmoon Bay
Stewart Island
750
Port Pegasus
Southwest Cape

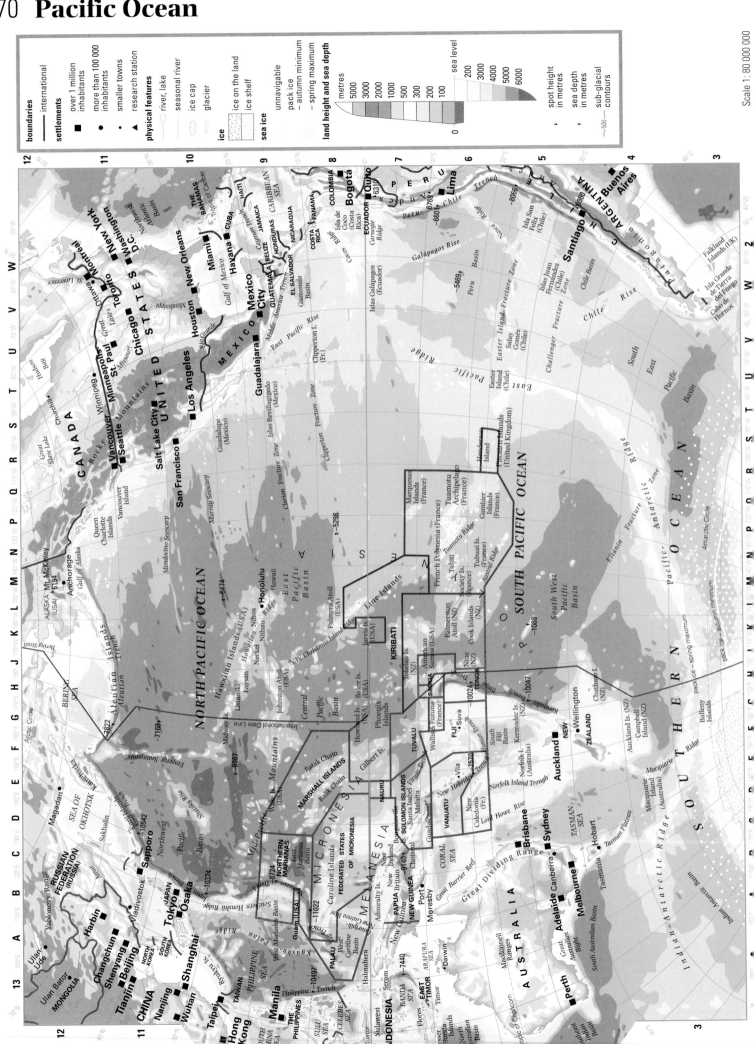

Scale 1 : 80 000 000

Antarctica map

SOUTHERN OCEAN

Mawson (Australia) · Cape Darnley · Davis (Australia) · Mirny (Russia) · Casey (Australia) · Dumont d'Urville (France)

Molodezhnaya (Russia) · Zhongshan (China) · Wilhelm II Land · Queen Mary Land · Wilkes Land · Adélie Land

Syowa (Japan) · Amery Ice Shelf · Princess Elizabeth Land

Enderby Land · Kemp Land · Lambert Glacier · Vostok (Russia) · George V Land

Novolazarevskaya (Russia) · Asuka (Japan) · Verteikaka Nunatak · 3630 · 1500 · 2000 · 2500

Maitri (India) · Dronning Maud Land · ANTARCTICA · South Magnetic Pole (1982)

SANAE (SA) · Neumayer (Germany) · Victoria Land · Transantarctic Mountains

SOUTH POLE 2800 metres above sea level · Amundsen-Scott (USA) · Scott Base (NZ) · McMurdo (USA)

Ross Ice Shelf · ROSS SEA · International Date Line

WEDDELL SEA · Halley (UK) · General Belgrano II (Argentina) · Filchner Ice Shelf · Berkner Island Ice Shelf · Coats Land

Ronne Ice Shelf · Ellsworth Land · Vinson Massif 4897 · Marie Byrd Land · AMUNDSEN SEA

Larsen Ice Shelf · Palmer Land · Graham Land · Antarctic Peninsula · Alexander Island · BELLINGSHAUSEN SEA

Rothera (UK) · Faraday (UK) · Palmer (USA) · General San Martín (Argentina)

Esperanza (Argentina) · Gen. Bernardo O'Higgins (Chile) · SOUTHERN OCEAN

Capitán Arturo Prat (Chile) · Comandante Ferraz (Brazil) · Arctowski (Poland) · King George I. (S. Korea) · Jubany (Argentina) · Bellingshausen (Russia) · Marsh (Chile) · Vicecomodoro Marambio (Argentina)

South Orkney Islands · South Shetland Islands · SCOTIA SEA · South Georgia (UK)

Tierra del Fuego (Argentina) · Cape Horn · Drake Passage · Antarctic Circle · Falkland Isles (UK) · SOUTH AMERICA

pack ice - average autumn minimum
pack ice - average spring maximum

Scale 1 : 40 000 000
0 400 800 1200 1600 2000 km

A section through the Antarctic ice sheet
(from the Bellingshausen Sea to Colvocoresses Bay)

metres 3000 2000 1000 SL 1000 2000

East Antarctic Ice Sheet · Transantarctic Mountains · Ross Ice Shelf · West Antarctic Ice Sheet

ice · sea level · land below sea level

horizontal scale 1 cm to 400 km

A

Arctic Ocean map

RUSSIAN FEDERATION (RUSSIA)

Verkhoyansk Range · Lena · Cherskogo Range · Verkhoyansk · Taymyr Peninsula · Nordvik · Dikson · Ob · N. Dvina · Arkhangelsk · St. Petersburg

Magadan · Kamchatka · Kazach'ye · LAPTEV SEA · Severnaya Zemlya · KARA SEA · Novaya Zemlya · Franz Josef Land · Murmansk · FINLAND · Helsinki · ESTONIA · LATVIA · LITHUANIA · BELARUS

Koryak Range · Kolyma Range · Kolyma · Kolyma Lowland · New Siberian Islands · Severnaya Zemlya · BARENTS SEA · Svalbard · North Cape · Tromsø · SWEDEN · Stockholm

Arctic Circle · EAST SIBERIAN SEA · Wrangel Island · 4321 · ARCTIC · NORTH POLE · -730 · -5449 · NORWEGIAN SEA · NORWAY · Oslo · Trondheim

Chukotsk Peninsula · Chukchi Range · CHUKCHI SEA · International Date Line · OCEAN · North Magnetic Pole (2003) · -3690 · GREENLAND SEA · Jan Mayen (Norway) · -3970 · Arctic Circle

BERING SEA · Bering Strait · C. Lisburne · -3800 · Patrick Island · Prince Patrick Island · -2875

Aleutian Islands (USA) · USA · Barrow · Prudhoe Bay · Brooks Range · Melville Island · Banks Island · Ellesmere Island · Alert · Greenland (Denmark) · ICELAND · Reykjavík · Hekla 1491

Anchorage · Mt McKinley (Denali) · Alaska Range · Yukon · Gulf of Alaska · CANADA · Victoria Island · Prince of Wales Island · Devon Island · Baffin Bay · Uummannaq · Upernavik · Mont Forel 3360 · Itoqqortoormiit · Denmark Strait

BEAUFORT SEA · Amundsen Gulf · Gulf of Boothia · Baffin Island · Nuuk · Kangerlussuaq · Kangaatsiaq

pack ice - average autumn minimum
pack ice - average spring maximum

Zenithal Equidistant Projection
© Oxford University Press

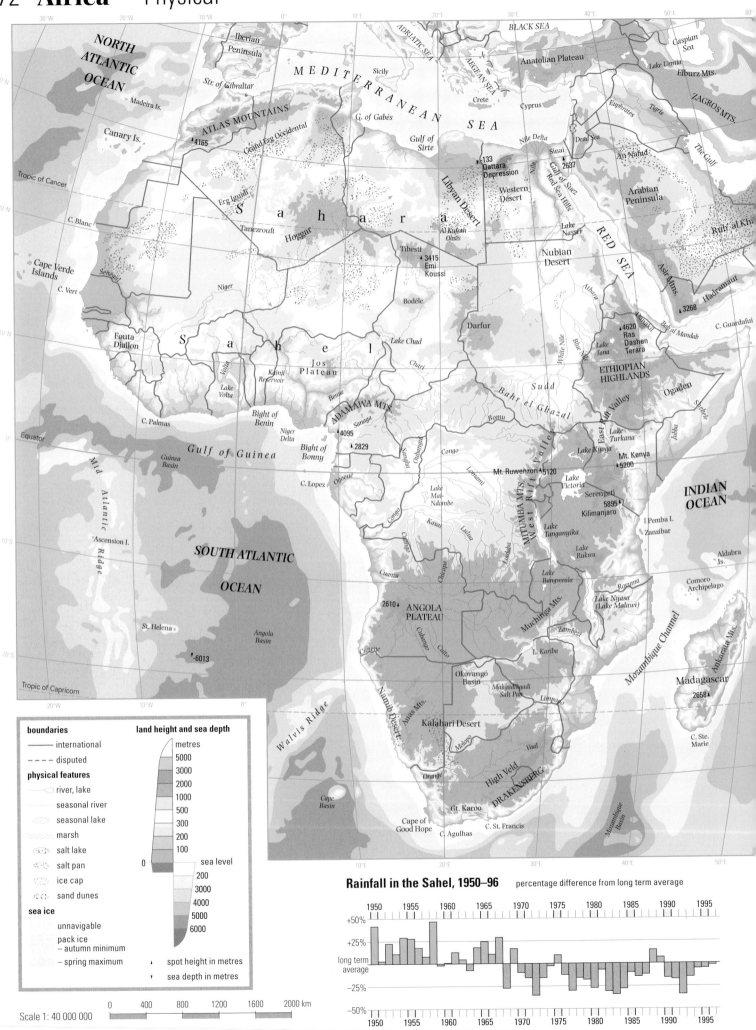

boundaries

——— international

- - - disputed

physical features

river, lake

seasonal river

seasonal lake

marsh

salt lake

salt pan

ice cap

sand dunes

sea ice

unnavigable

pack ice
– autumn minimum

– spring maximum

land height and sea depth

metres

5000
3000
2000
1000
500
300
200
100
0 sea level
200
3000
4000
5000
6000

▲ spot height in metres

▼ sea depth in metres

Scale 1: 40 000 000

0 400 800 1200 1600 2000 km

© Oxford University Press   Zenithal Equal Area Projection

Rainfall in the Sahel, 1950–96   percentage difference from long term average

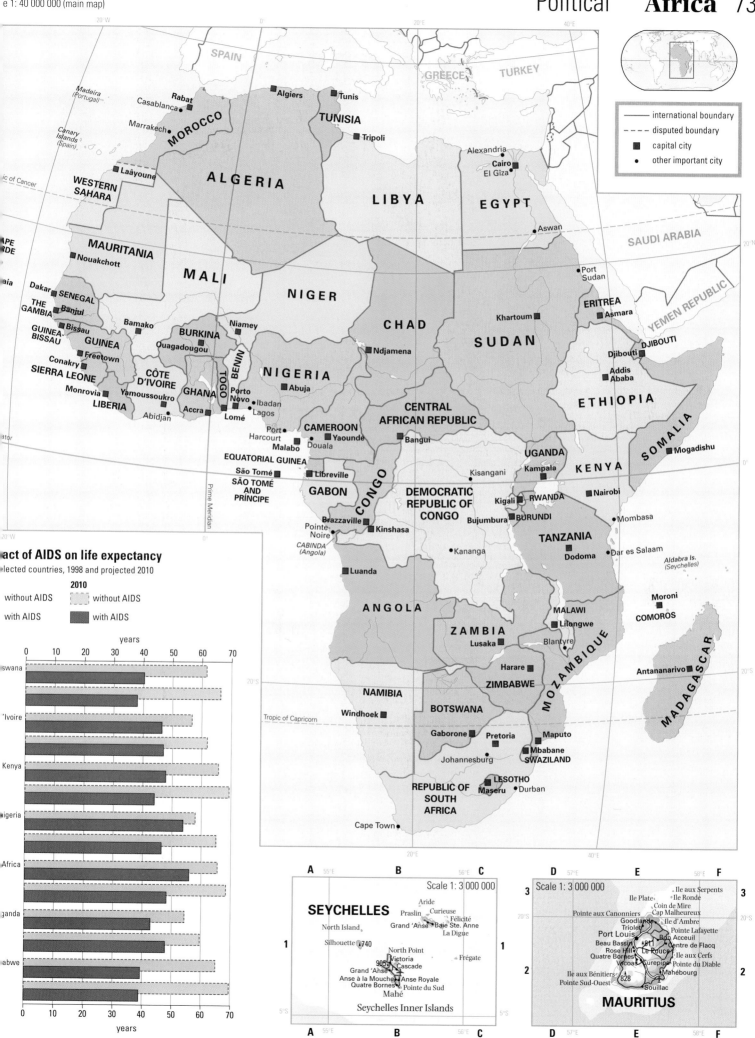

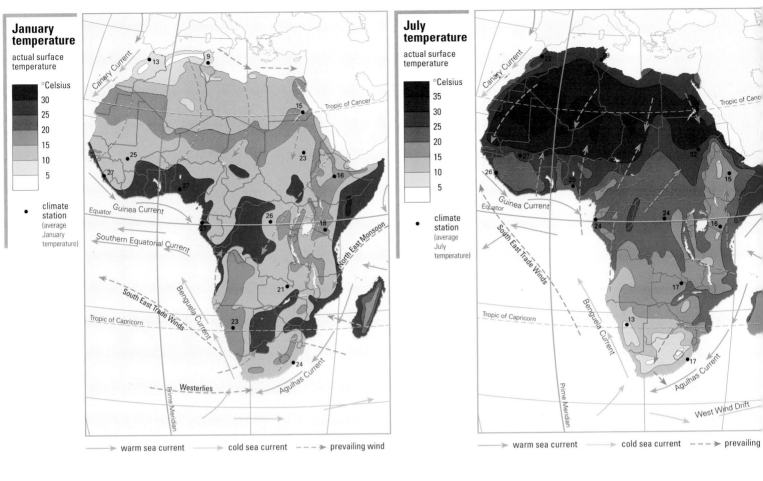

January temperature

actual surface temperature

°Celsius
- 30
- 25
- 20
- 15
- 10
- 5

● climate station (average January temperature)

Canary Current
Tropic of Cancer
Equator
Guinea Current
Southern Equatorial Current
South East Trade Winds
Benguela Current
Tropic of Capricorn
North East Monsoon
Westerlies
Agulhas Current
Prime Meridian

→ warm sea current → cold sea current - - → prevailing wind

July temperature

actual surface temperature

°Celsius
- 35
- 30
- 25
- 20
- 15
- 10
- 5

● climate station (average July temperature)

Canary Current
Tropic of Cancer
Equator
Guinea Current
South East Trade Winds
Benguela Current
Tropic of Capricorn
Agulhas Current
West Wind Drift
Prime Meridian

→ warm sea current → cold sea current - - → prevailing

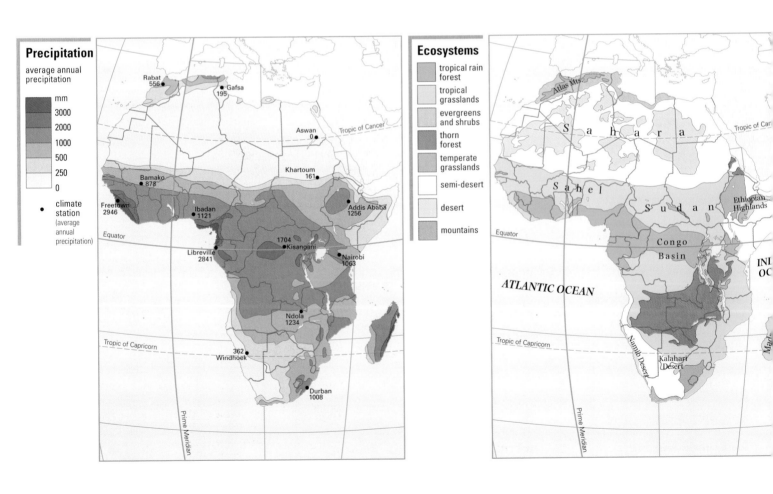

Precipitation

average annual precipitation

mm
- 3000
- 2000
- 1000
- 500
- 250
- 0

● climate station (average annual precipitation)

Rabat 556
Gafsa 195
Aswan 0
Tropic of Cancer
Khartoum 161
Bamako 878
Freetown 2946
Ibadan 1121
Addis Ababa 1256
Equator
Libreville 2841
Kisangani 1704
Nairobi 1063
Ndola 1234
Tropic of Capricorn
362 Windhoek
Durban 1008
Prime Meridian

Ecosystems

- tropical rain forest
- tropical grasslands
- evergreens and shrubs
- thorn forest
- temperate grasslands
- semi-desert
- desert
- mountains

Atlas Mts.
S a h a r a
Tropic of Cancer
Sahel
Sudan
Ethiopian Highlands
Equator
Congo Basin
INI OC
ATLANTIC OCEAN
Tropic of Capricorn
Namib Desert
Kalahari Desert
Prime Meridian

Zenithal Equal Area Projection   © Oxford Unive

ale 1: 55 000 000

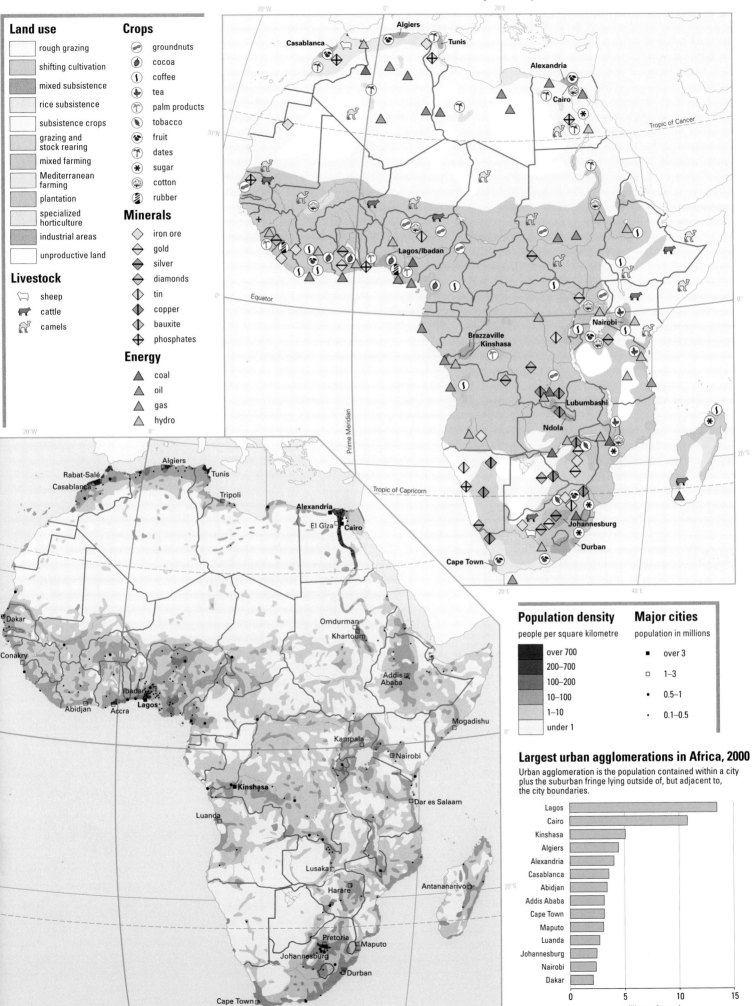

Land use
- rough grazing
- shifting cultivation
- mixed subsistence
- rice subsistence
- subsistence crops
- grazing and stock rearing
- mixed farming
- Mediterranean farming
- plantation
- specialized horticulture
- industrial areas
- unproductive land

Livestock
- sheep
- cattle
- camels

Crops
- groundnuts
- cocoa
- coffee
- tea
- palm products
- tobacco
- fruit
- dates
- sugar
- cotton
- rubber

Minerals
- iron ore
- gold
- silver
- diamonds
- tin
- copper
- bauxite
- phosphates

Energy
- coal
- oil
- gas
- hydro

Population density
people per square kilometre
- over 700
- 200–700
- 100–200
- 10–100
- 1–10
- under 1

Major cities
population in millions
- over 3
- 1–3
- 0.5–1
- 0.1–0.5

Largest urban agglomerations in Africa, 2000
Urban agglomeration is the population contained within a city plus the suburban fringe lying outside of, but adjacent to, the city boundaries.

Lagos
Cairo
Kinshasa
Algiers
Alexandria
Casablanca
Abidjan
Addis Ababa
Cape Town
Maputo
Luanda
Johannesburg
Nairobi
Dakar

0   5   10   15
millions of people

© Oxford University Press

Zenithal Equal Area Projection

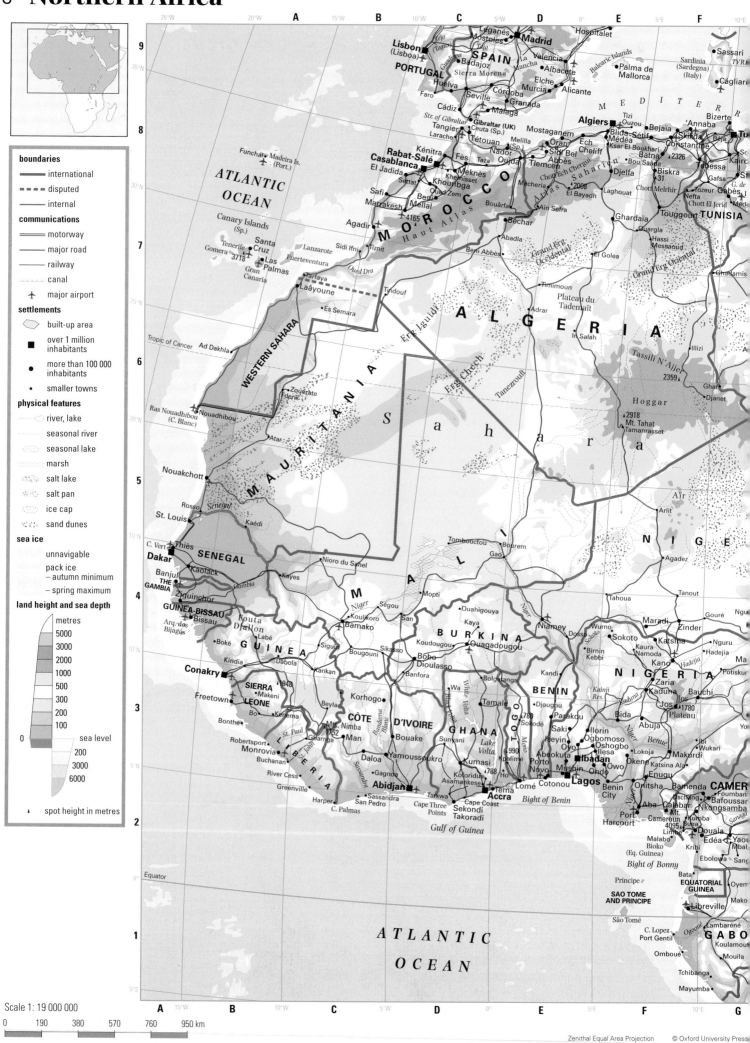

boundaries

	international
----	disputed
----	internal

communications

motorway
major road
railway
canal
✈ major airport

settlements

built-up area
■ over 1 million inhabitants
● more than 100 000 inhabitants
· smaller towns

physical features

river, lake
seasonal river
seasonal lake
marsh
salt lake
salt pan
ice cap
sand dunes

sea ice

unnavigable
pack ice
– autumn minimum
– spring maximum

land height and sea depth

metres
5000
3000
2000
1000
500
300
200
100
0   sea level
200
3000
6000

▲ spot height in metres

Scale 1: 19 000 000

0   190   380   570   760   950 km

Zenithal Equal Area Projection

© Oxford University Press

ITALY
15°E 20°E 25°E 30°E 35°E 40°E 45°E 50°E 55°E

FYRO MACEDONIA
Tiranë
ALBANIA
Bari
Táranto
Vesuvio 1277
Cosenza
Catanzaro
Messina
Reggio di Calabria
Catania
Siracusa
MALTA
aletta

GREECE
Thessaloníki
Ólympos 2917
Lárisa
Patras
Athens
Pelopónnisos
Peloponnese
IONIAN SEA
Kríti (Crete)
Iráklion
AEGEAN SEA
Dodekánisos (Dodecanese)
SEA OF CRETE

Istanbul
SEA OF MARMARA
İzmit
Bursa
İzmir
Eskişehir
Balıkesir
Denizli
Antalya
Mersin

TURKEY
Zonguldak
Ankara
Kızıl Irmak
Tuz Gölü
Konya
Adana
İskenderun
Sivas
Kayseri
3916
Malatya
Gaziantep
Urfa
Erzurum
Diyarbakır
Van Gölü
Ağrı Dağı (Mt. Ararat) 5123
Oru̇miyeh

SYRIA
Aleppo
Latakia
Homs
Damascus
Nicosia
CYPRUS
Limassol
LEBANON
Beirut
Haifa
Tel Aviv-Yafo
ISRAEL
Jerusalem
Dead Sea
Amman
JORDAN
Ma'ān
Aqaba
Elat
Mosul
Kirkūk
Baghdad
IRAQ
Tigris
Euphrates
An Nāsiriyah
Al Başrah
KUWAIT
Kuwait

IRAN
Tabrīz 4548
Tehran 5671
Rasht
Gorgān
Caspian Sea
Damāvand
Sabzevār
Qom
Eşfahān
Yazd
Kermānshāh
Shīrāz
Ābādān
Al Fuḩayḩ̄il
BAHRAIN
Manama
QATAR
Doha
Ad Dammām
Al Hufūf
UNITED ARAB EMIRATES
Bandar-e Lengeh
The Gulf
Zagros Mountains

Alexandria (El Iskandariya)
Damietta
Port Said
Suez Canal
Ismā'ilīya
Suez
El Mahalla el Kubra
El Giza
Cairo (El Qâ'hira)
El Faiyum
Beni Suef
El Minya
Asyût
El Khârga
Dakhla Oasis
Qasr Farâfra
Farâfra Oasis
Siwa
Qattara Depression -133

EGYPT
Sinai
2637
G. of Suez
Tabūk 2579
Aynūnah
Hurghada
Bûr Safâga
Al Wajh
Luxor
Quseir
Idfu
Aswân
Aswân Dam 1st Cataract
Lake Nasser
Râs Banâs
Medina
Yanbu al Baḩr
Jedda / Mecca
At Ṭā'if
Al Lith
Al Qunfudhah
Abhā

SAUDI ARABIA
An Nafūd
Al Jawf
Sākākah
Ḩā'il
Tayma
Khaybar
Unayzah
Buraydah
Shaqrā
Al Artāwīyah
Riyadh
Ad Dilam
Al Hariq
Layla
Harad
Tropic of Cancer
Rub' Al Khali
Say'ūn
W. al Masilah
Hadhramaut

LIBYA
Khums
Misratah
Gulf of Sirte
Benghazi
Al Bayda
Jabal al Akhdar
Darnah
Tubruq
Sidi Barrani
Sirte
Ajdabiya
Ras Lanuf
Zaltan
Jālū
's Sawdā' 840
1200
Jbha
Sirte Desert
Libyan Plateau

Great Sand Sea
Sarīr Calancio
Al Kufrah Oasis
Al Jawf
Libyan Desert
Jebel Abyad Plateau

2nd Cataract
Wadi Halfa
Selima Oasis
Nubian Desert
2260
Port Sudan
Suakin
Al Qunfudhah
3rd Cataract
Dongola
4th Cataract
Abu Hamed
5th Cataract
Berber
Ed Debba
Merowe
Atbara
Ed Damer
el Milk
Ras Kasar
RED SEA
Massawa
Arch. Kamaran
Dehalak
Jaza'ir Farasān
Jizan
Sabya
Najran
boundary undefined

CHAD
Aozou Strip
Tibesti 3265
Zouar
Emi Koussi 3415
Faya-Largeau
Dépression du Mourdi
Fada
Bodélé
Bodélé
Ndjamena
Chari
Bousso
Bongor
Lac Fitri
Ati
Abéché
Am Timan
Batha
Azoum
Mondou
Koumra
Sarh
Birao

1435
1852

SUDAN
Omdurman
White Nile Dam
Khartoum
Wad Medani
Kassala
Keren
Asmara
Teseney
Gedaref
Sennar
Er Roseires
Kosti
Umm Ruwaba
En Nahud
El Obeid
Nyala
El Fasher
Geneina
Jebel Marra 3071
Talodi
El Muglad
Kodok
Malakal
Bahr el Arab
Lol
Radom
Wau
Jur
Bahr el Jebel (White Nile)
Bor
Amadi
Juba
Yambio
Nimule 3187

ERITREA
Sana 3760
YEMEN REPUBLIC
Mukalla
Hodeida
Ta'izz
Dhamār 3268
Shuqra
Al Mukha
Madinat ash Sha'b
Bab al Mandab
Little Aden
Aden
Habban
2576
Mekele
Keren
Adwa
Adi
Assab
Gulf of Aden
Raas Caseyr

DJIBOUTI
Djibouti 150
Saylac
Berbera
Boosaaso
Xaafuun
Bender Bayla
Laascaanood
Ceerigaabo 2408
Dharoor
Boorama
Hargeysa

ETHIOPIA
Gonder
4620 Ras Dashen Terara
Debre Tabor
Lake Tana
3556
Debre Mark'os
4153
Abbai (Blue Nile)
4000
L. Abbe
Dese
Dire Dawa
Harer
Awash
Ahmar Mts.
Addis Ababa 3298
Nek'emte
Dembi Dolo
Gore
Jima
Sodo
Yirga Alem
4307
Mendebo Mts.
Ginir
Imi
Maji
Omo
1548
Negele
Lake Chamo
Gidole
Mega
Dolo Odo
Degeh Bur
Shebele
Genale
K'elafo
Gaalkacyo
Haud
Ogaden
Werder

SOMALIA
Buulobarde
Hobyo
Baydhabo
Marka
Mogadishu

CENTRAL AFRICAN REPUBLIC
Bossangoa
Bouar
Bozoum
Sibut
Bambari
Bria
Ouadda
Massif des Bongos 1055
Ndélé
Batangafo
Bangui
Berbérati
Carnot
Nola
Mbaïki
Libenge
Dongou
Impfondo
Budjala
Mbandaka

DEMOCRATIC REPUBLIC OF CONGO
Kisangani
Buta
Aketi
Bumba
Bondo
Niangara
Isiro
Mungbere
Mambasa
Lake Albert
Lake Edward
Mt. Karisimbi 4507
L. Kivu
Bukavu
Bujumbura
Kindu
Kibombo
Kasese
Opala
Ubundu
Ikela
Congo
Lomela
Busira
Tshuapa
Lac Mai-Ndombe
Inongo
Bandundu
Kasai
Sankuru
Dekese

UGANDA
Arua
Gulu
Moroto
Moyo
Lake Kyoga
Soroti
Masindi
Mubende
Kampala 3110
Fort Portal
Jinja
Entebbe
Owen Falls Dam
Lake Victoria
4321
Bukoba
Mwanza
Shinyanga

RWANDA
Kigali
Butare
Biharamulo

BURUNDI
2685
Bujumbura

KENYA
Eldoret
5200
Mt. Elgon 4321
Kisumu
Nakuru 2777
Thika
Mt. Kenya 5200
Nairobi
Machakos
Nanyuki
Garissa
Mado Gashi
Wajir
Marsabit
Moyale
Sardindida Plain
Luuq
East Rift Valley
Lake Turkana
Mega
Ginir
2805
Bura
Lamu
Pate I.
Kismaayo
Machakos

Eldoret
Nakuru
Kilimanjaro 5895
Moshi
Arusha
Voi
Mombasa
Pemba I.
L. Natron
L. Eyasi
3418
Tabora

INDIAN OCEAN

Equator
5°N
5°S
35°N
30°N
25°N
20°N
15°N
10°N
5°N
0°

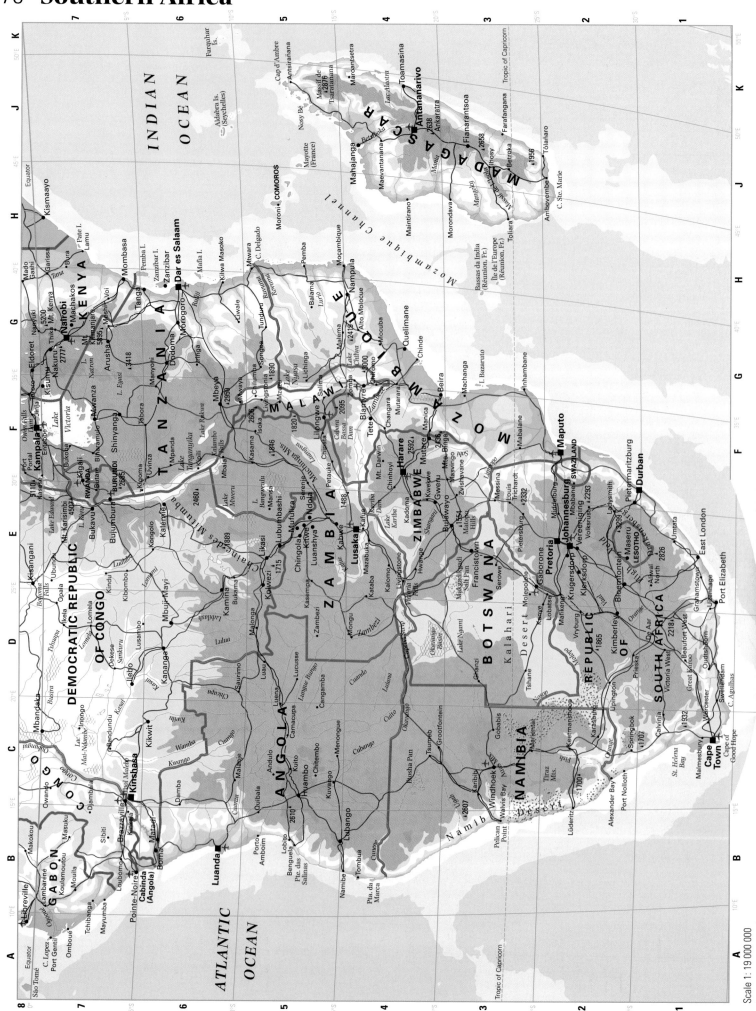

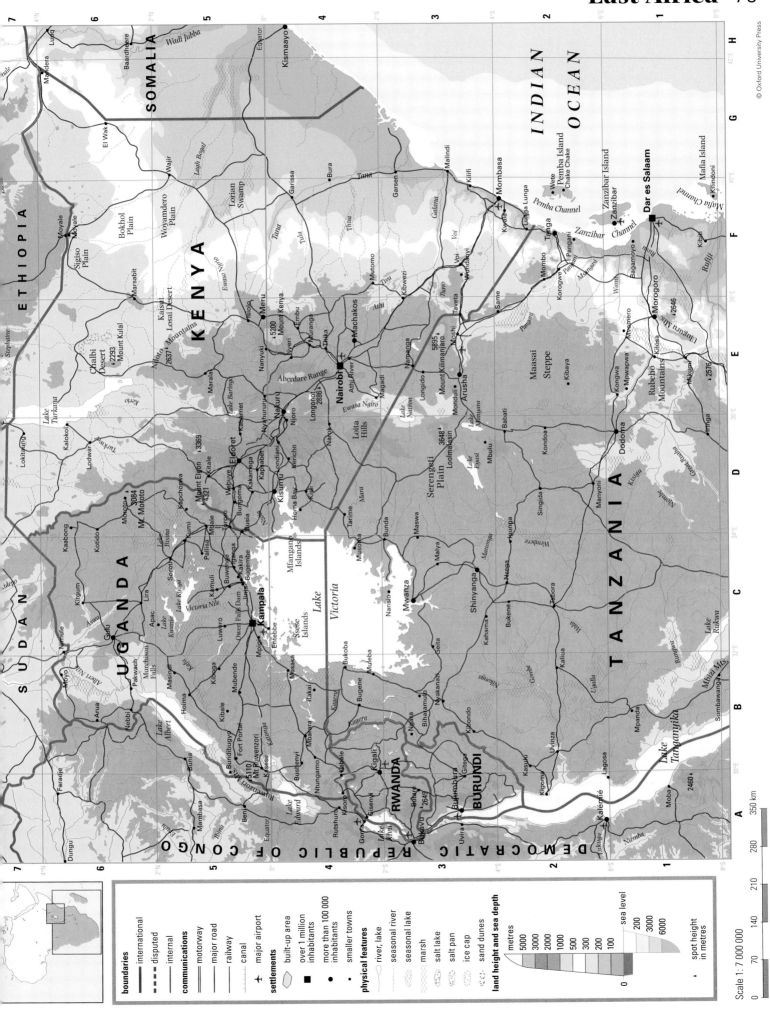

© Oxford University Press

INDIAN OCEAN

SOMALIA

ETHIOPIA

KENYA

UGANDA

SUDAN

DEMOCRATIC REPUBLIC OF CONGO

RWANDA

BURUNDI

TANZANIA

Lake Victoria

Lake Tanganyika

Zanzibar Island

Pemba Island

Mafia Island

Nairobi

Kampala

Dar es Salaam

Dodoma

Scale 1 : 7 000 000

boundaries
international
disputed
internal

communications
motorway
major road
railway
canal
major airport

settlements
built-up area
over 1 million inhabitants
more than 100 000 inhabitants
smaller towns

physical features
river, lake
seasonal river
seasonal lake
marsh
salt lake
salt pan
ice cap
sand dunes

land height and sea depth

metres
5000
3000
2000
1000
500
300
200
100
sea level
200
3000
6000

spot height in metres

0 70 140 210 280 350 km

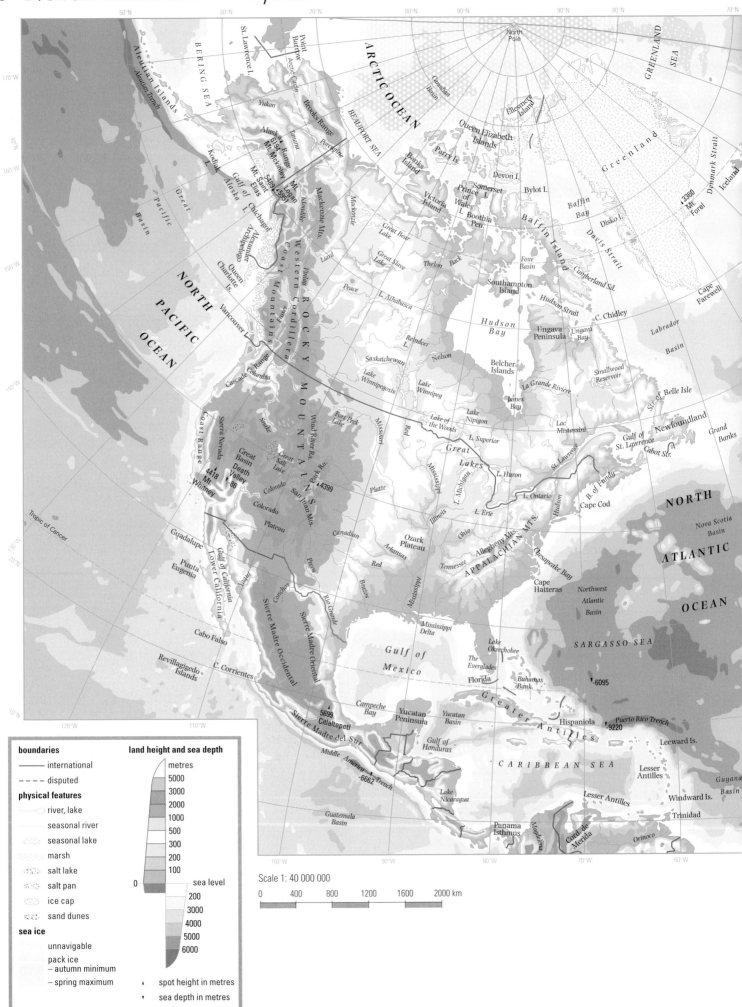

boundaries

— international

- - - disputed

physical features

river, lake

seasonal river

seasonal lake

marsh

salt lake

salt pan

ice cap

sand dunes

sea ice

unnavigable

pack ice
– autumn minimum
– spring maximum

▲ spot height in metres

▼ sea depth in metres

land height and sea depth

metres

5000
3000
2000
1000
500
300
200
100

0   sea level

200
3000
4000
5000
6000

Scale 1: 40 000 000

0   400   800   1200   1600   2000 km

© Oxford University Press   Oblique Mercator Projection

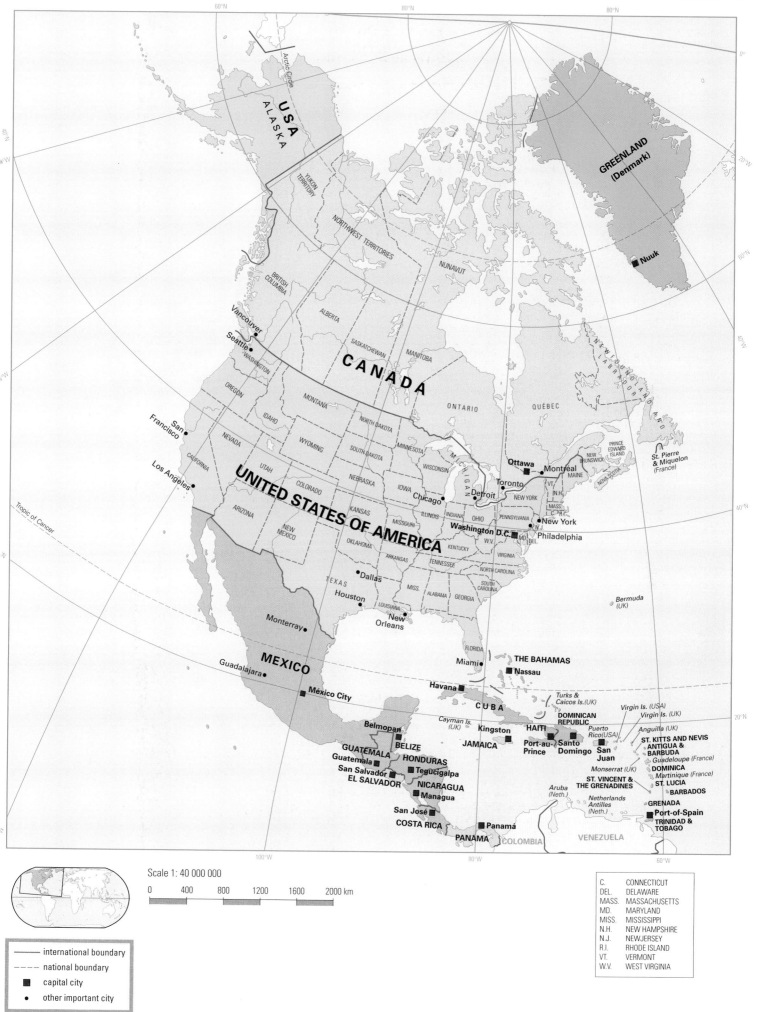

Scale 1: 40 000 000

0   400   800   1200   1600   2000 km

C.	CONNECTICUT
DEL.	DELAWARE
MASS.	MASSACHUSETTS
MD.	MARYLAND
MISS.	MISSISSIPPI
N.H.	NEW HAMPSHIRE
N.J.	NEWJERSEY
R.I.	RHODE ISLAND
VT.	VERMONT
W.V.	WEST VIRGINIA

—— international boundary

--- national boundary

■ capital city

• other important city

Oblique Mercator Projection   © Oxford University Press

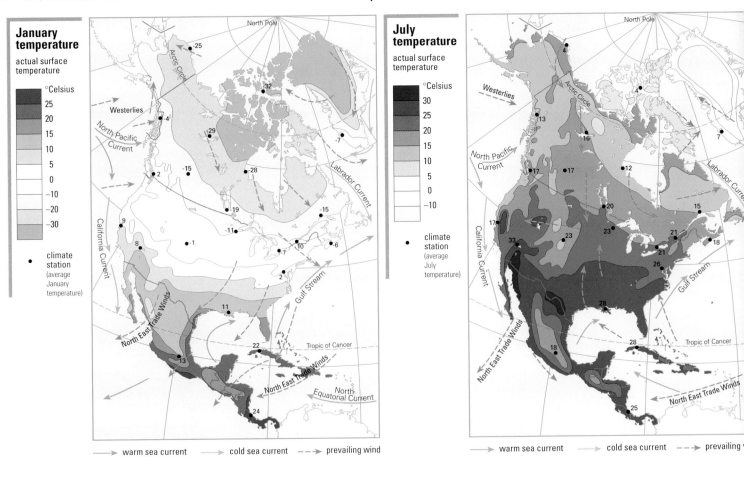

January temperature

actual surface temperature

°Celsius
25
20
15
10
5
0
−10
−20
−30

● climate station (average January temperature)

Westerlies

North Pacific Current

California Current

North East Trade Winds

Arctic Circle

North Pole

−25
−32
−4
−29
−7
−15
−28
2
−15
−19
9
−11
−5
8
−1
−7
10
−6
2
11
22
13
North East Trade Winds
Tropic of Cancer
North Equatorial Current
Gulf Stream
Labrador Current
24

→ warm sea current → cold sea current --→ prevailing wind

July temperature

actual surface temperature

°Celsius
30
25
20
15
10
5
0
−10

● climate station (average July temperature)

Westerlies

North Pacific Current

California Current

North East Trade Winds

Arctic Circle

North Pole

4
4
13
16
7
17
17
12
15
20
18
33
23
23
21
21
18
26
28
28
Tropic of Cancer
Gulf Stream
Labrador Current
North East Trade Winds
25

→ warm sea current → cold sea current --→ prevailing

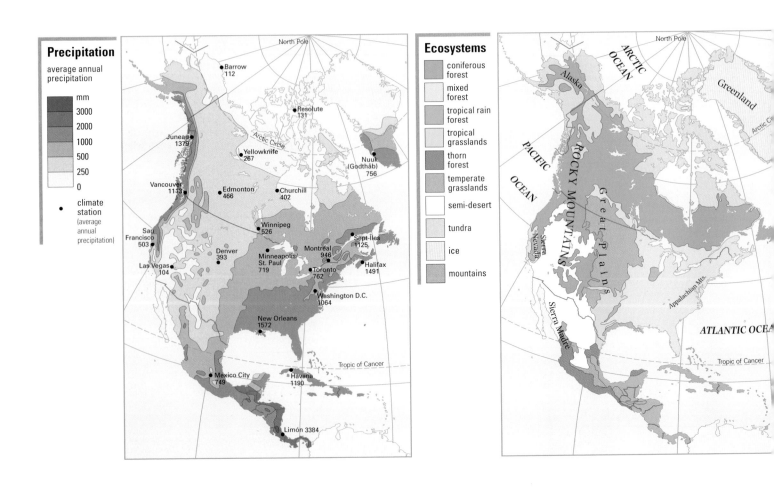

Precipitation

average annual precipitation

mm
3000
2000
1000
500
250
0

● climate station (average annual precipitation)

North Pole

Barrow 112
Resolute 131
Juneau 1379
Arctic Circle
Yellowknife 267
Nuuk (Godthåb) 756
Vancouver 1113
Edmonton 466
Churchill 402
San Francisco 503
Winnipeg 526
Sept-Îles 1125
Denver 393
Montréal 946
Las Vegas 104
Minneapolis/ St. Paul 719
Halifax 1491
Toronto 762
Washington D.C. 1064
New Orleans 1572
Tropic of Cancer
Mexico City 749
Havana 1190
Limón 3384

Ecosystems

coniferous forest
mixed forest
tropical rain forest
tropical grasslands
thorn forest
temperate grasslands
semi-desert
tundra
ice
mountains

North Pole

ARCTIC OCEAN
Alaska
Greenland
Arctic Ci
PACIFIC OCEAN
ROCKY MOUNTAINS
Great Plains
Sierra Nevada
Sierra Madre
Appalachian Mts.
ATLANTIC OCEA
Tropic of Cancer

Scale 1: 55 000 000

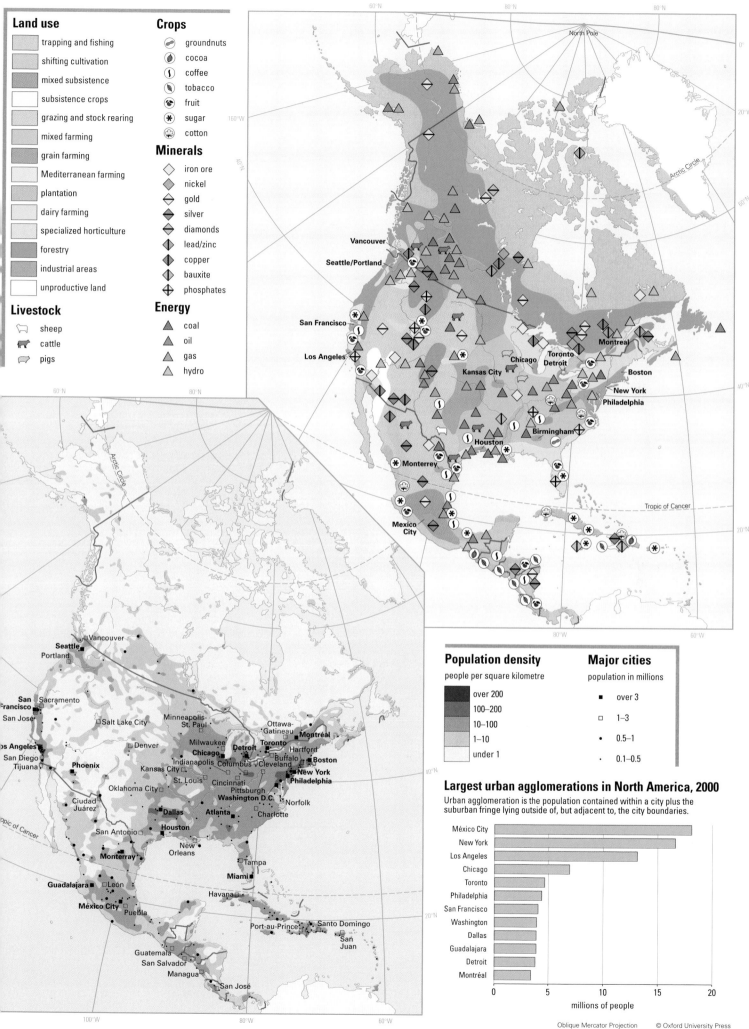

Land use

- trapping and fishing
- shifting cultivation
- mixed subsistence
- subsistence crops
- grazing and stock rearing
- mixed farming
- grain farming
- Mediterranean farming
- plantation
- dairy farming
- specialized horticulture
- forestry
- industrial areas
- unproductive land

Livestock

- sheep
- cattle
- pigs

Crops

- groundnuts
- cocoa
- coffee
- tobacco
- fruit
- sugar
- cotton

Minerals

- iron ore
- nickel
- gold
- silver
- diamonds
- lead/zinc
- copper
- bauxite
- phosphates

Energy

- coal
- oil
- gas
- hydro

Population density

people per square kilometre

- over 200
- 100–200
- 10–100
- 1–10
- under 1

Major cities

population in millions

- over 3
- 1–3
- 0.5–1
- 0.1–0.5

Largest urban agglomerations in North America, 2000

Urban agglomeration is the population contained within a city plus the suburban fringe lying outside of, but adjacent to, the city boundaries.

México City	
New York	
Los Angeles	
Chicago	
Toronto	
Philadelphia	
San Francisco	
Washington	
Dallas	
Guadalajara	
Detroit	
Montréal	

0   5   10   15   20
millions of people

Oblique Mercator Projection   © Oxford University Press

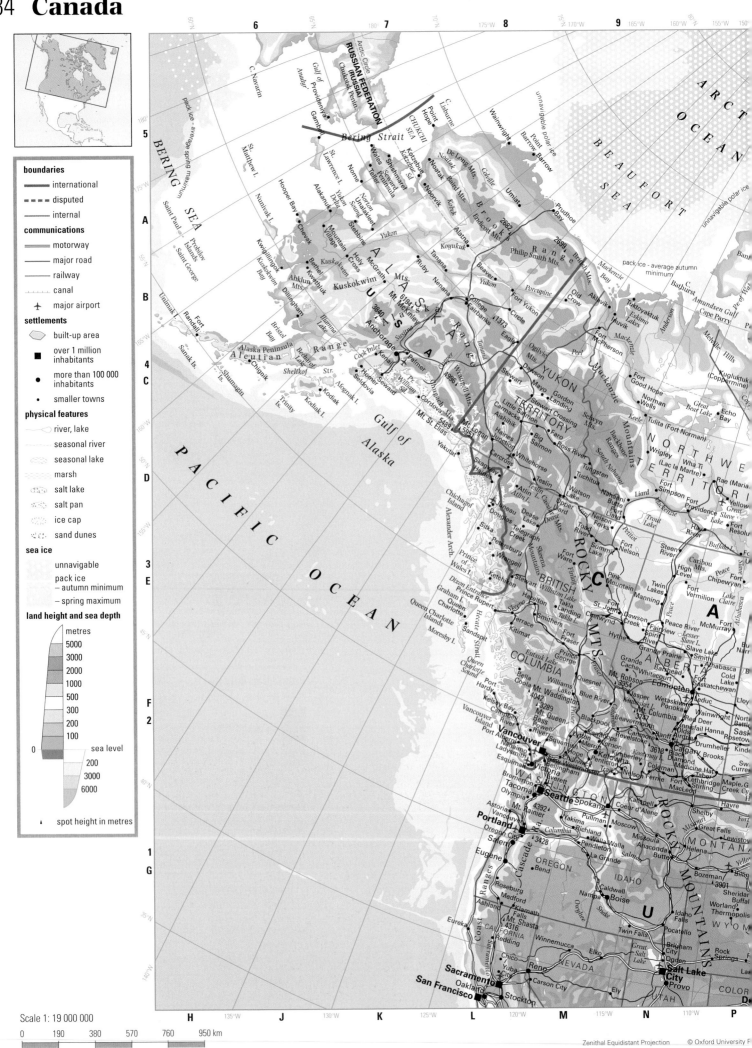

boundaries

━━━	international
╍╍╍	disputed
───	internal

communications

	motorway
	major road
	railway
⊥⊥⊥	canal
✈	major airport

settlements

⬡	built-up area
■	over 1 million inhabitants
●	more than 100 000 inhabitants
•	smaller towns

physical features

	river, lake
	seasonal river
	seasonal lake
	marsh
	salt lake
	salt pan
	ice cap
	sand dunes

sea ice

	unnavigable
	pack ice – autumn minimum
	– spring maximum

land height and sea depth

metres
5000
3000
2000
1000
500
300
200
100
0 sea level
200
3000
6000

▲ spot height in metres

Scale 1: 19 000 000

0   190   380   570   760   950 km

Zenithal Equidistant Projection   © Oxford University P

Greenland (Denmark)

ICELAND
Reykjavík
Hafnarfjördur
Ísafjördur
Vopnafjördur
Akureyri
Hekla 1491
Hafnarfjördur

Arctic Circle

Ellesmere Island
Axel Heiberg Island
Amund Ringnes I.
Ellef Ringnes I.
Queen Elizabeth Islands
Parry Islands
Bathurst I.
Cornwallis I.
Resolute
Devon Island
Jones Sound
Nares Strait
Hayes
Qaanaaq
Halvø
Uumannaq
Qimisseriarsuaq

Viscount Melville Sound
Peel Sound
Prince of Wales Island
Somerset Island
Prince Regent Inlet
Arctic Bay
Borden Penin.
Brodeur Penin.
Bylot Island
Pond Inlet

Baffin Bay

Upernavik
Nuussuaq
Oegertarsuatsiat

Davis Strait

Boothia Penin.
Gulf of Boothia
Brodeur Penin.

Baffin Island

Barnes Ice Cap 1250
Home Bay
Clyde River
Qeqertarsuaq
Disko
Ilulissat

McClintock Channel
Victoria Strait
King William Island
Gjoa Haven
Taloyoak
Boothia Penin.

Cambridge Bay
Kent Peninsula
Queen Maud Gulf

Melville Peninsula
Prince Charles I.
Foxe Basin
Nettilling Lake

Cumberland Penin.
Pangnirtung
Cumberland Sound
Amadjuak L.
Cape Dyer
Sisimiut
Maniitsoq
Nuuk

NUNAVUT

Pelly Lake
Garry Lake
Back
Thelon
Dubawnt Lake
Baker Lake
Yathkyed Lake
Nueltin Lake

Wager Bay
Southampton Island
Coral Harbour
Roes Welcome Sound
Foxe Channel
Cape Dorset
Salisbury I.
Nottingham I.
Meta Incognita Penin.
Iqaluit (Frobisher Bay)
Hall Penin.
Frobisher Bay
Kimmirut
Paamiut
Narsaq
Narsarsuaq
Nunap Isua
Qaqortoq
Nanortalik

Hudson Strait
C. Hopes Advance
Akpatok
C. Chidley
Button Is.

LABRADOR SEA

NORTH ATLANTIC OCEAN

Ivujivik
Déception
Ungava Bay (Baie d'Ungava)
Péninsule d'Ungava

Hudson Bay

Baker Lake
Rankin Inlet
Eskimo Point

Puvirnituq
Inukjuak
Lac Minto
Lac Payne
Rivière aux Feuilles
Koksoak
Kuujjuaq
George
Kaniapiskau
Torngat Mts.
Nutak
Nain
Davis Inlet
Makkovik
Hamilton Inlet
Cartwright
Battle Harbour
St. Anthony

NEWFOUNDLAND

Seal
C. Churchill
Churchill
C. Tatnam
North River
Nelson
York Factory
Fort Severn

Reindeer Lake
Wollaston Lake
Southern Indian Lake
Lynn Lake
Gillam
Thompson
Sipiwesk
Snow Lake
Wabowden

MANITOBA

Les Îles Belcher
Kuujjuarapik
Grande Rivière de la Baleine
Cape Henrietta Maria
Lake River
Winisk
Akimiski I.
James Bay
Attawapiskat
Eastmain
Waskaganish

Lac à l'Eau Claire
Lac Bienville
Schefferville
Réservoir de Caniapiscau
Labrador City
Wabush
Smallwood Reservoir
Happy Valley–Goose Bay
Melville Lake
Wolf Bay
Harrington Harbour

Grande Rivière
Chisasibi
Résr. La Grande 3
La Grande Rivière
Résr. La Grande 2
Monts Otish 1128
Lac Mistassini
Réservoir Manicouagan
Sept-Îles
Mingan
Natashquan
Gulf of St. Lawrence

QUÉBEC

Norway House
The Pas
Grand Rapids
Cedar Lake
Lake Winnipeg
Lake Winnipegosis
Lake Manitoba
Dauphin
Riverton
Selkirk
Winnipeg
Portage la Prairie
Brandon
Morden
Kenora
Lake of the Woods

ONTARIO

Gods Lake
Big Trout Lake
Sandy Lake
Pikangikum Lake
Pickle Lake
Lansdowne House
Fort Hope
Attawapiskat
Winisk L.
Albany
Moosonee
Hearst
Kapuskasing
Cochrane
Timmins
Rouyn-Noranda
Val-d'Or
Matagami
Chibougamau
Lac Matagami
Réservoir Gouin
La Tuque
Shawinigan
Trois-Rivières
Chicoutimi
Saguenay
Lac St. Jean
Roberval
Dolbeau

Sioux Lookout
Dryden
Auden
Nakina
Longlac
Geraldton
Terrace Bay
Nipigon
White River
Wawa
Chapleau
Foleyet
Kirkland Lake
New Liskeard
Mattawa
North Bay
Pembroke
Renfrew
Ottawa
Gatineau
Mont-Laurier
Maniwaki
Gracefield

Atikokan
Fort Frances
Thunder Bay
Lake Superior
Michipicoten
Sault Ste. Marie
Blind River
Sudbury
Manitoulin I.
Georgian Bay
Parry Sound
Midland
Owen Sound
Collingwood
Barrie
Orillia
Peterborough
Kingston
Brockville
Cornwall
Montréal
Sherbrooke
St-Jean
Drummondville
Victoriaville
Québec
Lévis
Rivière-du-Loup
Edmundston
Grand Falls
Woodstock
Fredericton
Saint John

NEW BRUNSWICK
NOVA SCOTIA
PRINCE EDWARD I.
Charlottetown
Moncton
Bathurst
Miramichi
Campbellton
Matane
Rimouski
Gaspé
Îles de la Madeleine
Cape Breton I.
Sydney
Glace Bay
Port Hawkesbury
Canso
Truro
Dartmouth
Halifax
Lunenburg
Bridgewater
Yarmouth
Shelburne
Bay of Fundy
Digby

St. Paul
Minneapolis
Duluth
Superior
MINNESOTA
WISCONSIN
Green Bay
Milwaukee
Madison
Chicago
Rockford
Michigan
Lake Michigan
Grand Rapids
Flint
Detroit
Windsor
Lake Huron
Lake Erie
Cleveland
Toledo
Columbus
Dayton
Indianapolis
Springfield
ILLINOIS
INDIANA
OHIO
Cincinnati
Pittsburgh
PENNSYLVANIA
Toronto
Hamilton
Kitchener
Guelph
London
St. Catharines
Buffalo
Rochester
Syracuse
Utica
Albany
NEW YORK
Boston
Hartford
Providence
New Haven
Bridgeport
New York
Newark
Philadelphia
Trenton
Atlantic City
Baltimore
Washington D.C.
MARYLAND
DELAWARE
VIRGINIA
WEST VIRGINIA
NEW JERSEY
VERMONT
N.H.
MASS.
MAINE
Manchester
Portland

SOUTH DAKOTA
NORTH DAKOTA
Fargo
Moorhead
Aberdeen
Jamestown
Bismarck
Sioux Falls
Sioux City
Yankton
NEBRASKA
Omaha
Lincoln
Council Bluffs
Des Moines
Cedar Rapids
Davenport
IOWA
Peoria
Springfield
MISSOURI

NORTH ATLANTIC OCEAN

boundaries
—— international
- - - disputed
—— internal

communications
═══ motorway
—— major road
—— railway
┼┼┼ canal
✈ major airport

settlements
⬡ built-up area
■ over 1 million inhabitants
● more than 100 000 inhabitants
• smaller towns

physical features
river, lake
seasonal river
seasonal lake
marsh
salt lake
salt pan
ice cap
sand dunes

sea ice
unnavigable
pack ice
– autumn minimum
– spring maximum

land height and sea depth
metres
5000
3000
2000
1000
500
300
200
100
0 sea level
200
3000
6000

▲ spot height in metres

Scale 1: 12 500 000

0   125   250   375   500   625 km

Conical Orthomorphic Projection   © Oxford University

PACIFIC OCEAN

CANADA

BRITISH COLUMBIA
ALBERTA
SASKATCHEWAN

WASHINGTON
OREGON
IDAHO
MONTANA
WYOMING
NEVADA
UTAH
CALIFORNIA
ARIZONA
NEW MEXICO
COLORADO

MEXICO
BAJA CALIFORNIA NORTE
BAJA CALIFORNIA SUR
SONORA
CHIHUAHUA
SINALOA
DURANGO
COAHUILA
NUEVO LEÓN

Vancouver
Seattle
Tacoma
Olympia
Portland
Salem
Eugene
San Francisco
San José
Oakland
Sacramento
Los Angeles
Long Beach
San Diego
Tijuana
Las Vegas
Phoenix
Salt Lake City
Denver
Colorado Springs
Ciudad Juárez
Monterrey
Calgary
Saskatoon
Regina
Winnipeg

Coordinate labels (top): G 95°W H 90°W J 85°W K 80°W L 75°W M 70°W N 65°W P 7

Canada / Quebec / Ontario region:
Norway House · Island Lake · Big Trout Lake · Akimiski I. · Attawapiskat · Eastmain · Lac Mistassini · Mingan · Île d'Anticosti
Sandy Lake · Winisk L. · James Bay · Waskaganish · QUÉBEC · Manicouagan · Sept-Îles · Honguedo Passage
Pikangikum L. · Pickle Lake · Lansdowne House · Fort Hope · Albany · Moosonee · Chibougamau · Betsiamites · Baie-Comeau · Matane · Ste-Anne-des-Monts · Gulf of St. Lawrence · Gaspé · Chandler · Bathurst
Riverton · Selkirk · Sioux Lookout · Dryden · ONTARIO · Hearst · Kapuskasing · Cochrane · Timmins · Val-d'Or · Rouyn-Noranda · La Tuque · Québec · NEW BRUNSWICK · Grand Falls · Miramichi · Richibucto
Winnipeg · Kenora · Lake of the Woods · Nipigon · Terrace Bay · White River · Chapleau · New Liskeard · Mattawa · Shawinigan · Trois-Rivières · Montréal · Sherbrooke · Moncton · Amherst · Saint John
Fargo · Moorhead · MINNESOTA · Duluth · Thunder Bay · Lake Superior · Michipicoten · Agawa · Sudbury · North Bay · Pembroke · Ottawa · Gatineau · Cornwall · VERMONT · MAINE · Bangor

United States cities (selected):
Winnipeg · Crookston · Bemidji · Grand Rapids · WISCONSIN · Green Bay · MICHIGAN · Sault Ste. Marie · Georgian Bay · Parry Sound · Huntsville · Kingston · Watertown · NEW HAMPSHIRE · Augusta · Portland · Concord · Manchester
Minneapolis · St. Paul · Eau Claire · Wausau · Appleton · Oshkosh · Milwaukee · Lansing · Detroit · Toronto · Hamilton · Rochester · Syracuse · Utica · Albany · Boston · Providence
Mankato · Rochester · Madison · Waukesha · Kenosha · Grand Rapids · Flint · Kalamazoo · Battle Creek · Toledo · Cleveland · Buffalo · NEW YORK · Hartford · New Haven · New York
Sioux City · IOWA · Des Moines · Cedar Rapids · Davenport · Chicago · Gary · South Bend · Fort Wayne · Lima · Akron · PENNSYLVANIA · Pittsburgh · Philadelphia · NEW JERSEY
Omaha · Lincoln · Council Bluffs · ILLINOIS · Peoria · Springfield · INDIANA · Indianapolis · Columbus · OHIO · Columbus · Dayton · Cincinnati · Wheeling · Baltimore · Washington D.C. · DELAWARE
Kansas City · Topeka · Lawrence · St. Louis · MISSOURI · Evansville · Louisville · KENTUCKY · Lexington · Frankfort · WEST VIRGINIA · Richmond · VIRGINIA · Norfolk · Virginia Beach
Wichita · Springfield · Nashville · Knoxville · NORTH CAROLINA · Winston-Salem · Greensboro · Raleigh · Durham · Cape Hatteras
Tulsa · Muskogee · Memphis · TENNESSEE · Chattanooga · Asheville · Charlotte · SOUTH CAROLINA · Columbia
Oklahoma City · Little Rock · ARKANSAS · Huntsville · Birmingham · Atlanta · GEORGIA · Augusta · Savannah · Charleston
Dallas · Shreveport · MISSISSIPPI · Jackson · ALABAMA · Montgomery · Columbus · Macon · Brunswick
Waco · LOUISIANA · Baton Rouge · New Orleans · Mobile · Pensacola · Tallahassee · Jacksonville · St. Augustine · Daytona Beach
Houston · Galveston · Gulf of Mexico · Mississippi Delta · Gainesville · Orlando · C. Canaveral · Melbourne
Corpus Christi · FLORIDA · Tampa · St. Petersburg · Sarasota · Ft. Pierce · West Palm Beach · Freeport · Grand Bahama · Great Abaco · Marsh Harbour
Brownsville · Fort Myers · Naples · The Everglades · Fort Lauderdale · Miami · Homestead · THE BAHAMAS · Nassau · New Providence I. · Eleuthera
Key West · Florida Keys · Florida Bay · C. Sable · Straits of Florida · Andros Town · Andros · Great Exuma · Long Island · San Salvador · Cat I.

Water bodies: Lake Superior · Lake Michigan · Lake Huron · Lake Erie · Lake Ontario · Gulf of Mexico · ATLANTIC OCEAN · Tropic of Cancer

Coordinate labels (side, right): 6 · 5 · 4 · 3 · 2 · 1 (45°N, 40°N, 35°N, 30°N, 25°N)

Coordinate labels (bottom): G 95°W H 90°W J 85°W K 80°W L

Oxford University Press

Main map labels

PACIFIC OCEAN

Gulf of Mexico

Bahía de Campeche

Golfo de Tehuantepec

Golfo de California

Baja California

Sierra Madre Occidental

Sierra Madre Oriental

Sierra Madre del Sur

Tropic of Cancer

United States

Los Angeles, Long Beach, San Bernardino, Riverside, San Diego, Tijuana, Ensenada, Mexicali, El Centro, Phoenix, Mesa, Tucson, Nogales, Yuma, Casa Grande, Ajo, Prescott, Kingman, Flagstaff, Winslow, Gallup, Albuquerque, Santa Fe, Las Vegas, Tucumcari, Clovis, Roswell, Carlsbad, Las Cruces, El Paso, Ciudad Juárez

ARIZONA, NEW MEXICO, COLORADO, COLORADO Plateau, Grand Canyon, Colorado River

Durango, Trinidad, Raton, Farmington, San Juan, Rio Grande, Arkansas, Lamar, Great Bend, Salina, Topeka, Columbia, St. Louis, ILLINOIS, Evansville, MISSOURI, Springfield, Jefferson City, Kansas City, Emporia, Wichita, Hutchison, Dodge City, Garden City, Liberal, Ponca City, Enid, Woodward, Amarillo, KANSAS, OKLAHOMA, Oklahoma City, Muskogee, Tulsa, Joplin, Fort Smith, ARKANSAS, Little Rock, North Little Rock, Fayetteville, Jonesboro, Jackson, Memphis, TENNESSEE, Florence, Tupelo, Columbus, Birmingham, Tuscaloosa

TEXAS, Lubbock, Plainview, Altus, Lawton, Duncan, Ardmore, Vernon, Wichita Falls, Abilene, Sweetwater, Odessa, Pecos, Fort Stockton, Sierra Blanca, Del Rio, Eagle Pass, San Antonio, Austin, Waco, Killeen, Edwards Plateau, Fort Worth, Dallas, Irving, Garland, Paris, Greenville, Texarkana, El Dorado, Greenwood, Greenville, Monroe, Shreveport, Longview, Tyler, Alexandria, LOUISIANA, Lafayette, Baton Rouge, Lake Charles, Beaumont, Port Arthur, Houston, Pasadena, Galveston, Corpus Christi, McAllen, Harlingen, Brownsville, Reynosa, New Orleans, Biloxi, Mobile, MISSISSIPPI, Natchez, Laurel, Hattiesburg, Meridian, Vicksburg, Jackson

Mexico

Ensenada, Vicente Guerrero, Rosario, San Fernando, El Arco, Santa Rosalía, Guaymas, Empalme, Ciudad Obregón, Navojoa, Los Mochis, Guamúchil, Culiacán, Quilá, La Paz, Cabo Falso, San José del Cabo, Mazatlán, El Salto, Villa Unión, Rosario, Acaponeta, Santiago Ixcuintla, Tepic, Pto. Vallarta, Cabo Corrientes, Tomatlán, Autlán, Colima, Manzanillo, Playa Azul

Hermosillo, Magdalena, Arizpe, Cananea, Nacozari, Agua Prieta, Nueva Casas Grandes, Buenaventura, Chihuahua, Aquiles Serdán, Ciudad Camargo, Hidalgo del Parral, El Fuerte, Santa Bárbara, San Francisco del Oro, Durango, Sombrerete, Fresnillo, Zacatecas, Villanueva, Aguascalientes, León, Irapuato, Celaya, Querétaro, Salamanca, Acámbaro, Morelia, Uruapan, Apatzingán, Colima

Ojinaga, Ciudad Acuña, Piedras Negras, Allende, Nueva Rosita, Sabinas, Monclova, Lampazos, Sabinas Hidalgo, Nuevo Laredo, Laredo, Gómez Palacio, Ciudad Lerdo, Torreón, San Pedro de las Colonias, Parras, Saltillo, Monterrey, Concepción, Linares, Hidalgo, Ciudad Victoria, La Pesca, Aldama, Ciudad Mante, Tampico, Ciudad Madero, Tamazunchale, Tuxpan, Molango, Poza Rica, Papantla, Cárdenas, Ciudad Valles, Río Verde, San Luis Potosí, Matehuala, Tula, Pachuca, Tulancingo, Jalapa Enríquez, Coatepec, Veracruz, Córdoba, Orizaba, Puebla, Mexico City, Nezahualcóyotl, Toluca, Cuernavaca, Xochimilco, Ixtaccihuatl, Popocatépetl, Citlaltépetl, Tehuacán, Acatlán, Tierra Blanca, Acayucan, Coatzacoalcos, Minatitlán, Villahermosa, Iguala, Chilpancingo, Acapulco, Huajuápan de León, Oaxaca, Ixtepec, Tuxtla Gutiérrez, S. Cristóbal, Comitán, Tonalá, Pijijiapan, Pochutla, Jamiltepec, Tehuantepec, Juchitán, Istmo de Tehuantepec

Mérida, Progreso, Campeche, Champotón, Yucatán, Ciudad del Carmen, Frontera, Chetumal, Valladolid, Ticul

Central America

BELIZE, Belize, Belmopan, Flores, Punta Gorda, Pto. Barrios, Puerto Cortés, GUATEMALA, Cobán, Guatemala City, Quezaltenango, Mazatenango, Huixtla, Tapachula, Antigua, Chiquimula, Zacapa, Santa Rosa, Sta. Ana, HONDURAS, San Pedro Sula, Tegucigalpa, Ahuachapán, Sonsonate, Nueva San Salvador, San Salvador, San Vicente, Zacatecoluca, San Miguel, Usulután, EL SALVADOR, NICARAGUA, Managua

Inset maps

Leeward Islands
Scale 1 : 5 000 000

Anguilla (UK), The Valley, St. Martin (Fr.), St. Maarten (Neths.), St. Barthélémy (Fr.), St. Eustatius (Neths.), Barbuda, Codrington, ANTIGUA AND BARBUDA, St. Kitts, Basseterre, Nevis, ST. KITTS AND NEVIS, St. John's, Antigua, Falmouth, Plymouth, Montserrat (UK), Grande Terre, Les Abymes, Pointe-à-Pitre, Basse Terre, Soufrière, Guadeloupe (Fr.), Marie Galente, Basse-Terre, Guadeloupe Passage, Dominica Passage, DOMINICA, Portsmouth, Marigot, Roseau, Morne Diablotins

Windward Islands
Scale 1 : 5 000 000

Mt. Pelée, Ste. Marie, Fort-de-France, Le François, Rivière-Pilote, Martinique (Fr.), St. Lucia Channel, Castries, ST. LUCIA, Vieux Fort, St. Vincent Passage, Chateaubelair, St. Vincent, Kingstown, Bequia, Mustique, Canouan, Union, Carriacou, ST. VINCENT AND THE GRENADINES, GRENADA, St. George's, Speightstown, Bridgetown, BARBADOS

Scale 1 : 15 000 000 (main map)
0 150 300 450 600 750 km

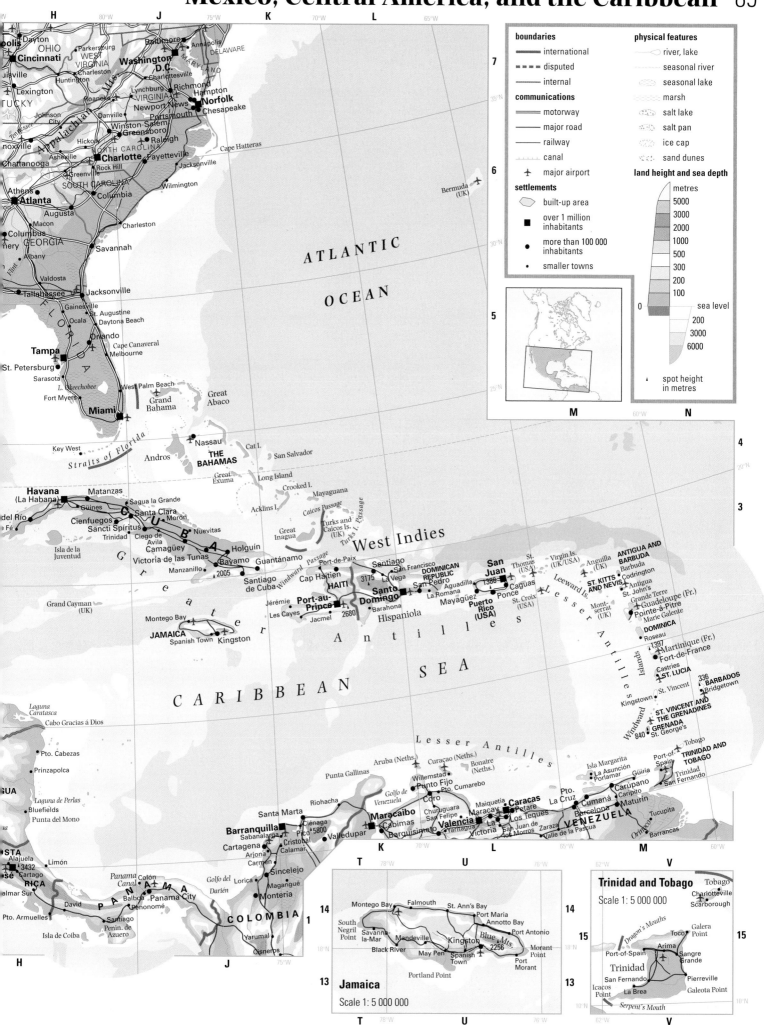

boundaries
- —— international
- ---- disputed
- —— internal

communications
- ═══ motorway
- —— major road
- —— railway
- ┼┼┼ canal
- ✈ major airport

settlements
- ⬡ built-up area
- ■ over 1 million inhabitants
- ● more than 100 000 inhabitants
- • smaller towns

physical features
- river, lake
- seasonal river
- seasonal lake
- marsh
- salt lake
- salt pan
- ice cap
- sand dunes

land height and sea depth

metres
5000
3000
2000
1000
500
300
200
100
0 sea level
200
3000
6000

▲ spot height in metres

ATLANTIC OCEAN

THE BAHAMAS

West Indies

Greater Antilles

CARIBBEAN SEA

Lesser Antilles

Windward Islands

Leeward Is.

CUBA
HAITI
DOMINICAN REPUBLIC
JAMAICA
PUERTO RICO (USA)

VENEZUELA

COLOMBIA

PANAMA

Jamaica
Scale 1: 5 000 000

Trinidad and Tobago
Scale 1: 5 000 000

© Oxford University Press

ATLANTIC

OCEAN

CARIBBEAN SEA

Lesser Antilles

Windward Islands

DOMINICA
Martinique (Fr.)
ST. LUCIA
BARBADOS
ST. VINCENT AND THE GRENADINES
GRENADA
TRINIDAD AND
TOBAGO
Port of Spain

PANAMA

COLOMBIA

VENEZUELA

GUYANA

SURINAME

French Guiana (France)

ECUADOR

PERU

BRAZIL

BOLIVIA

PARAGUAY

CHILE

ANDES

AMAZONAS

MATO GROSSO

Planalto de Mato Grosso

Mouths of the Amazon

Equator

Tropic of Capricorn

Bogotá
Medellín
Cali
Quito
Guayaquil
Lima
Caracas
Valencia
Maracaibo
Barranquilla
Georgetown
Paramaribo
Cayenne
Belém
Fortaleza
Recife
Salvador
Manaus
Brasília
Goiânia
Belo Horizonte
Rio de Janeiro
São Paulo
Curitiba
La Paz
Santa Cruz
Sucre
Asunción

© Oxford Universit

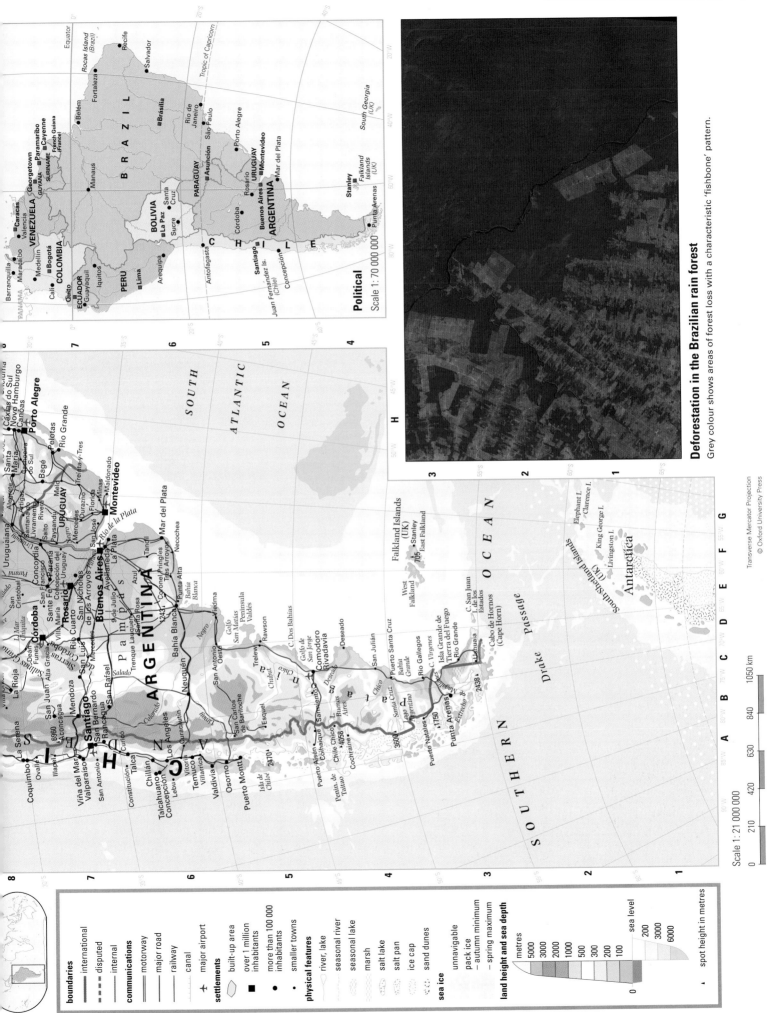

Political
Scale 1:70 000 000

Deforestation in the Brazilian rain forest
Grey colour shows areas of forest loss with a characteristic 'fishbone' pattern.

Scale 1:21 000 000

Transverse Mercator Projection
© Oxford University Press

0 210 420 630 840 1050 km

Scale 1: 70 000 00

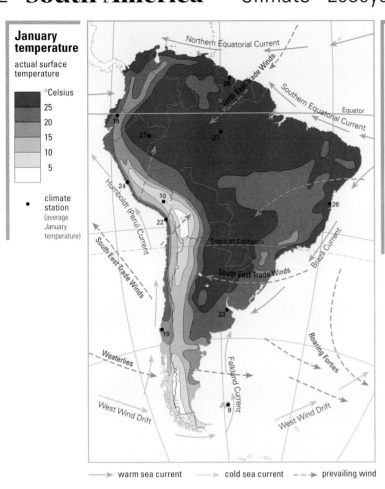

January temperature

actual surface temperature

°Celsius

25
20
15
10
5

● climate station (average January temperature)

Northern Equatorial Current
North East Trade Winds
Southern Equatorial Current
Equator
Humboldt (Peru) Current
South East Trade Winds
South East Trade Winds
Brazil Current
Tropic of Capricorn
Westerlies
Falkland Current
Roaring Forties
West Wind Drift
West Wind Drift

26
15
27
27
24
10
22
26
23
19
9

→ warm sea current   → cold sea current   --→ prevailing wind

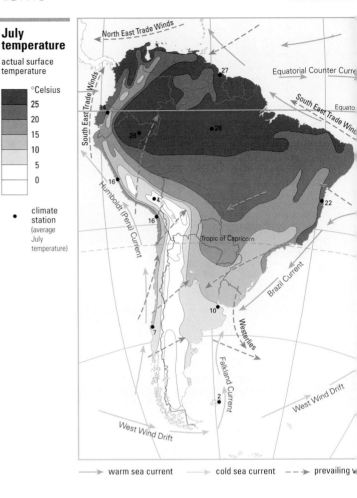

July temperature

actual surface temperature

°Celsius

25
20
15
10
5
0

● climate station (average July temperature)

North East Trade Winds
South East Trade Winds
Equatorial Counter Curre
South East Trade Wind
Equator
Humboldt (Peru) Current
Westerlies
Brazil Current
Tropic of Capricorn
Falkland Current
West Wind Drift
West Wind Drift

27
14
26
28
16
16
22
10
7
2

→ warm sea current   → cold sea current   --→ prevailing w

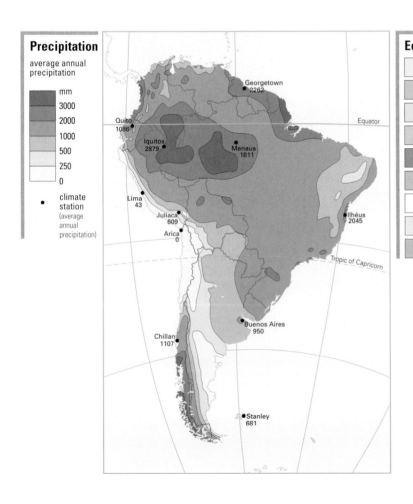

Precipitation

average annual precipitation

mm

3000
2000
1000
500
250
0

● climate station (average annual precipitation)

Georgetown 2262
Quito 1086
Iquitos 2879
Manaus 1811
Equator
Lima 43
Juliaca 609
Arica 0
Ilhéus 2045
Tropic of Capricorn
Chillan 1107
Buenos Aires 950
Stanley 681

Ecosystems

mixed forest
tropical rain forest
tropical grasslands
evergreens and shrubs
thorn forest
temperate grasslands
semi-desert
desert
mountains

ATLANTIC OCEAN
Llanos
Guiana Highlands
Amazon Basin
Selvas
Equate
ANDES
Mato Grosso
Brazilian Highlands
Atacama Desert
Gran Chaco
Tropic of Capric
PACIFIC OCEAN
ANDES
Pampa
Patagonia
SOUTHERN OCEAN

Oblique Mercator Projection   © Oxford Univer

cale 1: 45 000 000

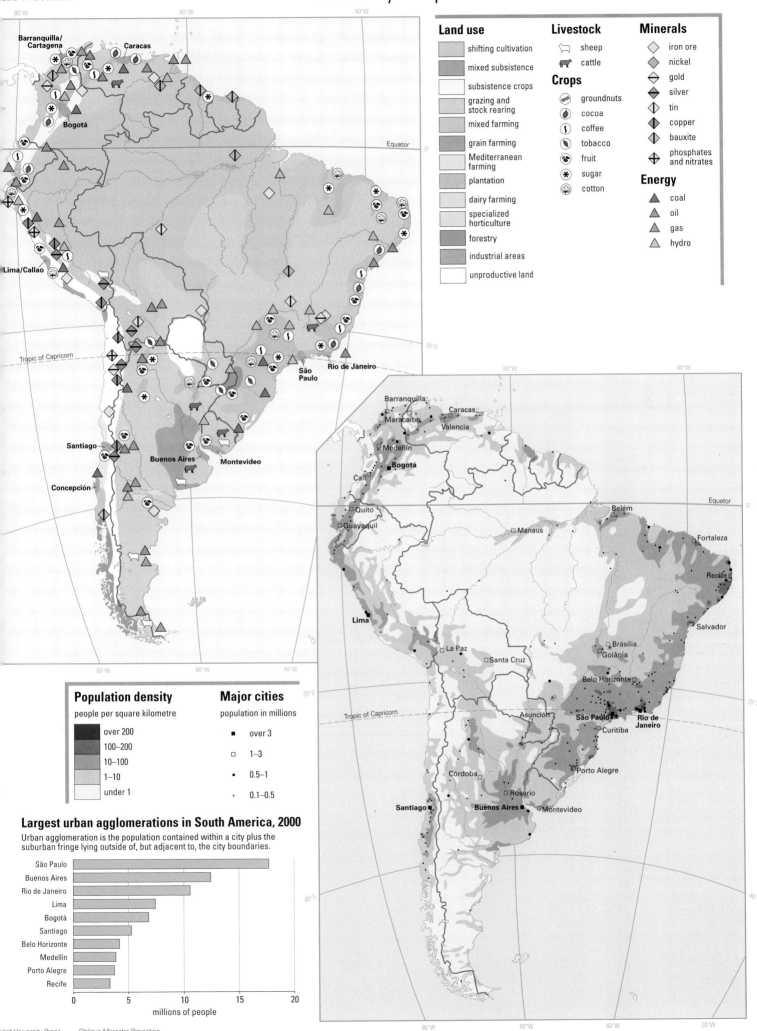

Land use

- shifting cultivation
- mixed subsistence
- subsistence crops
- grazing and stock rearing
- mixed farming
- grain farming
- Mediterranean farming
- plantation
- dairy farming
- specialized horticulture
- forestry
- industrial areas
- unproductive land

Livestock

- sheep
- cattle

Crops

- groundnuts
- cocoa
- coffee
- tobacco
- fruit
- sugar
- cotton

Minerals

- iron ore
- nickel
- gold
- silver
- tin
- copper
- bauxite
- phosphates and nitrates

Energy

- coal
- oil
- gas
- hydro

Population density

people per square kilometre

- over 200
- 100–200
- 10–100
- 1–10
- under 1

Major cities

population in millions

- over 3
- 1–3
- 0.5–1
- 0.1–0.5

Largest urban agglomerations in South America, 2000

Urban agglomeration is the population contained within a city plus the suburban fringe lying outside of, but adjacent to, the city boundaries.

São Paulo
Buenos Aires
Rio de Janeiro
Lima
Bogotá
Santiago
Belo Horizonte
Medellín
Porto Alegre
Recife

0   5   10   15   20

millions of people

The datasets below are explained on pages 1■

	Land		Population									Employment		
	Area	Arable and permanent crops	Total	Density	Change	Births	Deaths	Fertility	Infant mortality	Life expectancy	Urban	Agriculture	Industry	Servi■
			2002	2002	1990–2000	2002	2002	2001	2001	2001	2001	1990	1990	199■
	thousand km²	% of total	millions	persons per km²	%	births per 1000	deaths per 1000	children per mother	per 1000 live births	years	%	%	%	%■
Afghanistan	652	12.4	27.8	42.6	75.5	41	17	6.0	145	45	22	○○○	○○○	○○■
Albania	29	24.3	3.5	120.7	7.1	19	6	2.1	26	73	43	55	23	22
Algeria	2382	3.5	32.3	13.6	23.1	22	5	2.8	39	69	58	26	31	4■
Andorra	0.5	2.2	0.07	136.0	26.5	10	6	1.2	4	○○○	93	○○○	○○○	○○■
Angola	1247	2.8	10.6	8.5	25.9	46	26	6.8	154	40	35	75	8	1■
Antigua and Barbuda	0.4	18.2	0.07	167.5	6.0	19	6	2.4	12	74	37	○○○	○○○	○○■
Argentina	2780	9.8	38.3	13.8	13.2	18	8	2.6	16	74	88	12	32	5■
Armenia	30	18.8	3.3	110.0	-0.6	12	10	1.1	31	72	67	18	43	3■
Australia	7741	6.2	19.5	2.5	12.6	13	7	1.7	6	79	91	6	26	6■
Austria	84	17.6	8.2	97.6	5.4	10	10	1.3	5	78	67	8	38	5■
Azerbaijan	87	22.9	7.8	89.7	7.6	19	10	1.9	74	72	52	31	29	4■
Bahamas, The	14	0.7	0.3	21.4	14.7	19	9	2.1	13	67	89	5	16	7■
Bahrain	0.7	8.7	0.7	937.1	26.7	20	4	2.8	13	74	93	2	30	6■
Bangladesh	144	58.6	135.7	942.4	17.6	30	9	3.3	51	61	26	65	16	1■
Barbados	0.4	39.5	0.3	690.0	4.4	13	9	1.8	12	77	51	14	30	5■
Belarus	208	30.4	10.3	49.5	1.5	10	14	1.3	17	70	70	20	40	4■
Belgium	33	25.2	10.3	312.1	2.7	11	10	1.7	5	79	97	3	28	6■
Belize	23	3.9	0.3	11.3	30.5	31	6	3.7	34	72	48	33	19	4■
Benin	113	16.4	6.8	60.2	37.4	44	14	5.6	94	51	43	63	8	2■
Bhutan	47	3.4	2.1	44.7	25.5	35	14	4.7	74	63	7	94	2	■
Bolivia	1099	2.0	8.4	7.6	24.0	26	8	4.1	60	63	63	47	18	3■
Bosnia-Herzegovina	51	12.7	4.0	77.7	-13.3	13	8	1.6	15	74	43	○○○	○○○	3■
Botswana	582	0.6	1.6	2.7	20.9	26	29	3.9	80	45	49	46	20	3■
Brazil	8547	7.6	179.9	21.0	14.4	18	6	2.2	31	68	82	23	23	5■
Brunei	6	1.2	0.4	58.3	30.3	20	3	2.7	6	76	73	2	24	7■
Bulgaria	111	40.7	7.6	68.5	-12.3	8	14	1.3	14	71	68	13	48	3■
Burkina	274	12.6	12.9	47.1	32.2	45	19	6.8	104	46	17	92	2	■
Burundi	28	39.5	6.0	213.0	14.6	40	18	6.8	114	40	9	92	3	■
Cambodia	181	21.0	12.9	71.2	36.2	27	9	4.0	97	57	17	74	8	1■
Cameroon	475	15.1	15.4	32.4	31.1	36	15	4.9	96	48	50	70	9	21
Canada	9971	4.6	31.9	3.2	12.6	11	8	1.5	5	79	79	3	25	7■
Cape Verde	4	10.2	0.4	100.0	14.9	28	7	4.0	29	70	63	30	30	4■
Central African Republic	623	3.2	3.6	5.8	25.3	36	19	5.1	115	40	42	80	3	1■
Chad	1284	2.8	9.0	7.0	40.0	48	16	6.6	117	45	24	83	4	1■
Chile	757	3.0	15.5	20.5	15.4	16	6	2.4	10	76	86	19	25	5■
China	9598	14.1	1286.5	134.0	10.8	13	7	1.8	31	71	37	72	15	1■
Colombia	1139	3.8	41.0	36.0	20.8	22	6	2.6	19	72	76	27	23	5■
Comoros	2	52.9	0.6	307.0	34.8	39	9	6.8	59	60	34	78	9	1■
Congo	342	0.6	2.9	8.5	27.7	30	14	6.3	81	49	66	49	15	3■
Congo, Dem. Rep.	2345	3.4	55.0	23.5	36.8	46	15	6.9	129	41	29	68	13	1■
Costa Rica	51	9.9	3.8	74.5	22.6	20	4	2.5	9	78	60	26	27	47
Côte d'Ivoire	322	22.8	16.6	51.6	34.1	40	18	5.2	102	42	44	60	10	3■
Croatia	57	28.1	4.4	77.2	-5.0	13	11	1.4	7	74	58	16	34	5■
Cuba	111	40.3	11.2	100.9	5.7	12	7	1.5	7	77	76	19	30	51
Cyprus	9	15.5	0.8	85.2	11.3	13	8	1.7	5	78	70	14	30	5■
Czech Republic	79	42.2	10.3	130.4	-0.4	9	11	1.1	4	75	75	11	45	4■
Denmark	43	53.4	5.4	125.6	3.8	12	11	1.7	4	76	85	6	28	6■
Djibouti	23	○○○	0.5	19.4	22.1	41	19	5.9	100	46	84	○○○	○○○	○○○
Dominica	0.8	20.0	0.07	87.5	-1.6	17	7	1.8	14	73	71	○○○	○○○	○○○
Dominican Republic	49	32.2	8.6	175.5	18.9	24	7	3.1	41	67	66	25	29	46
Ecuador	284	10.6	13.4	47.2	25.2	25	5	3.3	24	71	63	33	19	4■
Egypt	1001	3.3	73.3	73.2	21.8	25	5	3.5	35	68	43	40	22	3■
El Salvador	21	38.5	6.4	304.8	20.1	28	6	3.5	33	70	61	36	21	4■
Equatorial Guinea	28	8.2	0.5	17.9	28.8	37	13	5.9	101	49	49	66	11	2■
Eritrea	118	4.3	4.3	36.4	40.5	40	13	5.9	72	53	19	80	5	1■

Legend:
○○○ no data
per capita for each person

ealth | Energy and trade | Quality of life

Purchasing power	Growth of PP	Energy consumption	Imports	Exports	Aid received (given)	Human Development Index	Health care	Food consumption	Safe water	Illiteracy male	Illiteracy female	Higher education	Cars	
2001	1990–2000	2000	2001	2001	2000	2001	1990–2002	2001	2000	2000	2000	1996	2000	
US$	%	kg oil equivalent per capita	US$ per capita	US$ per capita	million US$		doctors per 100 000 people	daily calories per capita	% access	%	%	students per 100 000 people	people per car	
○○○	○○○	○○○	○○○	○○○	142	○○○	○○○	○○○	13	○○○	○○○	165	644	Afghanistan
3880	2.7	521	378	88	319	0.735	133	2900	76	8	23	1087	36	Albania
5150	-0.1	956	315	651	162	0.704	85	2987	94	24	43	1238	34	Algeria
○○○	○○○	○○○	○○○	○○○	○○○	○○○	○○○	○○○	100	○○○	○○○	○○○	2	Andorra
1550	-1.8	584	293	544	307	0.377	5	1953	38	○○○	○○○	○○○	111	Angola
9870	2.8	○○○	○○○	○○○	10	0.798	17	2381	91	○○○	○○○	○○○	○○○	Antigua and Barbuda
11 690	3.0	1660	542	711	76	0.849	294	3171	79	3	3	3317	7	Argentina
2880	-2.5	542	234	88	216	0.729	305	1991	84	1	2	1886	1900	Armenia
25 780	2.9	5744	3310	3284	(987)	0.939	260	3126	100	○○○	○○○	5682	2	Australia
27 080	1.7	3524	9118	8678	(423)	0.929	302	3799	100	○○○	○○○	2988	2	Austria
3020	-7.3	1454	213	304	139	0.744	357	2474	○○○	○○○	○○○	2289	30	Azerbaijan
16 400	0.1	○○○	○○○	○○○	6	0.812	106	2777	96	6	4	○○○	4	Bahamas, The
14 410	1.7	9858	○○○	○○○	49	0.839	169	○○○	○○○	9	17	1402	5	Bahrain
1680	3.0	142	58	45	1172	0.502	20	2187	97	51	70	397	2808	Bangladesh
15 020	1.7	○○○	○○○	○○○	0	0.888	121	2992	100	0	0	2535	7	Barbados
8030	-1.4	2432	815	732	40	0.804	457	2925	100	0	0	3168	9	Belarus
28 210	1.8	5776	17 641	18 336	(820)	0.937	395	3682	○○○	○○○	○○○	3551	2	Belgium
5350	1.6	○○○	○○○	○○○	15	0.776	55	2886	76	7	7	○○○	29	Belize
1030	1.8	377	103	58	239	0.411	10	2455	63	48	76	256	260	Benin
1530	3.4	○○○	○○○	○○○	53	0.511	16	○○○	62	○○○	○○○	○○○	○○○	Bhutan
2380	1.6	592	197	148	477	0.672	130	2267	79	8	21	○○○	65	Bolivia
○○○	○○○	1096	○○○	○○○	1063	0.777	140	2845	○○○	○○○	○○○	○○○	34	Bosnia-Herzegovina
8810	2.3	○○○	1475	1444	31	0.614	26	2292	70	26	20	587	59	Botswana
7450	1.5	1077	338	337	322	0.777	158	3002	83	13	13	1424	11	Brazil
16 779	-0.7	5870	○○○	○○○	1	0.872	85	2814	○○○	5	12	516	2	Brunei
5950	-1.5	2299	926	649	311	0.795	344	2626	100	1	2	3110	5	Bulgaria
1020	2.4	○○○	45	18	336	0.330	3	2485	○○○	66	86	83	744	Burkina
590	-4.7	○○○	22	5	93	0.337	1	1612	52	44	60	○○○	650	Burundi
1520	2.0	○○○	110	114	399	0.556	30	1967	30	20	43	85	788	Cambodia
1670	-0.8	427	99	116	380	0.499	7	2242	62	21	36	○○○	152	Cameroon
27 870	1.9	8156	7363	8459	(1744)	0.937	186	3176	100	○○○	○○○	5953	2	Canada
4870	3.3	○○○	○○○	○○○	94	0.727	17	3308	74	16	34	○○○	133	Cape Verde
1180	-0.5	○○○	32	39	76	0.363	4	1949	60	40	65	○○○	422	Central African Republic
930	-0.8	○○○	44	22	131	0.376	3	2245	27	48	66	51	853	Chad
9420	5.2	1604	1116	1147	49	0.831	115	2868	94	4	4	2546	15	Chile
4260	9.2	905	188	206	1735	0.721	167	2963	75	8	22	473	369	China
5980	1.1	681	303	290	187	0.779	109	2580	91	8	8	1640	43	Colombia
1610	-2.4	○○○	○○○	○○○	19	0.528	7	1735	96	37	51	○○○	1	Comoros
580	-3.4	296	303	773	33	0.502	25	2221	51	13	26	○○○	119	Congo
765	-8.2	292	6	8	184	0.363	7	1535	45	27	50	212	525	Congo, Dem. Rep.
8080	3.0	861	1601	1222	12	0.832	178	2761	98	5	4	2830	22	Costa Rica
1470	0.4	433	174	235	352	0.396	9	2594	77	41	63	568	88	Côte d'Ivoire
8440	1.8	1775	1924	991	66	0.818	229	2678	95	1	3	1911	5	Croatia
○○○	3.7	1180	○○○	○○○	44	0.806	590	2643	95	3	3	1013	574	Cuba
20 780	3.1	3203	○○○	○○○	55	0.891	269	3302	100	1	5	1193	4	Cyprus
14 550	1.0	3931	3544	3240	438	0.861	308	3097	○○○	○○○	○○○	2009	3	Czech Republic
27 950	2.1	3644	8595	9776	(1664)	0.930	339	3454	100	○○○	○○○	3349	3	Denmark
2120	-3.9	○○○	○○○	○○○	71	0.462	13	2218	100	24	46	26	55	Djibouti
5040	○○○	○○○	○○○	○○○	16	0.776	49	2995	97	○○○	○○○	○○○	23	Dominica
5870	4.2	932	1044	653	62	0.737	216	2333	79	16	16	2223	53	Dominican Republic
3070	-0.3	647	411	347	147	0.731	138	2792	71	7	10	○○○	123	Ecuador
3790	2.5	726	189	59	1328	0.648	218	3385	95	33	56	1895	52	Egypt
4500	2.6	651	785	448	180	0.719	121	2512	74	19	24	1935	67	El Salvador
5640	18.9	○○○	○○○	○○○	21	0.664	25	○○○	43	8	26	○○○	143	Equatorial Guinea
970	1.1	○○○	○○○	○○○	176	0.446	5	1690	46	33	56	90	760	Eritrea

The datasets below are explained on pages 1

	no data
per capita	for each person

	Land		Population									Employment		
	Area	Arable and permanent crops	Total	Density	Change	Births	Deaths	Fertility	Infant mortality	Life expectancy	Urban	Agriculture	Industry	Serv
			2002	2002	1990–2000	2002	2002	2001	2001	2001	2001	1990	1990	19
	thousand km²	% of total	millions	persons per km²	%	births per 1000	deaths per 1000	children per mother	per 1000 live births	years	%	%	%	%
Estonia	45	25.2	1.4	31.1	-9.0	9	13	1.3	11	71	69	14	41	4
Ethiopia	1104	9.7	65.3	59.1	32.7	40	20	5.9	116	46	16	86	2	1
Fiji	18	15.6	0.9	47.6	12.8	23	6	3.3	18	69	50	46	15	3
Finland	338	6.4	5.2	15.4	3.6	11	10	1.7	4	78	59	8	31	6
France	552	35.4	59.9	108.5	4.6	13	9	1.9	4	79	76	5	29	6
French Guiana	91	0.1	0.2	2.0	48.9	22	5	3.6	○○○	76	79	○○○	○○○	○○
Gabon	268	1.8	1.3	4.9	13.0	37	11	4.3	60	57	82	51	16	3
Gambia, The	11	17.7	1.5	136.4	42.2	41	13	5.8	91	54	31	82	8	1
Georgia	70	15.3	5.0	70.9	-8.0	11	15	1.2	24	73	57	26	31	4
Germany	357	33.7	82.4	230.8	4.3	9	10	1.3	4	78	88	4	38	5
Ghana	239	22.2	20.2	84.5	27.2	27	10	4.3	57	58	36	59	13	2
Greece	132	29.3	10.6	80.3	4.4	10	10	1.3	5	78	60	23	27	5
Greenland	342	○○○	0.06	0.2	1.1	16	8	○○○	○○○	○○○	○○○	○○○	○○○	○○
Grenada	0.3	32.4	0.09	296.7	-3.3	23	8	2.4	20	65	39	○○○	○○○	○○
Guatemala	109	17.5	13.5	123.9	31.2	36	7	4.6	43	65	40	52	17	3
Guinea	246	6	8.8	35.8	25.8	43	16	5.5	109	49	28	87	2	1
Guinea-Bissau	36	9.7	1.3	36.1	29.1	39	17	6.0	130	45	32	85	2	1
Guyana	215	2.3	0.7	3.3	-6.0	18	9	2.5	54	63	37	22	25	5
Haiti	28	32.8	7.4	264.3	13.9	34	14	4.7	79	49	36	68	9	2
Honduras	112	16.3	6.5	58.0	31.0	32	6	4.4	31	69	54	41	20	3
Hungary	93	54.2	10.1	108.6	-2.3	9	13	1.3	8	72	65	15	38	4
Iceland	103	0.07	0.3	2.7	8.5	14	7	2.0	3	80	93	○○○	○○○	○○
India	3288	51.6	1034.2	314.5	19.2	24	9	3.2	67	63	28	64	16	20
Indonesia	1905	16.3	231.3	121.4	19.2	22	6	2.6	33	66	42	55	14	31
Iran	1633	11.8	67.5	41.3	17.8	17	6	2.5	35	70	65	39	23	38
Iraq	438	12.2	24.0	54.8	25.0	34	6	5.4	104	59	68	16	18	66
Ireland	70	15.4	3.9	55.7	8.2	15	8	1.9	6	77	59	14	29	57
Israel	21	20.9	6.0	285.7	29.5	19	6	2.9	6	79	92	4	29	67
Italy	301	37.9	57.9	192.4	1.6	9	10	1.3	4	79	67	9	31	60
Jamaica	11	24.9	2.7	245.5	7.7	18	5	2.4	17	76	57	25	23	52
Japan	378	12.9	127.1	336.2	2.4	10	8	1.3	3	81	79	7	34	59
Jordan	89	4.3	5.3	59.6	53.2	25	3	3.6	27	71	79	15	23	62
Kazakhstan	2717	11.1	16.7	6.1	0.2	18	11	1.8	61	66	56	22	32	46
Kenya	580	7.8	31.2	53.8	27.7	30	16	4.4	78	46	34	80	7	13
Kiribati	0.7	50.7	0.1	137.1	28.9	32	9	4.5	53	62	37	○○○	○○○	○○
Kuwait	18	0.4	2.1	116.7	-7.9	22	2	4.3	9	76	96	1	25	74
Kyrgyzstan	199	7.2	4.8	24.1	6.7	26	9	2.4	52	68	34	32	27	41
Laos	237	4.0	5.8	24.5	30.6	37	13	4.9	87	54	20	78	6	16
Latvia	65	29.1	2.4	36.9	-10.0	8	15	1.2	17	71	60	16	40	44
Lebanon	10	29.6	3.7	370.0	13.7	20	6	2.4	28	73	90	7	31	62
Lesotho	30	10.7	1.9	63.3	23.7	28	24	4.3	91	39	29	40	28	32
Liberia	111	2.9	3.3	29.7	44.5	46	18	6.6	157	50	45	○○○	○○○	○○○
Libya	1760	1.2	5.4	3.1	23.6	28	4	3.7	16	72	88	11	23	66
Liechtenstein	0.2	25.0	0.03	150.0	11.8	11	7	1.4	10	○○○	23	○○○	○○○	○○○
Lithuania	65	46.0	3.6	55.4	-2.2	10	13	1.3	8	72	69	18	41	41
Luxembourg	3	○○○	0.4	133.3	14.5	12	9	1.8	5	78	92	○○○	○○○	○○○
Macedonia, FYRO	26	24.7	2.1	80.8	7.8	13	8	1.9	22	73	60	21	40	39
Madagascar	587	5.3	16.5	28.1	34.6	42	12	5.8	84	53	30	78	7	15
Malawi	118	16.9	11.4	96.6	12.7	45	22	6.5	114	39	15	87	5	8
Malaysia	330	23.1	22.7	68.8	24.5	24	5	3.2	8	73	58	27	23	50
Maldives	0.3	10.0	0.3	1066.7	39.3	37	8	3.4	58	67	28	32	31	37
Mali	1240	3.8	11.3	9.1	29.9	48	19	6.8	141	48	31	86	2	12
Malta	0.3	28.1	0.4	1333.3	9.1	13	8	1.7	5	78	91	○○○	○○○	○○○
Marshall Islands	0.2	16.7	0.06	300.0	47.3	34	5	5.7	63	65	65	○○○	○○○	○○○
Mauritania	1026	0.5	2.8	2.7	34.4	43	13	4.7	120	52	59	55	10	35

alth | Energy and trade | Quality of life

Purchasing power	Growth of PP	Energy consumption	Imports	Exports	Aid received (given)	Human Development Index	Health care	Food consumption	Safe water	Illiteracy male	Illiteracy female	Higher education	Cars	
2001	1990–2000	2000	2001	2001	2000	2001	1990–2002	2001	2000	2000	2000	1996	2000	
US$	%	kg oil equivalent per capita	US$ per capita	US$ per capita	million US$		doctors per 100 000 people	daily calories per capita	% access	%	%	students per 100 000 people	people per car	
10 020	1.0	3303	3250	2504	64	0.833	307	3048	ooo	0	0	2965	3	Estonia
710	2.4	291	ooo	6	693	0.359	3	2037	24	53	69	74	1433	Ethiopia
5140	0.7	ooo	ooo	ooo	29	0.754	36	2789	47	5	9	757	17	Fiji
25 180	2.4	6409	6162	8328	(371)	0.930	306	3202	100	ooo	ooo	4418	3	Finland
25 280	1.3	4366	5427	5369	(4105)	0.925	303	3629	100	ooo	ooo	3541	2	France
ooo	ooo	ooo	ooo	ooo	ooo	ooo	ooo	ooo	ooo	ooo	ooo	ooo	7	French Guiana
5460	0.1	1271	ooo	ooo	12	0.653	ooo	2602	70	ooo	ooo	649	7	Gabon
1730	-0.3	ooo	ooo	ooo	49	0.463	4	2300	62	56	70	148	186	Gambia, The
2860	-12.4	533	156	56	170	0.746	487	2247	76	ooo	ooo	3149	12	Georgia
25 530	1.2	4131	6013	6946	(5030)	0.921	354	3567	ooo	ooo	ooo	2603	2	Germany
1980	1.8	400	154	86	609	0.567	6	2670	64	20	37	ooo	214	Ghana
17 860	1.8	2635	2581	827	(226)	0.892	392	3754	ooo	2	4	3138	4	Greece
ooo	ooo	ooo	ooo	ooo	ooo	ooo	ooo	ooo	ooo	ooo	ooo	ooo	ooo	Greenland
6720	2.9	ooo	ooo	ooo	17	0.738	50	2749	94	ooo	ooo	ooo	ooo	Grenada
3850	1.4	628	482	208	264	0.652	90	2203	92	24	39	804	84	Guatemala
1980	1.7	ooo	144	96	153	0.425	13	2362	48	ooo	ooo	112	488	Guinea
710	-1.1	ooo	ooo	ooo	80	0.373	17	2481	49	46	77	ooo	267	Guinea-Bissau
3750	5.0	ooo	ooo	ooo	108	0.740	48	2515	94	1	2	956	32	Guyana
1450	-2.7	256	125	17	208	0.467	25	2045	46	48	52	ooo	252	Haiti
2450	0.3	469	453	192	449	0.667	83	2406	90	25	25	985	165	Honduras
12 570	1.9	2448	3427	3109	252	0.837	361	3520	99	1	1	1903	4	Hungary
29 830	1.8	12 246	ooo	ooo	0	0.942	326	3231	ooo	ooo	ooo	2918	2	Iceland
2450	4.1	494	49	43	1487	0.590	48	2487	88	32	55	638	218	India
2940	2.5	706	145	264	1731	0.682	16	2904	76	8	18	1157	86	Indonesia
6230	1.9	1771	230	369	130	0.719	110	2931	95	17	31	1763	44	Iran
ooo	ooo	1190	ooo	ooo	76	ooo	ooo	2619	85	45	77	ooo	35	Iraq
27 460	6.5	3854	13 401	21 957	(235)	0.930	226	3666	ooo	ooo	ooo	3702	3	Ireland
19 330	2.2	3241	5665	4680	800	0.905	378	3512	99	3	7	3571	5	Israel
24 340	1.4	2974	4065	4196	(1376)	0.916	567	3680	ooo	1	2	3299	2	Italy
3650	0.4	1524	1311	493	10	0.757	140	2705	71	17	9	768	23	Jamaica
27 430	1.1	4136	2750	3179	(13 508)	0.932	197	2746	96	ooo	ooo	3131	3	Japan
4080	1.0	1061	970	437	552	0.743	205	2769	96	5	16	ooo	28	Jordan
6370	-3.1	2594	400	543	189	0.765	339	2477	91	0	1	2859	ooo	Kazakhstan
1020	-0.5	515	92	57	512	0.489	14	2058	49	11	24	ooo	174	Kenya
ooo	ooo	ooo	ooo	ooo	21	ooo	ooo	2922	47	ooo	ooo	ooo	ooo	Kiribati
18 690	-1.4	10 529	3482	8117	3	0.820	160	3170	100	16	20	1750	3	Kuwait
2710	-5.1	497	95	112	215	0.727	288	2882	77	ooo	ooo	1088	36	Kyrgyzstan
1610	3.9	ooo	81	59	281	0.525	61	2309	90	24	47	260	540	Laos
7870	-2.3	1541	1473	846	91	0.811	313	2809	ooo	0	0	2248	5	Latvia
4640	4.2	1169	2025	247	197	0.752	274	3184	100	8	20	2712	5	Lebanon
2670	2.1	ooo	357	124	42	0.510	7	2320	91	27	6	234	350	Lesotho
ooo	ooo	ooo	ooo	ooo	94	ooo	ooo	1946	ooo	30	63	ooo	310	Liberia
7570	ooo	3107	ooo	ooo	15	0.783	120	3333	72	9	32	ooo	11	Libya
ooo	ooo	ooo	ooo	ooo	ooo	ooo	ooo	ooo	ooo	ooo	ooo	ooo	2	Liechtenstein
7610	-2.9	2032	1672	1251	99	0.824	394	3384	ooo	0	1	2251	4	Lithuania
48 080	4.1	8409	ooo	ooo	(127)	0.930	253	ooo	ooo	ooo	ooo	640	2	Luxembourg
4860	-1.5	ooo	815	585	252	0.784	300	2552	99	ooo	ooo	1557	7	Macedonia, FYRO*
870	-0.9	ooo	48	19	322	0.468	11	2072	47	26	40	188	288	Madagascar
620	1.8	ooo	47	27	445	0.387	ooo	2168	57	26	54	58	644	Malawi
8340	4.4	2126	3291	3917	45	0.790	68	2927	95	9	17	1048	6	Malaysia
4520	5.4	ooo	ooo	ooo	19	0.751	40	2587	100	3	3	ooo	ooo	Maldives
810	1.3	ooo	66	41	360	0.337	5	2376	65	64	84	134	557	Mali
16 530	4.0	2088	ooo	ooo	21	0.856	263	3496	100	9	7	2183	2	Malta
ooo	ooo	ooo	ooo	ooo	63	ooo	ooo	ooo	ooo	ooo	ooo	ooo	ooo	Marshall Islands
1680	1.2	ooo	125	100	212	0.454	14	2764	37	49	70	365	280	Mauritania

ord University Press

The datasets below are explained on pages 1

		Land		Population									Employment		
		Area	Arable and permanent crops	Total	Density	Change	Births	Deaths	Fertility	Infant mortality	Life expectancy	Urban	Agriculture	Industry	Serv
				2002	2002	1990–2000	2002	2002	2001	2001	2001	2001	1990	1990	19
		thousand km²	% of total	millions	persons per km²	%	births per 1000	deaths per 1000	children per mother	per 1000 live births	years	%	%	%	%
Mauritius		2	52.0	1.2	600.0	9.9	16	7	1.9	17	72	42	17	43	4
Mexico		1958	13.9	103.4	52.8	18.8	22	5	2.9	24	73	75	28	24	4
Micronesia, Fed. States		0.7	51.4	0.1	142.9	22.6	31	6	4.9	20	66	27	ooo	ooo	c
Moldova		34	64.4	4.4	129.4	0.8	14	13	1.3	27	69	42	33	30	3
Monaco		0.002	ooo	0.03	15 000	5.7	10	13	ooo	5	ooo	100			
Mongolia		1567	0.8	2.7	1.7	18.0	21	7	2.5	61	63	57	32	22	4
Morocco		447	21.2	31.2	69.8	22.0	24	6	3.1	39	68	56	45	25	3
Mozambique		802	4.2	17.3	21.6	33.8	39	29	5.6	125	39	33	83	8	
Myanmar		677	15.0	42.3	62.5	8.4	20	12	3.1	77	57	28	73	10	1
Namibia		824	1.0	1.9	2.3	25.7	35	18	4.9	55	47	31	49	15	3
Nauru		0.02	ooo	0.01	500.0	24.8	27	7	4.4	25	61	100	ooo	ooo	c
Nepal		147	20.2	25.9	176.2	27.8	33	10	4.1	66	59	12	94	0	
Netherlands		41	22.9	16.1	392.7	6.3	12	9	1.7	5	78	90	5	26	●
New Zealand		271	12.1	3.9	14.4	13.7	14	8	2.0	6	78	86	10	25	
Nicaragua		130	21.1	5.0	38.5	32.1	27	5	4.1	36	69	57	28	26	
Niger		1267	4.0	10.8	8.5	32.1	50	22	8.0	156	46	21	90	4	
Nigeria		924	33.3	130.5	141.2	33.4	39	14	5.8	110	52	45	43	7	
Northern Marianas		0.5	17.4	0.08	154.0	6.3	20	2	ooo	ooo	ooo	ooo	ooo	ooo	
North Korea		121	16.6	22.2	183.5	8.3	19	7	2.1	23	70	59	38	32	
Norway		324	2.7	4.5	13.9	5.6	12	10	1.8	4	79	75	6	25	
Oman		213	0.4	2.7	12.7	42.9	38	4	4.7	12	72	77	44	24	
Pakistan		796	27.5	147.7	185.6	24.2	30	9	4.8	84	60	33	52	19	
Palau		0.5	21.7	0.02	40.0	23.4	19	7	2.6	28	67	71	ooo	ooo	
Panama		76	8.7	2.9	38.2	17.6	21	6	2.6	19	74	57	26	16	
Papua New Guinea		463	1.5	5.2	11.2	28.8	32	8	4.8	70	57	18	79	7	
Paraguay		407	5.6	5.9	14.5	31.9	31	5	4.2	26	71	57	39	22	
Peru		1285	3.3	27.9	21.7	22.9	23	6	2.9	30	69	73	36	18	
Philippines		300	33.5	83.0	276.7	24.8	27	6	3.5	29	70	59	46	15	
Poland		323	44.6	38.6	119.5	1.4	10	10	1.3	8	74	63	27	36	
Portugal		92	29.4	10.1	109.8	1.3	12	10	1.5	5	76	66	18	34	
Qatar		11	1.9	0.8	72.1	54.6	16	4	3.9	11	72	93	3	32	
Romania		238	41.3	22.3	93.7	-2.0	11	12	1.2	19	71	55	24	47	
Russian Federation		17 075	7.4	145.0	8.5	-1.4	10	14	1.3	18	67	73	14	42	
Rwanda		26	42.4	7.7	296.2	3.8	40	22	5.8	96	38	6	92	3	
St. Kitts and Nevis		0.4	22.2	0.04	100.0	-6.3	19	9	2.4	20	70	34	ooo	ooo	
St. Lucia		0.6	27.4	0.2	333.3	12.0	21	5	2.0	17	72	38	ooo	ooo	
St. Vincent & the Grenadines		0.4	28.2	0.1	250.0	8.4	18	6	2.3	22	74	56	ooo	ooo	
Samoa		3.0	43.0	0.2	66.7	5.3	16	6	4.5	20	70	22	ooo	ooo	
San Marino		0.06	16.7	0.03	500.0	14.8	11	8	1.2	6	80	89	ooo	ooo	
Sao Tome and Principe		1.0	42.7	0.2	170.0	33.9	42	7	6.1	57	69	48	ooo	ooo	
Saudi Arabia		2150	1.8	23.5	10.9	39.0	37	6	5.7	23	72	87	19	20	
Senegal		197	11.5	10.3	52.3	25.7	37	11	5.2	79	52	48	77	8	
Serbia and Montenegro		102	36.5	10.7	104.9	9.2	13	11	1.7	20	72	52	ooo	ooo	
Seychelles		0.5	15.6	0.08	160.0	8.0	17	7	2.1	13	73	65	ooo	ooo	
Sierra Leone		72	7.5	5.6	77.8	23.8	44	21	6.5	182	35	37	68	15	
Singapore		1	1.6	4.5	4500.0	37.6	13	4	1.4	3	78	100	0	36	
Slovakia		49	32.5	5.4	110.2	2.8	10	9	1.2	8	73	58	12	32	
Slovenia		20	10.0	1.9	95.0	1.7	9	10	1.3	4	76	49	6	46	
Solomon Islands		29	2.1	0.5	17.2	39.4	33	4	5.7	20	69	20	77	7	
Somalia		638	1.7	7.8	12.2	8.7	47	18	7.2	125	46	28	ooo	ooo	
South Africa		1221	12.9	42.7	35.0	13.7	19	17	2.9	56	51	58	14	32	
South Korea		99	19.1	48.0	484.8	10.7	13	6	1.5	5	75	82	18	35	
Spain		506	36.6	40.2	79.4	1.6	10	9	1.2	4	79	78	12	33	
Sri Lanka		66	29.0	19.6	297.0	11.9	16	6	2.0	17	72	23	48	21	
Sudan		2506	6.7	37.1	14.8	31.7	37	10	4.9	65	55	37	70	8	

ooo no data
per capita for each person

© Oxford University

alth   Energy and trade   Quality of life

Purchasing power	Growth of PP	Energy consumption	Imports	Exports	Aid received (given)	Human Development Index	Health care	Food consumption	Safe water	Illiteracy male	Illiteracy female	Higher education	Cars	
2001	1990–2000	2000	2001	2001	2000	2001	1990–2002	2001	2000	2000	2000	1996	2000	
US$	%	kg oil equivalent per capita	US$ per capita	US$ per capita	million US$		doctors per 100 000 people	daily calories per capita	% access	%	%	students per 100 000 people	people per car	
10 410	4.0	○○○	○○○	○○○	20	0.779	85	2995	100	12	19	632	26	Mauritius
8770	1.4	1567	1755	1579	-54	0.800	130	3160	86	7	11	1739	11	Mexico
○○○	○○○	○○○	○○○	○○○	108	○○○	○○○	○○○	○○○	○○○	○○○	○○○	○○○	Micronesia, Fed. States
2420	-9.5	671	213	131	123	0.700	325	2712	100	1	2	2143	25	Moldova
○○○	○○○	○○○	○○○	○○○	○○○	○○○	○○○	○○○	100	○○○	○○○	○○○	2	Monaco
1800	-0.3	○○○	177	96	218	0.661	254	1974	60	1	2	1767	104	Mongolia
3690	0.6	359	356	234	419	0.606	49	3046	82	38	64	1167	29	Morocco
1000	3.9	403	55	26	876	0.356	6	1980	60	40	71	40	233	Mozambique
1027	4.8	262	51	36	107	0.549	30	2822	68	11	20	590	1274	Myanmar
6700	1.8	587	956	906	152	0.627	29	2745	77	17	19	735	31	Namibia
○○○	○○○	○○○	○○○	○○○	7	○○○	○○○	○○○	○○○	○○○	○○○	○○○	○○○	Nauru
1450	2.4	343	52	27	390	0.499	4	2459	81	41	76	485	○○○	Nepal
26 440	2.2	4762	13 073	14 455	(3135)	0.938	251	3282	100	○○○	○○○	3018	3	Netherlands
19 130	1.8	4864	3509	3619	(113)	0.917	226	3235	○○○	○○○	○○○	3318	2	New Zealand
2366	0.6	542	342	117	562	0.643	61	2256	79	34	33	1209	98	Nicaragua
770	-1.0	○○○	38	24	211	0.292	4	2118	59	76	92	○○○	590	Niger
830	-0.4	710	88	164	185	0.463	19	2747	57	28	44	○○○	151	Nigeria
○○○	○○○	○○○	○○○	○○○	0	○○○	○○○	○○○	○○○	○○○	○○○	○○○	○○○	Northern Marianas
○○○	○○○	2071	○○○	○○○	201	○○○	○○○	2201	100	○○○	○○○	○○○	○○○	North Korea
30 440	3.1	5704	7191	12 857	(1264)	0.944	413	3382	100	○○○	○○○	4239	3	Norway
13 356	0.3	4046	○○○	○○○	46	0.755	137	○○○	39	20	38	695	13	Oman
1920	1.2	463	70	64	703	0.499	68	2457	88	43	72	○○○	161	Pakistan
○○○	○○○	○○○	○○○	○○○	29	○○○	○○○	○○○	79	○○○	○○○	○○○	○○○	Palau
5720	2.3	892	1040	335	17	0.788	117	2386	87	8	9	3025	15	Panama
2150	1.4	○○○	219	368	275	0.548	7	2193	42	29	43	○○○	136	Papua New Guinea
4400	-0.4	715	383	174	82	0.751	117	2576	79	6	8	948	66	Paraguay
4680	2.9	489	332	734	401	0.752	117	2610	77	5	15	3268	48	Peru
4360	1.1	554	407	436	578	0.751	124	2372	87	5	5	2958	110	Philippines
9280	4.5	2328	1296	920	1396	0.841	233	3397	○○○	0	0	1865	5	Poland
17 270	2.5	2459	3766	2373	(271)	0.896	312	3751	82	5	10	3242	3	Portugal
18 789	○○○	26 773	○○○	○○○	1	0.826	220	○○○	○○○	20	17	1518	4	Qatar
6980	-0.4	1619	693	511	432	0.773	191	3407	58	1	3	1819	10	Romania
8660	-4.6	4218	370	713	1565	0.779	423	3014	99	0	1	3006	9	Russian Federation
1000	-2.1	○○○	33	10	322	0.422	○○○	2086	41	26	40	○○○	889	Rwanda
11 730	4.7	○○○	○○○	○○○	4	0.808	117	2997	98	○○○	○○○	○○○	8	St. Kitts and Nevis
5200	0.9	○○○	○○○	○○○	11	0.775	518	2849	98	○○○	○○○	○○○	21	St. Lucia
5250	2.6	○○○	○○○	○○○	6	0.755	88	2609	93	○○○	○○○	○○○	16	St. Vincent & the Grenadines
5450	1.9	○○○	○○○	○○○	27	0.775	70	○○○	99	1	2	○○○	56	Samoa
○○○	○○○	○○○	○○○	○○○	○○○	○○○	○○○	○○○	○○○	○○○	○○○	○○○	1	San Marino
1792	-0.8	○○○	○○○	○○○	35	0.639	47	2567	○○○	○○○	○○○	○○○	3	Sao Tome and Principe
11 390	-1.2	5081	1529	3248	31	0.769	153	2841	95	17	33	1455	11	Saudi Arabia
1560	0.9	324	156	111	424	0.430	10	2277	78	53	72	297	104	Senegal
○○○	○○○	1289	461	181	638	○○○	○○○	2778	○○○	16	31	1625	5	Serbia and Montenegro
12 508	1.1	○○○	○○○	○○○	18	0.840	132	2461	○○○	○○○	○○○	○○○	12	Seychelles
480	-6.5	○○○	36	6	182	0.275	9	1913	28	○○○	○○○	○○○	131	Sierra Leone
24 910	4.7	6120	28 283	29 690	1	0.884	135	○○○	100	4	12	2730	10	Singapore
11 610	1.9	3234	2734	2339	113	0.836	322	2894	100	○○○	○○○	1897	4	Slovakia
18 160	2.8	3288	5093	4666	61	0.881	215	2935	100	0	0	2657	3	Slovenia
1680	-1.0	○○○	○○○	○○○	68	0.632	13	2272	71	○○○	○○○	○○○	○○○	Solomon Islands
○○○	○○○	○○○	○○○	○○○	○○○	○○○	○○○	○○○	○○○	○○○	○○○	○○○	876	Somalia
9510	-0.2	2514	655	669	488	0.684	443	2921	86	14	15	1841	11	South Africa
18 110	4.7	4119	2996	3199	-198	0.879	173	3055	92	1	4	6106	6	South Korea
20 150	2.3	3084	3621	2778	(1195)	0.918	436	3422	○○○	2	3	4254	2	Spain
3560	3.9	437	319	257	276	0.730	41	2274	83	6	11	474	87	Sri Lanka
1610	5.6	521	○○○	○○○	225	0.503	16	2288	75	31	54	○○○	398	Sudan

	○○○ no data
	per capita — for each person

	Land		Population									Employment		
	Area	Arable and permanent crops	Total	Density	Change	Births	Deaths	Fertility	Infant mortality	Life expectancy	Urban	Agriculture	Industry	Serv
			2002	2002	1990–2000	2002	2002	2001	2001	2001	2001	1990	1990	19
	thousand km²	% of total	millions	persons per km²	%	births per 1000	deaths per 1000	children per mother	per 1000 live births	years	%	%	%	
Suriname	163	0.4	0.4	2.5	9.2	20	7	2.8	26	71	75	21	18	6
Swaziland	17	10.4	1.2	70.6	27.1	30	19	5.9	106	38	27	40	22	3
Sweden	450	6.1	8.9	19.8	3.7	10	11	1.6	3	80	83	○○○	○○○	0
Switzerland	41	10.6	7.3	178.0	6.2	10	9	1.4	5	79	68	6	35	5
Syria	185	29.7	17.2	93.0	31.1	30	5	4.1	23	72	52	33	24	4
Taiwan	36	○○○	22.5	625.0	9.4	13	6	1.4	○○○	75	77	○○○	○○○	0
Tajikistan	143	6.0	6.7	46.9	20.8	33	9	2.4	53	68	28	41	23	3
Tanzania	945	4.9	35.3	37.4	34.6	40	17	5.6	104	44	33	84	5	
Thailand	513	35.1	63.6	124.0	11.2	17	7	1.8	24	69	20	64	14	2
Togo	57	40.5	5.3	93.0	36.0	36	11	5.8	79	50	34	66	10	2
Tonga	0.8	64.0	0.1	125.0	11.1	24	6	4.2	18	71	32	○○○	○○○	0
Trinidad and Tobago	5	23.8	1.1	220.0	-1.9	13	8	1.7	17	72	75	11	31	5
Tunisia	164	31.2	9.8	59.8	16.9	17	5	2.1	21	73	66	28	33	3
Turkey	775	34.4	67.3	86.8	17.1	18	6	2.5	36	70	66	53	18	2
Turkmenistan	488	3.5	4.7	9.6	23.2	28	9	2.2	76	67	45	37	23	
Tuvalu	0.02	○○○	0.01	500.0	18.2	21	7	2.4	40	67	18	○○○	○○○	0
Uganda	241	28.3	24.9	103.3	35.7	47	17	6.9	79	45	15	85	5	
Ukraine	604	55.7	48.4	80.1	-4.9	10	16	1.1	17	69	68	20	40	
United Arab Emirates	84	1.6	2.4	28.6	21.5	18	4	3.5	8	74	87	8	27	
United Kingdom	245	24.6	59.9	244.5	3.3	11	10	1.6	6	78	90	2	29	
United States of America	9364	18.6	287.7	30.7	10.3	14	9	2.1	7	77	77	3	28	
Uruguay	177	7.4	3.4	19.2	7.4	17	9	2.2	14	75	92	14	27	
Uzbekistan	447	10.8	25.6	57.3	20.0	26	8	2.7	52	69	37	34	25	
Vanuatu	12	9.8	0.2	16.7	23.3	25	8	5.3	34	68	22	○○○	○○○	
Venezuela	912	3.8	24.3	26.6	21.8	20	5	2.8	19	74	87	12	27	
Vietnam	332	22.2	80.6	242.8	18.8	20	6	2.3	30	69	25	71	14	
Western Sahara	252	0.008	0.3	1.2	28.1	46	17	6.8	○○○	○○○	95	○○○	○○○	
Yemen	528	3.2	18.7	35.4	45.4	43	9	7.2	79	59	25	61	17	
Zambia	753	7.0	10.2	13.4	22.1	40	24	5.7	112	33	40	75	8	
Zimbabwe	391	8.6	12.5	32.0	12.3	31	21	4.0	76	35	36	68	8	

Explanation of datasets

Land

Area — does not include areas of lakes and seas

Arable and permanent crops — percentage of total land area used for arable and permanent crops

Population

Total — estimate for mid 2002

Density — the total population of a country divided by its land area

Change — percentage change in population between 1990 and 2000. Negative numbers indicate a decrease

Births — number of births per one thousand people in one year

Deaths — number of deaths per one thousand people in one year

Fertility — average number of children born to child bearing women

Infant mortality — number of deaths of children under one year per 1000 live births

Life expectancy — number of years a baby born now can expect to live

Urban — percentage of the population living in towns and cities

Employment

Agriculture — percentage of the labour force employed in agriculture

Industry — percentage of the labour force employed in industry

Services — percentage of the labour force employed in services

Macedonia, FYRO*   Former Yugoslav Republic of Macedonia

Health | Energy and trade | Quality of life

GNP (US$ billion)	Purchasing power	Growth of PP	Energy consumption	Imports	Exports	Aid received (given)	Human Development Index	Health care	Food consumption	Safe water	Illiteracy male	Illiteracy female	Higher education	Cars	
	2001	1990–2000	2000	2001	2001	2000	2001	1990–2002	2001	2000	2000	2000	1996	2000	
US$	US$	%	kg oil equivalent per capita	US$ per capita	US$ per capita	million US$		doctors per 100 000 people	daily calories per capita	% access	%	%	students per 100 000 people	people per car	
.7	3310	3.0	○○○	○○○	○○○	34	0.762	45	2643	95	○○○	○○○	○○○	8	Suriname
.4	4690	0.2	○○○	○○○	○○○	13	0.547	15	2593	○○○	19	21	630	38	Swaziland
.9	24 670	1.6	5354	7099	8545	(1799)	0.941	311	3164	100	○○○	○○○	3116	2	Sweden
.5	31 320	0.2	3704	11 677	11 398	(890)	0.932	336	3440	100	○○○	○○○	2072	2	Switzerland
.6	3440	2.8	1137	258	326	158	0.685	142	3038	80	12	40	1559	107	Syria
○○○	○○○	○○○	○○○	4766	5462	0	○○○	○○○	○○○	○○○	○○○	○○○	○○○	5	Taiwan
.1	1150	-11.8	470	127	94	0142	0.677	207	1662	69	0	1	1895	○○○	Tajikistan
.2	540	0.1	457	46	22	1045	0.400	4	1997	54	16	34	57	735	Tanzania
.9	6550	3.3	1212	946	1010	641	0.768	24	2486	80	3	6	2252	37	Thailand
.3	1420	-0.4	338	132	92	70	0.501	8	2287	54	28	58	315	174	Togo
.2	○○○	○○○	○○○	○○○	○○○	21	○○○	○○○	○○○	100	○○○	○○○	○○○	19	Tonga
.2	9080	2.3	6660	○○○	○○○	-2	0.802	79	2756	86	1	2	787	6	Trinidad and Tobago
.1	6450	3.0	825	990	689	223	0.740	70	3293	99	19	39	1341	24	Tunisia
.3	6640	2.1	1181	598	462	325	0.734	127	3343	83	7	24	2301	17	Turkey
.0	4580	-8.0	2627	439	533	32	0.748	300	2738	58	○○○	○○○	2072	○○○	Turkmenistan
○○○	○○○	○○○	○○○	○○○	○○○	7	○○○	○○○	○○○	100	○○○	○○○	○○○	○○○	Tuvalu
.3	1250	3.8	○○○	60	22	819	0.489	5	2398	50	23	43	179	923	Uganda
.2	4150	-8.8	2820	328	338	541	0.766	299	3008	55	0	1	2996	10	Ukraine
oo	17 935	-1.6	10 175	○○○	○○○	4	0.816	177	3340	○○○	25	21	801	7	United Arab Emirates
.4	24 460	2.2	3962	5589	4596	(4501)	0.930	164	3368	100	○○○	○○○	3237	2	United Kingdom
.7	34 870	2.2	8148	4129	2556	(9955)	0.937	276	3766	100	○○○	○○○	5341	2	United States of America
.0	8710	2.6	923	917	614	17	0.834	375	2848	98	3	2	2458	11	Uruguay
8	2470	-2.4	2027	107	105	186	0.729	300	2197	85	0	1	○○○	○○○	Uzbekistan
.2	2710	-0.9	○○○	○○○	○○○	46	0.568	12	2565	88	○○○	○○○	○○○	50	Vanuatu
.2	5890	-0.6	2452	763	1163	77	0.775	203	2376	84	7	8	○○○	13	Venezuela
.6	2130	6.0	471	202	191	1700	0.688	52	2533	56	6	9	678	562	Vietnam
oo	○○○	○○○	○○○	○○○	○○○	○○○	○○○	○○○	○○○	○○○	○○○	○○○	○○○	○○○	Western Sahara
.3	770	2.3	201	128	216	265	0.470	22	2050	69	33	75	419	101	Yemen
3	790	-2.1	619	71	82	795	0.386	7	1885	64	15	29	238	107	Zambia
2	2340	0.4	809	119	137	178	0.496	14	2133	85	7	15	661	61	Zimbabwe

Explanation of datasets

Health

GNP Gross National Product (GNP) is the total value of goods and services produced in a country plus income from abroad.

Purchasing power Gross Domestic Product (GDP) is the total value of goods and services produced in a country. Purchasing power parity (PPP) is GDP per person, adjusted for the local cost of living

Growth of PP average annual growth (or decline, shown as a negative value in the table) in purchasing power. This figure shows whether people are becoming better or worse off

Energy and trade

Energy consumption consumption of commercial energy per person shown as the equivalent in kilograms of oil

Imports total value of imports per person shown in US dollars

Exports total value of exports per person shown in US dollars

Aid received (given) amount of economic aid a country has received. Negative values indicate that the repayment of loans exceeds the amount of aid received. Figures in brackets show aid given.

Quality of life

HDI Human Development Index (HDI) measures the relative social and economic progress of a country. It combines life expectancy, adult literacy, average number of years of schooling, and purchasing power. Economically more developed countries have an HDI approaching 1.0. Economically less developed countries have an HDI approaching 0.

Health care number of doctors in each country per 100 000 people

Food consumption average number of calories consumed by each person each day

Safe water percentage of the population with access to safe drinking water

Illiteracy percentage of men and women who are unable to read and write

Higher education number of students in higher education per 100 000 people

Cars the number of people for every car

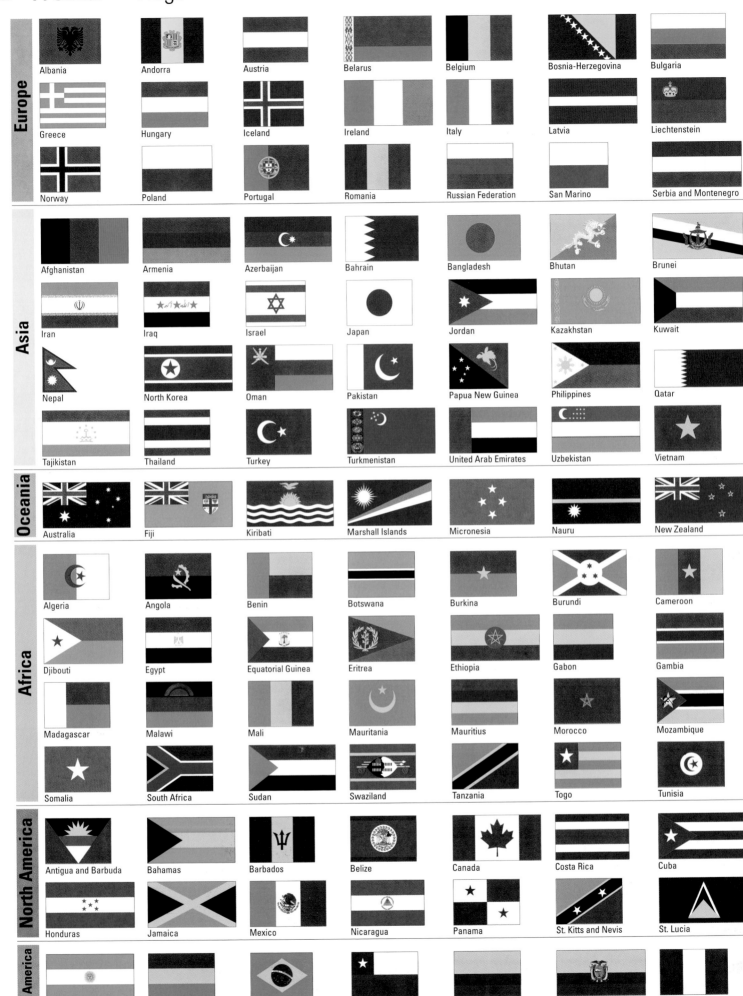

Europe

Albania · Andorra · Austria · Belarus · Belgium · Bosnia-Herzegovina · Bulgaria

Greece · Hungary · Iceland · Ireland · Italy · Latvia · Liechtenstein

Norway · Poland · Portugal · Romania · Russian Federation · San Marino · Serbia and Montenegro

Asia

Afghanistan · Armenia · Azerbaijan · Bahrain · Bangladesh · Bhutan · Brunei

Iran · Iraq · Israel · Japan · Jordan · Kazakhstan · Kuwait

Nepal · North Korea · Oman · Pakistan · Papua New Guinea · Philippines · Qatar

Tajikistan · Thailand · Turkey · Turkmenistan · United Arab Emirates · Uzbekistan · Vietnam

Oceania

Australia · Fiji · Kiribati · Marshall Islands · Micronesia · Nauru · New Zealand

Africa

Algeria · Angola · Benin · Botswana · Burkina · Burundi · Cameroon

Djibouti · Egypt · Equatorial Guinea · Eritrea · Ethiopia · Gabon · Gambia

Madagascar · Malawi · Mali · Mauritania · Mauritius · Morocco · Mozambique

Somalia · South Africa · Sudan · Swaziland · Tanzania · Togo · Tunisia

North America

Antigua and Barbuda · Bahamas · Barbados · Belize · Canada · Costa Rica · Cuba

Honduras · Jamaica · Mexico · Nicaragua · Panama · St. Kitts and Nevis · St. Lucia

S. America

Argentina · Bolivia · Brazil · Chile · Colombia · Ecuador · French Guiana

© Oxford University P

Croatia
 Czech Republic
 Denmark
 Estonia
 Finland
France
Germany

Lithuania
Luxembourg
Macedonia, FYRO
 Malta
Moldova
Monaco
 Netherlands

Slovakia
Slovenia
Spain
Sweden
Switzerland
Ukraine
 United Kingdom

 Cambodia
China
Cyprus
East Timor
Georgia
 India
 Indonesia

Kyrgyzstan
Laos
Lebanon
 Malaysia
 Maldives
 Mongolia
 Myanmar

Saudi Arabia
 Seychelles
 Singapore
 South Korea
 Sri Lanka
 Syria
Taiwan

 Yemen

 Northern Marianas
 Palau
 Samoa
 Solomon Islands
 Tonga
 Tuvalu
 Vanuatu

 Cape Verde
 Central African Republic
 Chad
 Comoros
 Congo
 Congo, Dem. Rep.
 Côte d'Ivoire

 Ghana
 Guinea
 Guinea-Bissau
 Kenya
 Lesotho
 Liberia
 Libya

 Namibia
 Niger
 Nigeria
 Rwanda
 Sao Tomé and Pirncipe
 Senegal
 Sierra Leone

Uganda
Zambia
Zimbabwe

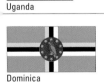 Dominica
 Dominican Republic
 El Salvador
 Greenland
 Grenada
 Guatemala
 Haiti

St. Vincent & the Grenadines
Trinidad and Tobago
United States of America

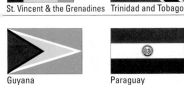 Guyana
 Paraguay
 Peru
 Suriname
 Uruguay
 Venezuela

How to use the index

To find a place on an atlas map use either
the grid code or latitude and longitude.

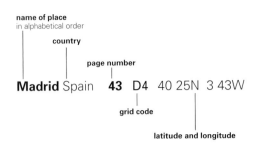

name of place
in alphabetical order

country

page number

Madrid Spain **43** D4 40 25N 3 43W

grid code

latitude and longitude

Grid code

Madrid Spain **43** D4 40 25N 3 43W

Madrid is in grid square D4

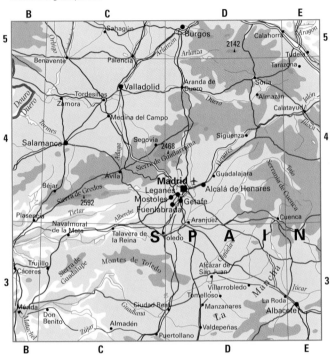

Latitude and longitude

Madrid Spain **43** D4 40 25N 3 43W

Madrid is at latitude 40 degrees, 25 minutes north and 3 degrees, 43 minutes west

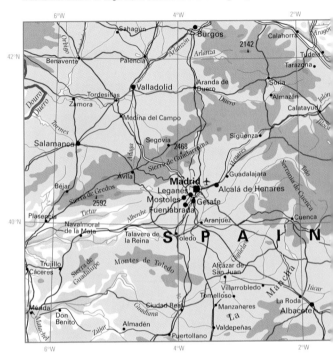

Geographical abbreviations

admin	administrative area
Arch.	Archipelago
b.	bay or harbour
c.	cape, point, or headland
can.	canal
co.	county
d.	desert
fj.	fjord
G.	Gunung; Gebel
g.	gulf
geog. reg.	geographical region
i.	island
is.	islands
Kep.	Kepulauan
l.	lake, lakes, lagoon
mt.	mountain, peak, or spot height
mts.	mountains
NP	National Park
P.	Pulau
p; pen	peninsula
Peg	Pegunungan
plat.	plateau
prov.	province
Pt.	Point
Pta.	Punta
Pte.	Pointe
Pto.	Porto; Puerto
r.	river
Ra.	Range
res.	reservoir
salt l.	salt lake
sd.	sound, strait, or channel
St.	Saint
Ste.	Sainte
Str.	Strait

sum.	summit
tn.	town or other populated place
v.	valley
vol.	volcano

Political abbreviations

Aust.	Australia
Bahamas	The Bahamas
CAR	Central African Republic
Col.	Columbia
CDR	Congo Democratic Republic
Czech Rep.	Czech Republic
Dom. Rep.	Dominican Republic
Eq. Guinea	Equatorial Guinea
Fr.	France
Med. Sea	Mediterranean Sea
Neths	Netherlands
NI	Northern Ireland
NZ	New Zealand
Philippines	The Philippines
PNG	Papua New Guinea
Port.	Portugal
RoI	Republic of Ireland
RSA	Republic of South Africa
Russia	Russian Federation
SM	Serbia and Montenegro
Sp.	Spain
Switz.	Switzerland
UAE	United Arab Emirates
UK	United Kingom
USA	United States of America
W. Indies	West Indies
Yemen	Yemen Republic

Name	Page	Grid	Lat.	Long.
chen Germany	44	C5	50 46N	6 06E
ten Belgium	41	B4	51 56N	6 35E
a Nigeria	76	F3	5 06N	7 21E
ādān Iran	57	M10	30 20N	48 15E
adla Algeria	76	D8	31 01N	2 43W
aetetuba Brazil	90	H13	1 45S	48 54W
akan Russia	55	M7	53 43N	91 25E
ancay Peru	90	C11	13 37S	72 52W
ashiri Japan	62	D4	44 02N	114 17E
beville Fr.	42	E6	50 06N	1 51E
éché Chad	77	K4	13 49N	20 49E
eokuta Nigeria	76	E3	7 10N	3 26E
erdeen UK	40	E5	57 10N	2 04W
erdeen USA	86	B6	46 58N	123 49W
nā Saudi Arabia	56	D2	18 14N	42 31E
djan Côte d'Ivoire	76	D3	5 19N	4 01W
lene UK	86	G3	32 27N	99 45W
u Dhabi UAE	57	N8	24 28N	54 25E
J Hadrīyah Saudi Arabia	57	M9	27 18N	48 59E
J Hamed Sudan	77	M5	19 32N	33 20E
uja Nigeria	76	F3	9 10N	7 11E
ū Kamāl Syria	56	D5	34 29N	40 56E
ū Mūsā UAE	57	P9	25 52N	55 03E
unā Brazil	90	D12	9 41S	65 20W
ambaro Mexico	88	D3	20 00N	100 42W
poneta Mexico	88	C4	22 30N	102 25W
pulco Mexico	88	E3	16 51N	99 56W
arigua Venezuela	90	D15	9 35N	69 12W
itlán Mexico	88	E3	18 12N	98 02W
yucán Mexico	88	E3	17 59N	94 58W
ra Ghana	76	D3	5 33N	0 15W
uacachi Bolivia	90	D10	16 01S	68 44W
ern Germany	41	G1	48 38N	8 04E
insk Russia	55	M8	56 20N	90 33E
ncagua mt. Argentina	91	C7	32 40S	70 02W
na Turkey	49	E2	37 00N	35 19E
Dakhla Western Sahara	76	A6	23 50N	15 58W
Dammām Saudi Arabia	57	N9	26 25N	50 06E
Dīlam Saudi Arabia	57	M8	23 59N	47 06E
Dir'īyah Saudi Arabia	57	M8	24 45N	46 32E
lis Ababa Ethiopia	77	N3	9 03N	38 42E
Diwānīyah Iraq	56	D5	32 00N	44 57E
laide Aust.	67	G4	34 56S	138 36E
n Yemen	56	E1	12 50N	45 03E
ud Romania	45	N3	46 07N	27 10E
oni India	58	D3	15 38N	77 16E
a Sp.	43	D2	36 45N	3 01W
n Algeria	76	D7	27 54N	0 17W
wa Ethiopia	77	N4	14 12N	38 56E
HANISTAN	57	H5/K6		
on Turkey	49	D2	38 46N	30 32E
dez Niger	76	F5	17 00N	7 56E
dir Morocco	76	C8	30 30N	9 40W
rtala India	59	G4	23 49N	91 15E
wa Canada	85	U3	47 22N	84 37W
n Fr.	42	E3	44 12N	0 38E
o Japan	63	C3	35 58N	139 35E
a India	58	D5	27 09N	78 00E
Turkey	49	F2	39 44N	43 04E
gento Italy	46	E2	37 19N	13 35E
nio Greece	47	J3	38 38N	21 25E
oppoli Italy	46	F4	40 21N	14 59E
adas Col.	90	B15	5 36N	75 30W
ascalientes Mexico	88	D4	21 51N	102 18W
les Serdan Mexico	88	C5	28 40N	105 57W
n Germany	41	F4	51 45N	7 54E
adabad India	58	C4	23 03N	72 40E
adnagar India	58	C3	19 08N	74 48E
achapán El Salvador	88	G2	13 57N	89 49W
aiz India	56	E5	31 17N	48 43E
o Greece	47	K3	38 15N	22 06E
Sefra Algeria	76	D8	32 45N	0 35W
rie Canada	84	N4	51 20N	114 00W
sur-l'Adour Fr.	42	D2	43 42N	0 15W
en-Provence Fr.	42	G2	43 31N	5 27E
es-Bains Fr.	42	G3	45 41N	5 55E
wl India	59	M9	23 43N	92 47E
-wakamatsu Japan	62	D3	37 30N	139 58E
cio Corsica	42	J1	41 55N	8 43E
n UAE	57	P9	25 4N	55 26E
r India	58	C5	26 29N	74 40E
SA	86	D3	32 24N	112 51W
ka Japan	63	B2	33 32N	133 42E
a NZ	69	D3	43 49S	172 58E
hi Japan	63	B2	34 39N	135 00E
CDR	77	K2	2 42N	23 51E
ubinsk Russia	49	G4	48 20N	46 10E
Japan	62	D3	39 44N	140 05E
vik Canada	84	J7	68 15N	135 02W
a India	58	D4	20 49N	77 05E
nes Iceland	48	K6	64 19N	22 05W
n USA	87	K5	41 04N	81 31W
Kazakhstan	54	H5	43 37N	51 11E
ubinsk Kazakhstan	54	H7	50 16N	57 13E
e Japan	63	B2	32 00N	130 12E
eyri Iceland	48	L7	65 41N	18 04W
ama state USA	87	J3	32 00N	87 00W
inhas Brazil	90	K11	12 09S	
ela Costa Rica	89	H2	10 00N	84 12W
mārah Iraq	56	E5	31 51N	47 10E
osa USA	86	E4	37 28N	105 54W
a Turkey	49	D2	36 32N	32 02E
cete Sp.	43	E3	39 00N	1 52W
a state USA	84	D6/F6	63 10N	157 30W
a, Gulf of USA	84	F5/G5	58 00N	147 00W
ete Sp.	43	E3	39 00N	1 52W
NIA	47	H4/J4		
y Aust.	66	C4	34 57S	117 54E
rah Iraq	57	M10	30 30N	47 50E
Al Bayda Libya	77	K8	32 00N	21 30E
Alberta province Canada	84	M4/N4	54 00N	117 30W
Albert Lea USA	87	H5	43 36N	93 16W
Albi Fr.	42	F2	43 56N	2 08E
Al Bi'r Saudi Arabia	56	C4	28 50N	36 16E
Albuquerque USA	86	E4	35 05N	106 38W
Albury Aust.	67	J3	36 03S	146 54E
Alcalá de Henares Sp.	43	D4	40 28N	3 22W
Alcalá la Real Sp.	43	C2	37 28N	3 55W
Alcamo Italy	46	E2	37 58N	12 58E
Alcañiz Sp.	43	E4	41 03N	0 09W
Aldama Mexico	88	E4	22 54N	98 05W
Aldan Russia	55	Q8	58 44N	124 22E
Alderney i. British Isles	40	E1	49 43N	2 12W
Alegrete Brazil	91	F8	29 45S	55 40W
Alençon Fr.	42	E5	48 25N	0 05E
Aleppo Syria	56	C6	36 14N	37 10E
Alès Fr.	42	F3	44 08N	4 05E
Alessándria Italy	46	C6	44 55N	8 37E
Ålesund Norway	48	C3	62 28N	6 11E
Alexander Bay tn. RSA	78	C3	28 40S	16 30E
Alexandra NZ	69	B2	45 15S	169 23E
Alexandria Egypt	77	L8	31 13N	29 55E
Alexandria Romania	45	M1	43 59N	25 19E
Algeciras Sp.	43	C2	36 08N	5 27W
ALGERIA	76	D7/F7		
Alghero Italy	46	C4	40 34N	8 19E
Algiers Algeria	76	E9	36 50N	3 00E
Al Hadīthah Iraq	56	C5	34 06N	42 25E
Al Hasakah Syria	56	D6	36 32N	40 44E
Al Hillah Iraq	56	D5	32 28N	44 29E
Al Hillah Saudi Arabia	57	M8	23 29N	46 50E
Al Hufūf Saudi Arabia	57	M9	25 20N	49 34E
Alicante Sp.	43	E3	38 21N	0 29W
Alice USA	87	G2	27 45N	98 06W
Alice Springs tn. Aust.	66	F5	23 42S	133 52E
Aligarh India	58	D5	27 54N	78 04E
Al Jahrah Kuwait	57	M9	29 22N	47 40E
Al Jamalīyah Qatar	57	N9	25 37N	51 03E
Al Jawf Libya	77	K6	24 12N	23 18E
Al Jawf Saudi Arabia	56	C4	29 49N	39 52E
Al Jubayl Saudi Arabia	57	M9	26 59N	49 40E
Al Kharj Saudi Arabia	57	M8	24 09N	47 19E
Al Khubar Saudi Arabia	57	N9	26 18N	50 13E
Al Khums Libya	77	G8	32 39N	14 16E
Al Kir'ānah Qatar	57	N8	24 59N	51 02E
Al Kūt Iraq	56	E5	32 30N	45 51E
Allahabad India	58	E5	25 27N	81 50E
Allende Mexico	88	D4	28 22N	100 50W
Allentown USA	87	L5	40 37N	75 30W
Alliance USA	86	F5	42 08N	102 54W
Al Lith Saudi Arabia	56	D3	20 10N	40 20E
Alloa UK	40	E5	56 07N	3 49W
Almada Port.	43	A3	38 40N	9 09W
Almadén Sp.	43	C3	38 47N	4 50W
Almansa Sp.	43	E3	38 52N	1 06W
Al Maṣna'ah Oman	57	P8	23 46N	57 39E
Almelo Neths	41	E5	52 21N	6 40E
Almendralejo Sp.	43	B3	38 41N	6 25W
Almere Neths	41	D5	52 22N	5 12E
Almería Sp.	43	D2	36 50N	2 26W
Al'met'yevsk Russia	49	H5	54 51N	52 23E
Al Mubarraz Saudi Arabia	57	M9	25 26N	49 37E
Al Muharraq Bahrain	57	N9	26 19N	50 35E
Al Mukhā Yemen	56	D1	13 20N	43 16E
Al Muqdādīyah Iraq	56	D5	33 58N	44 58E
Alor Setar Malaysia	64	C5	6 07N	100 21E
Alpine USA	86	F3	30 22N	103 40W
Alps mts. Europe	44	D3	46 00N	7 30E
Al Qāmishlī Syria	56	D6	37 03N	41 15E
Al Qunfudhah Saudi Arabia	56	D2	19 09N	41 07E
Al Salmiya Kuwait	57	M9	29 15N	48 14E
Alsdorf Germany	41	E3	50 53N	6 10E
Alsfeld Germany	41	H3	50 45N	9 16E
Alta Norway	48	F4	69 57N	23 10E
Alta Gracia Argentina	91	E7	31 42S	64 25W
Altamira Brazil	90	G13	3 13S	
Altamura Italy	47	G4	40 49N	16 34E
Altay China	60	F7	47 48N	88 07E
Altus USA	86	G3	34 39N	99 21W
Alva USA	87	G4	36 48N	98 40W
Al Wajh Saudi Arabia	56	C4	26 16N	32 28E
Al Wakrah Qatar	57	N9	25 10N	51 36E
Alwar India	58	D5	27 32N	76 35E
Alzey Germany	41	G2	49 45N	8 06E
Amadi Sudan	77	M3	5 32N	30 20E
Amagasaki Japan	63	C2	34 42N	135 23E
Amapá Brazil	90	G14	2 00N	50 50W
Amarillo USA	86	F4	35 14N	101 50W
Amazonas r. Brazil	90	G13	2 00S	53 00W
Ambala India	58	D6	30 19N	76 49E
Ambato Ecuador	90	B13	1 18S	78 39W
Amberg Germany	44	E4	49 26N	11 52E
Ambon Indonesia	65	H3	3 41S	128 10E
Ambovombe Madagascar	78	J2	25 10S	46 06E
Amdo China	60	F4	32 22N	91 07E
Ameca Mexico	88	D4	20 34N	104 03W
American Falls tn. USA	86	D5	42 47N	112 50W
American Samoa i. Pacific Ocean			70	
Amersfoort Neths	41	D5	52 09N	5 23E
Amfípoli Greece	47	K4	40 48N	23 52E
Amherst Canada	85	Y3	45 50N	64 14W
Amiens Fr.	42	F5	49 54N	2 18E
Amman Jordan	56	C5	31 04N	36 17E
Amol Iran	49	H2	36 27N	52 20E
Ampana Indonesia	65	G3	0 54S	121 35E
Amravati India	58	D4	20 58N	77 50E
Amritsar India	58	C6	31 35N	74 56E
Amsterdam Neths	41	C5	52 22N	4 54E
Amstetten Austria	44	F4	48 08N	14 52E
Amur r. Asia	61	N8	52 30N	126 30E
Amursk Russia	55	R7	50 16N	136 55E
Anaconda USA	86	D6	46 09N	112 56W
Anadyr' Russia	55	V9	64 50N	178 00E
Anamizu Japan	63	C3	37 14N	136 56E
Anan Japan	63	B2	33 54N	134 40E
Ananindeua Brazil	90	H13	1 22S	48 20W
Anantapur India	58	D2	14 42N	77 05E
Anápolis Brazil	90	H10	16 19S	48 58W
Anchorage USA	84	F6	61 10N	150 00W
Ancona Italy	46	E5	43 37N	13 31E
Andalsnes Norway	48	C3	62 33N	7 43E
Andaman Islands India	59	G2	12 00N	94 00E
Andenne Belgium	41	D3	50 29N	5 06E
Anderlecht Belgium	41	C3	50 50N	4 20E
Andermatt Switz.	44	D3	46 38N	8 36E
Andes mts. South America	90	B14/C6	10 00S	77 00W
Andizhan Uzbekistan	54	K5	40 40N	72 12E
Andkhvoy Afghanistan	57	J6	36 59N	65 08E
Andong South Korea	63	A3	36 37N	128 44E
ANDORRA	42	E2		
Andorra la Vella Andorra	42	E2	42 30N	1 30E
Andreyevka Kazakhstan	60	D7	45 53N	80 37E
Andros i. Bahamas	89	J4	24 00N	78 00W
Ándros i. Greece	47	L2	37 49N	24 54E
Andújar Sp.	43	C3	38 02N	4 03W
Angarsk Russia	55	N7	52 31N	103 55E
Angers Fr.	42	D4	47 29N	0 32W
ANGOLA	78	C5		
Angoulême Fr.	42	E3	45 40N	0 10E
Anguilla i. Leeward Islands	88	P10	18 14N	63 05W
Anjo Japan	63	C2	34 56N	137 05E
'Annaba Algeria	76	F9	36 55N	7 47E
An Nabk Saudi Arabia	56	C5	31 21N	37 20E
An Nabk Syria	56	C5	34 02N	36 43E
An Najaf Iraq	56	D5	31 59N	44 19E
Annapolis USA	87	L4	38 59N	76 30W
An Nāsirīyah Iraq	56	E5	31 04N	46 17E
Annecy Fr.	42	H3	45 54N	6 07E
Anniston USA	87	J3	33 38N	85 50W
Annotto Bay tn. Jamaica	89	U14	18 16N	76 47W
Anqing China	61	L4	30 46N	119 40E
Ansbach Germany	44	E4	49 18N	10 36E
Anse Royale Seychelles	73	B1	4 44S	55 31E
Anshan China	61	M6	41 05N	122 58E
Anshun China	61	J3	26 15N	105 51E
Antakya Turkey	49	E2	36 12N	36 10E
Antalya Turkey	49	D2	36 53N	30 42E
Antananarivo Madagascar	78	J4	18 52S	47 30E
Antarctica			71	
Antequera Sp.	43	C2	37 01N	4 34W
Antibes Fr.	42	H2	43 35N	7 07E
Antigua i. Antigua & Barbuda	88	Q9	17 09N	61 49W
ANTIGUA & BARBUDA	88	Q9		
Antofagasta Chile	90	C9	23 40S	70 23W
Antsiranana Madagascar	78	J5	12 19S	49 17E
Antwerpen Belgium	41	C4	51 13N	4 25E
Anuradhapura Sri Lanka	58	E1	8 20N	80 25E
Anxi China	60	G6	40 32N	95 57E
Anyang China	61	K5	36 04N	114 20E
Anyang South Korea	63	A3	37 23N	126 56E
Aomori Japan	62	D4	40 50N	140 43E
Aosta Italy	46	B6	45 43N	7 19E
Aoya Japan	63	B3	35 32N	133 59E
Aparri Philippines	65	G7	18 22N	121 40E
Apatity Russia	54	F10	67 32N	33 21E
Apeldoorn Neths	41	D5	52 13N	5 57E
Appennini mts. Italy	46	C6/F4		
Appleton USA	87	J5	44 17N	88 24W
'Aqaba Jordan	56	C4	29 32N	35 00E
Aquidauana Brazil	90	F9	20 27S	55 45W
Ara India	60	D3	25 31N	84 46E
Aracaju Brazil	90	K11	10 54S	37 07W
Aracati Brazil	90	K13	4 32S	37 45W
Arad Romania	45	K3	46 10N	21 19E
Araguaina Brazil	90	H12	7 16S	48 18W
Araguari Brazil	90	H10	18 38S	48 13W
Arak Iran	56	E5	34 05N	49 42E
Aral Sea f. Asia	54	H5/J6	45 00N	60 00E
Aral'sk Kazakhstan	54	J6	46 56N	61 43E
Arambag India	59	J2	22 50N	87 59E
Aranda de Duero Sp.	43	D4	41 40N	3 41W
Aranjuez Sp.	43	D4	40 02N	3 37W
Arao Japan	63	B2	32 58N	130 26E
Arapiraca Brazil	90	K12	9 45S	36 40W
'Ar'ar Saudi Arabia	56	D5	30 58N	41 03E
Araraquara Brazil	90	H9	21 46S	48 08W
Arbil Iraq	56	D6	36 12N	44 01E
Arctic Ocean			71	
Arda Bulgaria	47	L4	41 28N	25 37E
Ardabil Iran	56	E6	38 15N	48 18E
Ardmore USA	87	G3	34 11N	97 08W
Arendal Norway	48	C2	58 27N	8 56E
Arequipa Peru	90	C10	16 25S	71 32W
Arezzo Italy	46	D5	43 28N	11 53E
Argentan Fr.	42	D5	48 45N	0 01W
ARGENTINA	90/91	D6		
Århus Denmark	48	D2	56 15N	10 10E
Arica Chile	90	C10	18 30S	70 20W
Ariquemes Brazil	90	E12	9 55S	63 06W
Arizona state USA	86	D3	34 00N	112 00W
Arjona Col.	90	B16	10 14N	75 22W
Arkansas state USA	87	H3	34 00N	93 00W
Arkansas City USA	87	G4	37 03N	97 02W
Arkhangel'sk Russia	54	G9	64 32N	40 40E
Arles Fr.	42	G2	43 41N	4 38E
Arlon Belgium	41	D2	49 41N	5 49E
Armagh UK	40	C4	54 21N	6 39W
Armavir Russia	49	F4	44 59N	41 40E
ARMENIA	49	F3		
Armenia Col.	90	B14	4 32N	75 40W
Armentières Fr.	42	F6	50 41N	2 53E
Armidale Aust.	67	K4	30 32S	151 40E
Arnhem Neths	41	D5	52 00N	5 53E
Arnprior Canada	87	L6	45 26N	76 21W
Arnsberg Germany	41	G4	51 23N	8 04E
Arolsen Germany	41	H4	51 23N	9 00E
Ar Ramādī Iraq	56	D5	33 27N	43 19E
Ar Raqqah Syria	56	C6	35 57N	39 03E
Arras Fr.	42	F6	50 17N	2 46E
Ar Rayyān Qatar	57	N9	25 17N	51 27E
Árta Greece	47	J3	39 10N	20 59E
Artigas Uruguay	91	F7	30 25S	56 28W
Arua Uganda	79	B6	3 02N	30 56E
Aruba i. Neths	90	C16/D16	12 30N	70 00W
Arusha Tanzania	79	C3	3 23S	36 40E
Arzamas Russia	49	F6	55 24N	43 48E
Asahikawa Japan	62	D4	43 46N	142 23E
Asamankese Ghana	76	D3	5 45N	0 45W
Asansol India	59	F4	23 40N	86 59E
Asari Japan	63	B3	35 03N	132 16E
Aschaffenburg Germany	41	H2	49 58N	9 09E
Ascoli Piceno Italy	46	E5	42 52N	13 35E
Ashburton NZ	69	C3	43 54S	171 45E
Asheville USA	87	K4	35 35N	82 35W
Ash Fork USA	86	D4	35 13N	112 29W
Ashgabat Turkmenistan	54	H4	37 58N	58 24E
Ashikaga Japan	63	C3	36 21N	139 26E
Asmara Eritrea	77	N5	15 20N	38 58E
Assab Eritrea	77	P4	13 01N	42 47E
Assen Neths	41	E6	53 00N	6 34E
Assis Brazil	90	G9	22 37S	50 25W
Assisi Italy	46	E5	43 04N	12 37E
As Sulaymānīyah Iraq	56	E6	35 32N	45 27E
As Suwayq Oman	57	P8	23 49N	57 28E
Astana Kazakhstan	54	K7	51 10N	71 28E
Astara Azerbaijan	49	G2	38 27N	48 53E
Asti Italy	46	C6	44 54N	8 13E
Astorga Sp.	43	B5	42 27N	6 04W
Astoria USA	86	B6	46 12N	123 50W
Astrakhan' Russia	54	G6	46 22N	48 04E
Asunción Paraguay	90	F8	25 15S	57 40W
Aswān Egypt	77	M6	24 05N	32 56E
Aswān Dam Egypt	77	M6	23 40N	31 50E
Asyūt Egypt	77	M7	27 14N	31 07E
Atar Mauritania	76	B6	20 32N	13 08W
Atbara Sudan	77	M5	17 42N	34 00E
Atbasar Kazakhstan	54	J7	51 49N	68 18E
Atchison USA	87	G4	39 33N	95 09W
Athabasca Canada	84	N4	54 44N	113 15W
Athens Greece	47	K2	38 00N	23 44E
Athi River tn. Kenya	79	E4	1 27S	36 58E
Athlone Rol	40	C5	53 25N	7 56W
Ati Chad	77	J4	13 11N	18 20E
Atikokan Canada	85	S3	48 45N	91 38W
Atlanta USA	87	K3	33 45N	84 23W
Atlantic City USA	87	M4	39 23N	74 27W
Atlantic Ocean			6	
At Tā'if Saudi Arabia	56	D3	21 15N	40 21E
Attapu Laos	64	D6	14 51N	106 56E
Attawapiskat Canada	85	U4	53 00N	82 30W
Atyrau Kazakhstan	54	H6	47 08N	51 59E
Auch Fr.	42	E2	43 40N	0 36E
Auckland NZ	69	E6	36 51S	174 46E
Auden Canada	85	T4	50 14N	87 54W
Augsburg Germany	44	E4	48 21N	10 54E
Augusta Aust.	66	C4	34 19S	115 09E
Augusta USA	87	K3	33 29N	82 00W
Aurangābād India	58	D3	19 52N	75 22E
Aurich Germany	41	F6	53 28N	7 30E
Aurillac Fr.	42	F3	44 56N	2 26E
Austin USA	87	G3	30 18N	97 47W
AUSTRALIA	66/67			
Australian Capital Territory admin. Aust.	67	J3	35 00S	144 00E
AUSTRIA	44	E3/G3		
Autun Fr.	42	G4	46 58N	4 18E
Auxerre Fr.	42	F4	47 48N	3 35E
Avallon Fr.	42	F4	47 30N	3 54E
Aveiro Port.	43	A4	40 38N	8 40W
Avesta Sweden	48	E3	60 09N	16 10E
Avezzano Italy	46	E5	42 02N	13 26E
Avignon Fr.	42	G2	43 56N	4 48E
Avila Sp.	43	C4	40 39N	4 42W
Avilés Sp.	43	C5	43 33N	5 55W
Avranches Fr.	42	D5	48 42N	1 21W
Awaji-shima i. Japan	63	B2/C2	34 30N	134 45E
Awash Ethiopia	77	P3	9 01N	41 10E
Awbāri Libya	77	G7	26 35N	12 46E
Ayacucho Peru	90	C11	13 10S	74 15W
Ayaguz Kazakhstan	54	L6	47 59N	80 27E
Ayamonte Sp.	43	B2	37 13N	7 24W
Ayaviri Peru	90	C11	14 53S	70 35W
Aydin Turkey	49	M2	37 51N	27 51E
Ayers Rock mt. Aust.	66	F5	25 18S	131 18E
'Aynūnah Saudi Arabia	56	C4	28 06N	35 08E
Ayod Sudan	77	M3	8 08N	31 24E
Ayr UK	40	D4	55 28N	4 38W
Ayutthaya Thailand	64	C6	14 20N	100 35E
AZERBAIJAN	49	G2		
Azogues Ecuador	90	B13	2 46S	78 56W
Azuaga Sp.	43	C3	38 16N	5 40W
Azul Argentina	91	F6	36 46S	59 50W

B

Name	Page	Grid	Lat.	Long.
Baarn Neths	41	D5	52 13N	5 16E
Babati Tanzania	79	D2	4 13S	35 45E
Babruysk Belarus	45	P6	53 08N	29 10E
Bacabal Brazil	90	J13	4 15S	44 45W
Bacău Romania	45	N3	46 33N	26 58E
Bac Ninh Vietnam	64	D8	21 10N	106 04E
Bacolod Philippines	65	G6	10 38N	122 58E
Badajoz Sp.	43	B3	38 53N	6 58W
Badalona Sp.	43	G4	41 27N	2 15E
Baden Austria	44	H3	48 01N	16 14E
Baden Switz.	44	D3	47 28N	8 19E
Baden-Baden Germany	41	G1	48 45N	8 15E
Bad Essen Germany	41	G5	52 19N	8 21E
Bad Homburg Germany	41	G3	50 14N	8 37E

Name	Country	Page	Grid	Lat	Long
Bad Honnef	Germany	41	F3	50 38N	7 14E
Bad Iburg	Germany	41	G5	52 10N	8 03E
Bad Ischl	Austria	44	F3	47 43N	13 38E
Bad Kreuznach	Germany	41	F2	49 50N	7 51E
Bad Lippspringe	Germany	41	G4	51 47N	8 48E
Bad Salzuflen	Germany	41	G5	52 05N	8 45E
Baffin Bay	Canada/Greenland	85	X8/Z8	72 00N	65 00W
Baffin Island	Canada	85	U8/W7	68 30N	70 00W
Bafoussam	Cameroon	76	G3	5 31N	10 25E
Bafq	Iran	56	G5	31 35N	55 21E
Bagé	Brazil	91	G7	31 22S	54 06W
Baghdad	Iraq	56	D5	33 20N	44 26E
Baghlān	Afghanistan	57	J6	36 11N	68 44E
BAHAMAS, THE		89	J4		
Baharampur	India	59	K10	24 06N	88 15E
Bahawalpur	Pakistan	58	C5	29 24N	71 47E
Bahía Blanca	Argentina	91	E6	38 45S	62 15W
Bahraich	India	58	E5	27 35N	81 36E
BAHRAIN		57	N9		
Baia Mare	Romania	45	L3	47 39N	23 36E
Baicheng	China	61	M7	45 37N	122 48E
Baie-Comeau tn.	Canada	85	X3	49 12N	68 10W
Baiona	Sp.	43	A5	42 07N	8 51W
Baja California p.	Mexico	88	A6/C4	27 30N	113 00W
Baker	USA	86	C5	44 46N	117 50W
Bakersfield	USA	86	C4	35 25N	119 00W
Baku	Azerbaijan	49	G3	40 22N	49 53E
Balakovo	Russia	54	G7	52 04N	47 46E
Bālā Morghāb	Afghanistan	57	H6	35 35N	63 21E
Balashov	Russia	49	F5	51 31N	43 10E
Balassagyarmat	Hungary	45	J4	48 06N	19 17E
Balboa	Panama	89	J1	8 57N	79 33W
Balclutha	NZ	69	A4	46 14S	169 44E
Balearic Islands	Med. Sea	43	F3/H3	40 00N	2 00E
Baleshwar	India	59	J8	21 30N	86 56E
Bali i.	Indonesia	64	E2/F2	8 30S	115 00E
Balikesir	Turkey	49	C2	39 37N	27 51E
Balikpapan	Indonesia	65	F3	1 15S	116 50E
Balipar	India	59	M11	27 00N	92 30E
Balkhash	Kazakhstan	54	K6	46 50N	74 57E
Ballarat	Aust.	67	H3	37 36S	143 58E
Ballymena	UK	40	C4	54 52N	6 17W
Balsas	Mexico	88	E3	18 00N	99 44W
Bălți	Moldova	45	N3	47 44N	28 41E
Baltimore	USA	87	L4	39 18N	76 38W
Balurghat	India	59	K10	25 12N	88 50E
Balykchy	Kyrgyzstan	60	C6	42 22N	76 11E
Bam	Iran	57	P9	29 07N	58 20E
Bamako	Mali	76	C4	12 40N	7 59W
Bambari	CAR	77	K3	5 40N	20 37E
Bamberg	Germany	44	E4	49 54N	10 54E
Bamenda	Cameroon	76	G3	5 55N	10 09E
Banda Aceh	Indonesia	64	B5	5 30N	95 20E
Bandar-e 'Abbās	Iran	57	P9	27 12N	56 15E
Bandar Khomeyni	Iran	57	M10	30 40N	49 08E
Bandar Seri Begawan	Brunei	64	P11	4 53N	115 00E
Bandirma	Turkey	49	C3	40 21N	27 58E
Bandundu	CDR	78	C7	3 20S	17 24E
Bandung	Indonesia	64	D2	6 57S	107 34E
Banff	Canada	84	M4	51 10N	115 34W
Banfora	Burkina	76	D4	10 36N	4 45W
Bangalore	India	58	D2	12 58N	77 35E
Bangassou	CAR	77	K2	4 41N	22 48E
Bangkok	Thailand	64	C6	13 44N	100 30E
BANGLADESH		59	F4/G4		
Bangor	USA	87	N5	44 49N	68 47W
Bangui	CAR	77	J2	4 23N	18 37E
Banja Luka	Bosnia-Herzegovina	47	G6	44 47N	17 11E
Banjarmasin	Indonesia	64	E3	3 22S	114 33E
Banjul	The Gambia	76	A4	13 28N	16 39W
Bankura	India	59	J9	23 14N	87 04E
Banmi	Pakistan	58	C6	33 00N	70 30E
Banská Bystrica	Slovakia	45	J4	48 44N	19 10E
Banyuwangi	Indonesia	64	E2	8 12S	114 22E
Baoding	China	61	L5	38 54N	115 26E
Baoji	China	61	J4	34 23N	107 16E
Baotou	China	61	J6	40 38N	109 59E
Ba'qūbah	Iraq	56	D5	33 45N	44 40E
Baracaldo	Sp.	43	D5	43 17N	2 59W
Baranavichy	Belarus	45	N6	53 09N	26 00E
Barbacena	Brazil	90	J9	21 13S	43 47W
BARBADOS		88	S11		
Barbastro	Sp.	43	F5	42 02N	0 07E
Barbuda i.	Antigua & Barbuda	88	Q9	17 41N	61 48W
Barcaldine	Aust.	67	J6	23 33S	145 15E
Barcellona	Italy	46	F3	38 10N	15 15E
Barcelona	Sp.	43	G4	41 25N	2 10E
Barcelona	Venezuela	90	E16	10 08N	64 43W
Barcelonnette	Fr.	42	H3	44 24N	6 40E
Barcs	Hungary	45	H2	45 58N	17 30E
Barddhaman	India	59	F4	23 20N	88 00E
Bareilly	India	58	D5	28 20N	79 24E
Barengapara	India	59	L10	25 13N	90 12E
Barga	China	58	E6	30 55N	81 17E
Barharwa	India	59	J10	24 51N	87 49E
Bari	Italy	47	G4	41 07N	16 52E
Barinas	Venezuela	90	C15	8 36N	70 15W
Baripada	India	59	J8	21 56N	86 44E
Barisal	Bangladesh	59	L9	22 41N	90 20E
Bârlad	Romania	45	N3	46 14N	27 40E
Bar-le-Duc	Fr.	42	G4	48 46N	5 10E
Barletta	Italy	46	G4	41 20N	16 17E
Barnaul	Russia	55	L7	53 21N	83 45E
Barnstaple	UK	40	D2	51 05N	4 04W
Barquisimeto	Venezuela	90	D16	10 03N	69 18W
Barra do Corba	Brazil	90	H12	5 30S	45 12W
Barrancabermeja	Col.	90	C15	7 06N	73 54W
Barrancas	Venezuela	90	E15	8 45N	62 13W
Barranquilla	Col.	90	C17	11 10N	74 50W
Barre	USA	87	M5	44 13N	72 31W
Barreiras	Brazil	90	J11	12 09S	44 58W
Barreiro	Port.	43	A3	38 40N	9 05W
Barry	UK	40	E2	51 24N	3 18W
Barstow	USA	86	C3	34 55N	117 01W
Bartlesville	USA	87	G4	36 44N	95 59W
Barysaw	Belarus	45	P7	54 09N	28 30E
Basel	Switz.	44	C3	47 33N	7 36E
Basildon	UK	40	G2	51 34N	0 25W
Basingstoke	UK	40	F2	51 16N	1 05W
Basirhat	India	59	K9	22 39N	88 52E
Bassein	Myanmar	59			
Basse Terre i.	Lesser Antilles	88	Q9	16 10N	61 40W
Basseterre	St. Kitts & Nevis	88	P9	17 18N	62 43W
Bassum	Germany	41	G5	52 51N	8 44E
Bastia	Fr.	42	J2	42 14N	9 26E
Bastogne	Belgium	41	D3	50 00N	5 43E
Bastrop	USA	87	H3	32 49N	91 54W
Bata	Eq. Guinea	76	F2	1 51N	9 49E
Batakan	Indonesia	64	E3	4 03S	114 39E
Batala	India	58	D6	31 48N	75 17E
Batang	China	60	G4	30 02N	99 01E
Batangas	Philippines	65	G6	13 46N	121 01E
Batdâmbâng	Cambodia	64	C6	13 06N	103 13E
Bath	UK	40	E2	51 23N	2 22W
Bathinda	India	58	C6	30 10N	74 58E
Bathurst	Aust.	67	J4	33 27S	149 35E
Bathurst	Canada	85	X3	47 37N	65 40W
Batman	Turkey	49	F2	37 52N	41 02E
Baton Rouge	USA	87	H3	30 30N	91 10W
Batticaloa	Sri Lanka	58	E1	7 43N	81 42E
Battle Creek tn.	USA	87	J5	42 20N	85 21W
Bat'umi	Georgia	49	F3	41 37N	41 36E
Baturaja	Indonesia	64	C3	4 10S	104 10E
Baubau	Indonesia	65	G2	5 30S	122 37E
Bauchi	Nigeria	76	F4	10 16N	9 50E
Bauru	Brazil	90	H9	22 19S	49 07W
Bautzen	Germany	44	G5	51 11N	14 29E
Bayamo	Cuba	89	J4	20 23N	76 39W
Bayeux	Fr.	42	D5	49 16N	0 42W
Bayonne	Fr.	42	D2	43 30N	1 28W
Bayreuth	Germany	44	E4	49 27N	11 35E
Baytown	USA	87	H2	29 43N	94 59W
Baza	Sp.	43	D2	37 30N	2 45W
Beatrice	USA	87	G5	40 17N	96 45W
Beatty	USA	86	C4	36 54N	116 45W
Beaufort	USA	87	K3	32 26N	80 40W
Beaumont	USA	87	H3	30 04N	94 06W
Beaune	Fr.	42	G4	47 02N	4 50E
Beauvais	Fr.	42	F5	49 26N	2 05E
Beaver	USA	84	F7	66 22N	147 30W
Béchar	Algeria	76	D8	31 35N	2 17W
Beckley	USA	87	K4	37 46N	81 12W
Bedford	UK	40	F3	52 08N	0 29W
Beersheba	Israel	56	B5	31 15N	34 47E
Beeville	USA	87	G2	28 25N	97 47W
Behbehān	Iran	57	N10	30 34N	50 18E
Bei'an	China	61	N7	48 16N	126 36E
Beihai	China	61	J2	21 29N	109 10E
Beijing	China	61	L5	39 55N	116 26E
Beilen	Neths	41	E5	52 51N	6 31E
Beira	Mozambique	78	F4	19 49S	34 52E
Beirut	Lebanon	56	C5	33 52N	35 30E
Beiuş	Romania	45	L3	46 40N	22 21E
Beja	Port.	43	B3	38 01N	7 52W
Béja	Tunisia	76	F9	36 52N	9 13E
Bejaïa	Algeria	76	F9	36 49N	5 03E
Béjar	Sp.	43	C4	40 24N	5 45W
BELARUS		49	C5		
Belém	Brazil	90	H13	1 27S	48 29W
Belfast	UK	40	D4	54 35N	5 55W
Belfort	Fr.	42	H4	47 38N	6 52E
Belgaum	India	58	C3	15 54N	74 36E
BELGIUM		41	B3/D3		
Belgorod	Russia	54	F7	50 38N	36 36E
Belgrade	SM	47	J4	44 50N	20 30E
BELIZE		88	G3		
Belize	Belize	88	G3	17 29N	88 10W
Bellac	Fr.	42	E4	46 07N	1 04E
Bellary	India	58	D3	15 11N	76 54E
Bella Vista	Argentina	91	F8	28 31S	59 00W
Bellingham	USA	86	B6	48 45N	122 29W
Bellinzona	Switz.	44	D3	46 12N	9 01E
Bello	Col.	90	B15	6 20N	75 41W
Belmopan	Belize	88	G3	17 13N	88 48W
Belogorsk	Russia	55	Q7	50 55N	128 26E
Belo Horizonte	Brazil	90	J10	19 54S	43 54W
Belyy Yar	Russia	55	L8	58 28N	85 03E
Benavente	Sp.	43	C4	42 00N	5 40W
Bender-Bayla	Somalia	77	R3	9 30N	50 50E
Bendigo	Aust.	67	H3	36 48S	144 21E
Benevento	Italy	46	F4	41 08N	14 46E
Bengbu	China	61	L4	32 56N	117 27E
Benghazi	Libya	77	K8	32 07N	20 04E
Bengkulu	Indonesia	64	C3	3 46S	102 16E
Benguela	Angola	78	B5	12 34S	13 24E
Beni Abbès	Algeria	76	D8	30 11N	2 14W
Benicarló	Sp.	43	F4	40 25N	0 25E
Benidorm	Sp.	43	E3	38 33N	0 09W
Beni Mellal	Morocco	76	C8	32 22N	6 29W
BENIN		76	E4		
Benin City	Nigeria	76	F3	6 19N	5 41E
Beni Suef	Egypt	77	M7	29 05N	31 05E
Benson	USA	86	D3	31 58N	110 19W
Benxi	China	61	M6	41 21N	123 45E
Beppu	Japan	63	B2	33 18N	131 30E
Berber	Sudan	77	M5	18 01N	34 00E
Berbera	Somalia	77	Q4	10 28N	45 02E
Berbérati	CAR	77	J2	4 19N	15 51E
Berck	Fr.	42	E6	50 24N	1 35E
Berdyans'k	Ukraine	49	E4	46 45N	36 47E
Beregovo	Ukraine	45	L4	48 13N	22 39E
Berezovo	Russia	54	J9	63 58N	65 00E
Bérgamo	Italy	46	C6	45 42N	9 40E
Bergen	Norway	48	C6	60 23N	5 20E
Bergerac	Fr.	42	E3	44 50N	0 29E
Bergheim	Germany	41	E3	50 57N	6 38E
Berkåk	Norway	48	D3	62 48N	10 03E
Berlin	Germany	44	F6	52 32N	13 25E
Berlin	USA	87	M5	44 27N	71 13W
Bern	Switz.	44	C3	46 57N	7 26E
Bernalda	Italy	47	G4	40 24N	16 44E
Bertoua	Cameroon	77	G2	4 34N	13 42E
Betanzos	Sp.	43	A5	43 17N	8 13W
Bétaré Oya	Cameroon	77	G3	5 34N	14 09E
Bethlehem	Middle East	56	C5	31 42N	35 12E
Béthune	Fr.	42	F6	50 32N	2 38E
Betroka	Madagascar	78	H3	23 15S	46 07E
Betsiamites	Canada	85	X3	48 56N	68 40W
Betzdorf	Germany	41	F3	50 48N	7 52E
Beveren	Belgium	41	C4	51 13N	4 15E
Beyla	Guinea	76	C3	8 42N	8 39W
Beyneu	Kazakhstan	49	J4	45 18N	55 11E
Béziers	Fr.	42	F2	43 21N	3 13E
Bhadravati	India	58	D2	13 54N	75 38E
Bhagalpur	India	59	F5	25 14N	86 59E
Bhanga	Bangladesh	59	L9	23 24N	89 58E
Bharatpur	India	58	D5	27 14N	77 29E
Bharuch	India	58	C4	21 40N	73 02E
Bhatpara	India	59	K9	22 51N	88 24E
Bhavnagar	India	58	C4	21 46N	72 14E
Bhilwara	India	58	C5	25 23N	74 39E
Bhopal	India	58	D4	23 17N	77 28E
Bhubaneshwar	India	59	B4	20 13N	85 50E
Bhuj	India	58	B4	23 12N	69 54E
Bhusawal	India	58	D4	21 01N	75 50E
BHUTAN		59	G5		
Biała Podlaska	Poland	45	L6	52 03N	23 05E
Białystok	Poland	45	L6	53 09N	23 10E
Biarritz	Fr.	42	D4	43 29N	1 33W
Bibai	Japan	62	D4	43 21N	141 53E
Bida	Nigeria	76	F3	9 06N	5 59E
Biddeford	USA	87	M5	43 29N	70 27W
Biel	Switz.	44	C3	46 27N	8 13E
Bielefeld	Germany	44	D6	52 02N	8 32E
Bielsko-Biała	Poland	45	J4	49 50N	19 00E
Bielsk Podlaski	Poland	45	L6	52 47N	23 11E
Bien Hoa	Vietnam	64	D6	10 58N	106 50E
Biga	Turkey	49	M4	40 13N	27 14E
Bihać	Bosnia-Herzegovina	46	F6	44 49N	15 53E
Biharamulo	Tanzania	79	B3	2 37S	31 20E
Bijapur	India	58	D3	16 47N	75 48E
Bijār	Iran	56	E6	35 52N	47 39E
Bikaner	India	58	C5	28 01N	73 22E
Bilaspur	India	58	E4	22 51N	82 00E
Bila Tserkva	Ukraine	45	Q4	49 49N	30 10E
Bilbao	Sp.	43	D5	43 15N	2 56W
Billings	USA	86	E6	45 47N	108 30W
Biloxi	USA	87	J3	30 24N	88 55W
Binche	Belgium	41	C3	50 25N	4 10E
Bingen	Germany	41	F2	49 58N	7 55E
Binghamton	USA	87	L5	42 06N	75 55W
Bintulu	Malaysia	64	E4	3 10N	113 02E
Biratnagar	Nepal	59	F5	26 27N	87 17E
Birdsville	Aust.	67	G5	25 50S	139 20E
Birjand	Iran	57	E3	32 55N	59 10E
Birkenhead	UK	40	E3	53 24N	3 02W
Birkirkara	Malta	46	P8	35 54N	14 27E
Birmingham	UK	40	F3	52 30N	1 50W
Birmingham	USA	87	J3	33 30N	86 55W
Birobidzhan	Russia	55	R6	48 49N	132 54E
Birzebbuga	Malta	46	Q8	35 50N	14 31E
Bishkek	Kyrgyzstan	54	K5	42 53N	74 46E
Bishnupur	India	59	J9	23 05N	87 18E
Biskra	Algeria	76	F8	34 50N	5 41E
Bismarck	USA	86	F6	46 50N	100 48W
Bissau	Guinea-Bissau	76	A4	11 52N	15 39W
Bistriţa	Romania	45	M3	47 08N	24 30E
Bitburg	Germany	41	E2	49 58N	6 32E
Bitola	FYROM	47	J4	41 01N	21 21E
Biysk	Russia	55	L7	52 35N	85 16E
Bizerte	Tunisia	76	F9	37 18N	9 52E
Blackall	Aust.	67	J6	24 23S	145 27E
Black Diamond	Canada	84	N4	50 45N	114 12W
Blackpool	Canada	84	L4	51 33N	120 07W
Blackpool	UK	40	E3	53 50N	3 03W
Black River tn.	Jamaica	89	U14	18 02N	77 52W
Blackwell	USA	87	G4	36 47N	97 18W
Blagoevgrad	Bulgaria	47	K5	42 01N	23 05E
Blagoveshchensk	Russia	55	Q7	50 19N	127 30E
Blankenberge	Belgium	41	B4	51 19N	3 08E
Blantyre	Malawi	78	F4	15 46S	35 00E
Blenheim	NZ	69	H3	36 48S	144 21E
Blida	Algeria	76	E9	36 30N	2 50E
Bloemfontein	RSA	78	E2	29 07S	26 14E
Blois	Fr.	42	E4	47 36N	1 20E
Bloomington	USA	87	J4	39 10N	86 31W
Bloomington	USA	87	J5	40 29N	89 00W
Bludenz	Austria	44	D3	47 10N	9 50E
Bluefield	USA	87	K4	37 14N	81 17W
Bluff	NZ	69	B1	46 36S	168 20E
Blumenau	Brazil	90	H8	26 55S	49 07W
Blyth	UK	40	F4	55 07N	1 30W
Blythe	USA	86	D3	33 38N	114 35W
Bo	Sierra Leone	76	B3	7 58N	11 45W
Boa Vista	Brazil	90	E14	2 49N	60 40W
Böblingen	Germany	41	H1	48 41N	9 00E
Bobo Dioulasso	Burkina	76	D4	11 11N	4 18W
Bocholt	Germany	41	E4	51 49N	6 37E
Bochum	Germany	44	C5	51 28N	7 11E
Boden	Sweden	48	F4	65 50N	21 44E
Bodø	Norway	48	D4	67 18N	14 26E
Bogalusa	USA	87	J3	30 56N	89 53W
Bogor	Indonesia	64	D2	6 34S	106 45E
Bogotá	Col.	90	C14	4 38N	74 05W
Boise	USA	86	C5	43 38N	116 12W
Boise City	USA	86	F4	36 44N	102 31W
Bokaro	India	59	F4	23 46N	85 55E
Bolesławiec	Poland	45	G5	51 16N	15 34E
Bolhrad	Ukraine	45	P2	45 42N	28 3…
BOLIVIA		90	D10/E10		
Bollnäs	Sweden	48	E3	61 20N	16 2…
Bologna	Italy	46	D6	44 30N	11 2…
Bolton	UK	40	E3	53 35N	2 2…
Bolzano	Italy	46	D7	46 30N	11 2…
Boma	CDR	78	B6	5 50S	13 0…
Bondo	CDR	77	K2	1 22N	23 5…
Bongor	Chad	77	J4	10 18N	15 2…
Bonifacio	Corsica	42	J1	41 23N	9 1…
Bonn	Germany	44	C5	50 44N	7 0…
Boorama	Somalia	77	P3	9 56N	43 1…
Boppard	Germany	41	F3	50 14N	7 3…
Bor	Sudan	77	M3	6 18N	31 3…
Borås	Sweden	48	D2	57 44N	12 5…
Borāzjan	Iran	57	N9	29 16N	51 1…
Bordeaux	Fr.	42	D3	44 50N	0 3…
Borgholm	Sweden	48	E2	56 51N	16 4…
Borisoglebsk	Russia	49	F5	51 23N	42 0…
Borken	Germany	41	E4	51 50N	6 5…
Borken	Germany	41	H4	51 02N	9 1…
Borkum	Germany	41	E6	53 35N	6 4…
Borlänge	Sweden	48	E3	60 29N	15 2…
Borneo i.	Indonesia/Malaysia	64/65	D3/F5	1 00N	113 0…
Bornholm i.	Denmark	48	D2	55 02N	15 0…
Borşa	Romania	45	M3	47 39N	24 4…
Borūjerd	Iran	56	E5	33 55N	48 4…
Borzya	Russia	55	P7	50 24N	116 3…
BOSNIA-HERZEGOVINA		47	G6/H6		
Bossangoa	CAR	77	J3	6 27N	17 2…
Boston	UK	40	F3	52 29N	0 0…
Boston	USA	87	M5	42 20N	71 0…
Bothnia, Gulf of	Finland/Sweden	48	E3/F3	61 00N	19 1…
Botoşani	Romania	45	N3	47 44N	26 4…
BOTSWANA		78	D3/E3		
Bottrop	Germany	44	C5	51 31N	6 5…
Bouaké	Côte d'Ivoire	76	D3	7 42N	5 0…
Bouar	CAR	77	J3	5 58N	15 3…
Bouârfa	Morocco	76	D8	32 30N	1 5…
Bougouni	Mali	76	C4	11 25N	7 2…
Bouillon	Belgium	41	D2	49 47N	5 0…
Boulder	USA	86	E5	40 02N	105 1…
Boulogne-sur-Mer	Fr.	42	E6	50 43N	1 3…
Bourem	Mali	76	D5	16 59N	0 2…
Bourges	Fr.	42	F4	47 05N	2 2…
Bourke	Aust.	67	J4	30 09S	145 5…
Bournemouth	UK	40	F2	50 43N	1 5…
Bou Saâda	Algeria	76	E9	35 10N	4 0…
Bousso	Chad	77	J4	10 32N	16 4…
Bowman	USA	86	F6	46 11N	103 2…
Boxmeer	Neths	41	D4	51 39N	5 5…
Boxtel	Neths	41	D4	51 36N	5 5…
Bozeman	USA	86	D6	45 40N	111 0…
Bozoum	CAR	77	J3	6 16N	16 2…
Brad	Romania	45	L3	46 07N	22 2…
Bradenton	USA	87	K2	27 29N	82 3…
Bradford	UK	40	F3	53 48N	1 4…
Braga	Port.	43	A4	41 32N	8 2…
Bragança	Brazil	90	H13	1 02S	46 4…
Bragança	Port.	43	B4	41 47N	6 4…
Brahman Baria	Bangladesh	59	L9	23 58N	91 0…
Brahmapur	India	60	D1	19 21N	84 4…
Brahmaputra r.	India/Bangladesh	59	G5	26 40N	92 0…
Brăila	Romania	45	N2	45 17N	27 5…
Brandenburg	Germany	44	F6	52 25N	12 3…
Brandon	Canada	85	R3	49 50N	99 5…
Brasileia	Brazil	90	D11	10 59S	68 4…
Brasília	Brazil	90	H10	15 45S	47 5…
Braşov	Romania	45	M2	45 39N	25 3…
Bratislava	Slovakia	45	H4	48 10N	17 1…
Bratsk	Russia	55	N8	56 20N	101 1…
Braunau	Austria	44	F4	48 16N	13 0…
Braunschweig	Germany	44	E6	52 15N	10 3…
Brawley	USA	86	C3	32 59N	115 3…
Bray	Irish Rep.	40	C3	53 12N	6 0…
BRAZIL		90	F11/H11		
Brazzaville	Congo	78	C7	4 14S	15…
Breda	Neths	41	C4	51 35N	4…
Bregenz	Austria	44	D3	47 31N	9…
Bremen	Germany	44	D6	53 05N	8…
Bremerhaven	Germany	44	D6	53 33N	8…
Bremerton	USA	86	B6	47 34N	122…
Bremervörde	Germany	44	H6	53 29N	9…
Brenham	USA	87	G3	30 09N	96…
Brescia	Italy	46	D6	45 33N	10…
Brest	Belarus	49	C5	52 08N	23…
Brest	Fr.	42	B5	48 23N	4…
Bria	CAR	77	K3	6 32N	22…
Briançon	Fr.	42	H3	44 53N	6…
Bridgeport	USA	87	M5	41 12N	73…
Bridgetown	Barbados	88	S11	13 06N	59…
Brienz	Switz.	44	D3	46 46N	8…
Briey	Fr.	42	G5	49 15N	5…
Brig	Switz.	44	C3	46 19N	8…
Brighton	UK	40	F2	50 50N	0…
Brignoles	Fr.	42	H2	43 25N	6…
Brilon	Germany	41	G4	51 23N	8…
Brindisi	Italy	47	G4	40 37N	17…
Brisbane	Aust.	67	K5	27 30S	153…
Bristol	UK	40	E2	51 27N	2…
British Columbia province	Canada	84	K4/K5	56 50N	637…
Brive-la-Gaillarde	Fr.	42	E3	45 09N	…
Brno	Czech Rep.	45	H4	49 13N	16…
Brockton	USA	87	M5	42 06N	71…
Brody	Ukraine	45	M5	50 05N	25…
Broken Hill tn.	Aust.	67	H4	31 57S	141…
Brønnøysund	Norway	48	D4	65 38N	12…
Brookings	USA	87	G5	44 19N	96…
Brooks	Canada	84	N4	50 35N	111…
Broome	Aust.	66	D7	17 58S	122…
Browning	USA	86	D6	48 33N	113…

rownsville USA 87 G2 25 54N 97 30W
rownwood USA 86 G3 31 42N 98 59W
ruchsal Germany 41 G2 49 07N 8 35E
ruck an der Mur Austria 44 47 25N 15 17E
rugg Switz. 44 D3 47 29N 8 13E
rugge Belgium 41 B4 51 13N 3 14E
RUNEI 64 N10/Q10
runico Italy 46 D7 46 47N 11 57E
runssum Neths 41 50 57N 5 59E
runswick USA 87 K3 31 09N 81 30W
russels Belgium 41 C3 50 50N 4 21E
ryan USA 87 G3 30 41N 96 24W
ryansk Russia 54 F7 53 15N 34 09E
rzeg Poland 45 H5 50 52N 17 27E
ucaramanga Col. 90 C15 7 08N 73 10W
uchanan Liberia 76 B3 5 57N 10 02W
ucharest Romania 45 N2 44 25N 26 07E
uckeburg Germany 41 H5 52 16N 9 04E
udapest Hungary 45 J3 47 30N 19 03E
udjala CDR 77 J2 2 38N 19 48E
uea Cameroon 76 F2 4 09N 9 13E
uenaventura Col. 90 B14 3 54N 77 02W
uenaventura Mexico 88 C5 29 50N 107 30W
uenos Aires Argentina 91 F7 34 40S 58 30W
uffalo USA 87 L5 42 52N 78 55W
ugembe Uganda 79 C5 0 29N 33 15E
ugene Tanzania 79 B4 1 35S 31 08E
ugibba Malta 46 P8 35 57N 14 25E
uguľ'ma Russia 49 H5 54 33N 52 48E
uhuşi Romania 45 N3 46 44N 26 41E
ujumbura Burundi 79 A3 3 22S 29 19E
ukama CDR 78 E6 9 13S 25 52E
ukene Tanzania 79 C2 4 14S 32 53E
ukhara Uzbekistan 54 J4 39 47N 64 26E
ukittinggi Indonesia 64 C3 0 18S 100 20E
ukoba Tanzania 79 B4 1 19S 31 49E
ulawayo Zimbabwe 78 E3 20 10S 28 43E
ULGARIA 47 K5/M5
umba CDR 77 K2 2 10N 22 30E
unbury Aust. 66 C4 33 20S 115 34E
unda Tanzania 79 C4 2 03S 33 52E
undaberg Aust. 67 K6 24 50S 152 21E
undibugyo Uganda 79 B5 0 38N 30 02E
ungoma Kenya 79 D5 0 34N 34 34E
uôn Mê Thuột Vietnam 64 D6 12 41N 108 02E
ura Kenya 79 F4 1 06S 39 58E
uraydah Saudi Arabia 56 D4 26 20N 43 59E
urbach Germany 41 G3 50 45N 8 05E
urdur Turkey 49 D2 37 44N 30 17E
urgas Bulgaria 47 M5 42 30N 27 29E
urgos Sp. 43 D5 42 21N 3 41W
urhanpur India 58 D4 21 18N 76 08E
URKINA 76 D4
urnie Aust. 67 J2 41 03S 145 55E
ursa Turkey 49 C3 40 12N 29 04E
URUNDI 79 A3/B3
urwell USA 86 G5 41 48N 99 09W
ushehr Iran 57 N9 28 57N 50 52E
ushenyi Uganda 79 B4 0 31S 30 11E
usia Uganda 79 D5 0 28N 34 06E
ussum Neths 41 D5 52 16N 5 09E
uta CDR 77 K2 2 49N 24 50E
utare Rwanda 79 A3 2 35S 29 44E
ute USA 86 D6 46 00N 112 31W
utterworth Malaysia 64 C5 5 24N 100 22E
utuan Philippines 65 H5 8 56N 125 31E
uulobarde Somalia 77 Q2 3 50N 45 33E
uwenge Uganda 79 C5 0 45N 33 11E
ydgoszcz Poland 45 H6 53 16N 18 00E
ylot Island Canada 85 V8 73 13N 78 34W
ytom Poland 45 J5 50 21N 18 51E

abanatuan Philippines 65 G7 15 30N 120 58E
abano Canada 85 X3 47 40N 68 56W
abimas Venezuela 90 C16 10 26N 71 27W
abinda admin. Angola 78 B6 5 30S 12 20E
abo Brazil 90 K12 8 16S 35 00W
abo Catoche c. Mexico 88 G4 21 38N 87 08W
abo de Hornos c. Chile 91 D2 56 00S 67 15W
abo de São Vicente c. Port. 43 A2 37 01N 8 59W
abo Falso c. Mexico 88 B4 22 50N 110 00W
abo Finisterre c. Sp. 43 A5 42 52N 9 16W
aborca Mexico 88 B6 30 42N 112 10W
abo San Juan c. Argentina 91 E7 54 45S 63 46W
ačak SM 47 J5 43 54N 20 22E
aceres Sp. 43 B3 39 29N 6 23W
achoeira Brazil 90 K11 12 35S 38 59W
achoeira do Sol Brazil 91 G7 30 03S 52 52W
adiz Philippines 65 G6 10 57N 123 18E
adiz Sp. 43 B2 36 32N 6 18W
aen Fr. 42 D5 49 11N 0 22W
agayan de Oro Philippines 65 G6 8 29N 124 40E
agliari Italy 46 C3 39 13N 9 08E
aguas Puerto Rico 89 L3 18 41N 66 04W
ahors Fr. 42 E3 44 28N 0 26E
airns Aust. 67 J7 16 51N 145 43E
airo Egypt 77 M7 30 00N 31 15E
ajamarca Peru 90 B12 7 09S 78 32W
ajàzeiras Brazil 90 K12 6 52S 38 31W
akovec Croatia 44 G7 46 24N 16 26E
alabar Nigeria 76 F2 4 56N 8 22E
alahorra Sp. 43 E6 46 19N 1 58W
alais Fr. 42 E6 50 57N 1 52E
alama Chile 90 D9 22 30S 68 55W
alamar Col. 90 C16 10 16N 74 55W
alapan Philippines 65 G6 13 23N 121 10E
alatayud Sp. 43 E4 41 21N 1 39W
albayog Philippines 65 G6 12 04N 124 38E
alçoene Brazil 90 G14 2 30N 50 55W
aldwell USA 86 C5 43 39N 116 40W
algary Canada 84 N4 51 05N 114 05W
ali Col. 90 B14 3 24N 76 30W

Calicut India 58 D2 11 15N 75 45E
Caliente USA 86 D4 37 36N 114 31W
California state USA 86 C4 35 00N 119 00W
Callao Peru 90 B11 12 05S 77 08W
Calvi Corsica 42 J2 42 34N 8 44E
Calvinia RSA 78 C1 31 25S 19 47E
CAMBODIA 64 C6/D6
Cambrai Fr. 42 F6 50 10N 3 14E
Cambridge NZ 69 E6 37 53S 175 28E
Cambridge UK 40 G3 52 12N 0 07E
CAMEROON 76 G3
Cametá Brazil 90 H13 2 12S 49 30W
Camiri Bolivia 90 E9 20 08S 63 33W
Camocim Brazil 90 J13 2 55S 40 50W
Campbell River tn. Canada 84 K3 50 00N 125 18W
Campbellton Canada 85 X3 48 00N 66 30W
Campeche Mexico 88 F3 19 50N 90 30W
Câmpina Romania 45 M2 45 08N 25 44E
Campina Grande Brazil 90 K12 7 15S 35 50W
Campinas Brazil 90 H9 22 54S 47 06W
Campoalegre Col. 90 B14 2 49N 75 19W
Campo Grande Brazil 90 G9 20 24S 54 35W
Campo Mourão Brazil 90 G9 24 01S 52 24W
Campos Brazil 90 J9 21 46S 41 21W
Câmpulung Romania 45 M2 45 16N 25 02E
Cam Rahn Vietnam 64 D6 11 54N 109 14E
CANADA 84/85
Canakkale Turkey 49 C3 40 09N 26 25E
Canal du Midi Fr. 42 F2 43 20N 2 00E
Canary Islands Sp. 76 A7/B7 28 30N 15 10W
Canaveral, Cape USA 87 K2 28 28N 80 28W
Canberra Aust. 67 J3 35 18S 149 08E
Cancún Mexico 88 G4 21 09N 86 45W
Cangzhou China 61 L5 38 19N 116 54E
Canmore Canada 84 M4 51 07N 115 18W
Cannanore India 58 D2 11 53N 75 23E
Cannes Fr. 42 H2 43 33N 7 00E
Canôas Brazil 91 G8 28 55S 51 10W
Canso Canada 85 Y3 45 20N 61 00W
Canterbury UK 40 G2 51 17N 1 05E
Can Tho Vietnam 64 D6 10 03N 105 46E
Canton USA 87 K5 40 48N 81 23W
Cape Town RSA 78 C1 33 56S 18 28E
Cape York Peninsula Aust. 67 H8 12 30S 142 30E
Cap-Haïtien Haiti 89 K3 19 47N 72 17W
Capri i. Italy 46 F4 40 33N 14 15E
Caprivi Strip Namibia 78 D4 17 30S 27 50E
Cap Vert c. Senegal 76 A4 14 43N 17 33W
Caracal Romania 45 M2 44 07N 24 18E
Caracas Venezuela 90 D16 10 35N 66 56W
Caransebes Romania 45 L2 45 23N 22 13E
Caratinga Brazil 90 J10 19 50S 42 06W
Carcassonne Fr. 42 F2 43 13N 2 21E
Carcross Canada 84 J6 60 11N 134 41W
Cárdenas Mexico 88 E4 22 00N 99 41W
Cardiff UK 40 E2 51 30N 3 13W
Carei Romania 45 L3 47 40N 22 28E
Cariacica Brazil 90 J10 20 15S 40 23W
Caribbean Sea Central America 89 J3/L3 15 00N 75 00W
Caripito Venezuela 90 E16 10 07N 63 07W
Carlisle UK 40 E4 54 54N 2 55W
Carmacks Canada 84 H6 62 04N 136 21W
Carmarthen UK 40 D2 51 51N 4 20W
Carmen Col. 90 B15 9 46N 75 06W
Carnarvon Aust. 66 B6 24 51S 113 45E
Carnot CAR 77 J2 4 59N 15 56E
Carnsore Point Rol 40 C3 52 10N 6 22W
Carpathians mts. Europe 45 J4/M3 49 00N 22 00E
Carpentras Fr. 42 G3 44 03N 5 03E
Carson City USA 86 C4 39 10N 119 46W
Cartagena Col. 90 B16 10 24N 75 33W
Cartago Costa Rica 89 H1 9 50N 83 52W
Caruaru Brazil 90 K12 8 15S 35 55W
Carúpano Venezuela 90 E16 10 39N 63 14W
Casablanca Morocco 76 C8 33 39N 7 35W
Casa Grande USA 86 D3 32 52N 111 46W
Cascais Port. 43 A3 38 41N 9 25W
Cascavel Brazil 90 K13 4 10S 38 15W
Caserta Italy 46 F4 41 04N 14 20E
Casper USA 86 E5 42 50N 106 20W
Caspian Sea Asia 49 G3/H3 41 00N 50 00E
Cassino Italy 46 E4 41 29N 13 50E
Castellane Fr. 42 H2 43 50N 6 30E
Castellón de la Plana Sp. 43 E3 39 59N 0 03W
Castelnaudary Fr. 42 E2 43 18N 1 57E
Castelo Branco Port. 43 B3 39 50N 7 30W
Castelvetrano Italy 46 E2 37 41N 12 47E
Castlebar Rol 40 B3 53 52N 9 17W
Castres Fr. 42 F2 43 36N 2 14E
Castricum Neths 41 C5 52 33N 4 40E
Castries St. Lucia 88 R12 14 02N 60 59W
Castrovillari Italy 46 G3 39 48N 16 12E
Catània Italy 46 F2 37 31N 15 06E
Catanzaro Italy 47 G3 38 54N 16 36E
Catarman Philippines 65 G6 12 29N 124 35E
Cat Island Bahamas 89 J4 24 30N 75 30W
Caucaia Brazil 90 K13 3 44S 38 45W
Caucasus mts. Asia 49 F3/G3 43 00N 43 00E
Caxias Brazil 90 J13 4 53S 43 20W
Caxias do Sul Brazil 91 G8 29 14S 51 10W
Cayenne French Guiana 90 G14 4 55N 52 18W
Cebu Philippines 65 G6 10 17N 123 56E
Cecina Italy 46 D5 43 18N 10 31E
Cedar City USA 86 D4 37 40N 113 04W
Cedar Rapids tn. USA 87 H5 41 59N 91 39W
Ceduna Aust. 66 F4 32 07S 133 42E
Cefalù Italy 46 F3 38 03N 14 03E
Cegléd Hungary 45 J3 47 10N 19 47E
Celaya Mexico 88 D4 20 32N 100 48W
Celje Slovenia 46 F7 46 15N 15 16E
Celle Germany 44 E6 52 37N 10 05E

CENTRAL AFRICAN REPUBLIC 77 J3/K3
Cergy-Pontoise Fr. 42 F5 49 02N 2 04E
Cerignola Italy 46 F4 41 16N 15 54E
Cerro de Pasco Peru 90 B11 10 43S 76 15W
Cesena Italy 46 E6 44 09N 12 15E
Cetraro Italy 46 F3 39 32N 15 57E
Ceuta territory Sp. 43 C1 35 53N 5 19W
Chachapoyas Peru 90 B12 6 13S 77 54W
CHAD 77 J4/K4
Chāh Bahār Iran 57 H4 25 16N 60 41E
Chai Nat Thailand 64 C7 15 12N 100 00E
Chalkida Greece 47 K3 38 28N 23 36E
Châlons-sur-Marne Fr. 42 G5 48 58N 4 22E
Chalon-sur-Saône Fr. 42 G4 46 47N 4 51E
Chaman Pakistan 58 B6 30 55N 66 27E
Chambéry Fr. 42 G3 45 34N 5 55E
Chamonix Fr. 42 H3 45 55N 6 52E
Champaign USA 87 J5 40 07N 88 14W
Champotón Mexico 88 F3 19 20N 90 43W
Chānaral Chile 90 C8 26 23S 70 40W
Chandigarh India 58 D6 30 44N 76 54E
Chandpur Bangladesh 59 L9 23 15N 90 40E
Chandrapur India 58 D3 19 58N 79 21E
Changara Mozambique 78 F3 16 50S 33 17E
Changchun China 61 N6 43 53N 125 20E
Changde China 61 K3 29 03N 111 35E
Changi Singapore 65 T15 1 23N 103 59E
Changsha China 61 K3 28 10N 113 00E
Changwon South Korea 63 A3 35 14N 128 37E
Changzhi China 61 K5 36 05N 113 12E
Changzhou China 61 M4 31 39N 120 45E
Chaniá Greece 47 L1 35 31N 24 01E
Channel Islands British Isles 40 E1 49 30N 2 30W
Chanthaburi Thailand 64 C6 12 35N 102 08E
Chaoyang China 61 M6 41 36N 120 25E
Chaozhou China 61 L2 23 42N 116 36E
Chapecó Brazil 90 G8 27 14S 52 41W
Chapleau Canada 85 U3 47 50N 83 24W
Chardzhev Turkmenistan 54 J4 39 09N 63 34E
Charikār Afghanistan 57 J3 35 00N 69 11E
Charleroi Belgium 41 C3 50 25N 4 27E
Charles Canada 85 Q5 55 33N 101 01W
Charleston USA 87 L3 32 48N 79 58W
Charleville USA 87 J5 26 24S 146 14E
Charleville-Mézières Fr. 42 G5 49 46N 4 43E
Charlotte USA 87 K4 35 03N 80 50W
Charlottesville USA 87 L4 38 02N 78 29W
Charlottetown Canada 85 Y3 46 14N 63 09W
Charters Towers Aust. 67 J6 20 02S 146 20E
Chartres Fr. 42 F5 48 27N 1 30E
Châteaubriant Fr. 42 D4 47 43N 1 22W
Châteauroux Fr. 42 E4 46 49N 1 41E
Château-Thierry Fr. 42 F5 49 03N 3 24E
Châtelet Belgium 41 C3 50 24N 4 32E
Châtellerault Fr. 42 E4 46 49N 0 33E
Chatham Canada 85 U2 42 24N 82 11W
Châtillon-sur-Seine Fr. 42 G4 47 52N 4 35E
Chattanooga USA 87 J4 35 02N 85 18W
Chaumont Fr. 42 G5 48 07N 5 08E
Cheboksary Russia 54 G8 56 08N 47 12E
Chechon South Korea 63 A3 37 05N 128 09E
Cheju South Korea 63 A2 33 31N 126 29E
Chelm Poland 45 L5 51 08N 23 29E
Chelmsford UK 40 G2 51 44N 0 28E
Cheltenham UK 40 E2 51 54N 2 04W
Chelyabinsk Russia 54 J8 55 12N 61 25E
Chemnitz Germany 44 F5 50 50N 12 55E
Chengde China 61 L6 40 59N 117 52E
Chengdu China 61 H4 30 37N 104 06E
Chennai India 58 E2 13 05N 80 18E
Cherbourg Fr. 42 D5 49 38N 1 37W
Cheremkhovo Russia 55 N7 53 08N 103 01E
Cherepovets Russia 54 F8 59 09N 37 50E
Cherkasy Ukraine 49 D4 49 27N 32 04E
Chernihiv Ukraine 45 Q5 51 30N 31 18E
Chernivtsi Ukraine 45 M4 48 19N 25 52E
Chernyakhovsk Russia 48 F1 54 36N 21 48E
Cherokee USA 87 G5 42 45N 95 32W
Chervonograd Ukraine 45 M5 50 25N 24 10E
Chesapeake USA 87 L4 36 45N 76 15W
Chester UK 40 E3 53 12N 2 54W
Chetumal Mexico 88 G3 18 30N 88 17W
Chetwynd Canada 84 L5 56 30N 122 00W
Cheyenne USA 86 F5 41 08N 104 50W
Chiai Taiwan 61 M2 23 09N 120 11E
Chiang Mai Thailand 64 B7 18 48N 98 59E
Chiba Japan 63 D3 35 38N 140 07E
Chibougamau Canada 85 W3 49 56N 74 24W
Chicago USA 87 J5 41 50N 87 45W
Chiclayo Peru 90 B12 6 47S 79 47W
Chico USA 86 B4 39 46N 121 50W
Chieti Italy 46 F5 42 21N 14 10E
Chihuahua Mexico 88 C5 28 40N 106 06W
CHILE 90/91 C5/C8
Chile Chico Chile 91 C4 46 34S 71 44W
Chillán Chile 91 C4 36 37S 72 10W
Chilliwack Canada 84 L3 49 06N 121 56W
Chilpancingo Mexico 88 E3 17 33N 99 30W
Chilumba Malawi 78 F5 10 25S 34 18E
Chilung Taiwan 61 M3 25 10N 121 43E
Chimborazo mt. Ecuador 90 B13 1 29S 78 52W
Chimbote Peru 90 B12 9 04S 78 34W
CHINA 60/61
Chinchilla Aust. 67 K5 26 42S 150 35E
Chinde Mozambique 78 G4 18 35S 36 28E
Chindo South Korea 63 A2 34 28N 126 16E
Chingola Zambia 78 E5 12 31S 27 53E
Chinju South Korea 63 A3 35 10N 128 06E
Chioggia Italy 46 E6 45 13N 12 17E
Chios Greece 47 M3 38 23N 26 07E
Chipata Zambia 78 F5 13 40S 32 42E
Chiquimula Guatemala 88 G2 14 48N 89 32W
Chirchik Uzbekistan 54 J5 41 28N 69 31E

Chiromo Malawi 78 G4 16 33S 35 10E
Chisasibi Canada 85 V4 53 50N 79 01W
Chisinău Moldova 45 P3 47 00N 28 50E
Chita Russia 55 P7 52 03N 113 35E
Chittagong Bangladesh 59 L9 22 20N 91 48E
Chittoor India 58 D2 13 13N 79 06E
Chojnice Poland 45 H6 53 42N 17 32E
Cholet Fr. 42 D4 47 04N 0 53W
Choluteca Honduras 88 G2 13 15N 87 10W
Chonan South Korea 63 A3 36 50N 127 09E
Chon Buri Thailand 64 C6 13 24N 100 59E
Chongjin North Korea 61 N6 41 50N 129 55E
Chongju South Korea 63 A3 36 39N 127 27E
Chongqing China 61 J3 29 30N 106 35E
Chonju South Korea 63 A3 35 50N 127 50E
Chornobyl Ukraine 45 Q5 51 17N 30 15E
Christchurch NZ 69 D3 43 32S 172 38E
Chu Kazakhstan 60 B6 43 36N 73 43E
Chudovo Russia 49 D6 59 08N 31 41E
Chulucanas Peru 90 A12 5 08S 80 10W
Chumphon Thailand 64 B6 10 30N 99 11E
Chunchon South Korea 63 A3 37 56N 127 40E
Chunchura India 59 K9 22 55N 88 15E
Chungju South Korea 63 A3 36 59N 127 53E
Chur Switz. 44 D3 46 52N 9 32E
Churchill Canada 85 S5 58 45N 94 00W
Churchill Falls tn. Canada 85 Y4 53 35N 64 00W
Ciechenów Poland 45 K6 52 52N 20 38E
Ciénaga Col. 90 C16 11 01N 74 15W
Cienfuegos Cuba 89 H4 22 10N 80 27W
Cieza Sp. 43 E3 38 14N 1 25W
Cimislia Moldova 45 P3 46 30N 28 50E
Cincinnati USA 87 K4 39 10N 83 30W
Cirebon Indonesia 64 D2 6 46S 108 33E
Cirò Marina Italy 47 G3 39 22N 17 04E
Cisco USA 86 G3 32 23N 98 59W
Cisneros Col. 90 B15 6 32N 75 04W
Citlaltépetl mt. Mexico 88 E3 19 00N 97 18W
Ciucea Romania 45 L3 46 58N 22 50E
Ciudad Acuña Mexico 88 D5 29 20N 100 58W
Ciudad Bolívar Venezuela 90 E15 8 06N 63 36W
Ciudad del Este Paraguay 90 G8 25 32S 54 34W
Ciudad Guayana Venezuela 90 E15 8 22N 62 37W
Ciudad Juárez Mexico 88 C6 31 42N 106 29W
Ciudad Lerdo Mexico 88 D5 25 34N 103 30W
Ciudad Madero Mexico 88 E4 22 19N 97 50W
Ciudad Obregón Mexico 88 C5 27 28N 109 59W
Ciudad Real Sp. 43 D3 38 59N 3 55W
Ciudad Rodrigo Sp. 43 B4 40 36N 6 33W
Civitavecchia Italy 46 D5 42 05N 11 47E
Cizre Turkey 49 F2 37 21N 42 11E
Clarenville Canada 85 AA3 48 10N 54 00W
Clarksburg USA 87 K4 39 16N 80 22W
Clark's Harbour Canada 85 X2 43 25N 65 38W
Clarksville USA 87 J4 36 31N 87 21W
Clearwater USA 87 K2 27 57N 82 48W
Clermont-Ferrand Fr. 42 F3 45 47N 3 05E
Cleveland USA 87 K5 43 15N 75 50W
Clonmel Rol 40 C3 52 21N 7 42W
Cloppenburg Germany 41 D5 52 52N 8 02E
Clovis USA 86 F3 34 14N 103 13W
Cluj-Napoca Romania 45 L3 46 47N 23 37E
Clydebank UK 40 D4 55 54N 4 24W
Coatepec Mexico 88 E3 19 29N 96 59W
Coaticook Canada 85 W3 45 08N 71 40W
Coatzacoalcos Mexico 88 F3 18 10N 94 25W
Cobija Bolivia 90 D11 11 01S 68 45W
Coburg Germany 44 E5 50 15N 10 58E
Cochabamba Bolivia 90 D10 17 26S 66 10W
Cochin India 58 D1 9 56N 76 15E
Cochrane Canada 85 U3 49 04N 81 02W
Codajás Brazil 90 E13 3 55S 62 00W
Codó Brazil 90 J13 4 28S 43 51W
Coevorden Neths 41 E5 52 39N 6 45E
Cognac Fr. 42 D3 45 42N 0 19W
Coihaique Chile 91 C4 45 35S 72 08W
Coimbatore India 58 D2 11 00N 76 57E
Coimbra Port. 43 A4 40 12N 8 25W
Colchester UK 40 G2 51 54N 0 54E
Coleman Canada 84 N3 49 38N 114 28W
Coleraine UK 40 C4 55 08N 6 40W
Colima Mexico 88 D3 19 14N 103 41W
College USA 87 F6 64 54N 147 55W
Collie Aust. 66 C4 33 20S 116 06E
Colmar Fr. 42 H5 48 05N 7 21E
Cologne Germany 44 C5 50 56N 6 57E
COLOMBIA 90 C14
Colombo Sri Lanka 58 D1 6 55N 79 52E
Colorado state USA 86 E4/F4 39 00N 106 00W
Colorado Springs tn. USA 86 F4 38 50N 104 50W
Columbia USA 87 K3 34 00N 81 00W
Columbus USA 87 K3 39 59N 84 59W
Columbus USA 87 K5 39 59N 83 03W
Comacchio Italy 46 E6 44 42N 12 11E
Comilla Bangladesh 59 L9 23 28N 91 10E
Comino i. Malta 46 P9 36 01N 14 20E
Comitán Mexico 88 F3 16 18N 92 09W
Como Italy 46 C6 45 48N 9 05E
Comorin, Cape India 58 Q17 8 04N 77 35E
COMOROS 78 H5
Compiègne Fr. 42 F5 49 25N 2 50E
Comrat Moldova 45 P3 46 18N 28 40E
Conakry Guinea 76 B3 9 30N 13 43W
Concepción Chile 91 C4 36 50S 73 03W
Concepción Mexico 88 D4 24 38N 101 25W
Concepción Paraguay 90 F9 23 22S 57 26W
Concord USA 87 M5 43 13N 71 34W
Concordia Argentina 91 F7 31 25S 58 00W
Concordia USA 86 G4 39 35N 97 39W
Condom Fr. 42 E3 43 58N 0 23E
Conegliano Italy 46 E6 45 53N 12 18E
CONGO 76 C7
CONGO DEMOCRATIC REPUBLIC 78 D7/E7

Place	Page	Grid	Lat.	Long.
Connecticut state USA	87	M5	4100N	7300W
Constanța Romania	45	P2	4412N	2840E
Constantine Algeria	76	F9	3622N	640E
Cook, Mount NZ	69	C3	4336S	17009E
Cooktown Aust.	67	J7	1529S	14515E
Coolgardie Aust.	66	D4	3101S	12112E
Copenhagen Denmark	48	D2	5543N	1234E
Copiapó Chile	90	C8	2720S	7023W
Copper Harbor USA	87	J6	4728N	8754W
Coquimbo Chile	91	C8	2957S	7125W
Coral Canada	85	U4	5013N	8141W
Corbeil-Essonnes Fr.	42	F5	4836N	229E
Corbie Fr.	41	A2	4955N	231E
Córdoba Argentina	91	E7	3125S	6411W
Córdoba Mexico	88	E3	1855N	9655W
Córdoba Sp.	43	C2	3753N	446W
Corfu Greece	47	H3	3938N	1955E
Corinth USA	87	J3	3458N	8830W
Cork Rol	40	B2	5154N	828W
Çorlu Turkey	47	M4	4111N	2748E
Corner Brook tn. Canada	85	Z3	4859N	5758W
Cornwall Canada	85	W3	4502N	7445W
Coro Venezuela	90	D16	1120N	7000W
Corpus Christi USA	87	G2	2746N	9726W
Corrientes Argentina	90	F8	2730S	5848W
Corsica i. Fr.	42	J1/J2	4200N	900E
Corte Corsica	42	J2	4118N	908E
Corumbá Brazil	90	F10	1900S	5735W
Corvallis USA	86	B5	4434N	12316W
Cosenza Italy	46	G3	3917N	1616E
COSTA RICA	89	H1/H2		
Coștești Romania	45	M2	4440N	2453E
CÔTE D'IVOIRE	76	C3/D3		
Cotonou Benin	76	E3	624N	231E
Cotopaxi mt. Ecuador	90	B13	040S	7828W
Cottbus Germany	44	G5	5143N	1421E
Couvin Belgium	41	C3	5003N	430E
Coventry UK	40	F3	5225N	130W
Covilhã Port.	43	B4	4017N	730W
Covington USA	87	K4	3904N	8430W
Craiova Romania	45	L2	4418N	2347E
Crawley UK	40	F2	5107N	012W
Cremona Italy	46	D6	4508N	1001E
Crescent City USA	86	B5	4146N	12413W
Creston USA	87	H4	4104N	9420W
Crestview USA	87	J3	3044N	8634W
Créteil Fr.	42	F5	4847N	228E
Criciúma Brazil	91	H8	2845S	4925W
CROATIA	47	G6		
Cromwell NZ	69	B2	4503S	16912E
Crookston USA	87	G6	4747N	9636W
Crotone Italy	47	G3	3905N	1708E
Croydon Aust.	67	H7	1810S	14215E
Cruzeiro do Sul Brazil	90	C12	740S	7239W
CUBA	89	H4/K4		
Cúcuta Col.	90	C15	755N	7331W
Cuddalore India	58	D2	1143N	7946E
Cuddapah India	58	D2	1430N	7850E
Cuenca Ecuador	90	B13	254S	7900W
Cuenca Sp.	43	D4	4004N	207W
Cuernavaca Mexico	88	E3	1857N	9915W
Cuiabá Brazil	90	F10	1532S	5605W
Culiacán Mexico	88	C4	2450N	10721W
Cumaná Venezuela	90	E16	1029N	6412W
Cumberland USA	87	L4	3940N	7847W
Cumbernauld UK	40	C5	5557N	400W
Cuneo Italy	46	B6	4424N	733E
Cunnamula Aust.	67	J5	2804S	14540E
Curaçao i. Lesser Antilles	89	L2	1220N	6820W
Curacautin Chile	91	C6	3828S	7152W
Curicó Chile	91	C6	3500S	7115W
Curitiba Brazil	90	H8	2525S	4925W
Cuttack India	59	F4	2026N	8556E
Cuxhaven Germany	44	D6	5352N	842E
Cuzco Peru	90	C11	1332S	7159W
Cwmbran UK	40	E2	5139N	300W
CYPRUS	49	D1/D2		
CZECH REPUBLIC	44/45	G4/H4		
Częstochowa Poland	45	J5	5049N	1907E

D

Place	Page	Grid	Lat.	Long.
Dabola Guinea	76	B4	1048N	1102W
Dachau Germany	44	E4	4815N	1126E
Daet Philippines	65	G6	1407N	12258E
Daitō Japan	63	B3	3519N	13258E
Dakar Senegal	76	A4	1438N	1727W
Da Lat Vietnam	64	D6	1156N	10825E
Dalby Aust.	67	K5	2711S	15112E
Dalhart USA	86	F4	3605N	10232W
Dali China	60	H3	2533N	10009E
Dalian China	61	M5	3853N	12137E
Dallas USA	87	G3	3247N	9648W
Daloa Côte d'Ivoire	76	C3	656N	628W
Dalton USA	87	K3	3446N	8459W
Daman India	58	C4	2015N	7258E
Damascus Syria	56	C5	3330N	3619E
Damävand Iran	56	F6	3547N	5204E
Damävand mt. Iran	56	F6	3556N	5208E
Damba Angola	78	C6	644S	1520E
Damietta Egypt	77	M8	3124N	3148E
Dampier Aust.	66	C6	2045S	11642E
Da Nang Vietnam	64	D7	1604N	10814E
Danbury USA	87	M5	4124N	7326W
Dandong China	61	M6	4008N	12401E
Dannevirke NZ	69	F4	4012S	17606E
Daqing China	61	N7	4628N	12501E
Dārāb Iran	57	N9	2845N	5432E
Darbhanga India	59	F5	2610N	8554E
Dardanelles sd. Turkey	47	C3	4008N	2610E
Dar es Salaam Tanzania	79	F1	651S	3918E
Dargaville NZ	69	D7	3556S	17352E
Darjiling India	59	F5	2702N	8820E
Darling r. Aust.	67	H4	3030S	14400E
Darłowo Poland	45	H7	5426N	1625E
Darmstadt Germany	44	D4	4952N	839E
Darnah Libya	77	K8	3246N	2239E
Dartmouth Canada	85	Y2	4440N	6335W
Daru PNG	67	H9	905S	14310E
Darwin Aust.	66	F8	1223S	13044E
Dashkhovuz Turkmenistan	54	H5	4149N	5958E
Datong China	61	K6	4002N	11333E
Datu Piang Philippines	65	G5	702N	12430E
Daugava r. Latvia/Belarus/Russia	48	F2	5645N	2430E
Daugavpils Latvia	48	G2	5552N	2631E
Dauki India	59	L10	2510N	9200E
Dauphin Canada	85	R4	5109N	10005W
Davangere India	58	D2	1430N	7552E
Davao Philippines	65	H5	705N	12538E
Davenport USA	87	H5	4132N	9036W
David Panama	89	H1	826N	8226W
Davis Strait Canada/Greenland	85	Y7/Z6	6900N	6000W
Davos Switz.	44	D3	4647N	950E
Dawson Canada	84	H6	6404N	13924W
Dawson Creek tn. Canada	84	L5	5544N	12015W
Dayr az Zawr Syria	56	D6	3520N	4002E
Dayton USA	87	K4	3945N	8410W
Daytona Beach tn. USA	87	K2	2911N	8101W
Deán Funes Argentina	91	E7	3025S	6422W
Dease Lake tn. Canada	84	K5	5805N	13004W
Debrecen Hungary	45	K3	4730N	2137E
Debre Mark'os Ethiopia	77	N4	1019N	3741E
Debre Tabor Ethiopia	77	N4	1150N	3806E
Deh Bid Iran	57	N10	3037N	5312E
Dehra Dun India	58	D6	3019N	7803E
Deinze Belgium	41	B3	5059N	332E
Dej Romania	45	L3	4708N	2355E
Dekese CDR	78	D7	328S	2124E
Delaware state USA	87	L4	3900N	7500W
Delft Neths	41	C5	5200N	422E
Delhi India	58	D5	2840N	7714E
Delice Turkey	49	D2	3956N	3402E
Delicias Mexico	86	E2	2813N	10528W
Del Rio USA	86	F2	2923N	10056W
Delta USA	86	E4	3842N	10804W
Deming USA	86	E3	3217N	10746W
Denain Fr.	42	F6	5019N	324E
Denison USA	87	G3	3347N	9634W
Denizli Turkey	49	C2	3746N	2905E
DENMARK	48	C2/D2		
Denmark Strait Greenland/Iceland	85	FF7/GG7	6700N	2600W
Denpasar Indonesia	64	F2	840S	11514E
Denton USA	86	G3	3314N	9718W
Denver USA	86	E4	3945N	10500W
De Panne Belgium	41	A4	5106N	235E
Dera Ghazi Khan Pakistan	58	C6	3005N	7044E
Dera Ismail Khan Pakistan	58	C6	3151N	7056E
Derbent Russia	49	G3	4203N	4818E
Derby Aust.	66	D7	1719S	12338E
Derby UK	40	F3	5255N	130W
Dese Ethiopia	77	N4	1105N	3940E
Desierto de Atacama d. Chile	90	C9/D10	2230S	7000W
Des Moines USA	87	H5	4135N	9335W
Dessau Germany	44	F5	5151N	1215E
Detmold Germany	41	G5	5156N	853E
Detroit USA	87	K5	4223N	8305W
Deurne Belgium	41	D4	5128N	547E
Deventer Neths	41	E5	5215N	610E
Devil's Lake tn. USA	87	G6	4803N	9857W
Devonport Aust.	67	J2	4109S	14616E
Dezfúl Iran	56	E5	3223N	4828E
Dezhou China	61	L5	3729N	11611E
Dhahran Saudi Arabia	57	N9	2613N	5002E
Dhaka Bangladesh	59	L9	2342N	9022E
Dhamär Yemen	56	D1	1433N	4430E
Dhanbad India	59	F4	2347N	8632E
Dharwad India	58	D3	1530N	7504E
Dhule India	58	C4	2052N	7450E
Dibā al Hisn UAE	57	P9	2537N	5616E
Dibrugarh India	59	G5	2729N	9500E
Dickinson USA	86	F6	4654N	10248W
Diekirch Luxembourg	41	E2	4952N	610E
Diepholz Germany	41	D6	5237N	822E
Dieppe Fr.	42	E5	4955N	105E
Diest Belgium	41	D3	5058N	503E
Digby Canada	85	X2	4437N	6547W
Digne-les-Bains Fr.	42	H3	4405N	614E
Dijon Fr.	42	G4	4720N	502E
Dikson Russia	55	L11	7332N	8039E
Dikwa Nigeria	77	G4	1201N	1355E
Dili East Timor	65	H2	833S	12534E
Dimitrovgrad Bulgaria	47	L5	4203N	2534E
Dimitrovgrad Russia	49	G5	5414N	4937E
Dinajpur Bangladesh	59	K10	2538N	8844E
Dinan Fr.	42	C5	4827N	202W
Dinard Fr.	42	C5	4838N	203W
Dindigul India	58	D2	1023N	7800E
Dingwall UK	40	D5	5735N	429W
Dinslaken Germany	41	E4	5134N	643E
Dir Pakistan	58	C7	3512N	7157E
Dire Dawa Ethiopia	77	P3	935N	4150E
Dispur India	59	G5	2607N	9148E
Diu India	58	C4	2041N	7103E
Divinópolis Brazil	90	J9	2008S	4455W
Divriği Turkey	49	E2	3923N	3806E
Diyarbakir Turkey	49	F2	3755N	4014E
Djanet Algeria	76	F6	2434N	929E
Djelfa Algeria	76	E8	3443N	314E
DJIBOUTI	77	P4		
Djibouti Djibouti	77	P4	1135N	4311E
Dnepr r. Europe	48	Q6	5200N	3000E
Dnestr r. Ukraine	49	C4	4800N	2730E
Dnipro r. Europe	49	D4	4730N	3300E
Dniprodzerzhyns'k Ukraine	49	D4	4830N	3437E
Dnipropetrovs'k Ukraine	49	D4	4829N	3500E
Doboj Bosnia-Herzegovina	47	H6	4444N	1805E
Dobrich Bulgaria	47	M5	4334N	2751E
Dodge City USA	86	F4	3745N	10002W
Dodoma Tanzania	79	D1	610S	3540E
Dogonbadan Iran	57	N10	3021N	5048E
Doha Qatar	57	N9	2515N	5136E
Dokkum Neths	41	E6	5320N	600E
Dolbeau Canada	85	W3	4852N	7215W
Dolina Ukraine	45	L4	4900N	2359E
Dolo Odo Ethiopia	77	P2	411N	4203E
Dombas Norway	48	C3	6205N	907E
DOMINICA	88	Q8		
DOMINICAN REPUBLIC	89	L3		
Don r. Russia	54	G7	5000N	4100E
Don Benito Sp.	43	C3	3857N	552W
Doncaster UK	40	F3	5332N	107W
Donegal Rol	40	B4	5439N	807W
Donets'k Ukraine	49	E4	4800N	3750E
Dongchuan China	61	H3	2607N	10305E
Dông Hôi Vietnam	64	D7	1732N	10635E
Dongola Sudan	77	M5	1910N	3027E
Dordrecht Neths	41	C4	5148N	440E
Dornbirn Austria	44	D3	4725N	946E
Dorsten Germany	41	E4	5138N	658E
Dortmund Germany	44	C4	5132N	727E
Dos Hermanas Sp.	43	C2	3716N	555W
Dostyk Kazakhstan	60	D7	4513N	8230E
Dothan USA	87	J3	3112N	8525W
Douai Fr.	42	F6	5022N	305E
Douala Cameroon	76	F2	404N	943E
Douglas Isle of Man	40	D4	5409N	429W
Dourados Brazil	90	G9	2209S	5452W
Douro r. Port./Sp.	43	B4	4100N	830W
Dover UK	40	G2	5108N	119E
Dráma Greece	47	L4	4110N	2411E
Drammen Norway	48	D2	5945N	1015E
Dresden Germany	44	F5	5103N	1345E
Dreux Fr.	42	E5	4844N	123E
Drogheda Rol	40	C3	5343N	621W
Drohobyč Ukraine	45	L4	4922N	2333E
Drumheller Canada	84	M5	5128N	11240W
Drummondville Canada	85	W3	4550N	7230W
Dryden Canada	85	S3	4948N	9248W
Dubai UAE	57	P9	2514N	5517E
Dubbo Aust.	67	J4	3216S	14841E
Dublin Rol	40	C3	5320N	615W
Dublin USA	87	K3	3231N	8254W
Dubno Ukraine	45	M5	5026N	2543E
Dubrovnik Croatia	47	H5	4240N	1807E
Dubuque USA	87	H5	4230N	9041W
Dudhanai India	59	L10	2557N	9047E
Dudinka Russia	55	L10	6927N	8613E
Duero r. Sp./Port.	43	B4	4125N	630W
Duisburg Germany	44	C4	5126N	645E
Dülmen Germany	41	F4	5149N	717E
Duluth USA	87	H6	4645N	9210W
Dumfries UK	40	E4	5504N	337W
Dumka India	59	J10	2415N	8716E
Dunaújváros Hungary	45	J3	4700N	1855E
Dunav r. SM/Bulgaria	47	K5	4500N	2000E
Duncan USA	87	G3	3430N	9757W
Dundee UK	40	C2	5628N	300W
Dunedin NZ	69	C2	4553S	17030E
Dunfermline UK	40	E5	5604N	329W
Dunkerque Fr.	42	F6	5102N	223E
Dunkirk USA	87	L5	4229N	7921W
Dún Laoghaire Rol	40	C3	5317N	608W
Duque de Caxias Brazil	90	J9	2246S	4318W
Durango Mexico	88	D4	2401N	10440W
Durango Sp.	43	D5	4310N	238W
Durango USA	86	E4	3716N	10753W
Durant USA	87	G3	3359N	9624W
Durazno Uruguay	91	F7	3322S	5631W
Durban RSA	78	F2	2953S	3100E
Durgapur India	59	F4	2447N	8744E
Durg-Bhilai India	59	E4	2112N	8120E
Durham UK	40	F4	5447N	134W
Durham USA	87	L4	3600N	7854W
Durrës Albania	47	H4	4119N	1927E
Dushanbe Tajikistan	54	J4	3838N	6851E
Duyun China	61	J3	2616N	10729E
Dzhetygara Kazakhstan	54	J7	5214N	6110E

E

Place	Page	Grid	Lat.	Long.
Eagle USA	84	G6	6446N	14120W
Eastbourne UK	40	G2	5046N	017E
East Kilbride UK	40	D4	5546N	410W
East London RSA	78	E1	3300S	2754E
EAST TIMOR	65	H2		
Eau Claire tn. USA	87	H5	4450N	9130W
Ebolowa Cameroon	76	G2	256N	1111E
Ebro r. Sp.	43	D5	4300N	430W
Ech Cheliff Algeria	76	E9	3605N	115E
Ecija Sp.	43	C2	3733N	504W
ECUADOR	90	B13		
Ed Damer Sudan	77	M5	1737N	3359E
Ede Neths	41	D5	5203N	540E
Edéa Cameroon	76	G2	347N	1013E
Eden USA	87	L4	3630N	7946W
Edessa Greece	47	K4	4048N	2203E
Edinburgh UK	40	E4	5557N	313W
Edirne Turkey	49	C3	4140N	2634E
Edmonton Canada	84	N4	5334N	11325W
Edmundston Canada	85	X3	4722N	6820W
Edremit Turkey	47	M3	3934N	2701E
EGYPT	77	L7/M7		
Eindhoven Neths	41	D4	5126N	530E
Eisenach Germany	44	E5	5059N	1019E
Eisenstadt Austria	44	H3	4751N	1631E
Ekatahuna NZ	69	E4	4039S	17542E
Ekibastuz Kazakhstan	54	K7	5150N	7510E
Elat Israel	56	B4	2933N	3457E
Elâzig Turkey	49	E2	3841N	3914E
Elbasan Albania	47	J4	4107N	2005E
El Bayadh Algeria	76	E8	3340N	100E
Elbeuf Fr.	42	E5	4917N	101E
Elblag Poland	45	J7	5410N	1925E
El'brus mt. Russia	49	F3	4321N	4229E
Elburg Neths	41	D5	5227N	550E
El Callao Venezuela	90	E15	718N	6150W
El Centro USA	86	C3	3247N	11533W
Elche Sp.	43	E3	3816N	041W
Elda Sp.	43	E3	3829N	047W
Eldoret Kenya	79	D5	031N	3517E
Elektrostal' Russia	49	E5	5546N	3830E
Eleuthera i. Bahamas	87	L1	2505N	7630W
El Faiyûm Egypt	77	M7	2919N	3050E
El Fasher Sudan	77	L4	1337N	2522E
Elgin UK	40	E5	5739N	320W
El Giza Egypt	77	M7	3001N	3112E
El Golea Algeria	76	E8	3035N	251E
Elista Russia	54	G6	4618N	4414E
Elizabeth Aust.	67	G4	3445N	13839E
El Jadida Morocco	76	C8	3319N	835W
Elk Poland	45	L6	5351N	2220E
Elk City USA	86	G4	3425N	9926W
El Khârga Egypt	77	M7	2527N	3032E
Elkhart USA	87	J5	4152N	8556W
Elko USA	86	C5	4050N	11546W
El Minya Egypt	77	M7	2806N	3045E
Elmira USA	87	L5	4206N	7650W
El Obeid Sudan	77	M4	1311N	3010E
El Paso USA	86	E3	3145N	10630W
El Porvenir Mexico	88	C6	3115N	10548W
El Progreso Honduras	88	G3	1520N	8750W
El Reno USA	86	G4	3532N	9757W
El Salto Mexico	88	C4	2347N	10522W
EL SALVADOR	88	G2		
El Sueco Mexico	88	C5	2954N	10622W
El Tigre Venezuela	90	E15	844N	6418W
Eluru India	58	E3	1645N	8110E
Elvas Port.	43	B3	3853N	710W
Ely USA	86	D4	3915N	11453W
Elyria USA	87	K5	4122N	8206W
Emämrüd Iran	57	F6	3615N	5455E
Emba Kazakhstan	54	H6	4847N	5808E
Embrun Fr.	42	H3	4433N	630E
Embu Kenya	79	E4	031S	3726E
Emden Germany	44	C6	5323N	713E
Emerald Aust.	67	J6	2330S	14808E
Emmeloord Neths	41	D5	5243N	546E
Emmen Neths	41	E5	5247N	655E
Emmerich Germany	41	E4	5150N	615E
Empalme Mexico	88	B5	2800N	11049W
Emporia USA	87	G4	3824N	9610W
Emsdetten Germany	41	F5	5210N	732E
Encarnación Paraguay	91	F8	2720S	5550W
Endeh Indonesia	65	G2	851S	12140E
Engaru Japan	62	D4	4404N	14333E
Engel's Russia	54	G7	5130N	4607E
England country UK	40	E3/G3	5300N	200W
English Channel UK/Fr.	40	E1/F2	5000N	230W
Enid USA	87	G4	3624N	9754W
Enna Italy	46	F2	3734N	1416E
En Nahud Sudan	77	L4	1241N	2828E
Enniskillen UK	40	C4	5421N	738W
Enschede Neths	41	E5	5213N	655E
Ensenada Mexico	88	A6	3153N	11638W
Entebbe Uganda	79	C5	004N	3222E
Enugu Nigeria	76	F3	620N	728E
Epe Neths	41	D5	5221N	559E
Épinal Fr.	42	H5	4810N	628E
EQUATORIAL GUINEA	76	F2/G2		
Erding Germany	44	E4	4817N	1155E
Erechim Brazil	90	G8	2735S	5215E
Erenhot China	61	K6	4350N	11200E
Erfurt Germany	44	E5	5058N	1102E
Erie USA	87	K5	4207N	8005W
Erie, Lake Canada/USA	87	K5	4215N	8100W
ERITREA	77	P4		
Erkelenz Germany	41	E4	5105N	611E
Erlangen Germany	44	E4	4936N	1101E
Ermelo Neths	41	D5	5218N	533E
Erode India	58	D2	1121N	7743E
Er Roseires Sudan	77	M4	1152N	3423E
Erzincan Turkey	49	E2	3944N	3930E
Erzurum Turkey	49	F2	3957N	4117E
Esbjerg Denmark	48	C2	5528N	827E
Escanaba USA	87	J6	4547N	8704W
Eschweiler Germany	41	E4	5049N	611E
Escondido USA	86	C3	3307N	11705W
Esfahän Iran	56	F5	3241N	5141E
Eskilstuna Sweden	54	E8	5922N	1631E
Eskişehir Turkey	49	D2	3946N	3031E
Esmeraldas Ecuador	90	B14	056N	7940W
Esperance Aust.	66	D3	3349S	12157E
Espírito Santo i. Vanuatu	67	N7	1510S	16700E
Espoo Finland	54	F9	6010N	2445E
Esquel Argentina	91	C5	4255S	7120W
Esquimalt Canada	84	L4	4825N	12329W
Essen Germany	44	C5	5127N	655E
Esslingen Germany	44	D4	4845N	911E
Estância Brazil	90	K11	1115S	3723W
Estevan Canada	85	Q3	4909N	10300W
ESTONIA	48	G2		
Estremoz Port.	43	B3	3850N	735W
Esztergom Hungary	45	J3	4746N	1845E
Étaples Fr.	42	E6	5031N	138E
Etawah India	58	D5	2646N	7901E
ETHIOPIA	77	N3/P3		
Etna, Mount Italy	46	F2	3745N	1500E
Etten-Leur Neths	41	C4	5134N	435E
Eucla Aust.	66	E4	3140S	12853E
Eugene USA	86	B5	4403N	12304W
Eupen Belgium	41	E3	5038N	604E
Euphrates r. Asia	56	D5	3440N	4230E

ureka USA	86	B5	4049N 12410W
urooport Neths	41	C4	5155N 410E
vansville USA	87	J4	3800N 8733W
verest, Mount China/Nepal	59	F5	2759N 8656E
verett USA	86	B6	4759N 12214W
vora Port.	43	B3	3846N 741W
vreux Fr.	42	E5	4903N 111E
vvoia i. Greece	47	L3	3800N 2400E
xeter UK	40	E2	5043N 331W
xmouth Aust.	66	B6	2154S 11410E
yre, Lake Aust.	66	G5	2800S 13600E

ada Chad	77	K5	1714N 2132E
ăgăraş Romania	45	M2	4549N 2459E
ahraj Iran	57	P9	2858N 5852E
airbanks USA	84	F6	6450N 14750W
airmont USA	87	K4	3928N 8008W
airview Canada	84	M5	5603N 11828W
aisalabad Pakistan	58	C6	3125N 7309E
aizabad India	58	E5	2646N 8208E
alfurrias USA	87	G2	2717N 9810W
alkirk UK	40	E5	5559N 348W
alkland Islands South Atlantic Ocean	91	E3/F3	5230S 6000W
all River tn. USA	87	M5	4141N 7108W
almouth Jamaica	89	U14	1829N 7739W
alun Sweden	48	E3	6037N 1540E
amagusta Cyprus	49	D2	3507N 3357E
ano Italy	46	E5	4351N 1301E
arah Afghanistan	57	H5	3222N 6207E
arewell, Cape NZ	69	D4	4030S 17241E
argo USA	87	G6	4652N 9649W
aridabad India	58	D5	2824N 7718E
aridpur Bangladesh	59	K9	2329N 8931E
armington USA	86	E4	3643N 10812W
aro Canada	84	J6	6230N 13300W
aro Port.	43	B2	3701N 756W
asã Iran	57	N9	2856N 5338E
astov Ukraine	45	P5	5008N 2959E
aya Mauritania	76	B6	2230N 1230W

EDERATED STATES OF MICRONESIA
	70	E8/F8	
eilding NZ	69	E4	4014S 17534E
eira de Santana Brazil	90	K11	1217S 3853W
eldkirch Austria	44	D3	4715N 938E
elixstowe UK	40	G2	5158N 120E
engfeng China	61	K5	3700N 11400E
ergana Uzbekistan	54	K5	4023N 7119E
ermo Italy	46	E5	4309N 1344E
ernie Canada	84	M3	4930N 11500W
errara Italy	46	D6	4450N 1138E
erreñafe Peru	90	B12	642S 7945W
es Morocco	76	C8	3405N 500W
ethiye Turkey	49	C2	3637N 2906E
yzābād Afghanistan	57	K6	3706N 7034E
idenza Italy	46	D6	4452N 1004E
ier Albania	47	H4	4043N 1934E
igeac Fr.	42	F3	4432N 201E
igueira da Foz Port.	43	A4	4009N 851W
igueres Sp.	43	G5	4216N 257E
iJI	67	Q7	1700S 17800E
INLAND	48	G3	
iordland NZ	69	A2	4509S 16718E
irozabad India	58	D5	2709N 7824E
ishguard UK	40	D2	5159N 459W
lagstaff USA	86	D4	3512N 11138W
lekkefjord Norway	48	C2	5817N 640E
lensburg Germany	44	D7	5447N 927E
lers Fr.	42	D5	4845N 034W
lin Flon Canada	85	Q4	5450N 10200W
lint USA	87	K5	4303N 8340W
lorence Italy	46	D5	4347N 1115E
lorencia Col.	90	B14	137N 7537W
lores i. Indonesia	65	G2	830S 12100E
lorianópolis Brazil	91	H8	2735S 4831W
lorida Uruguay	91	F7	3404S 5614W
lorida state USA	87	K2	2800N 8200W
lorida Keys is. USA	87	K1	2500N 8000W
lorina Greece	47	J4	4048N 2126E
lorissant USA	87	H4	3849N 9024W
locşani Romania	45	N2	4541N 2712E
lix Fr.	42	E2	4257N 135E
oleyet Canada	87	U3	4805N 8226W
oligno Italy	46	E5	4257N 1243E
olkestone UK	40	G2	5105N 111E
ond du Lac USA	87	J5	4348N 8827W
ontainebleau Fr.	42	F5	4824N 242E
orbach Fr.	42	H5	4911N 654E
orbesganj India	59	J11	2619N 8715E
orel, Mount Greenland	85	DD7	6700N 3700W
ormentera i. Balearic Islands	43	F3	3841N 130E

ORMER YUGOSLAV REPUBLIC OF MACEDONIA
(FYROM)
	47	J4/K4	
ormosa Argentina	90	F8	2607S 5814W
ormosa Brazil	90	H10	1530S 4722W
orrest Aust.	66	E4	3049S 12803E
ortaleza Brazil	90	K13	345S 3835W
rt Bragg USA	86	B4	3929N 12346W
rt Collins USA	86	E5	4035N 10505W
rt Dodge USA	87	H5	4231N 9410W
rt Frances Canada	85	S3	4836N 9323W
rt Fraser Canada	84	L4	5403N 12430W
rt Good Hope Canada	84	K7	6616N 12837W
rt Lauderdale USA	87	K2	2608N 8008W
rt Liard Canada	84	L6	6014N 12328W
rt Macleod Canada	84	N3	4944N 11324W
rt McMurray Canada	84	N5	5645N 11127W
rt McPherson Canada	84	J7	6729N 13450W
rt Myers USA	87	K2	2639N 8151W

Fort Nelson Canada	84	L5	5848N 12244W
Fort Pierce USA	87	K2	2728N 8020W
Fort Portal Uganda	79	B5	040N 3017E
Fort Providence Canada	84	M6	6103N 11740W
Fort Randall USA	84	C5	5510N 16247W
Fort St. John Canada	84	L5	5614N 12055W
Fort Scott USA	87	H4	3752N 9443W
Fort Simpson Canada	84	L6	6146N 12115W
Fort Smith Canada	84	N6	6001N 11155W
Fort Smith USA	87	H4	3522N 9427W
Fort Stockton USA	86	F3	3054N 10254W
Fort Sumner USA	86	F3	3427N 10416W
Fort Wayne USA	87	J5	4105N 8508W
Fort William UK	40	D5	5649N 507W
Fort Worth USA	87	G3	3245N 9720W
Fort Yukon USA	84	F7	6635N 14520W
Foshan China	61	K2	2303N 11308E
Foumban Cameroon	76	G3	543N 1050E
Fourmies Fr.	42	G6	5001N 403E
Foz Sp.	43	B5	4334N 715W
Foz do Iguaçu Argentina	90	G8	2533S 5431W
Frameries Belgium	41	B3	5025N 354E
FRANCE	42		
Francistown Botswana	78	E3	2111S 2732E
Franeker Neths	41	D6	5311N 533E
Frankenberg Germany	41	G4	5103N 848E
Frankfort USA	87	K4	3811N 8453W
Frankfurt am Main Germany	44	D5	5006N 841E
Fraserburgh UK	40	F5	5742N 200W
Fredericksburg USA	87	L4	3818N 7730W
Fredericton Canada	85	X3	4557N 6640W
Frederikshavn Denmark	48	D2	5728N 1033E
Fredrikstad Norway	48	D2	5920N 1050E
Freeport Bahamas	87	L2	2630N 7842W
Freeport Canada	85	X2	4417N 6619W
Freeport USA	87	G2	2856N 9520W
Freetown Sierra Leone	76	B3	830N 1317W
Fréjus Fr.	42	H2	4326N 644E
Fremantle Aust.	66	C4	3207S 11544E
French Guiana territory Fr.	90	G14	500N 5300W
Fresnillo Mexico	88	D4	2310N 10254W
Fresno USA	86	C4	3641N 11947W
Fribourg Switz.	44	C3	4650N 710E
Friedberg Germany	41	G3	5020N 846E
Friedrichshafen Germany	44	D3	4739N 929E
Frobisher Bay Canada	85	X6	6215N 6500W
Frosinone Italy	46	E4	4138N 1322E
Fuchū Japan	63	C3	3540N 13929E
Fuenlabrada Sp.	43	D4	4016N 349W
Fuertaventura i. Canary Islands	76	B7	2825N 1400W
Fuji Japan	63	C3	3510N 13837E
Fujinomiya Japan	63	C3	3516N 13833E
Fuji-san mt. Japan	63	C3	3523N 13842E
Fujisawa Japan	63	C3	3520N 13929E
Fukui Japan	63	C3	3604N 13612E
Fukuoka Japan	63	B2	3339N 13021E
Fukushima Japan	62	D3	3744N 14028E
Fukuyama Japan	63	B2	3429N 13321E
Funabashi Japan	63	C3	3542N 13959E
Funchal Madeira	76	A8	3240N 1655W
Fürg Iran	57	P9	2819N 5510E
Fürth Germany	44	E4	4928N 1100E
Furukawa Japan	62	D3	3834N 14056E
Fushun China	61	M6	4150N 12354E
Fuxin China	61	M6	4204N 12139E
Fuzhou China	61	L3	2609N 11917E

G
Gabès Tunisia	76	G8	3352N 1006E
GABON	78	B7	
Gaborone Botswana	78	E3	2445S 2555E
Gadsden USA	87	J3	3400N 8600W
Gaeta Italy	46	E4	4113N 1336E
Gafsa Tunisia	76	F8	3428N 843E
Gainesville USA	87	K2	2937N 8221W
Gajol India	59	K10	2510N 8814E
Galashiels UK	40	E4	5537N 249W
Galaţi Romania	45	P2	4527N 2802E
Galesburg USA	87	H5	4058N 9022W
Galle Sri Lanka	58	E1	601N 8013E
Gallipoli Italy	47	F4	4128N 1533E
Gallup USA	86	E4	3232N 10846W
Galveston USA	87	H2	2917N 9448W
Galway RoI	40	B3	5316N 903W
GAMBIA, THE	76	A4	
Gäncä Azerbaijan	49	G3	4039N 4620E
Gander Canada	85	AA3	4900N 5415W
Gandia Sp.	43	E3	3859N 011W
Ganga r. India	58	E5	2500N 8330E
Ganganagar India	58	C6	2954N 7356E
Gangtok India	59	F5	2720N 8830E
Ganzhou China	61	K3	2545N 11451E
Gao Mali	76	D5	1619N 009W
Gap Fr.	42	H3	4433N 605E
Garanhuns Brazil	90	K12	853S 3628W
Garda Italy	46	D6	4534N 1043E
Garden City USA	86	F4	3757N 10054W
Garhbeta India	59	J9	2250N 8722E
Garland USA	87	G3	3255N 9637W
Garoua Cameroon	76	G3	917N 1322E
Garsen Kenya	79	G3	226S 4006E
Gary USA	87	J5	4134N 8720W
Garyarsa China	58	E6	3148N 8018E
Garzón Col.	90	B14	214N 7537W
Gaspé Canada	85	Y3	4850N 6430W
Gastonia USA	87	K4	3514N 8112W
Gatineau Canada	85	V3	4529N 7540W
Gatsugi Japan	62	C3	3829N 13930E
Gävle Sweden	48	E3	6041N 1710E
Gaya India	59	J10	2448N 8500E
Gaziantep Turkey	49	E2	3704N 3721E

Gbarnga Liberia	76	C3	702N 926W
Gdańsk Poland	45	J7	5422N 1841E
Gdynia Poland	45	J7	5431N 1830E
Gedaref Sudan	77	N4	1401N 3524E
Geelong Aust.	67	H3	3810S 14426E
Geita Tanzania	79	C3	252S 3210E
Gejiu China	61	H2	2325N 10305E
Gela Italy	46	F2	3704N 1415E
Geldrop Neths	41	D4	5125N 534E
Gelibolu Turkey	47	M4	4025N 2641E
Gembloux Belgium	41	C3	5034N 442E
Geneina Sudan	77	K4	1327N 2230E
Geneva Switz.	44	C3	4613N 609E
Genoa Italy	46	C6	4424N 856E
Gent Belgium	41	B4	5102N 342E
Georgetown Guyana	90	F15	646N 5810W
George Town Malaysia	64	C5	525N 10020E
Georgetown USA	87	L3	3323N 7918W
GEORGIA	49	F3	
Georgia state USA	87	K3	3300N 8300W
Gera Germany	44	F5	5051N 1211E
Geraldton Aust.	66	B5	2849S 14436E
Geraldton Canada	85	T3	4944N 8659W
GERMANY	44	C5/G5	
Germersheim Germany	41	G2	4914N 821E
Gerona Sp.	43	G4	4159N 249E
Getafe Sp.	43	D4	4018N 344W
Gexto Sp.	43	D5	4320N 259W
Ghadāmis Libya	76	F8	3008N 930E
Ghajnsielem Malta	46	P9	3601N 1418E
GHANA	76	D3	
Ghanzi Botswana	78	D3	2142S 2139E
Gharb Malta	46	P9	3604N 1413E
Ghardaïa Algeria	76	E8	3220N 340E
Gharyān Libya	77	G8	3210N 1301E
Ghāt Libya	76	G6	2458N 1011E
Ghaziabad India	58	D5	2839N 7726E
Ghazni Afghanistan	57	J5	3333N 6826E
Gibraltar territory UK	43	C2	3609N 521W
Gien Fr.	42	F4	4741N 237E
Giessen Germany	44	D5	5035N 842E
Gifu Japan	63	C3	3527N 13646E
Gijón Sp.	43	C5	4332N 540W
Gila Bend USA	86	D3	3256N 11242W
Gilgit Kashmir	58	C7	3554N 7420E
Gillam Canada	85	S5	5625N 9445W
Gillette USA	86	E5	4418N 10530W
Gillingham UK	40	G2	5102N 217W
Girardot Col.	90	C14	419N 7447W
Gisborne NZ	69	G5	3840S 17801E
Gitega Burundi	79	A3	326S 2956E
Giurgiu Romania	45	M1	4353N 2558E
Givet Fr.	41	C3	5008N 449E
Gizhiga Russia	55	U9	6200N 16034E
Gjirokastër Albania	47	J4	4004N 2009E
Gladstone Aust.	67	K6	2352S 15116E
Glasgow UK	40	D4	5553N 415W
Glazov Russia	49	H5	5809N 5241E
Gliwice Poland	45	J5	5020N 1840E
Globe USA	86	D3	3323N 11048W
Głogów Poland	45	H5	5140N 1606E
Gloucester UK	40	E2	5153N 214W
Glovertown Canada	85	AA3	4840N 5403W
Gmunden Austria	44	F3	4756N 1348E
Gniezno Poland	45	H6	5232N 1732E
Goalpara India	59	L11	2608N 9036E
Gobabis Namibia	78	C3	2230S 1858E
Gobi Desert Mongolia	60/61	G6/J6	4830N 10000E
Goch Germany	41	E4	5140N 609E
Godhra India	58	C4	2249N 7340E
Goes Neths	41	B4	5130N 354E
Goiânia Brazil	90	H10	1643S 4918W
Goiás Brazil	90	G10	1557S 5007W
Gold Coast tn. Aust.	67	K5	2759S 15322E
Goldsboro USA	87	L4	3523N 7800W
Goldsworthy Aust.	66	C6	2020S 11931E
Golfe de Gabès g. Tunisia	76	G8	3420N 1030E
Golfe de California g. Mexico	88	B5/C4	2700N 11100W
Golfo de Tehuantepec g. Mexico	88	E3/F3	1530N 9500W
Golfo di Genova g. Italy	46	C6	4400N 900E
Golfo di Táranto g. Italy	47	G3/G4	4000N 1700E
Golfo de Venézia g. Adriatic Sea	46	E6	4500N 1300E
Golmud China	60	F5	3622N 9455E
Goma CDR	79	A4	137S 2912E
Gonder Ethiopia	77	N4	1239N 3729E
Gondia India	58	E4	2123N 8014E
Good Hope, Cape of RSA	78	C1	3430S 1830E
Goodland USA	86	F4	3920N 10143W
Goodlands Mauritius	73	E2	2002S 5739E
Goondiwindi Aust.	67	K5	2830S 15017E
Gorakhpur India	58	E5	2645N 8323E
Gore NZ	69	B1	4606S 16856E
Gorgān Iran	56	F6	3650N 5429E
Gorizia Italy	46	E6	4557N 1337E
Gorno-Altaysk Russia	60	E8	5159N 8553E
Goroka PNG	67	J9	602S 14522E
Gorontalo Indonesia	65	G4	033N 12305E
Gostivar FYROM	47	J4	4147N 2055E
Göteborg Sweden	48	D2	5745N 1200E
Gotha Germany	44	E5	5057N 1043E
Gotland i. Sweden	48	E2	5730N 1840E
Gotō-retto is. Japan	63	A2	3245N 12845E
Gōtsu Japan	63	B2	3502N 13213E
Göttingen Germany	44	D5	5132N 957E
Gouda Neths	41	C5	5200N 442E
Goulburn Aust.	67	J4	3447S 14943E
Gouré Niger	76	G4	1359N 1015E
Governador Valadares — [not present]			

Granada Sp.	43	D2	3710N 335W
Gran Canaria i. Canary Islands	76	A7	2800N 1535W
Grand'Anse Seychelles	73	B1	440S 5525E
Grand Bahama i. Bahamas	89	J5	2700N 7800W
Grand Canyon USA	86	D4	3604N 11207W
Grand Cayman i. Caribbean Sea	89	H3	1920N 8115W
Grande Cache Canada	84	M4	5350N 11845W
Grande Prairie tn. Canada	84	M5	5510N 11852W
Grande Terre i. Lesser Antilles	88	Q9	1700N 6140W
Grand Falls tn. Canada	85	X3	4702N 6746W
Grand Forks USA	87	G6	4757N 9705W
Grand Island tn. USA	87	G5	4056N 9821W
Grand Junction tn. USA	86	E4	3904N 10833W
Grand Canyon USA	86	D4	3604N 11207W
Grand Lake Canada	85	Z3	4900N 5720W
Grand Rapids tn. Canada	85	R4	5312N 9919W
Grand Rapids tn. USA	87	J5	4257N 8640W
Grants Pass tn. USA	86	B5	4226N 13220W
Grasse Fr.	42	H2	4340N 556E
Graz Austria	44	G3	4705N 1522E
Great Abaco i. Bahamas	89	J5	2640N 7700W
Great Australian Bight b. Aust.	66	E4/F4	3300S 13000E
Great Bear Lake Canada	84	L7/M7	6600N 12000W
Great Bend USA	87	G4	3822N 9847W
Great Dividing Range mts. Aust.	67	H8/J3	3500S 14800E
Greater Antilles is. W. Indies	89	H4/L3	1900N 7800W
Great Falls tn. USA	86	D6	4730N 11116W
Great Salt Lake USA	86	D5	4110N 11240W
Great Slave Lake Canada	84	N6	6200N 11400W
Great Yarmouth UK	40	G3	5237N 144E
GREECE	47	J3/K3	
Greeley USA	86	F5	4026N 10443W
Green Bay tn. USA	87	J5	4432N 8800W
GREENLAND	85	BB8/EE8	
Greenock UK	40	D4	5557N 445W
Greensboro USA	87	L4	3603N 7950W
Greifswald Germany	44	F7	5406N 1324E
GRENADA	88	R11	
Grenchen Switz.	44	C3	4713N 724E
Grenoble Fr.	42	G3	4511N 543E
Greymouth NZ	69	C3	4227S 17112E
Griffin USA	87	K3	3315N 8417W
Grimsby UK	40	F3	5335N 005W
Gronau Germany	41	F5	5213N 702E
Groningen Neths	41	E6	5313N 635E
Grootfontein Namibia	78	C4	1932S 1805E
Grosseto Italy	46	D5	4246N 1107E
Groznyy Russia	54	G5	4321N 4542E
Grudziądz Poland	45	J6	5329N 1845E
Guadalajara Mexico	88	D4	2040N 10320W
Guadalajara Sp.	43	D4	4037N 310W
Guadalquivir r. Sp.	43	C2	3745N 530W
Guadeloupe i. Lesser Antilles	88	Q9	1630N 6130W
Guadiana r. Sp./Port.	43	B3	3830N 730W
Guadix Sp.	43	D2	3719N 308W
GUAM	70	E9	
Guamúchil Mexico	88	C5	2528N 10810W
Guangzhou China	61	K2	2308N 11320E
Guantánamo Cuba	89	J4	2009N 7514W
Guaqui Bolivia	90	D10	1638S 6850W
Guarapuava Brazil	90	G8	2522S 5128W
Guarda Port.	43	B4	4032N 717W
Guardiana r. Sp.	43	C3	3900N 400W
Guasave Mexico	86	C2	2534N 10827W
Guasdualito Venezuela	90	C15	715N 7040W
GUATEMALA	88	F3	
Guatemala City Guatemala	88	F2	1438N 9022W
Guayaquil Ecuador	90	A13	213S 7954W
Guaymas Mexico	88	B5	2759W 11054W
Guelph Canada	85	U2	4334N 8016W
Guéret Fr.	42	F4	4610N 152E
Guernsey i. British Isles	40	E1	4627N 235W
Guildford UK	40	F2	5114N 035W
Guilin China	61	K3	2521N 11011E
GUINEA	76	B4	
GUINEA-BISSAU	76	A4/B4	
Güines Cuba	89	H4	2250N 8202W
Güiria Venezuela	90	E16	1037N 6221W
Guiyang China	61	J3	2635N 10640E
Gujranwala Pakistan	58	C6	3206N 7411E
Gujrat Pakistan	58	C6	3235N 7406E
Gulbarga India	58	D3	1722N 7647E
Gulf, The Middle East	57	M9/N9	2720N 5100E
Gulu Uganda	79	C5	246N 3221E
Guntur India	58	E3	1620N 8027E
Gusev Russia	45	L7	5436N 2212E
Gushgy Turkmenistan	57	H6	3603N 6243E
Güstrow Germany	44	F6	5348N 1211E
Gütersloh Germany	41	G4	5154N 822E
Guthrie USA	87	G4	3553N 9726W
Guwahati India	59	G5	2610N 9145E
GUYANA	90	F14	
Gwalior India	58	D5	2612N 7809E
Gweru Zimbabwe	78	E4	1927S 2949E
Gyangze China	58	F5	2851N 8936E
Gympie Aust.	67	K5	2610S 15235E
Gyöngyös Hungary	45	J3	4746N 2000E
Györ Hungary	45	H3	4741N 1740E
Gyumri Armenia	49	F3	4047N 4351E

H
Haaksbergen Neths	41	E5	5209N 645E
Haarlem Neths	41	C5	5223N 439E
Haast NZ	69	B3	4353S 16903E
Hachinohe Japan	62	D4	4030N 14130E
Hachioji Japan	63	C3	3540N 13920E
Hadano Japan	63	C3	3525N 13910E
Hadejia Nigeria	76	G4	1230N 1003E
Haeju North Korea	61	N5	3804N 12540E

Place	Page	Grid	Lat	Long
Haenam South Korea	63	A2	3435N	12635E
Hagen Germany	44	C5	5122N	727E
Hagerstown USA	87	L4	3939N	7744W
Hagi Japan	63	B2	3425N	13122E
Ha Giang Vietnam	61	H2	2250N	10500E
Hagondange Fr.	42	H5	4916N	611E
Haguenau Fr.	42	H5	4849N	747E
Haifa Israel	56	B5	3249N	3459E
Haikou China	61	K2	2000N	11025E
Hä'il Saudi Arabia	56	D4	2731N	4145E
Hailar China	61	L7	4915N	11941E
Hainan Dao i. China	61	J1/K1	1850N	10950E
Haines USA	84	H15	5911N	13523W
Hai Phong Vietnam	61	J2	2050N	10641E
HAITI	89	K3		
Hajjiábád Iran	57	P9	2819N	5554E
Hakodate Japan	62	D4	4146N	14044E
Hakui Japan	63	C3	3655N	13646E
Hakusan Japan	63	C3	3610N	13654E
Halaib Sudan	77	N6	2212N	3635E
Halberstadt Germany	44	E5	5154N	1104E
Haldia India	59	K9	2202N	8805E
Halifax Canada	85	Y2	4438N	6335W
Halle Belgium	41	C3	5044N	414E
Halle Germany	44	E5	5128N	1158E
Hallein Austria	44	F3	4741N	1306E
Halls Creek tn. Aust.	66	E7	1817S	12738E
Halmahera i. Indonesia	65	H4	030S	12700E
Halmstad Sweden	48	D2	5641N	1255E
Haltern Germany	41	F4	5145N	710E
Halvö p. Greenland	85	X9	7600N	6730W
Hamada Japan	63	B2	3456N	13204E
Hamadān Iran	56	E5	3446N	4835E
Ḥamāh Syria	56	C5	3510N	3645E
Hamamatsu Japan	63	C2	3442N	13742E
Hamar Norway	48	D3	6057N	1055E
Hamburg Germany	44	E6	5333N	1000E
Hämeenlinna Finland	48	F3	6100N	2425E
Hameln Germany	44	D6	5206N	922E
Hamhung North Korea	61	N5	3954N	12735E
Hami China	60	F6	4237N	9332E
Hamilton Canada	85	U2	4315N	7950W
Hamilton NZ	69	E6	3747S	17517E
Hamilton USA	87	K4	3923N	8433W
Hamm Germany	44	C5	5140N	749E
Hammerdal Sweden	48	E3	6335N	1520E
Hammerfest Norway	48	F5	7040N	2344E
Hammond USA	87	J5	4136N	8730W
Hampton USA	87	L4	3702N	7623W
Hamrun Malta	46	P8	3553N	1429E
Hanau Germany	41	G3	5008N	855E
Handan China	61	K5	3635N	11431E
Hangzhou China	61	M4	3018N	12007E
Hanna Canada	84	N4	5138N	11156W
Hannibal USA	87	H4	3941N	9120W
Hannover Germany	44	D6	5223N	944E
Hannut Belgium	41	D3	5040N	505E
Hanoi Vietnam	61	J2	2101N	10552E
Hanover Canada	85	U2	4410N	8103W
Haora India	59	K9	2235N	8819E
Ḥaql Saudi Arabia	56	B4	2914N	3456E
Ḥaraḍ Saudi Arabia	57	M8	2412N	4912E
Harare Zimbabwe	78	F4	1750S	3103E
Harbin China	61	N7	4545N	12641E
Hardenberg Neths	41	E5	5234N	638E
Harderwijk Neths	41	D5	5221N	537E
Harlingen Neths	41	D5	5310N	525E
Harlingen USA	87	G2	2612N	9743W
Harrisburg USA	87	L5	4017N	7654W
Harrisonburg USA	87	L4	3827N	7854W
Harrogate UK	40	F3	5400N	133W
Hartford USA	87	M5	4100N	7200W
Hartlepool UK	40	F4	5441N	111W
Harwich UK	40	G2	5157N	117E
Hasselt Belgium	41	D3	5056N	520E
Hassi Messaoud Algeria	76	F8	3152N	543E
Hastings NZ	69	F5	3939S	17651E
Hastings USA	87	G5	4037N	9822W
Hattiesburg USA	87	J3	3120N	8919W
Hat Yai Thailand	64	C5	700N	10025E
Haugesund Norway	48	C2	5925N	516E
Havana Cuba	89	H4	2307N	8225W
Havre USA	86	D4	4834N	10940W
Hawaii i. Hawaiian Islands	70	L9	1950N	15750W
Hawaiian Islands Pacific Ocean	70	J10/L10	2500N	16600W
Hawera NZ	69	E5	3935S	17417E
Hawick UK	40	E4	5525N	247W
Hawkesbury Canada	85	L6	4536N	7437W
Hay River tn. Canada	84	M6	6051N	11542W
Hazebrouck Fr.	41	A3	5043N	232E
Hazelton Canada	84	K5	5516N	12718W
Haz-Zebbug Malta	46	P8	3552N	1426E
Hebi China	61	K5	3557N	11408E
Hechuan China	61	J4	3002N	10656E
Heerenveen Neths	41	D5	5257N	555E
Heerlen Neths	41	D3	5053N	559E
Hefei China	61	L4	3155N	11718E
Hegang China	61	P7	4736N	13030E
Heidelberg Germany	44	D4	4925N	842E
Heilbronn Germany	44	D4	4908N	914E
Heiloo Neths	41	C5	5236N	443E
Hekou China	61	H2	2230N	10400E
Helchteren Belgium	41	D4	5103N	523E
Helena USA	86	D6	4635N	11200W
Hellín Sp.	43	D3	3831N	143W
Helmond Neths	41	D4	5128N	540E
Helsingborg Sweden	48	D2	5603N	1243E
Helsinki Finland	48	F3	6008N	2500E
Henderson USA	86	D3	3601N	11500W
Hengelo Neths	41	E5	5216N	646E
Hengyang China	61	K3	2658N	11231E
Henryetta USA	87	G4	3527N	9600W

Place	Page	Grid	Lat	Long
Henzada Myanmar	64	B7	1736N	9526E
Herät Afghanistan	57	H5	3420N	6212E
Herborn Germany	41	G3	5041N	818E
Hereford UK	40	E3	5204N	243W
Herentals Belgium	41	C4	5111N	450E
Herford Germany	41	G5	5207N	841E
Herne Germany	41	F4	5132N	712E
Herstal Belgium	41	D3	5040N	538E
Hidalgo Mexico	88	E4	2416N	9928W
Higashi-Hiroshima Japan	63	B2	3427N	13243E
Hiketa Japan	63	B2	3413N	13423E
Hikigawa Japan	63	C2	3335N	13522E
Hildesheim Germany	44	D6	5209N	958E
Hilversum Neths	41	D5	5214N	510E
Himalaya mts. Asia	58/59	D6/G5	2800N	8500E
Himeji Japan	63	B2	3450N	13440E
Hirosaki Japan	62	D4	4034N	14028E
Hiroshima Japan	63	B2	3423N	13227E
Hisar India	58	D5	2910N	7545E
Hita Japan	63	B2	3319N	13055E
Hitachi Japan	63	D3	3635N	14040E
Hiwasa Japan	63	B2	3342N	13432E
Hjørring Denmark	48	C2	5728N	959E
Hobart Aust.	67	J2	4254S	14718E
Hobyo Somalia	77	Q3	520N	4830E
Hô Chi Minh Vietnam	64	D6	1046N	10643E
Hodeida Yemen	56	D1	1450N	4258E
Hoek van Holland Neths	41	C5	5159N	408E
Hof Germany	44	E5	5019N	1156E
Hofheim Germany	41	G3	5005N	826E
Höfn Iceland	48	L6	6416N	1510W
Hofu Japan	63	B2	3402N	13134E
Hohhot China	61	K6	4049N	11737E
Hoima Uganda	79	B5	126N	3121E
Hokitika NZ	69	C3	4243S	17058E
Hokkaidö i. Japan	62	D4	4330N	14300E
Holguin Cuba	89	J4	2054N	7615W
Homburg Germany	41	F2	4919N	720E
Homestead USA	87	K2	2529N	8029W
Homs Syria	56	C5	3442N	3640E
Homyel' Belarus	45	Q6	5225N	3100E
Honda Col.	90	C15	515N	7450W
HONDURAS	88	G2		
Hone Canada	85	Q5	5620N	10115W
Hongchon South Korea	63	A3	3740N	12751E
Hong Kong China	61	K2	2300N	11400E
Honiara Solomon Islands	67	L9	928S	15957E
Honjö Japan	62	D3	3922N	14002E
Honolulu Hawaiian Islands	70	L10	2119N	15750W
Honshü i. Japan	62/63	C3	3715N	13900E
Hoogezand Neths	41	E6	5310N	645E
Hoorn Neths	41	D5	5238N	503E
Hope Canada	84	L3	4921N	12128W
Hopkinsville USA	87	J4	3650N	8730W
Horonobe Japan	62	D4	4503N	14151E
Horsham Aust.	67	H3	3645S	14215E
Hörstel Germany	41	F5	5218N	736E
Hot Springs tn. USA	87	H3	3430N	9302W
Houhara NZ	69	D3	3448S	17306E
Houma China	61	K5	3536N	11116E
Houston USA	87	G2	2945N	9525W
Hovd Mongolia	60	F7	4800N	9143E
Howe, Cape Aust.	67	J3	3720S	14959E
Hrodna Belarus	45	L6	5340N	2350E
Hsinchu Taiwan	61	M2	2448N	12059E
Huacho Peru	90	B11	1105S	7736W
Huaide China	61	M6	4330N	12448E
Huainan China	61	L4	3241N	11700E
Huambo Angola	78	C5	1244S	1547E
Huancayo Peru	90	B11	1205S	7512W
Huang He r. China	61	K5	3800N	11100E
Huangshi China	61	L4	3013N	11505E
Huanuco Peru	90	B12	955S	7611W
Huashixia China	60	G5	3513N	9912E
Hude Germany	41	G6	5307N	828E
Hudson Bay Canada	85	T5/T6	6000N	8900W
Huê Vietnam	64	D7	1628N	10735E
Huelva Sp.	43	B2	3715N	656W
Huesca Sp.	43	E5	4208N	025W
Hughenden Aust.	67	H6	2050S	14410E
Hugo USA	87	G3	3401N	9531W
Huixtla Mexico	88	F3	1509N	9230W
Huizhou China	61	K2	2308N	11428E
Humaitá Brazil	90	E12	733S	6301W
Humboldt Canada	85	P4	5212N	10507W
Hunedoara Romania	45	L2	4545N	2254E
HUNGARY	45	H3/K3		
Hungnam North Korea	61	N5	3949N	12740E
Hunjiang China	61	N6	4154N	12623E
Huntington USA	87	K4	3824N	8226W
Huntly NZ	69	E6	3734S	17510E
Huntsville Canada	85	V3	4520N	7913W
Huntsville USA	87	J3	3444N	8635W
Hurghada Egypt	77	M7	2717N	3341E
Huron, Lake Canada/USA	87	K5/K6	4500N	8300W
Hürth Germany	41	E3	5052N	651E
Húsavik Iceland	48	L7	6603N	1717W
Husum Germany	44	D7	5429N	904E
Hutchinson USA	87	G4	3803N	9756W
Huzhou China	61	M4	3056N	12004E
Hwange Zimbabwe	78	E4	1822S	2629E
Hyderabad India	58	D3	1722N	7826E
Hyderabad Pakistan	58	B5	2523N	6824E
Hyères Fr.	42	H2	4307N	608E
Hythe Canada	84	M5	5518N	11933W
Hyüga Japan	63	B2	3225N	13138E

I

Place	Page	Grid	Lat	Long
Ianca Romania	45	N2	4506N	2729E
Iaşi Romania	45	N3	4709N	2738E
Ibadan Nigeria	76	E3	723N	356E

Place	Page	Grid	Lat	Long
Ibagué Col.	90	B14	425N	7520W
Ibb Yemen	56	D1	1403N	4410E
Ibbenbüren Germany	41	F5	5217N	744E
Ibiza Balearic Islands	43	F3	3854N	126E
Ibotirama Brazil	90	J11	1213S	4312W
Ibri Oman	57	G3	2315N	5635E
Ica Peru	90	B11	1402S	7548W
ICELAND	48	L7		
Ichikawa Japan	63	C3	3544N	13955E
Ichinomiya Japan	63	C3	3518N	13648E
Idaho state USA	86	D5	4400N	11500W
Idfu Egypt	77	M6	2458N	3250E
Ieper Belgium	41	A3	5051N	253E
Iganga Uganda	79	C5	037N	3329E
Iglesias Italy	46	C3	3919N	832E
Iguala Mexico	88	E3	1821N	9931W
Iguape Brazil	90	H9	2437S	4730W
Ihosy Madagascar	78	J3	2223S	4609E
Iida Japan	63	C3	3532N	13748E
Iisalmi Finland	48	G3	6334N	2708E
IJmuiden Neths	41	C5	5227N	437E
IJssel r. Neths	41	D5	5227N	515E
IJsselmeer l. Neths	41	D5	5250N	515E
Ikeda Japan	63	B2	3402N	13348E
Ikela CDR	78	D7	106S	2306E
Iksan South Korea	63	A3	3556N	12657E
Iława Poland	45	J6	5335N	1934E
Ilebo CDR	78	D7	420S	2035E
Ilesa Nigeria	76	E3	739N	438E
Ilgaz Turkey	49	D3	4055N	3337E
Ilhéus Brazil	90	K11	1450S	3906W
Iligan Philippines	65	G5	812N	12413W
Illinois state USA	87	J5	4000N	8900W
Iloilo Philippines	65	G6	1041N	12233E
Ilorin Nigeria	76	E3	832N	434E
Imabari Japan	63	B2	3404N	13259E
Imatra Finland	48	G3	6114N	2850E
Imazu Japan	63	C3	3525N	13601E
Imola Italy	46	D6	4422N	1143E
Imperatriz Brazil	90	H12	532S	4728W
Imperia Italy	46	C5	4353N	803E
Imphal India	59	G4	2447N	9355E
Inangahua NZ	69	C4	4152S	17157E
Inchon South Korea	63	A3	3730N	12638E
Independence USA	87	G4	3713N	9543W
INDIA	58/59	B4/F4		
Indiana state USA	87	J5	4000N	8600W
Indianapolis USA	87	J4	3945N	8610W
Indian Ocean	7			
INDONESIA	64/65	C3/H3		
Indore India	58	D4	2242N	7554E
Indus r. Pakistan	58	B5	2800N	6900E
Ingham Aust.	67	J7	1835S	14612E
Ingolstadt Germany	44	E4	4846N	1127E
Inhambane Mozambique	78	G3	2351S	3529E
Inner Hebrides is. UK	40	C5	5645N	645W
Innisfail Aust.	67	J7	1730S	14600E
Innsbruck Austria	44	E3	4717N	1125E
Ino Japan	63	B2	3333N	13323E
In Salah Algeria	76	E7	2720N	203E
Insein Myanmar	64	B7	1654N	9608E
Inta Russia	54	J10	6604N	6001E
Interlaken Switz.	44	C3	4642N	752E
Inuvik Canada	84	J7	6816N	13340W
Invercargill NZ	69	B1	4625S	16822E
Inverness Canada	85	Y3	4614N	6119W
Inverness UK	40	D5	5727N	415W
Ioánnina Greece	47	J3	3940N	2051E
Iónia Nisiá is. Greece	47	H3	3900N	2000E
Ios i. Greece	47	L2	3600N	2500E
Iowa state USA	87	H5	4200N	9400W
Iowa City USA	87	H5	4139N	9131W
Ipatinga Brazil	90	J10	1932S	4230W
Ipiales Col.	90	B14	052N	7738W
Ipoh Malaysia	64	C4	436N	10105E
Ipswich UK	40	G3	5204N	110E
Ipu Brazil	90	J13	432S	4044W
Iqaluit tn. Canada	85	X6	6345N	6830W
Iquitos Peru	90	C13	351S	7313W
Irákleio Greece	47	L1	3520N	2508E
IRAN	56/57	F5/G5		
Irapuato Mexico	88	D4	2040N	10130W
IRAQ	56	D5		
Irbid Jordan	56	C5	3233N	3551E
Irian Jaya admin. Indonesia	65	J3/L3	300S	13300E
Iringa Tanzania	79	D1	749S	3539E
Irkutsk Russia	55	N7	5218N	10415E
Ironwood USA	87	H6	4625N	9008W
Irrawaddy r. Myanmar	64	B7	2000N	9500E
Irtysh r. Asia	54	K8	5730N	7230E
Irún Sp.	43	E5	4320N	148W
Irving USA	87	G3	3249N	9657W
Isafjördur Iceland	48	K7	6605N	2308W
Ise Japan	63	C2	3429N	13641E
Iserlohn Germany	41	F4	5123N	742E
Isesaki Japan	63	C3	3619N	13911E
Iseyin Nigeria	76	E3	759N	340E
Ishinomaki Japan	62	D3	3825N	14118E
Isiolo Kenya	79	E5	022N	3738E
Isiro CDR	77	L2	250N	2740E
Iskenderun Turkey	49	E2	3637N	3608E
Isla d'Elba i. Italy	46	D5	4200N	1000E
Isla Grande de Tierra del Fuego i. Chile/Argentina	91	D3	5400S	6730W
Islamabad Pakistan	58	C6	3340N	7308E
Islampur India	59	K11	2616N	8811E
Isla San Felix i. Chile	70	U5	2623S	8005W
Islas Galápagos i. Ecuador	70	S7	005S	9000W
Isle of Man British Isles	40	D4	5415N	415W
Ismâ'iliya Egypt	77	M8	3036N	3216E
Ispica Italy	46	F2	3647N	1455E
ISRAEL	56	B5/C5		
Issoire Fr.	42	F3	4533N	315E
Istanbul Turkey	49	C3	4102N	2857E
Istres Fr.	42	G2	4330N	459E

Place	Page	Grid	Lat	Long
Itabaiana Brazil	90	K11	1042S	3737W
Itabuna Brazil	90	K11	1448S	3918W
Itaguí Col.	90	B15	613N	7540W
Itaituba Brazil	90	F13	415S	5556W
Itajaí Brazil	90	H8	2650S	4839W
ITALY	46	D5/E5		
Itapipoca Brazil	90	K13	329S	3935W
Itaqui Brazil	91	F8	2910S	5630W
Itzehoe Germany	44	D6	3703N	932
Ivano-Frankivs'k Ukraine	45	M4	4840N	2440
Ivanovo Russia	54	G8	5700N	4100
Ivdel' Russia	54	J9	6045N	6030
Ivujivik Canada	85	V6	6225N	7754W
Iwaki Japan	62	D3	3703N	14058
Iwakuni Japan	63	B2	3410N	13209
Iwamatsu Japan	63	B2	3306N	13231
Iwamizawa Japan	62	D4	4312N	14147
Iwate Japan	62	D3	3959N	14114
Ixtepec Mexico	88	E3	1630N	9510W
Izhevsk Russia	54	H8	5649N	5311
Izmayil Ukraine	45	P2	4520N	2848
Izmir Turkey	49	C2	3825N	2710
Izuhara Japan	63	A2	3412N	12918
Izumi Japan	62	D3	3819N	14051
Izumo Japan	63	B3	3522N	13246
Izu-shotö is. Japan	63	C2	3420N	13920

J

Place	Page	Grid	Lat	Long
Jabalpur India	58	D4	2310N	7959
Jablonec Czech Rep.	44	G5	5044N	1510
Jaboatão Brazil	90	K12	805S	3500W
Jaca Sp.	43	E5	4234N	033W
Jackson USA	87	H3	3220N	9011W
Jacksonville USA	87	K3	3020N	8140W
Jacobabad Pakistan	58	B5	2816N	6830
Jacobina Brazil	90	J11	1113S	4030W
Jaén Sp.	43	D2	3746N	348W
Jaffna Sri Lanka	58	E1	940N	8001
Jagdalpur India	58	E3	1904N	8205
Jaipur India	58	D5	2653N	7550
Jaisalmer India	58	C4	2652N	7056
Jakarta Indonesia	64	C2	608S	10645
Jaläläbäd Afghanistan	57	K5	3426N	7025
Jalandhar India	58	D6	3118N	7540
Jalapa Enriquez Mexico	88	E3	1932N	9656W
Jaleshwar India	59	J8	2147N	8714
Jalgaon India	58	D4	2101N	7539
Jalpaiguri India	59	K11	2629N	8847
Jālū Libya	77	K7	2902N	2133
JAMAICA	89	J3		
Jambi Indonesia	64	C3	134S	10337
Jamiltepec Mexico	88	E3	1616N	9751W
Jammu India	58	C6	3243N	7454
Jammu and Kashmir state Southern Asia	58	D6	2940N	7630
Jamnagar India	58	C4	2228N	7006
Jamshedpur India	59	F4	2247N	8612
Janesville USA	87	J5	4242N	8902W
Jangipur India	59	K10	2427N	8804
JAPAN	62/63			
Jarocin Poland	45	H5	5159N	1730
Jarú Brazil	90	E11	1024S	6245W
Jasło Poland	45	K4	4945N	2128
Jasper Canada	84	M4	5255N	11805W
Jastrowie Poland	45	H6	5325N	1650
Jaunpur India	58	E5	2544N	8241
Jawa i. Indonesia	64	D2/E2	700S	11000
Jayapura Indonesia	65	L3	237S	14039
Jedda Saudi Arabia	56	C3	2130N	3910
Jefferson City USA	87	H4	3833N	9210W
Jēkabpils Latvia	48	F2	5622N	2550
Jelenia Góra Poland	45	G5	5055N	1545
Jelgava Latvia	48	F2	5639N	2340
Jember Indonesia	64	E2	807S	11345
Jena Germany	44	E5	5056N	1135
Jequié Brazil	90	J11	1352S	4006W
Jerez de la Frontera Sp.	43	B2	3641N	608W
Jersey i. British Isles	40	E1	4913N	207W
Jerusalem Israel/Jordan	56	C5	3147N	3513
Jessore Bangladesh	59	K9	2310N	8912
Jever Germany	41	F6	5334N	756
Jhansi India	58	D5	2527N	7834
Jhelum Pakistan	58	C6	3256N	7344
Jhenida Bangladesh	59	K9	2332N	8909
Jiamusi China	61	P7	4659N	13029
Ji'an China	61	L3	2708N	11500
Jiangmen China	61	K2	2240N	11305
Jiangyuan China	61	M4	3015N	12052
Jiaxing China	60	G5	3947N	9814
Jilin China	61	N6	4353N	12635
Jima Ethiopia	77	N3	739N	3647
Jiménez Mexico	86	F2	2708N	10455W
Jinan China	61	L5	3641N	11700
Jingdezhen China	61	L3	2917N	11712
Jinhua China	61	L3	2906N	11940
Jining China	61	K6	4058N	11301
Jining China	61	L5	3525N	11640
Jinja Uganda	79	C5	027N	3314
Jinxi China	61	M6	4107N	12106
Jinzhou China	61	M6	4107N	12106
Jiujiang China	61	L3	2941N	11603
Jixi China	61	P7	4517N	13100
Jīzān Saudi Arabia	56	D1	1656N	4233
João Pessoa Brazil	90	K12	706S	3453W
Jodhpur India	58	C5	2618N	7308
Jöetsu Japan	63	C3	3706N	13815
Jogjphapa India	59	L11	2624N	9034
Johannesburg RSA	78	E2	2610S	2802
Johnson City USA	87	K4	3620N	8223W
Johnstown USA	87	L4	4020N	7856W
Johor Bahru Malaysia	65	S15	127N	10345
Joinville Brazil	90	H8	2620S	4855W
Jonesboro USA	87	H4	3550N	9041W
Jönköping Sweden	48	D2	5745N	1410

Name	Page	Grid	Lat	Long
oplin USA	87	H4	3704N	9431W
ORDAN	56	C5		
os Nigeria	76	F3	954N	853E
owai India	59	M10	2526N	9216E
uàzeiro Brazil	90	J12	925S	4030W
uàzeiro do Norte Brazil	90	K12	710S	3918W
uba Sudan	77	M2	450N	3135E
uchitán Mexico	88	E3	1627N	9505W
uiz de Fora Brazil	90	J9	2147S	4323W
uliaca Peru	90	C10	1529S	7009W
unagadh India	58	C4	2132N	7032E
unction City USA	87	G4	3902N	9651W
undiaí Brazil	90	J9	2310S	4654W
uneau USA	84	J5	5820N	13420W
urong Singapore	65	S14	121N	10343E
urong Island Singapore	65	S14	116N	10342E
ylland p. Denmark	48	C2	5500N	900E
yväskylä Finland	48	G3	6216N	2550E
K				
2 mt. China/India	60	C5	3547N	7630E
aabong Uganda	79	D6	331N	3409E
abale Uganda	79	A4	115S	2959E
abarnet Kenya	79	D5	032N	3545E
abe Japan	63	B2	3431N	13229E
abwe Zambia	78	E5	1429S	2825E
adoma Zimbabwe	78	E4	1821S	2955E
aduna Nigeria	76	F4	1028N	725E
aesong North Korea	63	A3	3759N	12630E
afue Zambia	78	E4	1544S	2810E
aga	63	C3	3620N	13615E
agoshima Japan	63	B2	3137N	13032E
ahama Tanzania	79	C3	350S	3236E
aiapoi NZ	69	D6	4323S	17239E
aifeng China	61	K4	3447N	11420E
aikohe NZ	69	D7	3525S	17348E
aikoura NZ	69	D3	4224S	17341E
ainan Japan	63	C2	3409N	13512E
airouan Tunisia	76	G9	3542N	1001E
aiserslautern Germany	44	C4	4927N	747E
aitaia NZ	69	D7	3507S	17316E
ajaani Finland	48	G3	6414N	2737E
akamega Kenya	79	D5	017N	3445E
akamigahara Japan	63	C3	3525N	13650E
akinada India	58	E3	1659N	8220E
akira Uganda	79	C5	031N	3318E
akogawa Japan	63	B2	3449N	13452E
akunodate Japan	63	D3	3937N	14035E
alamáta Greece	47	K2	3702N	2207E
alamazoo USA	87	J5	4217N	8536W
alat Pakistan	58	B5	2901N	6638E
alémié CDR	78	E6	557S	2910E
alevala Russia	48	H4	6515N	3108E
algoorlie Aust.	66	D4	3049S	12129E
alibo Philippines	65	G6	1142N	12220E
aliningrad reg. Russia	48	F1	5440N	2100E
aliningrad Russia	48	F1	5440N	2030E
alinkavichy Belarus	45	P6	5208N	2919E
alispell USA	86	D6	4812N	11419W
alisz Poland	45	J5	5146N	1802E
aliua Tanzania	79	B2	504S	3148E
almar Sweden	48	E2	5639N	1620E
almthout Belgium	41	C4	5123N	429E
alokol Kenya	79	D6	338N	3555E
alomo Zambia	78	E4	1702S	2629E
aluga Russia	54	F7	5431N	3616E
amaishi Japan	62	D3	3918N	14152E
ameda Japan	62	C3	3754N	13908E
amensk-Ural'skiy Russia	54	J8	5629N	6149E
amina CDR	78	E6	846S	2500E
amloops Canada	84	L4	5039N	12024W
amo Japan	62	C3	3740N	13905E
amojima Japan	63	B2	3402N	13414E
ampala Uganda	79	C5	019N	3235E
ampen Neths	41	D5	5233N	555E
amp'o South Korea	63	A3	3548N	12930E
ampóng Cham Cambodia	64	D6	1159N	10526E
ampot Cambodia	64	C6	1037N	10411E
ampung Luminin Brunei	64	P11	441N	11443E
amuli Uganda	79	C5	054N	3306E
amyshin Russia	54	G7	5005N	4524E
ananga CDR	78	D6	553S	2226E
anazawa Japan	63	C3	3635N	13638E
andahár Afghanistan	57	J5	3135N	6545E
andalaksha Russia	54	F10	6709N	3231E
andi Benin	76	E4	1105N	259E
andla India	58	C4	2303N	7011E
andy Sri Lanka	58	E1	717N	8040E
angnung South Korea	63	A3	3748N	12752E
ankakee USA	87	J5	4108N	8752W
ankan Guinea	76	C4	1022N	911W
annapolis USA	87	K4	3530N	8036W
ano Nigeria	76	F4	1200N	831E
anpur India	58	E5	2627N	8014E
ansas state USA	86/87	G4	3800N	9800W
ansas City USA	87	H4	3902N	9433W
ansk Russia	55	M8	5611N	9548E
ansŏng South Korea	63	A3	3820N	12828E
anuma Botswana	78	D3	2459S	2519E
aohsiung Taiwan	61	M2	2236N	12017E
aolack Senegal	76	A4	1409N	1608W
apfenberg Austria	44	G3	4727N	1518E
aposvár Hungary	45	H3	4621N	1749E
arasabet Kenya	79	D5	010N	3507E
apuskasing Canada	85	U3	4925N	8226W
arabük Turkey	49	D4	4112N	3236E
arachi Pakistan	58	B4	2451N	6702E
araganda Kazakhstan	54	K6	4953N	7307E
araj Iran	56	F6	3548N	5058E
asburg Namibia	78	C2	2800S	1843E
asjok Norway	48	G4	6927N	2530E
Karbalā' Iraq	56	D5	3237N	4403E
Karcag Hungary	45	K3	4719N	2053E
Karibib Namibia	78	C3	2159S	1551E
Karimganj India	59	M10	2450N	9221E
Kariya Japan	63	C3	3500N	13700E
Karlino Poland	45	G7	5402N	1552E
Karlovac Croatia	46	F6	4530N	1534E
Karlovy Vary Czech Rep.	44	F5	5013N	1252E
Karlskoga Sweden	48	D2	5919N	1433E
Karlskrona Sweden	48	E2	5610N	1535E
Karlsruhe Germany	44	D4	4900N	824E
Karlstad Sweden	48	D2	5924N	1332E
Karnal India	60	C3	2941N	7659E
Karnobat Bulgaria	47	M5	4238N	2659E
Kars Turkey	49	F3	4035N	4305E
Karsakpay Kazakhstan	54	J6	4747N	6643E
Karshul Iran	57	N10	3007N	5305E
Karwar India	58	C2	1450N	7409E
Kasama Zambia	78	F5	1010S	3111E
Kasaragod India	58	C2	1230N	7459E
Kasempa Zambia	78	E5	1328S	2548E
Kasese Uganda	79	B5	010N	3006E
Kāshān Iran	56	F5	3359N	5135E
Kashi China	60	C5	3929N	7602E
Kashima Japan	62	D3	3742N	14058E
Kashiwazaki Japan	63	C3	3722N	13833E
Kaskinen Finland	48	F3	6223N	2110E
Kasli Russia	54	K6	5553N	6044E
Kásos i. Greece	47	M1	3520N	2655E
Kassala Sudan	77	N5	1524N	3630E
Kassel Germany	44	D5	5118N	930E
Kastoriá Greece	47	J4	4033N	2115E
Kasugai Japan	63	C3	3515N	13657E
Kasulu Tanzania	79	B2	434S	3006E
Kasur Pakistan	58	C6	3107N	7430E
Kataba Zambia	78	E4	1602S	2503E
Katerini Greece	47	K4	4015N	2230E
Katha Myanmar	60	G2	2411N	9620E
Katherine Aust.	66	F8	1429S	13220E
Kathmandu Nepal	59	F5	2742N	8519E
Katihar India	60	E3	2534N	8734E
Katowice Poland	45	J5	5015N	1859E
Katrineholm Sweden	48	E2	5859N	1615E
Katsina Nigeria	76	F4	1300N	732E
Katsina Ala Nigeria	76	F3	710N	930E
Katsuta Japan	63	D3	3624N	14032E
Kaunas Lithuania	48	F1	5452N	2355E
Kavajë Albania	47	H4	4110N	1935E
Kavála Greece	47	L4	4056N	2425E
Kawanishi Japan	62	D3	3801N	14001E
Kawaraichi Japan	63	C3	3538N	13556E
Kawasaki Japan	63	C3	3530N	13945E
Kawerau NZ	69	F5	3805S	17642E
Kaya Burkina	76	D4	1304N	109W
Kayes Mali	76	B4	1426N	1128W
Kayseri Turkey	49	E2	3842N	3528E
KAZAKHSTAN	54	H6/J6		
Kazan' Russia	54	G8	5545N	4910E
Kearney USA	86	G5	4042N	9904W
Kecskemét Hungary	45	J3	4656N	1943E
Kediri Indonesia	64	E2	745S	11201E
Keetmanshoop Namibia	78	C2	2636S	1808E
Kefallonia i. Greece	47	J3	3800N	2000E
Kefamenanu Indonesia	65	G2	931S	12429E
Keflavik Iceland	48	K6	6401N	2235W
Kells Rol	40	C3	5344N	653W
Kelowna Canada	84	M3	4950N	11929W
Kelsey Bay tn. Canada	84	K4	5022N	12529W
Kemerovo Russia	55	L8	5525N	8605E
Kemi Finland	48	F4	6546N	2434E
Kempten Germany	44	E3	4744N	1019E
Kenai USA	84	E6	6035N	15119W
Kendal UK	40	E4	5420N	245W
Kendari Indonesia	65	G3	357S	12236E
Kenema Sierra Leone	76	B3	757N	1111W
Kengtung Myanmar	60	G2	2115N	9940E
Kénitra Morocco	76	C8	3420N	634W
Kenora Canada	85	S3	4947N	9426W
Kentucky state USA	87	J4/K4	3700N	8500W
KENYA	79	E5/F5		
Kep. Aru i. Indonesia	65	J2	600S	13430E
Kep. Maluku is. Indonesia	65	H3	400S	12700E
Kep. Mentawai is. Indonesia	64	B2	200S	9900E
Kep. Sula is. Indonesia	65	G3/H3	150S	12450E
Kep. Tanimbar is. Indonesia	65	J2	730S	13130E
Kerch' Ukraine	49	E4	4522N	3627E
Kerema PNG	67	J9	759S	14546E
Keren Eritrea	77	N5	1546N	3830E
Kericho Kenya	79	D4	022S	3515E
Kerkrade Neths	41	E5	5052N	604E
Kérkyra i. Greece	47	H3	3900N	1900E
Kermān Iran	57	P10	3018N	5705E
Kerpen Germany	41	E4	5052N	637E
Kerrville USA	86	G3	3003N	9909W
Ketchikan USA	84	J5	5525N	13140W
Ketrzyn Poland	45	K6	5405N	2124E
Key West USA	87	K1	2434N	8148W
Khabarovsk Russia	55	R6	4832N	13508E
Khairpur Pakistan	58	B5	2732N	6846E
Khammam India	58	E3	1715N	8011E
Khānābad Afghanistan	57	J6	3642N	6908E
Khānaqin Iraq	56	E5	3421N	4522E
Khandwa India	58	D4	2149N	7623E
Kharagpur India	59	F4	2223N	8722E
Kharkiv Ukraine	49	E4	5000N	3615E
Khartoum Sudan	77	M5	1533N	3235E
Khāsh Iran	57	H4	2814N	6115E
Khaskovo Bulgaria	47	L4	4157N	2532E
Khawr Fakkan UAE	57	P9	2521N	5621E
Khaybar Saudi Arabia	56	C4	2500N	3900E
Khemisset Morocco	76	C8	3350N	603W
Kherson Ukraine	49	D4	4639N	3238E
Khiva Uzbekistan	54	J5	4125N	6049E
Khmel'nyts'kyy Ukraine	45	N4	4925N	2659E
Khorog Tajikistan	54	K4	3722N	7132E
Khorramābād Iran	56	E5	3329N	4821E
Khorramshahr Iran	57	M10	3025N	4809E
Khotin Ukraine	45	N4	4830N	2631E
Khouribga Morocco	76	C8	3254N	657W
Khowai India	59	L10	2405N	9136E
Khulna Bangladesh	59	K9	2249N	8934E
Kibiti Tanzania	79	F1	743S	3856E
Kiboga Uganda	79	B5	056N	3146E
Kibombo CDR	78	E7	358S	2554E
Kibondo Tanzania	79	B3	335S	3042E
Kibwezi Kenya	79	E2	2425S	3758E
Kiel Germany	44	E5	5420N	1008E
Kielce Poland	45	K5	5051N	2039E
Kieta PNG	67	L9	615S	15537E
Kiev Ukraine	45	Q5	5025N	3030E
Kigali Rwanda	79	B4	156S	3004E
Kigoma Tanzania	79	A2	452S	2936E
Kii-Nagashima Japan	63	C2	3411N	13620E
Kikori PNG	67	H9	725S	14413E
Kikwit CDR	78	C6	502S	1851E
Kilifi Kenya	79	F3	336S	3951E
Kilimanjaro mt. Tanzania	79	E3	304S	3722E
Kilkenny Rol	40	C3	5239N	715W
Kilkis Greece	47	K4	4059N	2252E
Killarney Canada	85	R3	4912N	9940W
Killeen USA	87	G3	3108N	9744W
Kilmarnock UK	40	D4	5536N	430W
Kilosa Tanzania	79	E1	650S	3659E
Kilwa Masoko Tanzania	78	G6	855S	3931E
Kilyos Turkey	47	N4	4114N	2902E
Kimberley Canada	84	M3	4940N	11558W
Kimberley RSA	78	D2	2845S	2446E
Kimchaek North Korea	61	N6	4041N	12912E
Kimchon South Korea	63	A3	3607N	12808E
Kincardine Canada	85	U2	4411N	8138W
Kindersley Canada	84	P4	5127N	10908W
Kindia Guinea	76	B4	1003N	1249W
Kingman USA	86	D4	3512N	11402W
King's Lynn UK	40	G3	5245N	024E
Kingsport USA	87	K4	3633N	8234W
Kingston Canada	85	V2	4414N	7630W
Kingston Jamaica	89	U13	1758N	7648W
Kingston upon Hull UK	40	F3	5345N	020W
Kingstown St. Vincent and The Grenadines	88	R11	1312N	6114W
Kingsville USA	87	G2	2732N	9753W
Kinkala Congo	78	B7	418S	1449E
Kinleith NZ	69	E3	3815S	17556E
Kinshasa CDR	78	C7	418S	1518E
Kipili Tanzania	78	F6	730S	3039E
Kirchhain Germany	41	E4	5049N	855E
Kirchhundern Germany	41	G4	5105N	805E
KIRIBATI	70	H8/L7		
Kirikkale Turkey	49	D2	3951N	3332E
Kirkağaç Turkey	47	M3	3906N	2740E
Kirkcaldy UK	40	E5	5607N	310W
Kirkcudbright UK	40	D4	5450N	403W
Kirkland Lake tn. Canada	85	U3	4810N	8002W
Kirklareli Turkey	47	M4	4145N	2712E
Kirksville USA	87	H5	4012N	9235W
Kirkūk Iraq	56	D5	3528N	4426E
Kirkwall UK	40	E6	5859N	258W
Kirov Russia	54	G8	5800N	4938E
Kirovohrad Ukraine	49	D4	4831N	3215E
Kiryū Japan	63	C3	3626N	13918E
Kisakata Japan	62	C3	3913N	13954E
Kisangani CDR	77	L2	033N	2514E
Kisarazu Japan	63	C3	3522N	13955E
Kishanganj India	59	J11	2608N	8757E
Kishiwada Japan	63	C2	3428N	13522E
Kisii Kenya	79	D4	042S	3446E
Kiskunhalas Hungary	45	J3	4626N	1929E
Kismaayo Somalia	77	P1	025S	4231E
Kiso-Fukushima Japan	63	C3	3552N	13740E
Kisoro Uganda	79	A4	117S	2941E
Kisumu Kenya	79	D4	003N	3447E
Kitakami Japan	63	D3	3918N	14105E
Kitakata Japan	62	C3	3738N	13952E
Kita-Kyūshū Japan	63	B2	3352N	13049E
Kitale Kenya	79	D5	101N	3500E
Kitami Japan	62	D4	4351N	14354E
Kitchener Canada	85	U2	4327N	8030W
Kitgum Uganda	79	C6	319N	3253E
Kitimat Canada	84	K4	5405N	12838W
Kitwe Zambia	78	E5	008S	3030E
Kitzbühel Austria	44	F3	4727N	1223E
Kladno Czech Rep.	44	F5	5010N	1407E
Klagenfurt Austria	44	G3	4638N	1420E
Klaipėda Lithuania	48	F2	5543N	2107E
Klang Malaysia	64	C4	303N	10125E
Klatovy Czech Rep.	44	F4	4924N	1317E
Klerksdorp RSA	78	D2	2652S	2639E
Kleve Germany	41	E4	5147N	608E
Kłodzko Poland	45	H5	5028N	1640E
Klöfta Norway	48	D2	6004N	1106E
Klosterneuburg Austria	44	H4	4819N	1620E
Kluang Malaysia	64	C4	201N	10319E
Knoxville USA	87	K4	3600N	8357W
Kōbe Japan	63	C2	3440N	13512E
Koblenz Germany	44	C5	5021N	736E
Kobryn Belarus	45	M6	5216N	2422E
Kocaeli Turkey	54	C4	4047N	2955E
Koch Bihar India	59	F5	2618N	8932E
Kōchi Japan	63	B2	3333N	13332E
Kochubey Russia	49	G4	4425N	4632E
Kodiak USA	84	E5	5749N	15230W
Kodiak Island USA	84	E5	5720N	15340W
Kodok Sudan	77	M3	951N	3207E
Koforidua Ghana	76	D3	601N	012W
Kōfu Japan	63	C3	3543N	13834E
Kohat Pakistan	58	C6	3337N	7130E
Kohima India	59	G5	2540N	9408E
Kohtla-Järve Estonia	48	G2	5928N	2720E
Kokand Uzbekistan	54	K5	4033N	7055E
Kokkola Finland	48	F3	6245N	3006E
Kokomo USA	87	J5	4030N	8609W
Kokshetau Kazakhstan	54	J7	5318N	6925E
Kokura Japan	63	B2	3354N	13052E
Kolding Denmark	48	C2	5529N	930E
Kolhapur India	58	C3	1640N	7420E
Kolín Czech Rep.	44	G5	5002N	1511E
Kolkata India	59	F4	2230N	8820E
Koło Poland	45	J6	5212N	1837E
Kołobrzeg Poland	45	G7	5410N	1535E
Kolomna Russia	49	E6	5505N	3845E
Kolomyya Ukraine	45	M4	4831N	2500E
Kolvereid Norway	48	D3	6453N	1135E
Kolwezi CDR	78	E5	1045S	2525E
Komárno Slovakia	45	J3	4746N	1805E
Komatsu Japan	63	C3	3625N	13627E
Komotiní Greece	47	L4	4106N	2525E
Kômpóng Saôm Cambodia	64	C6	1028N	10328E
Kondoa Tanzania	79	D2	454S	3547E
Kondūz Afghanistan	57	J6	3645N	6851E
Kongolo CDR	78	E6	520S	2700E
Kongwa Tanzania	79	E1	612S	3625E
Konin Poland	45	J6	5212N	1812E
Köniz Switz.	44	C3	4656N	725E
Konosha Russia	54	G9	6058N	4008E
Konotop Ukraine	49	D5	5115N	3314E
Konstanz Germany	44	D3	4740N	910E
Konya Turkey	49	D2	3751N	3230E
Konz Germany	41	E2	4942N	635E
Koper Slovenia	46	E6	4531N	1344E
Kopychintsy Ukraine	45	M4	4910N	2558E
Korbach Germany	44	D5	5116N	853E
Korçë Albania	47	J4	4037N	2047E
Korhogo Côte d'Ivoire	76	C3	922N	531W
Kórinthos Greece	47	K2	3756N	2255E
Kōriyama Japan	62	D3	3723N	14022E
Korla China	60	E6	4148N	8610E
Korogwe Tanzania	79	F2	509S	3829E
Korosten' Ukraine	49	C5	5100N	2830E
Kortrijk Belgium	41	B3	5050N	317E
Kós i. Greece	47	M2	3645N	2710E
Ko Samui i. Thailand	64	C5	930N	10000E
Kościan Poland	45	H6	5205N	1638E
Košice Slovakia	45	K4	4844N	2115E
Kosovska Mitrovica SM	47	J5	4254N	2052E
Kosti Sudan	77	M4	1311N	3228E
Kostroma Russia	54	G8	5746N	4059E
Kostrzyn Poland	44	G6	5235N	1440E
Koszalin Poland	45	H7	5410N	1610E
Kota India	58	D5	2511N	7558E
Kotabaru Indonesia	65	F3	315S	11615E
Kota Bharu Malaysia	64	C5	608N	10214E
Kotabumi Indonesia	64	C3	452S	10459E
Kota Kinabalu Malaysia	65	F5	559N	11604E
Kotamobagu Indonesia	65	G4	046N	12421E
Kotel'nich Russia	49	G6	5818N	4820E
Kotido Uganda	79	D6	300N	3409E
Kotka Finland	48	G3	6026N	2655E
Kotlas Russia	54	G9	6115N	4635E
Kotri Pakistan	58	B5	2522N	6818E
Kotzebue USA	84	C7	6651N	16240W
Koudougou Burkina	76	D4	1315N	223W
Koulamoutou Gabon	78	B7	112S	1229E
Koulikoro Mali	76	C4	1255N	731W
Koumra Chad	77	J3	856N	1732E
Kourou French Guiana	90	G15	508N	5237W
Kouvola Finland	48	G3	6054N	2645E
Kovel' Ukraine	45	M5	5113N	2443E
Kovrov Russia	49	F6	5623N	4121E
Kozáni Greece	47	J4	4018N	2148E
Kpalimé Togo	76	E3	655N	044E
Kragujevac SM	47	J5	4401N	2055E
Kraków Poland	45	J5	5003N	1955E
Kraljevo SM	47	J5	4344N	2041E
Kranj Slovenia	46	F7	4615N	1420E
Krasnodar Russia	54	F6	4502N	3900E
Krasnotur'insk Russia	54	K9	5947N	6013E
Krasnoufimsk Russia	49	J6	5636N	5746E
Krasnovodsk Turkmenistan	54	H5	4001N	5300E
Krasnoyarsk Russia	55	M8	5605N	9246E
Krasnyy Kut Russia	49	G5	5058N	4700E
Kratie Cambodia	64	D6	1230N	10603E
Krefeld Germany	44	C5	5120N	632E
Kremenchuk Ukraine	49	D4	4903N	3325E
Kremenets Ukraine	45	M5	5005N	2548E
Krishnanagar India	59	K9	2325N	8830E
Kristiansand Norway	48	C2	5808N	801E
Kristianstad Sweden	48	D2	5602N	1410E
Kristiansund Norway	48	C3	6306N	758E
Kriti i. Greece	47	L1	3500N	2500E
Kronshtadt Russia	48	G3	6000N	2940E
Krotoszyn Poland	45	H5	5141N	1727E
Krugersdorp RSA	78	E2	2606S	2746E
Kruševac SM	47	J5	4334N	2120E
Krym' p. Ukraine	49	D4	4600N	3400E
Kryvyy Rih Ukraine	49	D4	4755N	3324E
Ksar El Boukhari Algeria	76	E9	3555N	247E
Kuala Lumpur Malaysia	64	C4	309N	10142E
Kuantan Malaysia	64	C4	348N	10319E
Kubokawa Japan	63	B2	3313N	13309E
Kuching Malaysia	64	D4	133N	11021E
Kufstein Austria	44	F3	4736N	1211E
Kuglugtuk Canada	84	M7	6749N	11512W
Kuito Angola	78	C5	1221S	1656E
Kukës Albania	47	J5	4205N	2024E
Kuldiga Latvia	48	F2	5658N	2158E
Kulti India	59	J9	2343N	8654E
Kuma Japan	63	B2	3339N	13254E
Kumagaya Japan	63	C3	3609N	13922E
Kumamoto Japan	63	B2	3250N	13042E
Kumano Japan	63	C2	3407N	13608E
Kumanovo FYROM	47	J5	4207N	2140E
Kumasi Ghana	76	D3	645N	135W
Kumba Cameroon	76	F2	439N	926E

Kumbakonam India 58 D2 1059N 7924E
Kŭmhwa South Korea 63 A3 3812N 12728E
Kumi South Korea 63 A3 3606N 12822E
Kumi Uganda 79 C5 128N 3355E
Kŭmnyŏng South Korea 63 A2 3332N 12644E
Kundat Malaysia 65 F5 654N 11650E
Kungrad Uzbekistan 54 H5 4306N 5854E
Kunming China 61 H3 2504N 10241E
Kunsan South Korea 63 A3 3557N 12642E
Kununurra Aust. 66 E7 1542S 12850E
Kuopio Finland 48 G3 6254N 2740E
Kupang Indonesia 65 G1 1013S 12338E
Kurashiki Japan 63 B2 3436N 13343E
Kure Japan 63 B2 3414N 13232E
Kure Japan 63 B2 3320N 13315E
Kuressaare Estonia 48 F2 5922N 2840E
Kurgan Russia 54 J8 5530N 6520E
Kurino Japan 63 B2 3157N 13042E
Kurnool India 58 D3 1551N 7801E
Kursk Russia 54 F7 5145N 3614E
Kurtalan Turkey 56 D6 3755N 4144E
Kurume Japan 63 B2 3320N 13029E
Kushikino Japan 63 B2 3145N 13016E
Kushiro Japan 62 D4 4258N 14424E
Kustanay Kazakhstan 54 J7 5315N 6340E
Kütahya Turkey 49 C2 3925N 2956E
K'ut'aisi Georgia 49 F3 4215N 4244E
Kutno Poland 45 J6 5213N 1920E
Kuujjuarapik Canada 85 V5 5515N 7741W
Kuusamo Finland 48 G4 6557N 2915E
Kuvango Angola 78 C5 1427S 1620E
KUWAIT 57 M9
Kuwait Kuwait 57 M9 2920N 4800E
Kuytun China 60 D6 4430N 8500E
Kuzuba Japan 63 B2 3246N 13142E
Kwale Kenya 79 F2 412S 3927E
Kwangju South Korea 63 A3 3507N 12652E
Kwekwe Zimbabwe 78 E4 1855S 2949E
Kyauktaw Myanmar 59 M8 2048N 9259E
Kykládes is. Greece 47 L2 3700N 2500E
Kyoga, Lake Uganda 79 C5 200N 3400E
Kyŏngju South Korea 63 A3 3552N 12912E
Kyōto Japan 63 C3 3502N 13545E
KYRGYZSTAN 54 K5
Kyūshū i. Japan 63 B2 3320N 13100E
Kyustendil Bulgaria 47 K5 4226N 2240E
Kyyiv Ukraine 45 Q5 5025N 3030E
Kyzyl Russia 55 M7 5145N 9428E
Kyzylorda Kazakhstan 54 J5 4425N 6528E

L

Laascaanood Somalia 77 Q3 835N 4655E
Laâyoune Western Sahara 76 B7 2710N 1311W
Labasa Fiji 67 Q7 1625S 17924E
la Baule-Escoublac Fr. 42 C4 4718N 222W
Labé Guinea 76 B4 1117N 1211W
Labrador City Canada 85 X4 5254N 6650W
Lábrea Brazil 90 E12 720S 6446W
La Brea Trinidad & Tobago 90 V15 1014N 6137W
Laccadive Islands India 58 C1/C2 1100N 7200E
la Chaux-de-Fonds Switz. 44 C3 4707N 651E
la Ciotat Fr. 42 G2 4310N 536E
Ladysmith Canada 84 L3 4857N 12350W
Ladysmith RSA 78 E2 2834S 2947E
Lae PNG 67 J9 643S 14701E
Lafayette USA 87 H3 3012N 9218W
Lafayette USA 87 J5 3025N 8654W
La Fé Cuba 89 H4 2202N 8415W
la Flèche Fr. 42 D4 4742N 004W
Laghouat Algeria 76 E8 3349N 255E
Lago di Como l. Italy 46 C6 4600N 900E
Lago di Garda l. Italy 46 D6 4500N 1000E
Lago Maggiore l. Italy 46 C6 4600N 800E
Lagos Nigeria 76 E3 627N 328E
Lagos Port. 43 A2 3705N 840W
La Grande USA 86 C6 4521N 11805W
La Grange USA 87 J3 3320N 8501W
La Guaira Venezuela 90 D16 1038N 6655W
Lagunillas Venezuela 90 C16 1017N 7116W
Lahore Pakistan 58 C6 3134N 7422E
Lahr Germany 41 F1 4820N 750E
Lahti Finland 48 G3 6100N 2540E
Lajes Brazil 91 G8 2748S 5020W
La Junta USA 86 F4 3759N 10334W
Lake Charles tn. USA 87 H3 3013N 9313W
Lakeland USA 87 K2 2802N 8159W
Lakeport USA 86 B4 3904N 12246W
Lakeview USA 86 B5 4213N 12021W
Lakselv Norway 48 F5 7003N 2455E
Lalitpur India 58 D4 2442N 7824E
Lalmanir Hat Bangladesh 59 K10 2551N 8934E
Lamar USA 86 F4 3804N 10237W
Lamego Port. 43 B4 4105N 749W
Lamía Greece 47 K3 3855N 2226E
Lampazos Mexico 88 D5 2700N 10030W
Lampertheim Germany 41 G2 4936N 827E
Lamu Kenya 79 P1 217S 4054E
Lancaster UK 40 E4 5403N 248W
Lancaster USA 86 C3 3441N 11809W
Lancaster USA 87 K4 3943N 8237W
Lancaster USA 87 L5 4001N 7619W
Landau Germany 41 G2 4912N 807E
Landerneau Fr. 42 B5 4827N 416W
Landshut Germany 41 F4 4831N 1210E
Landskrona Sweden 48 D2 5553N 1250E
Langen Germany 41 G6 5337N 836E
Langenselbold Germany 41 H3 5011N 902E
Langon Fr. 42 D3 4433N 014W
Langres Fr. 42 G4 4753N 520E
Langsa Indonesia 64 B4 428N 9759E
Langwedel Germany 41 H5 5259N 912E
Länkäran Azerbaijan 49 G2 3845N 4850E

Lannion Fr. 42 C5 4844N 327W
Lansing USA 87 K5 4244N 8534W
Lanzarote i. Canary Islands 76 B7 2900N 1338W
Lanzhou China 61 H5 3601N 10345E
Laoag Philippines 65 G7 1814N 12036E
Lao Cai Vietnam 61 H2 2230N 10357E
Laon Fr. 42 F5 4934N 337E
La Oroya Peru 90 B11 1136S 7554W
LAOS 64 C7/D7
La Paz Bolivia 90 D10 1630S 6810W
La Paz Mexico 88 B4 2410N 11017W
La Plata Argentina 91 F6 3452S 5755W
Lapua Finland 48 F3 6257N 2300E
Lapu-Lapu Philippines 65 G6 1018N 12358E
L'Aquila Italy 46 E5 4222N 1324E
Larache Morocco 76 C9 3512N 610W
Laramie USA 86 E5 4120N 10538W
Laredo USA 86 G2 2732N 9922W
La Rioja Argentina 91 D8 2926S 6650W
Lárisa Greece 47 K3 3938N 2225E
Larkana Pakistan 58 B5 2732N 6818E
Larnaca Cyprus 49 D1 3454N 3329E
Larne UK 40 D4 5451N 549W
La Rochelle Fr. 42 D4 4610N 110W
La Roda Sp. 43 D3 3913N 215W
Las Cruces USA 86 E3 3218N 10647W
La See d'Urgel Sp. 43 F5 4222N 127E
La Serena Chile 91 C8 2954S 7118W
la Seyne-sur-Mer Fr. 42 G2 4306N 553E
Lashio Myanmar 60 F3 2258N 9748E
Las Palmas Canary Islands 76 A7 2808N 1527W
La Spézia Italy 46 C6 4407N 948E
Las Vegas USA 86 C4 3610N 11510W
Las Vegas USA 86 E4 3536N 10515W
Latacunga Ecuador 90 B13 058S 7836W
Latakia Syria 56 C6 3531N 3547E
Latina Italy 46 E4 4128N 1253E
La Tuque Canada 85 W3 4726N 7247W
Latur India 58 D3 1824N 7634E
LATVIA 48 G2
Launceston Aust. 67 J2 4125S 14707E
Laurel USA 87 J3 3141N 8909W
Lauria Italy 46 F4 4003N 1550E
Lausanne Switz. 44 C3 4632N 639E
Laut i. Indonesia 65 F3 440S 11600E
Lautoka Fiji 67 Q7 1736S 17728E
Laval Fr. 42 D5 4804N 045W
La Vega Dom. Rep. 89 K3 1915N 7033W
La Victoria Venezuela 90 D16 1016N 6721W
Lawrence USA 87 G4 3858N 9515W
Lawton USA 87 G3 3436N 9825W
Laylá Saudi Arabia 56 E3 2216N 4645E
LEBANON 56 C5
Lebanon USA 87 H4 3740N 9240W
Lebrija Sp. 43 B2 3655N 610W
Lecce Italy 47 H4 4021N 1811E
le Creusot Fr. 42 G4 4648N 427E
Leduc Canada 84 N4 5317N 11330W
Leeds UK 40 F3 5350N 135W
Leer Germany 41 C6 5315N 728E
Leeuwarden Neths 41 D6 5312N 548E
Leeward Islands Lesser Antilles 89 M3 1730N 6400W
Lefkáda i. Greece 47 J3 3845N 2040E
Le François Martinique 89 R12 1437N 6054W
Leganés Sp. 43 D4 4020N 346W
Legnica Poland 45 H5 5112N 1610E
le Havre Fr. 42 E5 4930N 006E
Leicester UK 40 F3 5238N 105W
Leiden Neths 41 C5 5210N 430E
Leidschendam Neths 41 C5 5205N 424E
Leipzig Germany 44 F5 5120N 1225E
Leiria Port. 43 A3 3945N 849W
Leivadiá Greece 47 K3 3826N 2253E
Lelystad Neths 41 D5 5232N 529E
le Mans Fr. 42 E4 4800N 012E
Lemmer Neths 41 D5 5250N 543E
Leningrad USA 87 H4 4003N 550E
Leninsk-Kuznetskiy Russia 55 L7 5444N 8613E
Lennestadt Germany 41 G4 5107N 804E
Lens Fr. 42 F6 5026N 250E
Leoben Austria 44 G3 4723N 1506E
León Mexico 88 D4 2110N 10142W
León Nicaragua 89 G2 1224N 8652W
León Sp. 43 C5 4235N 534W
Leonding Austria 44 G4 4819N 1417E
Leonora Aust. 66 D5 2854S 12120E
le Puy Fr. 42 F3 4503N 353E
Léré Chad 77 G3 941N 1417E
Lerwick UK 40 F7 6009N 109W
Les Abymes Guadeloupe 88 Q9 1615N 6131W
Les Cayes Haiti 89 K3 1815N 7346W
Leskovac SM 47 K5 4300N 2157E
LESOTHO 78 E2
les Sables-d'Olonne Fr. 42 D4 4630N 147W
Lésvos i. Greece 47 M3 3900N 2600E
Leszno Poland 45 H5 5151N 1635E
Lethbridge Canada 84 N3 4943N 11248W
le Touquet-Paris-Plage Fr. 42 F6 5013N 136E
Letpadan Myanmar 64 B7 1746N 9545E
Leuven Belgium 41 C4 5053N 442E
Levanto Italy 46 C6 4410N 937E
Leverkusen Germany 44 C5 5102N 659E
Levice Slovakia 45 J4 4813N 1835E
Levin NZ 69 E4 4037S 17517E
Lévis Canada 85 W3 4647N 7112W
Lewistown USA 86 E6 4704N 10926W
Lexington USA 87 K4 3803N 8430W
Leyte i. Philippines 65 G6/H6 1050N 12500E
Lezhe Albania 47 J4 4146N 1939E
Lhasa China 60 F3 2941N 9110E
Lhaze China 60 E3 2908N 8743E
Lhokseumawe Indonesia 64 B5 509N 9709E
Lianyungang China 61 L4 3437N 11910E

Liaoyang China 61 M6 4116N 12312E
Liaoyuan China 61 N6 4253N 12510E
Libenge CDR 77 J2 339N 1839E
Liberal USA 86 F4 3703N 10056W
Liberec Czech Rep. 44 G5 5048N 1505E
LIBERIA 76 B3/C3
Libourne Fr. 42 D3 4455N 014W
Libreville Gabon 77 F2 030N 925E
LIBYA 77 G7/K7
Licata Italy 46 E2 3707N 1357E
Lichinga Mozambique 78 G5 1319S 3513E
Lida Belarus 49 C5 5350N 2519E
LIECHTENSTEIN 44 D3
Liège Belgium 41 5038N 535E
Lienz Austria 44 F3 4651N 1250E
Liepāja Latvia 48 F2 5630N 2100E
Lier Belgium 41 C5 5108N 435E
Liestal Switz. 44 C3 4729N 743E
Likasi CDR 78 E5 1058S 2647E
Lille Fr. 42 F6 5039N 305E
Lillehammer Norway 48 D3 6106N 1027E
Lilongwe Malawi 78 F5 1358S 3349E
Lima Peru 90 B11 1204S 7703W
Lima USA 87 K5 4043N 8406W
Limassol Cyprus 49 D1 3404N 3303E
Limbang Malaysia 64 P11 445N 11459E
Limbe Cameroon 76 F2 358N 910E
Limburg Germany 44 D5 5023N 804E
Limerick Rol 40 B3 5204N 838W
Limnos i. Greece 47 L3 3900N 2500E
Limoges Fr. 42 E3 4550N 115E
Limoux Fr. 42 F2 4303N 213E
Linares Mexico 88 E4 2454N 9938W
Linares Sp. 43 D3 3805N 338W
Lincoln UK 40 F3 5314N 033W
Lincoln USA 87 G5 4049N 9641W
Linden Germany 41 G3 5032N 839E
Linden Guyana 90 F15 559N 5819W
Lingen Germany 44 C6 5232N 719E
Linhares Brazil 90 K10 1922S 4004W
Linköping Sweden 48 E2 5825N 1535E
Linsell Sweden 48 D3 6210N 1350E
Linton USA 86 F6 4617N 10014W
Linxia China 61 H5 3531N 10308E
Linz Austria 44 G4 4819N 1418E
Lipetsk Russia 54 F7 5237N 3936E
Lipova Romania 45 K3 4605N 2143E
Lippstadt Germany 44 D5 5141N 820E
Lira Uganda 79 C6 215N 3254E
Lisbon Port. 43 A3 3844N 908W
Lisburn UK 40 C4 5431N 603W
Lisieux Fr. 42 E5 4909N 014E
Lismore Aust. 67 K5 2848S 15317E
Lisse Neths 41 C5 5216N 434E
Lithgow Aust. 67 K4 3330S 15009E
LITHUANIA 48 F2
Little Aden Yemen 56 D1 1247N 4455E
Little Falls tn. USA 87 H6 4558N 9420W
Little Rock USA 87 H3 3442N 9217W
Little Salmon Canada 84 J6 6230N 13459W
Liuzhou China 61 J2 2417N 10915E
Liverpool UK 40 E3 5325N 255W
Livingston USA 86 D6 4540N 11033W
Livingstone Zambia 78 E4 1752S 2552E
Livingstonia Malawi 78 F5 1035S 3410E
Livorno Italy 46 D5 4333N 1018E
Liwale Tanzania 78 G6 947S 3800E
Ljubljana Slovenia 46 F7 4604N 1430E
Ljusdal Sweden 48 E3 6157N 1605E
Llanelli UK 40 D2 5142N 410W
Llanes Sp. 43 C5 4325N 445W
Lleida Sp. 43 F4 4137N 038E
Lloydminster Canada 84 P4 5318N 11000W
Lobatse Botswana 78 E2 2511S 2540E
Lobito Angola 78 B4 1220S 1334E
Locarno Switz. 44 D3 4610N 848E
Loches Fr. 42 E4 4708N 100E
Lockhart USA 82 G3 2954N 9714W
Lodwar Kenya 79 D6 306N 3534E
Łódź Poland 45 J5 5149N 1928E
Loei Thailand 64 C7 1732N 10140E
Logan USA 86 D5 4145N 11150W
Logroño Sp. 43 D5 4228N 226W
Loire r. Fr. 42 C4 4717N 209W
Loja Ecuador 90 B13 359S 7916W
Loja Sp. 43 C2 3710N 409W
Lokeren Belgium 41 B4 5106N 359E
Lokitaung Kenya 79 D7 416N 3545E
Lolland i. Denmark 48 D1 5445N 1120E
Loloda Indonesia 65 H4 139N 12737E
Lombok i. Indonesia 65 F2 830S 11630E
Lomé Togo 76 E3 610N 121E
Lomela CDR 78 D7 219S 2315E
Lommel Belgium 41 D4 5114N 519E
Lomphat Cambodia 64 D6 1330N 10700E
Londiani Kenya 79 D4 010S 3536E
London Canada 85 U2 4258N 8115W
London UK 40 F2 5130N 010W
Londonderry UK 40 C4 5459N 719W
Londrina Brazil 90 G9 2318S 5113W
Long Beach tn. USA 86 C3 3347N 11815W
Long Branch USA 87 M5 4017N 7359W
Longford Rol 40 C3 5344N 747W
Longido Tanzania 79 E3 244S 3641E
Long Island Bahamas 89 J4/K4 2320N 7500W
Longlac Canada 85 T3 4947N 8634W
Longreach Aust. 67 H6 2328S 14415E
Longuyon Fr. 42 G5 4927N 536E
Long Xuyen Vietnam 64 D6 1023N 10525E
Löningen Germany 41 F5 5245N 747E
Lora del Rio Sp. 43 C2 3739N 532W
Lorain USA 87 K5 4128N 8211W
Lorca Sp. 43 E2 3740N 141W
Loreto Italy 46 E5 4336N 1336E

Loreto Mexico 86 D2 2601N 11121W
Lorient Fr. 42 C4 4745N 321W
Los Angeles Chile 91 C6 3728S 7223W
Los Angeles USA 86 C3 3400N 11815W
Los Mochis Mexico 88 C5 2548N 10900W
Losser Neths 41 F5 5216N 701E
Los Teques Venezuela 90 D16 1025N 6701W
Louangphrabang Laos 64 C7 1953N 10210E
Loubomo Congo 78 B7 409S 1247E
Loudéac Fr. 42 C5 4811N 245W
Lough Neagh l. UK 40 C4 5435N 630W
Louisiana state USA 87 H3 3200N 9200W
Louis Trichardt RSA 78 E3 2301S 2943W
Louisville USA 87 J4 3813N 8548W
Lourdes Fr. 42 D2 4306N 002E
Louviers Fr. 42 E5 4913N 107E
Lovech Bulgaria 47 L5 4308N 2445E
Lowell USA 87 M5 4238N 7119W
Lower Hutt NZ 69 E4 4113S 17458E
Lowestoft UK 40 G3 5229N 145E
Łowicz Poland 45 J6 5206N 1955E
Loznica SM 47 H6 4431N 1914E
Lozova Ukraine 49 E4 4854N 3620E
Luanda Angola 78 B6 850S 1317E
Luanshya Zambia 78 E5 1309S 2824E
Luarca Sp. 43 B5 4333N 631W
Luau Angola 78 D5 1042S 221E
Lubango Angola 78 B5 1455S 1333E
Lübbecke Germany 41 G5 5219N 834E
Lubbock USA 86 F3 3335N 10153W
Lübeck Germany 44 E6 5352N 1041E
Lubin Poland 45 H5 5123N 1612E
Lublin Poland 45 L5 5118N 2233E
Lubumbashi CDR 78 E5 1141S 2726E
Lucca Italy 46 D5 4350N 1030E
Lucena Philippines 65 G6 1357N 12136E
Lucena Sp. 43 C2 3725N 429W
Luckenwalde Germany 44 F6 5205N 1311E
Lucknow India 58 E5 2650N 8056E
Lucusse Angola 78 D5 1233S 2054E
Lüdenscheid Germany 41 F4 5113N 738E
Lüderitz Namibia 78 C2 2638S 1510E
Ludhiana India 58 D6 3056N 7552E
Ludvika Sweden 48 E3 6008N 1511E
Ludwigshafen Germany 44 D4 4929N 824E
Ludwigslust Germany 44 E6 5320N 1118E
Luena Angola 78 C5 1147S 1951E
Lufkin USA 87 H3 3121N 9447W
Luga Russia 49 C5 5842N 2959E
Lugano Switz. 44 D3 4601N 857E
Lugo Sp. 43 B5 4300N 733W
Lugoj Romania 45 K2 4541N 2156E
Luhans'k Ukraine 49 E4 4835N 3922E
Łuków Poland 45 L5 5157N 2222E
Luleå Sweden 48 F4 6535N 2210E
Lüleburgaz Turkey 47 M4 4125N 2727E
Lumberton USA 87 L3 3437N 7902W
Lund Sweden 48 D2 5542N 1311E
Lüneburg Germany 44 E6 5315N 1024E
Lunenburg Canada 85 Y2 4423N 6421W
Lunéville Fr. 42 H5 4835N 630E
Lunga Lunga Kenya 79 F2 435S 3910E
Lunglei India 59 M9 2254N 9243E
Luninyets Belarus 45 N6 5218N 2652E
Luoshan China 61 K4 3112N 11438E
Luoyang China 61 K4 3447N 11224E
Lusaka Zambia 78 E4 1526S 2824E
Lusambo CDR 78 D7 459S 2326E
Lushnjë Albania 47 J4 4057N 1940E
Lustenau Austria 44 D3 4726N 934E
Luton UK 40 F2 5153N 025W
Lutong Malaysia 64 N10 429N 11406E
Luts'k Ukraine 45 M5 5042N 2515E
Luwero Uganda 79 C5 047N 3229E
LUXEMBOURG 41 D2/E2
Luxembourg Luxembourg 41 E2 4937N 608E
Luxor Egypt 77 M7 2541N 3224E
Luzern Switz. 44 D3 4703N 817E
Luzhou China 61 J3 2855N 10524E
Luziânia Brazil 90 H10 1616S 4757W
Luzon i. Philippines 65 G7 1500N 12200E
L'viv Ukraine 45 M4 4950N 2400E
Lycksele Sweden 48 E4 6434N 1844E
Lyme Bay UK 40 E2 5040N 255W
Lynchburg USA 87 L4 3724N 7900W
Lynn Lake tn. Canada 85 Q5 5651N 10102W
Lyons Fr. 42 G3 4546N 450E
Lyttelton NZ 69 D3 4336S 17240E
Lytton Canada 84 L4 5012N 12131W

M

Ma'an Jordan 56 C5 3011N 3543E
Ma'anshan China 61 L4 3149N 11830E
Maaseik Belgium 41 D4 5108N 555E
Maastricht Neths 41 D3 5051N 542E
Mabalane Mozambique 78 F3 2351S 3226E
McAlester USA 87 G3 3456N 9546W
McAllen USA 87 G2 2613N 9815W
Macao China 61 K2 2213N 11336E
Macapá Brazil 90 G14 004N 5104W
Macarata Italy 46 E5 4318N 1327E
McComb USA 87 H3 3113N 9030W
McCook USA 86 F5 4013N 10033W
Maceió Brazil 90 K12 940S 3544W
Machakos Kenya 79 E4 132S 3716E
Machala Ecuador 90 B13 320S 7957W
Machiques Venezuela 90 C16 1004N 7237W
Mackay Aust. 67 J6 2110S 14911E
Mackenzie r. Canada 84 J7 6700N 13200W
Mackinaw City USA 85 T4 4547N 8444W
McKinley, Mount USA 84 E6 6202N 15100W
McKinney USA 87 G3 3314N 9635W

Name	Page	Grid	Lat	Long
âcon Fr.	42	G4	46 18N	4 50E
acon USA	87	K3	32 49N	83 37W
cPherson USA	87	G4	38 22N	97 41W
ADAGASCAR	78	H2/J5		
adang PNG	67	J9	5 14S	145 45E
adaripur Bangladesh	59	L9	23 09N	90 11E
adeira Islands Atlantic Ocean	76	A8	32 45N	17 00W
adinat ash Sha'b Yemen	56	D1	12 50N	44 56E
adinat Zâyid UAE	57	N8	23 34N	53 48E
adison USA	87	J5	43 04N	89 22W
adiun Indonesia	64	E2	7 37S	111 33E
ado Gashi Kenya	77	N2	0 45N	39 11E
adrid Sp.	43	D4	40 25N	3 43W
adurai India	58	D1	9 55N	78 07E
aebashi Japan	63	C3	36 24N	139 04E
aevantanana Madagascar	78	J4	16 57S	46 50E
afikeng RSA	78	E2	25 53S	25 39E
afraq Jordan	56	C5	32 20N	36 12E
agadan Russia	55	T8	59 38N	150 50E
agadi Kenya	79	E4	1 52S	36 19E
agdalena Mexico	88	B6	30 38N	110 59W
agdeburg Germany	44	E6	52 08N	11 37E
agelang Indonesia	64	E2	7 28S	110 11E
agnitogorsk Russia	54	H7	53 28N	59 06E
agwe Myanmar	60	G2	20 08N	94 55E
ahajanga Madagascar	78	J4	15 40S	46 20E
ahân Iran	57	P10	30 04N	57 17E
ahé i. Seychelles	73	B1	4 40S	55 30E
ahébourg Mauritius	73	E2	20 24S	57 42E
ahilyow Belarus	45	Q6	53 54N	30 20E
ahón Balearic Islands	43	H3	39 54N	4 15E
aidstone UK	40	G2	51 17N	0 32E
aiduguri Nigeria	76	G4	11 53N	13 16E
aine state USA	87	N6	45 00N	70 00W
ainz Germany	44	D4	50 00N	8 16E
aiquetía Venezuela	90	D16	10 38N	66 59W
aitland Aust.	67	K4	32 33S	151 33E
aizuru Japan	63	C3	35 30N	135 20E
ajene Indonesia	65	F3	3 33S	118 59E
akat Kazakhstan	49	H4	47 37N	53 14E
akeni Sierra Leone	76	B3	8 57N	12 02W
akhachkala Russia	54	G5	42 59N	47 30E
akó Hungary	45	K3	46 11N	20 30E
akokou Gabon	76	G2	0 38N	12 47E
akurdi Nigeria	76	F3	7 44N	8 35E
alabo Eq. Guinea	76	F2	3 45N	8 48E
alaga Sp.	43	C2	36 43N	4 25W
alakal Sudan	77	M3	9 31N	31 40E
alang Indonesia	64	E2	7 59S	112 45E
alanje Angola	78	C6	9 32S	16 20E
alatya Turkey	49	E2	38 22N	38 18E
ALAWI	78	F5		
ALAYSIA	64/65	C5/E5		
albork Poland	45	J7	54 02N	19 01E
ALDIVES	59	N12/N17		
aldonado Uruguay	91	G7	34 57S	54 59W
ale Maldives	59	N15	4 10N	73 29E
alegaon India	58	C4	20 32N	74 38E
alema Mozambique	78	F3	14 57S	37 25E
ALI	76	C4/D5		
alinau Malaysia	64	P10	4 03N	114 43E
alindi Kenya	79	G3	3 14S	40 06E
allaig UK	40	D5	57 00N	5 50W
allorca i. Balearic Islands	43	G3	39 50N	2 30E
almédy Belgium	41	E3	50 26N	6 02E
almesbury RSA	78	C1	33 28S	18 43E
almö Sweden	48	D2	55 35N	13 00E
almyzh Russia	49	H6	56 31N	50 43E
alonga CDR	78	D1	10 26S	23 10E
ALTA	46	P8/Q8		
alta USA	86	E6	48 22N	107 51W
aluku is. Indonesia	65	H3	4 00S	127 00E
alya Tanzania	79	C3	2 59S	33 31E
in Côte d'Ivoire	76	C3	7 31N	7 37W
anacor Balearic Islands	43	G3	39 35N	3 12E
anado Indonesia	65	G4	1 32N	124 55E
anagua Nicaragua	88	G2	12 06N	86 18W
anali India	58	D6	32 12N	77 06E
anama Bahrain	57	N9	26 12N	50 38E
anaus Brazil	90	F13	3 06S	60 00W
nchester UK	40	E3	53 30N	2 15W
ndal Norway	48	C2	58 02N	7 30E
ndalay Myanmar	60	G2	21 57N	96 04E
ndera Kenya	79	G6	3 53N	41 50E
ndeville Jamaica	89	U14	18 02N	77 31W
nfredonia Italy	46	F4	41 37N	15 55E
ngalia Romania	45	P1	43 48N	28 36E
ngalore India	58	C2	12 54N	74 51E
ngaweka NZ	69	E5	39 49S	176 05E
ngonui NZ	69	D7	34 59S	173 32E
nhattan USA	87	G4	39 11N	96 35W
nica Mozambique	78	F4	18 56S	32 52E
nicoré Brazil	90	E12	5 48S	61 16W
nicouagan Canada	85	X4	50 40N	68 45W
nila Philippines	65	G6	14 37N	120 58E
nisa Turkey	47	M3	38 36N	27 29E
nitoba province Canada	85	R5	55 15N	100 00W
nitowoc USA	87	J5	44 04N	87 40W
niwaki Canada	85	V3	46 22N	75 58W
nizales Col.	90	B15	5 03N	75 32W
nkato USA	87	H5	44 10N	94 00W
nnar Sri Lanka	58	D1	8 58N	79 54E
nsfield USA	87	K5	40 46N	82 31W
nta Ecuador	90	A13	0 59S	80 44W
ntes-la-Jolie Fr.	42	E4	48 59N	1 43E
ntua Italy	46	D6	45 10N	10 47E
nukau NZ	69	E6	37 00S	174 52E
nyoni Tanzania	79	D2	5 46S	34 50E
Manzanares Sp.	43	D3	39 00N	3 23W
Manzanillo Cuba	89	J4	20 21N	77 21W
Manzanillo Mexico	88	D3	19 00N	104 20W
Manzhouli China	61	L7	46 36N	117 28E
Maoming China	61	K2	21 50N	110 56E
Maple Creek tn. Canada	84	P3	49 55N	109 28W
Maputo Mozambique	78	F2	25 58S	32 35E
Marabá Brazil	90	H12	5 23S	49 10W
Maracaibo Venezuela	90	C16	10 44N	71 37W
Maracay Venezuela	90	D16	10 20N	67 28W
Maradi Niger	76	F4	13 29N	7 10E
Maralal Kenya	79	E5	1 06N	36 42E
Marbella Sp.	43	C2	36 31N	4 53W
Marble Bar tn. Aust.	66	C6	21 16S	119 45E
Marburg Germany	44	D5	50 49N	8 36E
Mardan Pakistan	58	C6	34 14N	72 05E
Mar del Plata Argentina	91	F6	38 00S	57 32W
Mardin Turkey	49	F2	37 19N	40 43E
Margate UK	40	G2	51 24N	1 24E
Maria Elena Chile	90	D9	22 18S	69 40W
Maribor Slovenia	46	F7	46 34N	15 38E
Mariehamn Finland	48	E3	60 05N	19 55E
Mariental Namibia	78	C3	24 36S	17 59E
Marignane Fr.	42	G2	43 25N	5 12E
Marigot Dominica	88	Q8	15 32N	61 18W
Marijampolė Lithuania	48	F1	54 31N	23 20E
Marília Brazil	90	G9	22 13S	49 58W
Maringá Brazil	90	G9	23 26S	52 02W
Marion USA	87	K5	40 35N	83 08W
Marka Somalia	77	P2	1 42N	44 47E
Marl Germany	41	F4	51 40N	7 06E
Marmande Fr.	42	E3	44 30N	0 10E
Maroantsetra Madagascar	78	J4	15 23S	49 44E
Maroua Cameroon	77	G4	10 35N	14 20E
Marquette USA	87	J6	46 33N	87 23W
Marrakesh Morocco	76	C8	31 49N	8 00W
Marsabit Kenya	79	F6	2 20N	37 59E
Marsala Italy	46	E2	37 48N	12 27E
Marsalforn Malta	46	P9	36 04N	14 16E
Marseilles Fr.	42	G2	43 18N	5 22E
MARSHALL ISLANDS	70	G9/H8		
Martapura Indonesia	64	E3	3 31S	114 45E
Martigny Switz.	44	C3	46 07N	7 05E
Martigues Fr.	42	G2	43 24N	5 03E
Martin Slovakia	45	J4	49 04N	18 55E
Martinique i. Lesser Antilles	88	R12	14 30N	61 00W
Martinsville USA	87	L4	36 43N	79 53W
Marton NZ	69	E4	40 05S	175 23E
Martos Sp.	43	C2	37 44N	3 58W
Marudi Malaysia	64	N10	4 12N	114 20E
Marvejois Fr.	42	F3	44 33N	3 18E
Mary Turkmenistan	54	J4	37 42N	61 54E
Maryborough Aust.	67	K5	25 32S	152 36E
Maryland state USA	87	L4	39 00N	77 00W
Marysville USA	86	B4	39 10N	121 34W
Masai Malaysia	65	T15	1 29N	103 53E
Masaka Uganda	79	B4	0 20S	31 44E
Masan South Korea	63	A3	35 10N	128 35E
Masaya Nicaragua	88	G2	11 59N	86 03W
Maseru Lesotho	78	E2	29 19S	27 29E
Mashhad Iran	57	G6	36 16N	59 34E
Mashike Japan	62	D4	43 52N	141 32E
Mashiz Iran	57	P9	29 54N	56 35E
Masindi Uganda	79	B5	1 41N	31 45E
Mason City USA	87	H5	43 10N	93 10W
Massa Italy	46	D5	44 02N	10 09E
Massachusetts state USA	87	M5	42 00N	72 00W
Massawa Eritrea	77	N5	15 42N	39 25E
Massena USA	87	M5	44 56N	74 57W
Massif Central mts. Fr.	42	F3	45 00N	3 30E
Masterton NZ	69	E4	40 57S	175 39E
Masuda Japan	63	B2	34 42N	131 51E
Masuku Gabon	78	B7	1 40S	13 31E
Masvingo Zimbabwe	78	F3	20 05S	30 50E
Matadi CDR	78	B6	5 50S	13 32E
Matagalpa Nicaragua	88	G2	12 52N	85 58W
Matagami Canada	85	V3	49 45N	77 45W
Matale Sri Lanka	58	E1	7 28N	80 37E
Matamoros Mexico	88	D5	25 33N	103 51W
Matamoros Mexico	88	E5	25 50N	97 31W
Matane Canada	85	X3	48 50N	67 31W
Matanzas Cuba	89	H4	23 04N	81 35W
Matara Sri Lanka	58	E1	5 57N	80 32E
Mataram Indonesia	65	F2	8 36S	116 07E
Mataró Sp.	43	G4	41 32N	2 27E
Mataura NZ	69	B1	45 45S	168 50E
Matehuala Mexico	88	D4	23 40N	100 40W
Matera Italy	47	G4	40 40N	16 37E
Mathura India	58	D5	27 30N	77 42E
Matosinhos Port.	43	A4	41 08N	8 45W
Maṭraḥ Oman	57	P8	23 31N	58 18E
Matsue Japan	63	C3	35 46N	139 04E
Matsue Japan	63	B3	35 29N	133 04E
Matsumoto Japan	63	C3	36 18N	137 58E
Matsuyama Japan	63	B2	33 50N	132 47E
Mattawa Canada	85	V3	46 19N	78 42W
Maturin Venezuela	90	E15	9 45N	63 10W
Maubeuge Fr.	42	F6	50 17N	3 58E
MAURITANIA	76	B5/C6		
MAURITIUS	73			
Mayagüez Puerto Rico	89	L3	18 13N	67 09W
Mayenne Fr.	42	D4	48 18N	0 37W
Maykop Russia	54	G5	44 37N	40 48E
May Pen Jamaica	89	U13	17 58N	77 15W
Mazabuka Zambia	78	E4	15 50S	27 47E
Mazamet Fr.	42	F2	43 30N	2 22E
Mazara del Vallo Italy	46	E2	37 40N	12 34E
Mazâr-e Sharif Afghanistan	57	J6	36 42N	67 06E
Mazatenango Guatemala	88	F2	14 31N	91 30W
Mazatlán Mexico	88	C4	23 11N	106 25W
Mazyr Belarus	45	P6	52 02N	29 10E
Mbabane Swaziland	78	F2	26 20S	31 08E
Mbaiki CAR	77	J2	3 53N	18 01E
Mbala Zambia	78	F6	8 50S	31 24E
Mbale Uganda	79	D5	1 05N	34 10E
Mbalmayo Cameroon	76	G2	3 30N	11 31E
Mbandaka CDR	77	J2	0 03N	18 28E
Mbarara Uganda	79	B4	0 36S	30 38E
Mbeya Tanzania	78	F6	8 54S	33 29E
Mbuji-Mayi CDR	78	D6	6 10S	23 39E
Meadville USA	87	K5	41 38N	80 10W
Meaux Fr.	42	F5	48 58N	2 54E
Mecca Saudi Arabia	56	C3	21 26N	39 49E
Mechelen Belgium	41	C4	51 02N	4 29E
Mecheria Algeria	76	D8	33 31N	0 20W
Medan Indonesia	64	B4	3 35N	98 39E
Médéa Algeria	76	E9	36 15N	2 48E
Medellín Col.	90	B15	6 15N	75 36W
Medenine Tunisia	76	G8	33 24N	10 25E
Medford USA	86	B5	42 20N	122 52W
Medias Romania	45	M3	46 10N	24 21E
Medicine Hat Canada	84	N4	50 03N	110 41W
Medina Saudi Arabia	56	C3	24 30N	39 35E
Medina del Campo Sp.	43	C4	41 18N	4 55W
Medinipur India	59	F4	22 25N	87 24E
Mediterranean Sea	46	B2/E2	36 00N	15 00E
Meekatharra Aust.	66	C5	26 30S	118 30E
Meerut India	58	D5	29 00N	77 42E
Meiktila Myanmar	64	B8	20 53N	95 54E
Meinerzhagen Germany	41	F4	51 06N	7 38E
Meizhou China	61	L2	24 19N	116 13E
Mekele Ethiopia	77	N4	13 32N	39 33E
Mekong r. Asia	64	C8	16 00N	105 00E
Melaka Malaysia	64	C4	2 11N	102 14E
Melbourne Aust.	67	H3	37 45S	144 58E
Melbourne USA	87	K2	28 04N	80 38W
Meleuz Russia	49	J5	52 55N	55 55E
Melfort Canada	85	Q4	52 52N	104 38W
Melilla territory Sp.	43	D1	35 17N	2 57W
Melitopol' Ukraine	49	E4	46 51N	35 22E
Melle Germany	41	G5	52 12N	8 21E
Mellieha Malta	46	P8	35 58N	14 22E
Melo Uruguay	91	G7	32 22S	54 10W
Melun Fr.	42	F5	48 32N	2 40E
Melville Canada	85	Q4	50 57N	102 49W
Memmingen Germany	44	E3	47 59N	10 11E
Memphis USA	87	J4	35 10N	90 00W
Mempuing Malaysia	65	U16	1 31N	104 02E
Mende Fr.	42	F3	44 32N	3 30E
Mendi PNG	67	H9	6 13S	143 39E
Mendoza Argentina	91	D7	32 48S	68 52W
Mengdingjie China	60	G2	23 03N	99 03E
Menongue Angola	78	C5	14 36S	17 48E
Menorca i. Balearic Islands	43	G4/H3	39 45N	4 15E
Menton Fr.	42	H2	43 47N	7 30E
Mentor USA	87	K5	41 42N	81 22W
Meoqui Mexico	86	E2	28 17N	105 29W
Meppel Neths	41	E5	52 42N	6 12E
Meppen Germany	41	F5	52 41N	7 18E
Merano Italy	46	D7	46 41N	11 10E
Merced USA	86	B4	37 17N	120 29W
Mercedes Argentina	91	D7	33 41S	65 28W
Mercedes Uruguay	91	F7	34 15S	58 02W
Mergui Myanmar	64	B6	12 26N	98 34E
Mérida Mexico	88	G4	20 59N	89 39W
Mérida Sp.	43	B3	38 55N	6 20W
Mérida Venezuela	90	C15	8 24N	71 08W
Méridian USA	87	J3	32 21N	88 42W
Mérignac Fr.	42	D3	44 50N	0 36W
Merowe Sudan	77	M5	18 30N	31 49E
Merritt Canada	84	L4	50 09N	120 49W
Mersin Turkey	49	D2	36 47N	34 37E
Mersing Malaysia	64	C4	2 26N	103 50E
Merthyr Tydfil UK	40	E2	51 46N	3 23W
Meru Kenya	79	E5	0 05N	37 38E
Merzifon Turkey	49	D3	40 52N	35 28E
Merzig Germany	41	E2	49 27N	6 39E
Mesa USA	86	D3	33 25N	111 50W
Meschede Germany	41	G4	51 21N	8 16E
Mesolóngi Greece	47	J3	38 21N	21 26E
Messina Italy	47	F3	38 13N	15 33E
Messina RSA	78	E3	22 23S	30 00E
Metz Fr.	42	H5	49 07N	6 11E
Mexicali Mexico	88	A6	32 36N	115 30W
MEXICO	88	C5/E3		
Mexico City Mexico	88	E3	19 25N	99 10W
Mexico, Gulf of Mexico	88	F4/G4	25 00N	90 00W
Meymaneh Afghanistan	57	H6	35 55N	64 47E
Miami USA	87	K2	25 45N	80 15W
Miäneh Iran	56	E6	37 23N	47 45E
Mianwali Pakistan	58	C6	32 32N	71 33E
Miass Russia	54	J7	55 00N	60 08E
Michigan state USA	87	J5/K5	45 00N	85 00W
Michigan, Lake Canada/USA	87	J5/J6	45 00N	87 00W
Michipicoten Canada	85	U3	47 57N	84 55W
Michurinsk Russia	49	F5	52 54N	40 30E
Middelburg Neths	41	B4	51 30N	3 36E
Middelburg RSA	78	E2	31 28S	25 01E
Middlesbrough UK	40	F4	54 35N	1 14W
Midland USA	87	V2	44 45N	79 53W
Midland USA	86	F3	32 00N	102 09W
Międzyrzec Poland	45	G6	52 27N	15 34E
Mieres Sp.	43	C5	43 15N	5 46W
Mikawa Japan	63	C3	36 30N	136 30E
Mikhaylovka Russia	49	F5	50 04N	43 15E
Mikkeli Finland	48	G3	61 44N	27 15E
Mikumi Tanzania	79	E1	7 24S	36 59E
Milagro Ecuador	90	B13	2 11S	79 36W
Milan Italy	46	C6	45 28N	9 12E
Milas Turkey	47	M2	37 19N	27 48E
Mildura Aust.	67	H4	34 14S	142 13E
Miles City USA	86	E6	46 24N	105 48W
Milford USA	86	D4	38 22N	113 00W
Milford Haven UK	40	D2	51 44N	5 02W
Milford Sound tn. NZ	69	A2	44 41S	167 56E
Millau Fr.	42	F3	44 06N	3 05E
Milton NZ	69	B1	46 07S	169 58E
Milton Keynes UK	40	F3	52 02N	0 42W
Milwaukee USA	87	J5	43 03N	87 56W
Minä Abdallāh Kuwait	57	M9	29 00N	48 08E
Mina Jebel Ali UAE	57	P9	25 00N	55 04E
Minamata Japan	63	B2	32 13N	130 23E
Minas Uruguay	91	F7	34 20S	55 15W
Minä 'Sa'ûd Kuwait	57	M9	28 43N	48 08E
Minatitlán Mexico	88	F3	17 59N	94 32W
Mindanao i. Philippines	65	G5/H5	8 00N	125 00E
Minden Germany	44	D6	52 18N	8 54E
Minden USA	87	H3	32 26N	93 17W
Mindoro i. Philippines	65	G6	13 00N	121 00E
Mingäcevir Azerbaijan	49	G3	40 45N	47 03E
Mingan Canada	85	Y4	50 19N	64 02W
Minicoy Island India	59	N17	8 29N	73 01E
Minneapolis USA	87	H5	45 00N	93 15W
Minnedosa Canada	85	R4	50 14N	99 50W
Minnesota state USA	87	H6	47 00N	95 00W
Minot USA	86	F6	48 16N	101 19W
Minsk Belarus	49	C5	53 51N	27 30E
Miramichi Canada	85	X3	65 30N	47 02W
Miranda de Ebro Sp.	43	D5	42 41N	2 57W
Miri Malaysia	64	M10	4 23N	114 00E
Mirpur Khas Pakistan	58	B5	25 33N	69 05E
Mirzapur India	58	E5	25 09N	82 34E
Misawa Japan	62	D4	40 42N	141 26E
Miskolc Hungary	45	K4	48 07N	20 47E
Misool i. Indonesia	65	J3	1 50S	129 55E
Misratah Libya	77	G8	32 23N	15 00E
Mississippi r. USA	87	H3	35 00N	90 00W
Mississippi state USA	87	H3/J3	32 00N	90 00W
Missoula USA	86	D6	46 52N	114 00W
Missouri r. USA	87	H4	39 00N	93 00W
Missouri state USA	87	H4	38 00N	93 00W
Misumi Japan	63	B2	32 37N	130 28E
Mitchell Aust.	67	J5	26 29S	147 57E
Mitchell USA	87	G5	43 40N	98 01W
Mito Japan	63	D3	36 22N	140 29E
Miyako Japan	62	D3	39 38N	141 59E
Miyakonojō Japan	63	B2	31 43N	131 02E
Miyazaki Japan	63	B2	31 56N	131 27E
Miyoshi Japan	63	B2	34 50N	132 49E
Mława Poland	45	K6	53 08N	20 20E
Mobaye CAR	77	K2	4 19N	21 11E
Mobile USA	87	J3	30 40N	88 05W
Moçambique Mozambique	78	H4	15 03S	40 45E
Mocuba Mozambique	78	G4	16 52S	36 57E
Módena Italy	46	D6	44 39N	10 55E
Modesto USA	86	B4	37 37N	121 00W
Mödling Austria	45	H4	48 06N	16 18E
Moe i. Aust.	67	J3	38 09S	146 22E
Moers Germany	41	E4	51 27N	6 36E
Mogadishu Somalia	77	Q2	2 02N	45 21E
Mogocha Russia	55	P7	53 44N	119 45E
Mohe China	61	M8	52 55N	122 27E
Mo-i-Rana Norway	48	D4	66 18N	14 00E
Mojave USA	86	C4	35 02N	118 11W
Moji Japan	63	B2	33 57N	130 58E
Mokau NZ	69	E5	38 42S	174 37E
Mokolo Cameroon	77	G4	10 49N	13 54E
Mokp'o South Korea	63	A2	34 50N	126 25E
MOLDOVA	45	P3		
Molepolole Botswana	78	E3	24 25S	25 30E
Molfetta Italy	47	G4	41 12N	16 36E
Mollendo Peru	90	C10	17 00S	72 00W
Mölndal Sweden	48	D2	57 40N	12 00E
Mombasa Kenya	79	F2	4 04S	39 40E
Mombo Tanzania	79	F2	4 53S	38 17E
MONACO	42	H2		
Monahans USA	86	F3	31 35N	102 54W
Monção Brazil	90	H13	3 30S	45 15W
Monclova Mexico	88	D5	26 55N	101 25W
Moncton Canada	85	Y3	46 04N	64 50W
Mondovi Italy	46	B6	44 23N	7 49E
Monduli Tanzania	79	E3	3 17S	36 22E
Monemvasia Greece	47	K2	36 41N	23 03E
Monfalcone Italy	46	E6	45 49N	13 32E
MONGOLIA	60	E7/L7		
Mongu Zambia	78	D4	15 13S	23 09E
Monopoli Italy	47	G4	40 57N	17 18E
Monroe USA	87	H3	32 31N	92 06W
Monrovia Liberia	76	B3	6 20N	10 46W
Mons Belgium	41	B3	50 28N	3 58E
Montabaur Germany	41	F3	50 26N	7 50E
Montana Bulgaria	47	K5	43 25N	23 11E
Montana state USA	86	E6	47 00N	111 00W
Montargis Fr.	42	F4	48 00N	2 44E
Montauban Fr.	42	E3	44 01N	1 20E
Montbéliard Fr.	42	H4	47 31N	6 48E
Mont Blanc mt. Fr./Italy	42	H3	45 50N	6 52E
Montceau-les-Mines Fr.	42	G4	46 40N	4 23E
Mont-de-Marsan Fr.	42	D2	43 54N	0 30W
Montdidier Fr.	42	F5	49 39N	2 35E
Monte Carlo Monaco	42	H2	43 44N	7 25E
Montego Bay tn. Jamaica	89	U14	18 27N	77 56W
Montélimar Fr.	42	G3	44 33N	4 45E
Montemor-o-Novo Port.	43	A3	38 38N	8 13W
Montepulciano Italy	46	D5	43 05N	11 46E
Monterey USA	86	B4	36 35N	121 55W
Montería Col.	90	B15	8 45N	75 54W
Montero Bolivia	41	C3	17 20S	63 15W
Monterrey Mexico	88	D5	25 40N	100 20W
Montes Claros tn. Brazil	90	J10	16 45S	43 52W
Montevideo Uruguay	91	F7	34 55S	56 10W
Montgomery USA	87	J3	32 22N	86 20W
Mont-Laurier tn. Canada	85	V3	46 33N	75 31W
Montluçon Fr.	42	F4	46 20N	2 36E
Montmagny Canada	85	W3	46 59N	70 33W
Montmorillon Fr.	42	E4	46 26N	0 52E
Monto Aust.	67	K6	24 53S	151 06E
Montoro Sp.	43	C3	38 02N	4 23W
Montpellier Fr.	42	F2	43 36N	3 53E
Montréal Canada	85	W3	45 32N	73 36W
Montreux Switz.	44	C3	46 27N	6 55E

Name	Page	Grid	Lat	Long
Montrose USA	86	E4	38 29N	107 53W
Montserrat i. Lesser Antilles	88	P9	16 45N	62 14W
Monywa Myanmar	60	G2	22 05N	95 12E
Monza Italy	46	C6	45 35N	9 16E
Moora Aust.	66	C4	30 40S	116 01E
Moorhead USA	87	G6	46 51N	96 44W
Moose Jaw Canada	84	P4	50 23N	105 35W
Moosonee Canada	85	U4	51 18N	80 39W
Mopti Mali	76	D4	14 29N	4 10W
Mora Sweden	48	D3	61 00N	14 30E
Moradabad India	58	D5	28 50N	78 45E
Morant Point Jamaica	89	U13	17 55N	76 12W
Moratuwa Sri Lanka	58	D1	6 47N	79 53E
Morcenx Fr.	42	D3	44 02N	0 55W
Morden Canada	85	R3	49 12N	98 05W
Morelia Mexico	88	D3	19 40N	101 11W
Morgantown USA	87	L4	39 38N	79 57W
Mori Japan	62	D4	42 07N	140 33E
Morioka Japan	62	D3	39 43N	141 08E
Morlaix Fr.	42	C5	48 35N	3 50W
MOROCCO	76	C8/D8		
Morogoro Tanzania	79	E1	6 49S	37 40E
Morón Cuba	89	J4	22 08N	78 39W
Morondava Madagascar	78	H3	20 19S	44 17E
Moroni Comoros	78	H5	11 40S	43 16E
Moroto Uganda	79	D6	2 32N	34 41E
Morrinsville NZ	69	E6	37 39S	175 32E
Moscow Russia	54	F8	55 45N	37 42E
Moscow USA	86	C6	46 44N	117 00W
Mosel r. Germany/Fr.	44	C4	50 00N	7 00E
Moselle r. Fr.	42	H5	48 30N	6 00E
Mosgiel NZ	69	C2	45 53S	170 21E
Moshi Tanzania	79	E3	3 21S	37 19E
Mosjøen Norway	48	D4	65 50N	13 10E
Moss Norway	48	D2	59 26N	10 41E
Mossoró Brazil	90	K12	5 10S	37 18W
Most Czech Rep.	44	F5	50 31N	13 39E
Mosta Malta	46	P8	35 55N	14 25E
Mostaganem Algeria	76	E9	35 45N	0 05E
Mostar Bosnia-Herzegovina	47	G5	43 20N	17 50E
Móstoles Sp.	43	D4	40 19N	3 53W
Mosul Iraq	56	D6	36 21N	43 08E
Mosůlp'o South Korea	63	A2	33 20N	126 17E
Motoyama Japan	63	B2	33 45N	133 36E
Motril Sp.	43	D2	36 45N	3 31W
Motueka NZ	69	D4	41 07S	173 01E
Mouila Gabon	78	B7	1 50S	11 02E
Moulins Fr.	42	F4	47 00N	3 48E
Moulmein Myanmar	64	B7	16 30N	97 39E
Moundou Chad	77	J3	8 35N	16 01E
Mount Cook tn. NZ	69	C3	43 44S	170 06E
Mount Gambier tn. Aust.	67	H3	37 51S	140 50E
Mount Hagen tn. PNG	67	H9	5 54S	144 13E
Mount Isa tn. Aust.	67	G6	20 50S	139 29E
Mount Magnet tn. Aust.	66	C5	28 06S	117 50E
Mount Morgan tn. Aust.	67	K6	23 40S	150 25E
Mount Vernon tn. USA	87	J4	38 19N	88 52W
Mouscron Belgium	41	B3	50 44N	3 14E
Moyvore Rol	40	B3/B4	54 00N	9 00W
Moyale Ethiopia	79	F6	3 32N	39 04E
Moyale Kenya	79	F6	3 31N	39 04E
Moyo Uganda	79	B6	3 40N	31 43E
Moyobamba Peru	90	B12	6 04S	76 56W
MOZAMBIQUE	78	F3/G5		
Mpanda Tanzania	79	B1	6 21S	31 01E
Mpigi Uganda	79	C5	0 15S	32 20E
Mtwara Tanzania	79	H5	10 17S	40 11E
Mubende Uganda	79	B5	0 36N	31 23E
Mudanjiang China	61	N6	44 36N	129 42E
Mufulira Zambia	78	E5	12 30S	28 12E
Mukachevo Ukraine	45	L4	48 26N	22 45E
Mukalla Yemen	56	E1	14 34N	49 09E
Muleba Tanzania	79	B4	1 43S	31 41E
Mulegé Mexico	88	B5	26 54N	112 00W
Mulgrave Canada	85	Y3	45 36N	61 25W
Mulhouse Fr.	42	H4	47 45N	7 21E
Mullingar Rol	40	C3	53 32N	7 20W
Multan Pakistan	58	C6	30 10N	71 36E
Mumbai India	58	C3	18 56N	72 51E
Muncie USA	87	J5	40 11N	85 22W
Mungbere CDR	77	L2	2 40N	28 25E
Munger India	59	J10	25 22N	86 28E
Mungla Bangladesh	59	K9	22 18N	89 34E
Munich Germany	44	E4	48 08N	11 35E
Münster Germany	44	C5	51 58N	7 37E
Muranga Kenya	79	E4	0 43S	37 09E
Murban UAE	57	N8	23 58N	53 40E
Murchison NZ	69	D4	41 50S	172 20E
Murcia Sp.	43	E2	37 59N	1 08W
Murfreesboro USA	87	J4	35 50N	86 25W
Murmansk Russia	54	F10	68 59N	33 08E
Murom Russia	54	G8	55 34N	42 04E
Muroran Japan	62	D4	42 21N	140 59E
Muroto Japan	62	B2	33 13N	134 11E
Murray r. Aust.	67	H3	35 30S	144 00E
Murupara NZ	69	F5	38 27S	176 42E
Murwara India	58	E4	23 49N	80 28E
Muş Turkey	49	F2	38 45N	41 30E
Musay'id Qatar	57	M8	24 59N	51 33E
Muscat Oman	57	P8	23 37N	58 38E
Mushin Nigeria	76	E3	6 30N	3 22E
Muskegon USA	87	J5	43 13N	86 15W
Muskogee USA	87	G4	35 35N	95 21W
Musoma Tanzania	79	C4	1 30S	33 48E
Mustique i. Lesser Antilles	88	R11	12 39N	61 15W
Mutarara Mozambique	78	G4	17 30S	35 06E
Mutare Zimbabwe	78	F4	18 58S	32 40E
Mutomo Kenya	79	F4	1 50S	38 15E
Muzaffarnagar India	58	D5	29 28N	77 42E
Muzaffarpur India	59	F5	26 07N	85 23E
Mwanza Tanzania	79	C3	2 31S	32 56E
Mwaya Tanzania	78	F6	9 33S	33 56E
MYANMAR	64	B7		
Myingyan Myanmar	60	G2	21 25N	95 20E
Myitkyina Myanmar	60	G3	25 24N	97 25E
Mykolayiv Ukraine	49	D4	46 57N	32 00E
Mysore India	58	D2	12 18N	76 37E
Myszków Poland	45	J5	50 35N	19 21E
My Tho Vietnam	64	D6	10 21N	106 21E
Mytilini Greece	47	M3	39 06N	26 34E
Mytishchi Russia	49	E6	55 54N	37 47E
Mzuzu Malawi	78	F5	11 31S	34 00E

N

Name	Page	Grid	Lat	Long
Naas Rol	40	C3	53 13N	6 39W
Nabid Iran	57	P9	29 43N	57 37E
Nacogdoches USA	87	H3	31 36N	94 40W
Nadiad India	58	C4	22 42N	72 55E
Nador Morocco	76	D9	35 10N	3 00W
Nadur Malta	46	P9	36 03N	14 17E
Nadym Russia	54	K10	65 25N	72 40E
Naestved Denmark	48	D2	55 14N	11 47E
Naga Philippines	65	G6	13 36N	123 12E
Nagahama Japan	63	B2	33 37N	132 30E
Nagano Japan	63	C3	36 39N	138 10E
Nagaoka Japan	63	C3	37 27N	138 50E
Nagaon India	59	G5	26 20N	92 41E
Nagasaki Japan	63	A2	32 45N	129 52E
Nagato Japan	63	B2	34 22N	131 11E
Nagercoil India	58	D1	8 11N	77 30E
Nagornyy Russia	55	Q8	55 57N	124 54E
Nagoya Japan	63	C3	35 08N	136 53E
Nagpur India	58	D4	21 10N	79 12E
Nagqu China	59	G6	31 29N	92 03E
Nahanni Butte Canada	84	L6	61 30N	123 20W
Nahari Japan	63	B2	33 25N	134 01E
Nairobi Kenya	79	E4	1 17S	36 50E
Najrān Saudi Arabia	56	D2	17 37N	44 40E
Nakamura Japan	63	B2	33 02N	132 58E
Nakatsu Japan	63	B2	33 37N	131 11E
Nakhodka Russia	55	R5	42 53N	132 54E
Nakhon Phanom Thailand	64	C7	17 22N	104 50E
Nakhon Sawan Thailand	64	B7	15 42N	100 10E
Nakina Canada	85	T4	50 11N	86 43W
Nakuru Kenya	79	E4	0 16S	36 05E
Nal'chik Russia	54	G5	43 31N	43 38E
Namanga Kenya	79	E3	2 31S	36 49E
Namangan Uzbekistan	54	K5	40 59N	71 41E
Nam Dinh Vietnam	61	J2	20 25N	106 12E
Namibe Angola	78	B4	15 10S	12 09E
NAMIBIA	78	C3		
Namie Japan	62	D3	37 28N	140 58E
Nampa USA	86	C5	43 35N	116 34W
Nampo North Korea	61	N5	38 51N	125 10E
Nampula Mozambique	78	G4	15 09S	39 14E
Namur Belgium	41	C3	50 28N	4 52E
Namwŏn South Korea	63	A3	35 23N	127 23E
Nanaimo Canada	84	L3	49 08N	123 58W
Nanao Japan	63	C3	37 03N	136 58E
Nanchang China	61	L3	28 33N	115 58E
Nanchong China	61	J4	30 54N	106 06E
Nancy Fr.	42	H5	48 42N	6 12E
Nänded India	58	D3	19 11N	77 21E
Nanga Eboko Cameroon	76	G2	4 38N	12 21E
Nanjing China	61	L4	32 03N	118 47E
Nanning China	61	J2	22 50N	108 19E
Nanping China	61	L3	26 40N	118 07E
Nantes Fr.	42	D4	47 14N	1 35W
Nantong China	61	M4	32 06N	121 04E
Nanyang China	61	K4	33 06N	112 31E
Nan'yō Japan	62	D3	38 04N	140 06E
Nanyuki Kenya	79	E5	0 01N	37 05E
Naogaon Bangladesh	59	K10	24 49N	88 59E
Napier NZ	69	F3	39 30S	176 54E
Naples Italy	46	F4	40 50N	14 15E
Naples USA	87	K2	26 09N	81 48W
Nara Japan	63	C2	34 41N	135 49E
Narayanganj Bangladesh	59	L9	23 36N	90 28E
Narbonne Fr.	42	F2	43 11N	3 00E
Narok Kenya	79	D4	1 06S	35 51E
Narrogin Aust.	66	C4	32 57S	117 07E
Naruto Japan	63	B2	34 11N	134 37E
Narva Estonia	48	G2	59 22N	28 17E
Narvik Norway	48	E4	68 26N	17 25E
Nar'yan Mar Russia	54	H10	67 37N	53 02E
Nashik India	58	C3	20 00N	73 52E
Nashua USA	87	M5	42 44N	71 28W
Nashville USA	87	J4	36 10N	86 50W
Nassau Bahamas	89	J5	25 05N	77 20W
Nässjö Sweden	48	D2	57 40N	14 40E
Natal Brazil	90	K12	5 46S	35 15W
Natashquan Canada	85	Y4	50 10N	61 50W
Natchez USA	87	H3	31 32N	91 24W
NAURU	67	N10		
Navadwip India	59	K9	23 25N	88 22E
Navoi Uzbekistan	54	J5	40 04N	65 20E
Navojoa Mexico	88	C5	27 04N	109 28W
Navsari India	58	C4	20 58N	73 01E
Nawabganj Bangladesh	59	K10	24 35N	88 21E
Naxcivan Azerbaijan	49	G2	39 13N	45 24E
Náxos i. Greece	47	L2	37 00N	25 00E
Naxxar Malta	46	P8	35 55N	14 27E
Nayoro Japan	62	D4	44 21N	142 30E
Nazca Peru	90	C11	14 53S	74 54W
Nazilli Turkey	47	M2	37 55N	28 19E
Nazwá Oman	57	G3	22 56N	57 33E
Ndélé CAR	77	K3	8 25N	20 38E
Ndjamena Chad	77	J4	12 10N	14 59E
Ndola Zambia	78	E5	13 00S	28 39E
Néapoli Greece	47	K2	36 31N	23 03E
Nebbi Uganda	79	B6	2 29N	31 04E
Nebitdag Turkmenistan	54	H4	39 31N	54 24E
Nebraska state USA	86	F5	42 00N	102 00W
Necochea Argentina	91	F6	38 31S	58 46W
Needles USA	86	D3	34 51N	114 36W
Neepawa Canada	85	R4	50 14N	99 29W
Nefta Tunisia	76	F8	33 53N	7 50E
Neftekamsk Russia	49	H6	56 06N	54 14E
Negele Ethiopia	77	N3	5 20N	39 35E
Negombo Sri Lanka	58	D1	7 13N	79 51E
Negritos Peru	90	A13	4 42S	81 18W
Negros i. Philippines	65	G5/G6	10 00N	123 00E
Neijiang China	61	J3	29 32N	105 03E
Neiva Col.	90	B14	2 58N	75 15W
Nellore India	58	D2	14 29N	80 00E
Nelson Canada	84	M3	49 29N	117 17W
Nelson NZ	69	D4	41 16S	173 17E
Nemuro Japan	62	E4	43 22N	145 36E
Nenana USA	84	F6	64 35N	149 20W
Nenjiang China	61	N7	49 10N	125 15E
NEPAL	58/59	E5/F5		
Nerchinsk Russia	55	P7	52 02N	116 38E
Neryungri Russia	55	Q8	56 39N	124 38E
NETHERLANDS	41	D5/E5		
Netzahualcóyotl Mexico	88	E3	19 24N	99 02W
Neubrandenburg Germany	44	F6	53 33N	13 16E
Neuchâtel Switz.	44	C3	46 55N	6 56E
Neufchâteau Belgium	41	D2	49 51N	5 26E
Neufchâteau Fr.	42	G5	48 21N	5 42E
Neufchâtel-en-Bray Fr.	42	E5	49 44N	1 26E
Neumünster Germany	44	D7	54 05N	9 59E
Neunkirchen Germany	41	F2	49 21N	7 10E
Neuquén Argentina	91	D6	38 55S	68 05W
Neuruppin Germany	44	F6	52 56N	12 49E
Neuss Germany	44	C5	51 12N	6 42E
Neustadt Germany	41	G2	49 21N	8 08E
Neustrelitz Germany	44	F6	53 22N	13 05E
Neuwied Germany	41	F3	50 26N	7 28E
Nevada state USA	86	C4	39 00N	118 00W
Nevel'sk Russia	62	D5	46 39N	141 49E
Nevers Fr.	42	F4	47 00N	3 09E
Nevinnomyssk Russia	49	F3	44 38N	41 59E
Nevis i. St. Kitts and Nevis	88	P9	17 10N	62 34W
New Albany USA	87	J4	38 17N	85 50W
New Amsterdam Guyana	90	F15	6 18N	57 30W
Newark USA	87	K5	40 03N	82 25W
Newark USA	87	M5	40 44N	74 24W
New Bedford USA	87	M5	41 38N	70 55W
New Bern USA	87	L4	35 05N	77 04W
New Braunfels USA	87	G2	29 43N	98 09W
New Brunswick province Canada	85	X3	47 30N	66 00W
Newburgh USA	87	M5	41 30N	74 00W
New Caledonia i. Pacific Ocean	67	M6/N6	22 00S	165 00E
Newcastle Aust.	67	K4	32 55S	151 46E
Newcastle USA	86	F5	43 52N	104 14W
Newcastle upon Tyne UK	40	F4	54 59N	1 35W
New Delhi India	58	D5	28 37N	77 14E
Newfoundland i. Canada	85	Z3	48 15N	57 00W
Newfoundland province Canada	85	Y5/AA3	52 30N	62 30W
New Guinea i. Pacific Ocean	66/67	F10/J9	5 00S	141 00E
New Hampshire state USA	87	M5	43 00N	72 00W
New Haven USA	87	M5	41 18N	72 55W
New Iberia USA	87	H2	30 00N	91 51W
New Ireland i. PNG	67	K10	3 15S	152 30E
New Jersey state USA	87	M4	40 00N	75 00W
New Liskeard Canada	85	V3	47 31N	79 41W
New London USA	87	M5	41 21N	72 06W
Newman Aust.	66	C6	23 20S	119 34E
New Mexico state USA	86	E3	35 00N	107 00W
New Orleans USA	87	H2	30 00N	90 03W
New Plymouth NZ	69	E3	39 04S	174 04E
Newport UK	40	E2	51 35N	3 00W
New South Wales state Aust.	67	H4/K4	32 00S	145 00E
Newtownabbey UK	40	D4	54 40N	5 54W
New Westminster Canada	84	L3	49 10N	122 58W
New York USA	87	M5	40 40N	73 50W
New York state USA	87	L5	43 00N	76 00W
NEW ZEALAND	69			
Neyshābūr Iran	57	G6	36 13N	58 49E
Nguigmi Niger	76	G4	14 19N	13 06E
Nguru Nigeria	76	G4	12 53N	10 30E
Nha Trang Vietnam	64	D6	12 15N	109 10E
Niagara Falls tn. USA	87	L5	43 06N	79 04W
Niamey Niger	76	E4	13 32N	2 05E
Niangara CDR	77	L2	3 45N	27 54E
NICARAGUA	88/89	G2/H2		
Nicastro Italy	46	G3	38 59N	16 20E
Nice Fr.	42	H2	43 42N	7 16E
Nicobar Islands India	59	G1	8 30N	94 00E
Nicosia Cyprus	49	D2	35 11N	33 23E
Nienburg Germany	44	D6	52 38N	9 13E
Nieuwegein Neths	41	D4	52 00N	5 05E
Nieuwpoort Belgium	41	A4	51 08N	2 45E
NIGER	76	E5/G5		
NIGERIA	76	F4/G4		
Niigata Japan	62	C3	37 58N	139 02E
Niihama Japan	63	B2	33 57N	133 15E
Nijmegen Neths	41	D4	51 50N	5 52E
Nikkō Japan	63	C3	36 45N	139 37E
Nikol'sk Russia	49	G6	59 32N	45 27E
Nikopol' Ukraine	49	D4	47 34N	34 25E
Nikšić SM	47	H5	42 48N	18 56E
Nile r. Sudan/Egypt	77	M7	27 30N	31 40E
Nîmes Fr.	42	G2	43 50N	4 21E
Nimule Sudan	77	M2	3 35N	32 03E
9 de Julio tn. Argentina	91	E6	35 28S	60 58W
Ningbo China	61	M3	29 54N	121 33E
Ninh Binh Vietnam	61	J2	20 14N	106 00E
Niort Fr.	42	D4	46 19N	0 27W
Nipigon Canada	85	T3	49 02N	88 26W
Nirasaki Japan	63	C3	35 45N	138 27E
Niš SM	47	J5	43 20N	21 54E
Nistru r. Moldova	45	N4	47 30N	28 30E
Niterói Brazil	90	J9	22 54S	43 06W
Nitra Slovakia	45	J4	48 19N	18 04E
Niue i. Pacific Ocean	70	K6	19 02S	169 55W
Nivelles Belgium	41	C3	50 36N	4 20E
Nizamabad India	58	D3	18 40N	78 05E
Nizhneangarsk Russia	55	N8	55 48N	109 35E
Nizhniy Novgorod Russia	54	G8	56 20N	44 00E
Nizhniy Tagil Russia	54	J8	58 00N	59 58E
Njoro Kenya	79	D4	0 20S	35 57E
Nkongsamba Cameroon	76	F2	4 59N	9 53E
Nobeoka Japan	63	B2	32 36N	131 40E
Noda Japan	62	D4	40 05N	141 50E
Nogales Mexico	88	B6	31 20N	111 00W
Nogales USA	86	D3	31 20N	110 56W
Noheji Japan	62	D4	40 51N	141 08E
Nola CAR	77	J2	3 28N	16 08E
Nome USA	84	B6	64 30N	165 30W
None Japan	63	B2	33 30N	130 17E
Nong Khai Thailand	64	C7	17 52N	102 44E
Nonthaburi Thailand	64	C6	13 48N	100 11E
Norden Germany	41	F6	53 36N	7 12E
Nordenham Germany	41	G6	53 30N	8 30E
Nordhausen Germany	44	E5	51 31N	10 48E
Nordhorn Germany	41	F5	52 26N	7 05E
Norfolk USA	87	L4	36 54N	76 18W
Noril'sk Russia	55	L10	69 21N	88 02E
Normanton Aust.	67	H7	17 40S	141 05E
Norrköping Sweden	48	E2	58 35N	16 10E
Norseman Aust.	66	D4	32 15S	121 47E
Northam Aust.	66	C4	31 40S	116 40E
Northampton Aust.	66	B5	28 27S	114 33E
Northampton UK	40	F3	52 14N	0 54W
North Battleford Canada	84	P4	52 47N	108 17W
North Bay tn. Canada	85	V3	46 20N	79 28W
North Cape NZ	69	D7	34 25S	173 03E
North Carolina state USA	87	L4	36 00N	80 00W
North Dakota state USA	86/87	F6/G6	47 00N	102 00W
Northern Ireland country UK	40	C4/D4	54 40N	7 00W
NORTHERN MARIANAS	70	E9/F9		
Northern Territory territory Aust.	66	F6/G6	19 00S	132 00E
North Island NZ	69	D5/G5	39 00S	176 00E
NORTH KOREA	61	N5/N6		
North Platte USA	86	F5	41 09N	100 45W
North Pole Arctic Ocean	71		90 00N	
Northwest Territories territory Canada	84	L6/N6	65 15N	115 00W
Norton USA	86	G4	39 51N	99 53W
NORWAY	48	C2/F4		
Norwich UK	40	G3	52 38N	1 18E
Noshiro Japan	62	D4	40 13N	140 00E
Nottingham UK	40	F3	52 58N	1 10W
Nouadhibou Mauritania	76	A6	20 54N	17 01W
Nouakchott Mauritania	76	A5	18 09N	15 58W
Nouméa New Caledonia	67	N6	22 16S	166 27E
Nova Friburgo Brazil	90	J9	22 16S	42 34W
Nova Iguaçu Brazil	90	J9	22 46S	43 23W
Novara Italy	46	C6	45 27N	8 37E
Nova Scotia province Canada	85	Y2/Y3	44 30N	65 00W
Novgorod Russia	54	F8	58 30N	31 20E
Novi Sad SM	47	H6	45 15N	19 51E
Novocheboksarsk Russia	49	G6	56 05N	47 27E
Novo Hamburgo Brazil	91	G8	29 37S	51 07W
Novokazalinsk Kazakhstan	54	J6	45 48N	62 06E
Novokuybyshevsk Russia	49	H5	53 05N	49 55E
Novokuznetsk Russia	55	L7	53 45N	87 12E
Novomoskovsk Russia	49	E5	54 06N	38 15E
Novorossiysk Russia	54	F4	44 44N	37 46E
Novoshakhtinsk Russia	49	E4	47 46N	39 55E
Novosibirsk Russia	55	L7	55 04N	83 05E
Novotroitsk Russia	49	J5	51 07N	58 18E
Nowa Sól Poland	45	G5	51 49N	15 41E
Nowy Sącz Poland	45	K4	49 39N	20 40E
Ntungamo Uganda	79	B4	0 51S	30 16E
Nuevitas Cuba	89	J4	21 34N	77 18W
Nuevo Laredo Mexico	88	E5	27 39N	99 30W
Nu Jiang r. China/Myanmar	60	G2/G3	25 00N	99 00E
Nukus Uzbekistan	54	H5	42 28N	59 07E
Numazu Japan	63	C3	35 08N	138 52E
Nunavut province Canada	85	Q7/S7/J	66 00N	100 00W
Nunspeet Neths	41	D5	52 22N	5 45E
Nuoro Italy	46	C4	40 20N	9 22E
Nuremberg Germany	44	E4	49 27N	11 05E
Nusaybin Turkey	49	F2	37 05N	41 11E
Nuuk Greenland	85	AA6	64 10N	51 44W
Nyahururu Kenya	79	E5	0 04N	36 21E
Nyakanazi Tanzania	79	B3	3 00S	31 15E
Nyala Sudan	77	K4	12 01N	24 50E
Nyaunglebin Myanmar	64	B7	17 59N	96 44E
Nyeri Kenya	79	E4	0 23S	36 56E
Nyingchi China	59	G5	29 32N	94 28E
Nyíregyháza Hungary	45	K3	47 57N	21 43E
Nykøbing Denmark	48	D1	54 47N	11 53E
Nyköping Sweden	48	E2	58 45N	17 00E
Nyngan Aust.	67	J4	31 34S	147 11E
Nysa Poland	45	H5	50 30N	17 20E
Nzega Tanzania	79	C2	4 13S	33 11E

O

Name	Page	Grid	Lat	Long
Oakland USA	86	B4	37 50N	122 15W
Oak Ridge tn. USA	87	K4	36 02N	84 11W
Oamaru NZ	69	C2	45 06S	170 59E
Oaxaca Mexico	88	E3	17 05N	96 41W
Ob' r. Russia	54	J10	65 30N	66 00E
Oba Canada	85	U3	48 38N	84 11W
Obama Japan	63	C2	35 32N	135 45E
Oban UK	40	D5	56 25N	5 29W
Oberhausen Germany	44	C5	51 27N	6 50E
Oberursel Germany	41	G3	50 13N	8 35E
Obihiro Japan	62	D4	42 56N	143 12E
Obninsk Russia	49	E6	55 04N	36 37E
Ocala USA	87	K2	29 11N	82 08W
Ocaña Col.	90	C15	8 16N	73 21W
Ocatlán Mexico	88	D4	20 21N	102 42W
Ōda Japan	63	B3	35 10N	132 29E
Odate Japan	62	D4	40 18N	140 34E

dawara Japan 63 C3 35 15N 139 08E
demiş Turkey 47 N3 38 11N 27 58E
dense Denmark 45 D2 55 24N 10 25E
der r. Europe 44 G6 52 00N 15 30E
dessa Ukraine 49 D4 46 30N 30 46E
dessa USA 86 F3 31 50N 102 23W
elde Germany 41 G4 51 50N 8 08E
fenburg Germany 44 C4 48 29N 7 57E
unato Japan 62 D3 39 04N 141 43E
ga Japan 62 C3 39 56N 139 47E
gaki Japan 63 C3 35 22N 136 36E
bomoso Nigeria 76 E3 8 05N 4 11E
gden USA 86 D5 41 14N 111 59W
hai NZ 69 A2 45 56S 167 57E
hio state USA 87 K5 40 00N 83 00W
ita Japan 63 B2 33 15N 131 36E
inaga Mexico 88 D5 29 35N 104 26W
fya Japan 63 C3 37 18N 138 49E
kara Pakistan 58 C6 30 49N 73 31E
kaya Japan 63 C3 36 03N 138 00E
kayama Japan 63 B2 34 40N 133 54E
azaki Japan 63 C2 34 58N 137 10E
lene Nigeria 76 F3 7 31N 6 14E
cha Russia 55 S7 53 35N 143 01E
lahoma state USA 87 G4 36 00N 98 00W
lahoma City USA 87 G4 35 28N 97 33W
loppe Japan 62 D4 44 29N 143 09E
tyabr'sk Kazakhstan 49 J4 49 27N 57 21E
tyabr'skiy Russia 55 T7 52 43N 156 14E
land i. Sweden 48 E2 56 45N 51 50E
bia Italy 46 C4 40 56N 9 30E
d Crow Canada 84 H7 67 34N 139 43W
denburg Germany 44 D6 53 08N 8 13E
denzaal Neths 41 E5 52 19N 6 55E
dham UK 40 E3 53 33N 2 07W
ds Canada 84 N4 51 50N 114 06W
enek Russia 55 P10 68 28N 112 18E
ñão Port. 43 B2 37 01N 7 50W
inda Brazil 90 K12 8 00S 34 51W
omouc Czech Rep. 45 H4 49 38N 17 15E
ongapo Philippines 65 G6 14 49N 120 17E
sztyn Poland 45 K6 53 48N 20 29E
ten Switz. 44 C3 47 22N 7 55E
teniţa Romania 45 N2 44 05N 26 40E
ympia USA 86 B6 47 03N 122 53W
nagari Japan 62 D3 39 29N 140 29E
nagh UK 40 C4 54 36N 7 18W
naha USA 87 G5 41 15N 96 00W
MAN 56/57 F2/G3
nbetsu Japan 62 D4 42 54N 143 57E
nboué Gabon 78 A7 1 38S 9 20E
ndurman Sudan 77 M5 15 37N 32 29E
ninato Japan 62 D4 41 15N 141 10E
noto Japan 62 D3 39 50N 141 52E
nsk Russia 54 K8 55 00N 73 22E
nura Japan 63 A2 32 56N 129 58E
nuta Japan 63 B2 33 02N 130 26E
dal India 59 J9 23 35N 87 11E
do Nigeria 76 E3 7 05N 4 55E
rio Romania 45 N3 46 15N 26 45E
itsha Nigeria 76 F3 6 10N 6 47E
omichi Japan 63 B2 34 25N 133 11E
slow Aust. 66 C6 21 41S 115 12E
tario province Canada 85 S4/U4 51 00N 91 00W
tario USA 86 C3 34 04N 117 38W
tario, Lake Canada/USA 87 L5 43 45N 78 00W
tonagon USA 87 J6 46 52N 89 18W
stende Belgium 44 A4 51 13N 2 55E
sterhout Neths 41 C4 51 39N 4 52E
ala CDR 78 D7 0 40S 24 20E
ava Czech Rep. 45 H4 49 58N 17 55E
ole Poland 45 H5 50 40N 17 56E
orto Port. 43 A4 41 09N 8 37W
otiki NZ 69 F5 38 01S 177 17E
adea Romania 45 K3 47 03N 21 55E
ai India 58 D5 26 00N 79 26E
an Algeria 76 D9 35 45N 0 38W
an Argentina 90 E9 23 07S 64 16W
ange r. Fr. 42 G3 44 08N 4 48E
ange USA 87 H3 30 05N 93 43W
angeburg USA 87 K3 33 28N 80 53W
betello Italy 46 D5 42 27N 11 07E
du Turkey 49 41 00N 37 52E
egon state USA 86 B5/C5 44 00N 120 00W
egon City USA 86 B6 45 21N 122 36W
ekhovo-Zuyevo Russia 49 E6 55 47N 39 00E
el Russia 54 F7 52 58N 36 04E
em USA 86 D5 40 20N 114 45W
enburg Russia 54 H7 51 50N 55 00E
ense Sp. 43 B4 42 20N 7 52W
ihuela Sp. 43 E3 38 05N 0 56W
noco r. Venezuela 90 E15 8 00N 64 00W
istano Italy 46 C4 39 54N 8 36E
zaba Mexico 88 E3 18 51N 97 08W
kney Islands is. UK 40 E6 59 00N 3 00W
ando USA 87 K2 28 33N 81 21W
eans Fr. 42 E4 47 54N 1 54E
oco Philippines 65 G6 11 01N 124 36E
sköldsvik Sweden 48 E3 63 19N 18 45E
ha Belarus 49 D5 54 30N 30 23E
sk Russia 54 H7 51 13N 58 35E
ova Romania 45 L2 44 42N 22 22E
igueira Sp. 43 B5 43 43N 8 13W
ona Italy 46 F5 42 21N 14 24E
iguela Iran 56 D6 37 40N 45 04E
ro Bolivia 90 D10 17 59S 67 08W
rieto Italy 46 E5 42 43N 12 06E
aka Japan 63 C2 34 40N 135 30E
mamambe Japan 62 D4 42 33N 140 22E
awa Canada 85 V2 43 53N 78 51W
kosh USA 87 J5 44 01N 88 32W
nogbo Nigeria 76 E3 7 50N 4 35E
k Croatia 47 H6 45 33N 18 41E

Oslo Norway 48 D2 59 56N 10 45E
Osmaniye Turkey 49 E2 37 04N 36 15E
Osnabrück Germany 44 D6 52 17N 8 03E
Osorno Chile 91 C5 40 35S 73 14W
Oss Neths 41 D4 51 46N 5 31E
Östersund Sweden 48 D3 63 10N 14 40E
Östervall Sweden 48 E3 62 20N 15 20E
Ostrava Czech Rep. 45 J4 49 50N 18 15E
Ostróda Poland 45 J6 53 42N 19 59E
Ōsumi-shotō is. Japan 63 B2 30 30N 130 30E
Oswego USA 87 L5 43 27N 76 31W
Ōtake Japan 63 B2 34 14N 132 12E
Otaki NZ 69 E4 40 46S 175 09E
Otaru Japan 62 D4 43 14N 140 59E
Otavalo Ecuador 90 B14 0 13N 78 15W
Otira NZ 69 C3 42 50S 171 34E
Ōtoineppu Japan 62 D4 44 44N 142 18E
Otranto Italy 47 H4 40 08N 18 30E
Ōtsu Japan 63 C3 35 00N 135 50E
Ōtsu Japan 63 D3 36 50N 140 47E
Ottawa Canada 85 V3 45 24N 75 38W
Ottawa USA 87 G4 38 35N 95 16W
Ottumwa USA 87 H5 41 02N 92 26W
Ouagadougou Burkina 76 D4 12 20N 1 40W
Ouargla Algeria 76 F8 32 00N 5 16E
Oudenaarde Belgium 41 B3 50 50N 3 37E
Oudtshoorn RSA 78 D1 33 35S 22 12E
Oued Zem Morocco 76 C8 32 55N 6 33W
Ouesso Congo 77 J2 1 38N 16 03E
Oujda Morocco 76 D8 34 41N 1 45W
Oulu Finland 48 F4 65 02N 25 27E
Outer Hebrides is. UK 40 C5/C6 58 00N 7 00W
Ovalle Chile 91 C7 30 33S 71 16W
Övertorneå Sweden 48 F4 66 22N 23 40E
Oviedo Sp. 43 C5 43 21N 7 18W
Owando Congo 78 C7 0 27S 15 44E
Owani Japan 62 D4 40 30N 140 32E
Owase Japan 63 C2 34 03N 136 12E
Owensboro USA 87 J4 37 45N 87 05W
Owen Sound tn. Canada 85 U2 44 34N 80 56W
Owo Nigeria 76 F3 7 10N 5 39E
Oxford UK 40 F2 51 46N 1 15W
Oxnard USA 86 C3 34 11N 119 10W
Oya Japan 62 D3 38 48N 141 35E
Oyama Japan 63 C3 36 18N 139 48E
Oyem Gabon 76 G2 1 34N 11 31E
Oyo Nigeria 76 E3 7 50N 3 55E
Ozieri Italy 46 C4 40 35N 9 01E
Ozuki Japan 63 B2 34 04N 131 02E

P
Paamiut Greenland 85 BB6 62 05N 49 30W
Pabianice Poland 45 J5 51 40N 19 20E
Pabna Bangladesh 59 K10 24 00N 89 15E
Pacasmayo Peru 90 B12 7 27S 79 33W
Pachuca Mexico 88 E4 20 10N 98 44W
Pacific Grove USA 86 B4 36 36N 121 56W
Pacific Ocean 70
Padang Indonesia 64 C3 1 00S 100 21E
Paderborn Germany 44 D5 51 43N 8 44E
Padilla Bolivia 90 E10 19 18S 64 20W
Padua Italy 46 D6 45 24N 11 53E
Paducah USA 87 J4 37 03N 88 36W
Paeroa NZ 69 E6 37 23S 175 40E
Pagadian Philippines 65 G5 7 50N 123 30E
Pagatan Indonesia 64 F3 3 36S 115 58E
Paisley UK 40 D5 55 50N 4 26W
Paita Peru 90 A12 5 11S 81 09W
Pakanbaru Indonesia 64 C4 0 33N 101 30E
PAKISTAN 58 B5/C5
Pakwach Uganda 79 B6 2 28N 31 30E
Pakxé Laos 64 D6 15 00N 105 55E
PALAU 70 D8 7 30N 134 30E
Palawan i. Philippines 65 F5/F6 10 00N 119 00E
Palembang Indonesia 64 C3 2 59S 104 45E
Palencia Sp. 43 C5 41 01N 4 32W
Palermo Italy 46 E3 38 08N 13 23E
Palestine USA 87 G3 31 45N 95 39W
Palghat India 58 D2 10 46N 76 42E
Pallisa Uganda 79 1 10N 33 43E
Palma de Mallorca Balearic Islands 43 G3 39 35N 2 39E
Palmar Sur Costa Rica 89 H1 8 57N 83 28W
Palmer USA 84 F6 61 35N 149 10W
Palmerston NZ 69 C2 45 29S 170 43E
Palmerston North NZ 69 E4 40 22S 175 37E
Palmira Col. 90 B14 3 33N 76 17W
Palmyra Syria 56 C5 34 40N 38 10E
Palomares Mexico 88 E3 17 10N 95 04W
Palopo Indonesia 65 G3 3 01S 120 12E
Palu Indonesia 65 F3 0 54S 119 52E
Pamiers Fr. 42 E2 43 07N 1 36E
Pamplona Col. 90 C15 7 24N 72 38W
Pamplona Sp. 43 E5 42 49N 1 39W
PANAMA 89 H1/J1
Panama Canal Panama 89 J1 9 00N 80 00W
Panama City Panama 89 J1 8 57N 79 30W
Panay i. Philippines 65 G6 11 00N 122 00E
Pančevo SM 47 J6 44 52N 20 40E
Pandan Malaysia 64 S16 1 32N 103 47E
Panevėžys Lithuania 48 F2 55 44N 24 21E
Pangkalpinang Indonesia 64 D3 2 05S 106 09E
Panipat India 58 D5 29 24N 76 58E
Pápa Hungary 45 H3 47 20N 17 29E
Papantla Mexico 88 E4 20 30N 97 21W
PAPUA NEW GUINEA 67 H9/K9
Paraburdoo Aust. 66 C5 23 15S 117 45E
PARAGUAY 90 F9
Paraguay r. Paraguay/Argentina 90 F8/F9 26 30S 58 00W
Parakou Benin 76 E3 9 23N 2 40E
Paramaribo Suriname 90 F15 5 52N 55 14W
Paramonga Peru 90 B11 10 42S 77 50W
Paraná Argentina 91 E7 31 45S 60 30W

Paraná r. Paraguay/Argentina 90 F8 27 00S 56 00W
Paranaíba r. Brazil 90 H10 18 00S 49 00W
Paranaguá Brazil 90 H8 25 32S 48 36W
Paraparaumu NZ 69 E4 40 55S 175 00E
Pardubice Czech Rep. 45 G5 50 03N 15 45E
Parepare Indonesia 65 F3 4 00S 119 40E
Paris Fr. 42 F5 48 52N 2 20E
Parkano Finland 48 F3 62 03N 23 00E
Parkersburg USA 87 K4 39 17N 81 33W
Parma Italy 46 D6 44 48N 10 19E
Parnaíba Brazil 90 J13 2 58S 41 46W
Pärnu Estonia 48 F2 58 28N 24 30E
Páros Greece 47 L2 37 04N 25 06E
Parry Sound tn. Canada 85 V3 45 21N 80 03W
Parthenay Fr. 42 D4 46 39N 0 14W
Pasadena USA 87 G2 29 42N 95 14W
Pascagoula USA 87 J3 30 21N 88 32W
Paşcani Romania 45 N3 47 14N 26 46E
Pasco USA 86 C6 46 15N 119 07W
Passau Germany 44 F4 48 35N 13 28E
Passo Fundo Brazil 91 G8 28 16S 52 20W
Pasto Col. 90 B14 1 12N 77 17W
Patan India 58 C4 23 51N 72 11E
Patan Nepal 59 F5 27 40N 85 20E
Patea NZ 69 E4 39 45S 174 28E
Paterson USA 87 M5 40 55N 74 08W
Pathankot India 58 D6 32 16N 75 43E
Patiala India 58 D6 30 21N 76 27E
Patna India 59 F5 25 37N 85 12E
Patos Brazil 90 K12 6 55S 37 15W
Patras Greece 47 J3 38 14N 21 44E
Pau Fr. 42 D2 43 18N 0 22W
Pavia Italy 46 C6 45 12N 9 09E
Pavlikeni Bulgaria 47 L5 43 14N 25 20E
Pavlodar Kazakhstan 54 K7 52 21N 76 59E
Pavlohrad Ukraine 49 E4 48 34N 35 50E
Pazardzhik Bulgaria 47 L5 42 10N 24 20E
Paya Lebar Singapore 65 T15 1 21N 103 53E
Paysandu Uruguay 91 F7 32 21S 58 05W
Peace River tn. Canada 84 M5 56 15N 117 18W
Peč SM 47 J5 42 40N 20 19E
Pechora Russia 54 H10 65 14N 57 18E
Pecos USA 86 F3 30 00N 102 00W
Pécs Hungary 45 J3 46 04N 18 15E
Pedreiras Brazil 90 J13 4 32S 44 40W
Pegu Myanmar 64 B7 17 18N 96 31E
Pekalongan Indonesia 64 D2 6 54S 109 37E
Pelentong Malaysia 65 S16/T16 1 33N 103 50E
Pelotas Brazil 91 G7 31 45S 52 20W
Pemba Mozambique 79 H5 13 00S 40 30E
Pemba Tanzania 79 F2 5 05S 39 44E
Pembroke Canada 85 V3 45 49N 77 08W
Penanjong Brunei 64 P11 4 50N 114 40E
Pendleton USA 86 C6 45 40N 118 46W
Penedo Brazil 90 K11 10 16S 36 33W
Pennsylvania state USA 87 L5 41 00N 78 00W
Penonomé Panama 89 H1 8 30N 80 20W
Penrith UK 40 E4 54 40N 2 44W
Pensacola USA 87 J3 30 26N 87 12W
Penticton Canada 84 M3 49 29N 119 38W
Penza Russia 54 G7 53 11N 45 00E
Penzance UK 40 D2 50 07N 5 33W
Peoria USA 87 J5 40 43N 89 38W
Pereira Col. 90 B14 4 47N 75 46W
Périgueux Fr. 42 E3 45 12N 0 44E
Perm' Russia 54 H8 58 01N 56 10E
Pernik Bulgaria 47 K5 42 36N 23 03E
Péronne Fr. 42 F5 49 56N 2 57E
Perpignan Fr. 42 F2 42 42N 2 54E
Perth Aust. 66 C4 31 58S 115 49E
Perth UK 40 E5 56 42N 3 28W
PERU 90 B11/C11
Perugia Italy 46 E5 43 07N 12 23E
Peruweiz Belgium 41 B3 50 30N 3 35E
Pervoural'sk Russia 49 J6 56 56N 59 55E
Pesaro Italy 46 E5 43 54N 12 54E
Pescara Italy 46 F5 42 27N 14 13E
Peshawar Pakistan 58 C6 34 01N 71 40E
Pessac Fr. 42 D3 44 49N 0 37W
Petah Tiqwa Israel 56 B5 32 05N 34 53E
Petaluma USA 86 B4 38 13N 122 39W
Petare Venezuela 90 D16 10 31N 66 50W
Petauke Zambia 79 14 15S 31 20E
Peterborough Aust. 67 G4 33 00S 138 51E
Peterborough Canada 85 V2 44 19N 78 20W
Peterborough UK 40 F3 52 35N 0 15W
Peterhead UK 40 F5 57 30N 1 46W
Petershagen Germany 41 D5 52 23N 8 59E
Petrolina Brazil 90 J12 9 22S 40 30W
Petropavlovsk Kazakhstan 54 J7 54 53N 69 13E
Petroşani Romania 45 L4 45 25N 23 22E
Petrozavodsk Russia 54 F9 61 46N 34 19E
Pforzheim Germany 44 D4 48 53N 8 41E
Phangnga Thailand 64 B5 8 29N 98 31E
Phan Thiet Vietnam 64 D6 10 56N 108 06E
Phatthalung Thailand 64 C5 7 36N 100 02E
Phetchaburi Thailand 64 B6 13 05N 99 58E
Philadelphia USA 87 L4 40 00N 75 10W
Philippeville Belgium 41 C3 50 12N 4 33E
PHILIPPINES, THE 65 G7/H5
Phnom Penh Cambodia 64 C6 11 35N 104 55E
Phoenix USA 86 D3 33 30N 112 03W
Phôngsali Laos 64 H2 21 40N 102 06E
Phuket Thailand 64 B5 7 52N 98 22E
Piacenza Italy 46 C6 45 03N 9 41E
Piatra Neamţ Romania 45 N3 46 53N 26 23E
Picos Brazil 90 J12 7 05S 41 24W
Picton NZ 69 E4 41 18S 174 00E
Piedras Negras Mexico 88 D5 28 40N 100 32W
Pierre USA 86 F5 44 23N 100 20W
Pietermaritzburg RSA 78 F2 29 36S 30 24E
Pietersburg RSA 78 E2 23 54S 29 23E
Pijijiapan Mexico 88 F3 15 42N 93 12W
Piła Poland 45 H6 53 09N 16 44E

Pilar Paraguay 90 F8 26 51S 58 20W
Pimenta Bueno Brazil 90 E11 11 40S 61 14W
Pinar del Río Cuba 89 H4 22 24N 83 42W
Pine Bluff USA 87 H3 34 13N 92 00W
Pingdingshan China 61 K4 33 50N 113 20E
P'ingtung Taiwan 61 M2 22 40N 120 30E
Pingxiang China 61 J2 22 06N 106 44E
Pingxiang China 61 K3 27 35N 113 46E
Pinsk Belarus 49 C5 52 08N 26 01E
Piombino Italy 46 D5 42 56N 10 32E
Piraeus Greece 47 K2 37 57N 23 42E
Pirapora Brazil 90 J10 17 20S 44 54W
Pisa Italy 46 D5 43 43N 10 24E
Pisco Peru 90 B11 13 46S 76 12W
Písek Czech Rep. 44 F4 49 18N 14 10E
Pistoia Italy 46 D5 43 56N 10 55E
Piteå Sweden 48 F4 65 19N 21 30E
Piteşti Romania 45 M2 44 51N 24 51E
Pitt Island NZ 67 R2 44 30S 176 30W
Pittsburgh USA 87 L5 40 26N 80 00W
Pittsfield USA 87 M5 42 27N 73 15W
Piura Peru 90 A12 5 15S 80 38W
Plainview USA 86 F3 34 12N 101 43W
Plasencia Sp. 43 B4 40 02N 6 05W
Plattsburgh USA 87 M5 44 42N 73 29W
Plauen Germany 44 F5 50 29N 12 08E
Pleven Bulgaria 47 L5 43 25N 24 04E
Płock Poland 45 J6 52 32N 19 40E
Ploieşti Romania 45 M2 44 57N 26 01E
Plovdiv Bulgaria 47 L5 42 08N 24 45E
Plunge Lithuania 48 F2 55 52N 21 49E
Plymouth Montserrat 88 P9 16 42N 62 13W
Plymouth UK 40 D2 50 23N 4 10W
Plzeň Czech Rep. 44 F4 49 45N 13 25E
Po r. Italy 46 D6 45 00N 10 00E
Pocatello USA 86 D5 43 05N 112 26W
Podgorica SM 47 H5 42 28N 19 17E
Podol'sk Russia 54 F8 55 23N 37 32E
Pohang South Korea 63 A3 36 00N 129 26E
Pointe-à-Pitre Guadeloupe 88 Q9 16 14N 61 32W
Point Hope tn. USA 84 B7 68 20N 166 50W
Point-Noire tn. Congo 78 B7 4 46S 11 53E
Poitiers Fr. 42 E4 46 35N 0 20E
Pokhara Nepal 58 E5 28 14N 83 58E
POLAND 45 J6/K6
Polatsk Belarus 48 G2 55 29N 28 47E
Policoro Italy 47 G4 40 12N 16 40E
Poltava Ukraine 49 D4 49 35N 34 35E
Ponca City USA 87 G4 36 41N 97 04W
Ponce Puerto Rico 89 L3 18 01N 66 36W
Pondicherry India 58 D2 11 59N 79 50E
Pond Inlet tn. Canada 85 V8 72 40N 77 59W
Ponferrada Sp. 43 B5 42 33N 6 35W
Ponoka Canada 84 N4 52 42N 113 33W
Ponta Grossa Brazil 90 G8 25 07S 50 09W
Pont-à-Mousson Fr. 42 H5 48 55N 6 03E
Ponta Porã Brazil 90 F9 22 27S 55 39W
Ponte Leccia Corsica 42 J2 42 28N 9 12E
Pontevedra Sp. 43 A5 42 25N 8 39W
Pontianak Indonesia 64 D3 0 05S 109 16E
Popacatepetl mt. Mexico 88 E3 19 02N 98 38W
Popayán Col. 90 A3 2 27N 76 32W
Poperinge Belgium 41 A3 50 52N 2 44E
Poplar Bluff tn. USA 87 H4 36 16N 90 25W
Popondetta PNG 67 J9 8 45S 148 15E
Poprad Slovakia 45 K4 49 03N 20 18E
Porbandar India 58 B4 21 04N 69 40E
Pordenone Italy 46 E6 45 58N 12 39E
Pori Finland 48 F3 61 28N 21 45E
Porirua NZ 69 E4 41 08S 174 50E
Poronaysk Russia 55 S6 49 13N 143 05E
Portadown UK 40 C4 54 26N 6 27W
Portage la Prairie Canada 85 R3 49 58N 98 20W
Port Alberni Canada 84 L3 49 11N 124 49W
Portalegre Port. 43 B3 39 17N 7 25W
Portales USA 86 F3 34 12N 103 20W
Port Angeles USA 86 B6 48 06N 123 26W
Port Antonio Jamaica 89 U14 18 10N 76 27W
Port Arthur USA 87 H2 29 55N 93 56W
Port Augusta Aust. 66 G4 32 30S 137 27E
Port-au-Prince Haiti 89 K3 18 33N 72 20W
Porta Westfalica Germany 41 G5 52 12N 8 55E
Port Blair Andaman Islands 59 G2 11 40N 92 44E
Port Chalmers NZ 69 C2 45 49S 170 37E
Port-de-Paix Haiti 89 K3 19 56N 72 52W
Port Dickson Malaysia 64 C4 2 31N 102 48E
Port Elizabeth RSA 78 E1 33 58S 25 36E
Port Gentil Gabon 78 A7 0 40S 8 50E
Port Harcourt Nigeria 76 F2 4 43N 7 05E
Port Hardy Canada 84 K4 50 41N 127 30W
Port Hawkesbury Canada 85 Y3 45 37N 61 22W
Port Hedland Aust. 66 C6 20 24S 118 36E
Port Huron USA 87 K5 42 59N 82 28W
Portimão Port. 43 A3 37 08N 8 32W
Portland Aust. 67 H3 38 21S 141 38E
Portland USA 86 B6 45 32N 122 40W
Portland USA 87 M5 43 41N 70 16W
Portlaoise RoI 40 C3 53 02N 7 17W
Port Lincoln Aust. 66 G4 34 43S 135 49E
Port Louis Mauritius 73 C2 20 10S 57 30E
Port Macquarie Aust. 67 K4 31 28S 152 25E
Port Morant Jamaica 89 U13 17 53N 76 20W
Port Moresby PNG 67 J9 9 30S 147 07E
Porto Alegre Brazil 91 G7 30 03S 51 10W
Porto Amboim Angola 78 B5 10 47S 13 43E
Portoferraio Italy 46 D5 42 49N 10 20E
Port-of-Spain Trinidad & Tobago 89 V15 10 38N 61 31W
Pôrto Grande Brazil 90 G14 0 43N 51 23W
Porto Novo Benin 76 E3 6 30N 2 47E
Porto Tórres Italy 46 C4 40 51N 8 24E
Porto-Vecchio Corsica 42 J1 41 35N 9 16E
Pôrto Velho Brazil 90 E12 8 45S 63 54W
Portoviejo Ecuador 90 A13 1 07S 80 28W

Port Pirie Aust. 66 G4 33 11S 138 01E
Port Said Egypt 77 M8 31 17N 32 18E
Portsmouth UK 40 F2 50 48N 1 05W
Portsmouth USA 87 L4 36 50N 76 20W
Port Sudan Sudan 77 N5 19 38N 37 07E
PORTUGAL 43 A3/B3
Posadas Argentina 90 F8 27 27S 55 50W
Potenza Italy 46 F4 40 38N 15 48E
P'ot'i Georgia 49 F3 42 11N 41 41E
Potiskum Nigeria 76 G4 11 40N 11 03E
Potosí Bolivia 90 D10 19 34S 65 45W
Potsdam Germany 44 F6 52 24N 13 04E
Poughkeepsie USA 87 M5 41 43N 73 56W
Pouthisat Cambodia 64 C6 12 27N 103 40E
Poza Rica Mexico 88 E4 20 34N 97 26W
Poznań Poland 45 H6 52 25N 16 53E
Prabumulih Indonesia 64 C3 3 29S 104 14E
Prague Czech Rep. 44 G5 50 06N 14 26E
Prato Italy 46 D5 43 53N 11 06E
Pratt USA 87 G4 37 40N 98 45W
Praya Indonesia 65 F2 8 38S 116 15E
Prescott USA 86 D3 34 34N 112 28W
Presidente Prudente Brazil 90 G9 22 09S 51 24W
Prešov Slovakia 45 K4 49 00N 21 10E
Presque Isle tn. USA 87 N6 46 42N 68 01W
Preston UK 40 E3 53 46N 2 42W
Pretoria RSA 78 E2 25 45S 28 12E
Price USA 86 D4 39 35N 110 49W
Prieska RSA 78 D2 29 40S 22 45E
Prievidza Slovakia 45 J4 48 47N 18 35E
Prilep FYROM 47 J4 41 20N 21 32E
Prince Albert Canada 85 P4 53 13N 105 45W
Prince Edward Island province Canada 85 Y3 46 30N 63 00W
Prince George Canada 84 L4 53 55N 122 49W
Prince of Wales Island USA 84 J5 56 00N 132 00W
Prince Rupert Canada 84 J4 54 09N 130 20W
Principe i. Gulf of Guinea 76 F2 1 37N 7 27E
Priština SM 47 J5 42 39N 21 20E
Prizren SM 47 J5 42 12N 20 43E
Probolinggo Indonesia 64 E2 7 45S 113 12E
Progreso Mexico 88 G4 21 20N 89 40W
Prokhladnyy Russia 49 F3 43 46N 44 03E
Prokop'yevsk Russia 55 L7 53 55N 86 45E
Propriá Brazil 90 K11 10 15S 36 51W
Propriano Corsica 42 J1 41 40N 8 54E
Providence USA 87 M5 41 50N 71 28W
Provins Fr. 42 F5 48 34N 3 18E
Provo USA 86 D5 40 15N 111 40W
Prudhoe Bay tn. USA 84 F8 70 05N 148 20W
Prüm Germany 41 E3 50 12N 6 25E
Pruszków Poland 45 K6 52 10N 20 47E
Przemyśl Poland 45 L4 49 48N 22 48E
Przeworsk Poland 45 L5 50 04N 22 30E
Pskov Russia 54 E8 57 48N 28 26E
Ptsich Belarus 45 P6 52 11N 28 51E
Pucallpa Peru 90 C12 8 21S 74 33W
Puchon South Korea 63 A3 37 29N 126 45E
Pudasjärvi Finland 48 G4 65 25N 26 50E
Puebla Mexico 88 E3 19 03N 98 10W
Pueblo USA 86 F4 38 17N 104 38W
Puerto Aisén Chile 91 C4 45 27S 72 58W
Puerto Armuelles Panama 89 H1 8 19N 82 51W
Puerto Barrios Guatemala 88 G3 15 41N 88 32W
Puerto Berrío Col. 90 C15 6 28N 74 28W
Puerto Cabello Venezuela 90 D16 10 29N 68 02W
Puerto Cabezas Nicaragua 89 H2 14 02N 83 24W
Puerto Cortés Honduras 88 G3 15 50N 87 55W
Puerto de Morelos Mexico 88 G4 20 49N 86 52W
Puerto La Cruz Venezuela 90 E16 10 14N 64 40W
Puertollano Sp. 43 C3 38 41N 4 07W
Puerto Maldonado Peru 90 D11 12 37S 69 11W
Puerto Montt Chile 91 C3 41 28S 73 00W
Puerto Natales Chile 91 C3 51 41S 72 15W
Puerto Peñasco Mexico 88 B6 31 20N 113 33W
Puerto Princesa Philippines 65 F5 9 46N 118 45E
PUERTO RICO 89 L3
Puerto Santa Cruz Argentina 91 D3 50 03S 68 35W
Puerto Vallarta Mexico 88 C4 20 36N 105 15W
Pukekohe NZ 69 E6 37 12S 174 54E
Pula Croatia 46 E6 44 52N 13 52E
Pulacayo Bolivia 90 D9 20 25S 66 41W
Pulau Dolak i. Indonesia 65 K2 7 45S 138 15E
Pulau Juling i. Malaysia 65 U16 1 32N 104 01E
Puławy Poland 45 K5 51 26N 21 59E
Pulkkila Finland 48 G3 64 16N 25 50E
Pullman USA 86 C6 46 46N 117 09W
Pune India 58 C3 18 34N 73 58E
Punggol Singapore 65 T15 1 24N 103 54E
Puno Peru 90 C10 15 53S 70 03W
Punta Alta Argentina 91 E6 38 50S 62 00W
Punta Arenas Chile 91 C3 53 10S 70 56W
Puntarenas Costa Rica 89 H2 10 00N 85 00W
Punto Fijo Venezuela 90 C16 11 50N 70 16W
Puquio Peru 90 C11 14 44S 74 07W
Puri India 59 F3 19 49N 85 54E
Purmerend Neths 41 C5 52 30N 4 56E
Purnia India 59 F5 25 47N 87 28E
Puruliya India 59 J9 23 20N 86 23E
Pusan South Korea 63 A3 35 05N 129 02E
Puttalam Sri Lanka 58 D1 8 02N 79 50E
Pyatigorsk Russia 54 G5 44 04N 43 06E
Pyè Myanmar 64 B7 18 50N 95 14E
Pyinmana Myanmar 64 B7 19 45N 96 13E
Pyongyang North Korea 61 N5 39 00N 125 47E
Pyrénées mts. Fr./Sp. 42 E2 42 50N 0 30E
Pýrgos Greece 47 J2 37 40N 21 27E
Pýrgos Greece 47 L1 35 00N 25 10E

Q
Qaanaaq Greenland 85 X9 77 30N 69 00W
Qaidam Pendi China 60 F5/G5 37 30N 94 00E
Qasr Farâfra Egypt 77 L7 27 03N 28 00E

QATAR 57 N8/N9
Qazvin Iran 56 E6 36 16N 50 00E
Qeshm Iran 57 P9 26 58N 56 17E
Qeys Iran 57 N9 26 32N 53 58E
Qiemo China 60 E5 38 08N 85 33E
Qila Saifullah Pakistan 58 B6 30 42N 68 30E
Qingdao China 61 M5 36 04N 120 22E
Qinhuangdao China 61 L5 39 55N 119 37E
Qionghai China 61 K1 19 17N 110 30E
Qiqihar China 61 M7 47 23N 124 00E
Qom Iran 56 F5 34 39N 50 57E
Qomishēh Iran 56 F5 32 01N 51 55E
Quang Ngai Vietnam 64 D7 15 00N 108 50E
Quang Tri Vietnam 64 D7 16 46N 107 11E
Quanzhou China 61 L2 24 53N 118 36E
Qu'Appelle Canada 85 Q4 50 33N 103 54W
Quatre Bornes Mauritius 73 E2 20 15S 57 28E
Quatre Bornes Seychelles 73 B1 4 45S 55 30E
Québec Canada 85 W3 46 50N 71 15W
Québec province Canada 85 V4/X4 50 00N 75 00W
Queen Charlotte Canada 84 J4 53 18N 132 04W
Queensland state Aust. 67 H8/K5 23 00S 143 00E
Queenstown Aust. 67 J2 42 07S 145 33E
Queenstown NZ 69 B2 45 02S 168 40E
Queenstown Singapore 65 S14 1 18N 103 48E
Quelimane Mozambique 78 G4 17 53S 36 51E
Querétaro Mexico 88 D4 20 38N 100 23W
Quesnel Canada 84 L4 53 03N 122 31W
Quetta Pakistan 58 B6 30 15N 67 00E
Quezaltenango Guatemala 88 F2 14 50N 91 30W
Quezon City Philippines 65 G6 14 39N 121 02E
Quibala Angola 78 B5 10 48S 14 59E
Quibdó Col. 90 B15 5 40N 76 38W
Quilá Mexico 88 C4 24 26N 107 11W
Quillacollo Bolivia 90 D10 17 26S 66 16W
Quilon India 58 D1 8 53N 76 38E
Quimper Fr. 42 B4 48 00N 4 06W
Quincy USA 87 H4 39 55N 91 22W
Qui Nhon Vietnam 64 D6 13 47N 109 11E
Quito Ecuador 90 B13 0 14S 78 30W

R
Raahe Finland 48 F3 64 42N 24 30E
Raalte Neths 41 E5 52 23N 6 16E
Raba Indonesia 65 F2 8 27S 118 45E
Rabat Malta 46 P8 35 53N 14 24E
Rabat-Salé Morocco 76 C8 34 02N 6 51W
Rabaul PNG 67 K10 4 13S 152 11E
Rach Gia Vietnam 64 D5 10 00N 105 05E
Racibórz Poland 45 J5 50 05N 18 10E
Rădăuţi Romania 45 M3 47 49N 25 58E
Radford USA 87 K4 37 07N 80 34W
Radom Poland 45 K5 51 26N 21 10E
Radomsko Poland 45 J5 51 04N 19 25E
Radstadt Austria 44 F3 47 23N 13 28E
Rae Canada 84 M6 62 55N 115 55W
Raetihi NZ 69 E5 39 26S 175 17E
Rafsanjân Iran 57 P10 30 25N 56 00E
Ragusa Italy 46 F2 36 56N 14 44E
Raichur India 58 D3 16 15N 77 20E
Raiganj India 59 K10 25 37N 88 12E
Raigarh India 58 E4 21 53N 83 28E
Rainier, Mount USA 86 B6 46 25N 121 45W
Raipur India 58 E4 21 16N 81 42E
Rajahmundry India 58 E3 17 01N 81 52E
Rajapalaiyam India 58 D1 9 26N 77 36E
Rajkot India 58 C4 21 18N 70 53E
Rajshahi Bangladesh 59 K10 24 24N 88 40E
Raleigh USA 87 L4 35 46N 78 39W
Ramgarh Bangladesh 59 L9 22 59N 91 43E
Râmnicu Sărat Romania 45 N2 45 24N 27 06E
Râmnicu Vâlcea Romania 45 M2 45 06N 24 21E
Rampur India 58 D5 28 50N 79 05E
Rampur India 58 D6 31 26N 77 37E
Rancagua Chile 91 C7 34 10S 70 45W
Ranchi India 59 F4 23 22N 85 20E
Randers Denmark 48 D2 56 28N 10 03E
Rangiora NZ 69 D3 43 19S 172 36E
Rangpur Bangladesh 59 K10 25 45N 89 21E
Rankin Inlet tn. Canada 85 S6 62 45N 92 05W
Ransiki Indonesia 65 J3 1 27S 134 12E
Rantauprapat Indonesia 64 B4 2 05N 99 46E
Rapallo Italy 46 C6 44 21N 9 13E
Rapid City USA 86 F5 44 06N 103 14W
Ra's al Khaymah UAE 57 P9 25 46N 55 56E
Ra's-e Barkan Iran 57 M10 30 02N 49 30E
Rasht Iran 56 E6 37 18N 49 38E
Ras Lanuf Libya 77 J8 30 31N 18 34E
Rastatt Germany 44 D4 48 51N 8 13E
Rat Buri Thailand 64 B6 13 30N 99 50E
Ratlam India 58 D4 23 18N 75 06E
Ratno Ukraine 45 M5 51 40N 24 32E
Raton USA 86 F4 36 45N 104 27W
Raudhatain Kuwait 57 M9 29 52N 47 41E
Rauma Finland 48 F3 61 09N 21 30E
Raurkela India 59 F4 22 16N 85 01E
Ravenna Italy 46 E6 44 25N 12 12E
Ravensburg Germany 44 D4 47 47N 9 37E
Ravensthorpe Aust. 66 D4 33 34S 120 01E
Rawalpindi Pakistan 58 C6 33 40N 73 08E
Rawlins USA 86 E5 41 46N 107 16W
Raymondville USA 87 G2 26 30N 97 48W
Razgrad Bulgaria 47 M5 43 31N 26 33E
Reading UK 40 F2 51 28N 0 59W
Reading USA 87 L5 40 20N 75 55W
Rechitsa Belarus 45 P5 52 21N 30 23E
Recife Brazil 90 L12 8 06S 34 53W
Recklinghausen Germany 44 C5 51 37N 7 11E
Reconquista Argentina 91 F8 29 08S 59 38W
Red Bluff USA 86 B5 40 11N 122 16W
Red Deer Canada 84 N4 52 15N 113 48W
Red Sea Middle East 56 C4/C2 26 00N 36 00E

Red Wing USA 87 H5 44 33N 92 31W
Reedsport USA 86 B5 43 42N 124 05W
Reefton NZ 69 C3 42 07S 171 52E
Regensburg Germany 44 F4 49 01N 12 07E
Reggio di Calabria Italy 46 F3 38 06N 15 39E
Reggio nell'Emilia Italy 46 D6 44 42N 10 37E
Regina Canada 85 Q4 50 30N 104 38W
Reims Fr. 42 G5 49 15N 4 02E
Reinosa Sp. 43 C5 43 01N 4 09W
Rembang Indonesia 64 E2 6 45S 111 22E
Remscheid Germany 41 F4 51 11N 7 11E
Rendsburg Germany 44 D7 54 19N 9 39E
Renfrew Canada 85 V3 45 28N 76 44W
Renkum Neths 41 D5 51 58N 5 44E
Rennes Fr. 42 D5 48 06N 1 40W
Reno USA 86 C4 39 32N 119 49W
REPUBLIC OF IRELAND 40 A3/C3
REPUBLIC OF SOUTH AFRICA 78 D1/D2
Requena Sp. 43 E3 39 29N 1 08W
Resistencia Argentina 90 F8 27 28S 59 00W
Resolute Canada 85 S8 74 40N 95 00W
Rethel Fr. 42 G5 49 31N 4 22E
Réthymno Greece 47 L1 35 23N 24 28E
Reus Sp. 43 F4 41 10N 1 06E
Reutlingen Germany 44 D4 48 30N 9 13E
Revelstoke Canada 84 M4 51 02N 118 12W
Rewa India 58 E4 24 32N 81 18E
Reykjavik Iceland 48 K6 64 09N 21 58W
Reynosa Mexico 88 E5 26 05N 98 18W
Rēzekne Latvia 48 G2 56 30N 27 22E
Rheden Neths 41 E5 52 01N 6 02E
Rhein r. Germany 44 C4 50 30N 8 00E
Rheinau Germany 41 F1 48 40N 7 57E
Rheinbach Germany 41 E3 50 37N 6 57E
Rheine Germany 44 C6 52 17N 7 26E
Rhode Island state USA 87 M5 41 00N 71 00W
Rhodes Greece 49 C2 36 26N 28 13E
Rhondda UK 40 E2 51 40N 3 30W
Rhône r. Switz./Fr. 42 G3 45 00N 4 50E
Ribeirão Prêto Brazil 90 H9 21 09S 47 48W
Riberalta Bolivia 90 D11 10 59S 66 06W
Richibucto Canada 85 Y3 46 42N 64 54W
Richland USA 86 C6 46 17N 119 17W
Richmond Aust. 67 H6 20 45S 143 05E
Richmond NZ 69 D4 41 31S 173 39E
Richmond USA 87 L4 37 34N 77 27W
Ried Austria 44 F4 48 13N 13 29E
Riesa Germany 44 F5 51 18N 13 18E
Riga Latvia 48 F2 56 53N 24 08E
Rijeka Croatia 46 F6 45 20N 14 27E
Rijssen Neths 41 E5 52 18N 6 31E
Rimini Italy 46 E6 44 03N 12 34E
Rimouski Canada 85 X3 48 27N 68 32W
Rio Branco tn. Brazil 90 D12 9 59S 67 49W
Rio Cuarto tn. Argentina 91 E7 33 08S 64 20W
Rio de Janeiro tn. Brazil 90 J9 22 53S 43 17W
Rio Gallegos tn. Argentina 91 D3 51 35S 68 10W
Rio Grande tn. Brazil 91 D3 53 45S 67 46W
Rio Grande tn. Brazil 91 G7 32 03S 52 08W
Rio Grande tn. Mexico 88 D4 23 50N 103 02W
Rio Grande r. Mexico/USA 86 E3/F3 30 00N 105 00W
Riohacha Col. 90 C16 11 34N 72 58W
Rio Verde tn. Brazil 90 G10 17 50S 50 55W
Rio Verde tn. Mexico 88 D4 21 58N 100 00W
Rivera Uruguay 91 F7 30 52S 55 30W
River Cess tn. Liberia 76 C3 5 28N 9 32W
Rivers tn. Canada 85 Q4 50 02N 100 14W
Riverside USA 86 C3 33 59N 117 22W
Riverton Canada 85 R4 51 00N 97 00W
Riverton NZ 69 B1 46 22S 168 01E
Rivière-du-Loup tn. Canada 85 X3 47 49N 69 32W
Rivière-Pilote tn. Martinique 88 R12 14 29N 60 54W
Rivne Ukraine 45 N5 50 39N 26 10E
Riyadh Saudi Arabia 57 M8 24 39N 46 46E
Roanne Fr. 42 G4 46 02N 4 05E
Roanoke USA 87 L4 37 15N 79 58W
Robertsport Liberia 76 B3 6 45N 11 22W
Roberval Canada 85 W3 48 31N 72 16W
Roblin Canada 85 Q4 51 15N 101 20W
Rochefort Fr. 42 D4 45 57N 0 58W
Rochester USA 87 L5 43 12N 77 37W
Rockford USA 87 J5 42 16N 89 06W
Rockhampton Aust. 67 K6 23 22S 150 32E
Rock Hill tn. USA 87 K3 34 55N 81 01W
Rock Springs tn. USA 86 E5 41 35N 109 13W
Rocky Mountains Canada/USA 84 K5/P2 55 00N 125 00W
Rodez Fr. 42 F3 44 21N 2 34E
Ródos i. Greece 47 M2 36 10N 28 00E
Roermond Neths 41 D4 51 12N 6 00E
Roeselare Belgium 41 B3 50 57N 3 08E
Rolla USA 87 H4 37 56N 91 55W
Roma Aust. 67 J5 26 34S 148 48E
Roman Romania 45 N3 46 56N 26 56E
ROMANIA 45 L2/M2
Romans-sur-Isère Fr. 42 G3 45 03N 5 03E
Rome Italy 46 E4 41 53N 12 30E
Romorantin-Lanthenay Fr. 42 E4 47 22N 1 44E
Ronda Sp. 43 C2 36 45N 5 10W
Rondonópolis Brazil 90 G10 16 29S 54 37W
Ronse Belgium 41 B3 50 45N 3 36E
Roosendaal Neths 41 C4 51 32N 4 28E
Roquetas de Mar Sp. 43 D2 36 46N 2 35W
Rosario Argentina 91 E7 33 00S 60 40W
Rosário Brazil 90 J13 3 00S 44 15W
Rosarito Mexico 88 B5 28 38N 114 02W
Rosarno Italy 46 F3 38 29N 15 59E
Roseau Dominica 89 Q8 15 18N 61 23W
Roseburg USA 86 B5 43 13N 123 21W
Rose Hill tn. Mauritius 73 E2 20 14S 57 27E
Rosenheim Germany 44 F3 47 51N 12 09E
Rosetown Canada 84 P4 51 34N 107 59W

Roşiori de Vede Romania 45 M2 44 06N 25 0
Roskilde Denmark 48 D2 55 39N 12 0
Roslavl' Russia 49 D5 53 57N 32 5
Rossano Italy 47 G3 39 35N 16 3
Rosslare RoI 40 C3 52 15N 6 22
Rosso Mauritania 76 A5 16 29N 15 5
Rossosh' Russia 49 E5 50 12N 39
Ross River tn. Canada 84 J6 62 02N 132 28
Rostock Germany 44 F7 54 06N 12 0
Rostov Russia 49 E6 57 11N 39
Rostov-na-Donu Russia 54 F4 47 15N 39 4
Roswell USA 86 F3 33 24N 104 33
Rotenburg Germany 41 H6 53 07N 9 2
Rotorua NZ 69 E5 38 08S 176 1
Rotterdam Neths 41 C4 51 54N 4 2
Roubaix Fr. 42 F6 50 42N 3 1
Rouen Fr. 42 E5 49 26N 1 0
Rouyn-Noranda Canada 85 V3 48 15N 79 00
Rovaniemi Finland 48 G4 66 29N 25 4
Rovigo Italy 46 D6 45 04N 11 4
Rowta India 59 M11 26 50N 92 2
Roxas Philippines 65 G6 11 36N 122 4
Roxburgh NZ 69 B2 45 33S 169 1
Royan Fr. 42 D3 45 38N 1 0
Rožňava Slovakia 45 K4 48 40N 20 3
Rtishchevo Russia 49 F5 52 16N 43 4
Rubtsovsk Russia 54 L7 51 43N 81 1
Rudnyy Kazakhstan 54 J7 53 00N 63 0
Rugao China 61 M4 32 27N 120 3
Rugby UK 40 F3 52 23N 1 15
Ruhr r. Germany 44 D5 51 00N 7 0
Runanga NZ 69 C3 42 24S 171 1
Ruse Bulgaria 47 M5 43 50N 25 5
Rusk USA 87 G3 31 49N 95 1
Russas Brazil 90 K13 4 56S 38 0
Russell Canada 85 Q4 50 47N 101 1
Russell NZ 69 E7 35 16S 174
Russell USA 87 G4 38 54N 98 5
Rüsselsheim Germany 41 G3 50 00N 8
RUSSIAN FEDERATION 54/55
Rust'avi Georgia 49 G3 41 34N 45
Ruston USA 87 H3 32 32N 92 3
Ruth USA 86 D4 39 16N 114 5
Rutland USA 87 M5 43 37N 72 5
Rutog China 60 C4 33 27N 79
Ruwais UAE 57 N8 24 07N 52
Ružomberok Slovakia 45 J4 49 04N 19 1
RWANDA 79 A3/B3
Ryazan' Russia 54 F7 54 37N 39
Rybinsk Russia 54 F8 58 03N 38
Rybnik Poland 45 J5 50 07N 18 3
Ryōtsu Japan 62 C3 38 05N 138 2
Ryukyu Islands Japan 61 M2/P4 27 30N 128 0
Rzeszów Poland 45 L5 50 04N 22 0
Rzhev Russia 49 D6 56 15N 34

S
Sa'ādatābād Iran 57 P9 29 40N 55 5
Saalfeld Germany 44 E5 50 39N 11 2
Saarbrücken Germany 44 C4 49 15N 6 5
Saarlouis Germany 41 E2 49 20N 6 4
Šabac SM 47 H6 44 45N 19 4
Sabadell Sp. 43 G4 41 33N 2 0
Sabhā Libya 77 H7 27 02N 14 2
Sabinas Mexico 88 D5 27 50N 101 0
Sabinas Hidalgo Mexico 88 D5 26 33N 100 1
Sabyā Saudi Arabia 56 D2 17 07N 42 3
Sabzevār Iran 56 G6 36 15N 57 3
Sacramento USA 86 B4 38 32N 121 3
Saeki Japan 63 B2 32 58N 131 5
Safi Morocco 76 C8 32 20N 9 1
Saga Japan 63 B2 33 16N 130
Saga Japan 63 B2 33 04N 130 1
Sagamihara Japan 63 C3 35 34N 139
Sagar India 58 D4 23 50N 78 4
Saginaw USA 87 K5 43 25N 83 5
Sagua la Grande Cuba 89 H4 22 48N 80 0
Saguenay Canada 85 W3 48 26N 71 0
Sagunto Sp. 43 E3 39 40N 0 1
Sahagún Sp. 43 C5 42 23N 5 0
Sahara Desert North Africa 76/77 C6/L6 22 50N
Saharanpur India 58 D5 29 58N 77
Saharsa India 59 J10 25 54N 86 3
Sahiwal Pakistan 58 C6 30 41N 73
Sahm Oman 57 P8 24 11N 56
Sahuayo Mexico 88 D4 20 05N 102 4
Sa'īdābād Iran 57 P9 29 36N 55
Saidpur Bangladesh 59 K10 25 48N 89
Saijo Japan 63 B2 33 55N 133 1
St. Albans UK 40 F2 51 46N 0 2
St. Andrews UK 40 E5 56 20N 2 4
St. Ann's Bay tn. Jamaica 89 U14 18 26N 77
St. Augustine USA 87 K2 29 54N 81 1
St-Brieuc Fr. 42 C5 48 31N 2 4
St. Catharines Canada 85 V2 43 10N 79 1
St-Chamond Fr. 42 G3 45 29N 4
St-Cloud Fr. 42 H6 45 34N 94 1
St-Dié Fr. 42 H5 48 17N 6 5
St-Dizier Fr. 42 G5 48 38N 4
Ste. Marie Martinique 88 R12 14 47N 61 0
Saintes Fr. 42 D3 45 44N 0
St-Étienne Fr. 42 G3 45 26N 4 2
St. Gallen Switz. 44 D3 47 25N 9
St-Gaudens Fr. 42 E2 43 07N 0
St. George's Grenada 88 R11 12 04N 61 4
St-German en-Laye Fr. 42 F5 48 54N 2
St-Ghislain Belgium 41 B3 50 27N 3
St-Girons Fr. 42 E2 42 59N 1
St. Helens UK 40 E3 53 28N 2
St. Helier Channel Islands 40 E1 49 12N 2 0
St-Hubert Belgium 41 D3 50 02N 5
St. Ignace USA 87 K6 45 53N 84

Ingbert Germany 41 F2 49 17N 7 06E
Jean-de-Luz Fr. 42 D2 43 23N 1 39W
int John Canada 85 X3 45 16N 66 03W
John's Antigua & Barbuda 88 Q9 17 08N 61 50W
John's Canada 85 AA3 47 34N 52 41W
Joseph USA 87 H4 39 45N 94 51W
Kitts i. St. Kitts & Nevis 88 P9 17 21N 62 48W
KITTS AND NEVIS 88 P9
Laurent French Guiana 90 G15 5 29N 54 03W
Lawrence r. Canada/USA 85 X3 46 55N 55 24W
Lô Fr. 42 D5 49 07N 1 05W
Louis Senegal 76 A5 16 01N 16 30W
Louis USA 87 H4 38 40N 90 15W
LUCIA 88 R11/R12
Malo Fr. 42 C5 48 39N 2 00W
Martin Lesser Antilles 88 P10 18 04N 63 04W
Moritz Switz. 44 D3 46 30N 9 51E
Nazaire Fr. 42 C4 47 17N 2 12W
Niklaas Belgium 41 C4 51 10N 4 09E
Omer Fr. 42 F6 50 45N 2 15E
Paul USA 87 H5 45 00N 93 10W
Petersburg Russia 54 F8 59 55N 30 25E
Petersburg USA 87 K2 27 45N 82 40W
nt-Pierre & Miquelon is. Atlantic Ocean 85 Z3 47 00N 56 20W
Pölten Austria 45 G4 48 13N 15 37E
Quentin Fr. 42 F5 49 51N 3 17E
Stephen Canada 85 X3 45 12N 67 18W
Tropez Fr. 42 H2 43 16N 6 39E
Truiden Belgium 41 D3 50 49N 5 11E
Vincent i. St. Vincent and The Grenadines 88 R11 13 15N 61 12W
VINCENT AND THE GRENADINES 88 R11
With Belgium 41 E3 50 15N 6 07E
Lai Japan 63 C2 34 35N 135 28E
Läkah Saudi Arabia 56 D4 29 59N 40 12E
ata Japan 62 C3 38 55N 139 51E
halin r. Russia 55 S7 50 00N 143 00E
hon Nakhon Thailand 64 C7 17 12N 104 09E
Nigeria 76 E3 8 39N 3 25E
alah Oman 56 F2 17 00N 54 04E
amanca Mexico 88 D4 20 34N 101 12W
amanca Sp. 43 C4 40 58N 5 40W
avat Russia 49 J5 53 19N 55 54E
dus Latvia 48 F2 56 38N 22 30E
em India 58 D2 11 38N 78 08E
erno Italy 46 F4 40 40N 14 46E
gótarján Hungary 45 J4 49 05N 19 47E
gueiro Brazil 90 K12 8 04S 39 05W
hli Turkey 47 N3 38 29N 28 08E
ma Malawi 78 F5 13 45S 34 29E
na USA 87 G4 38 53N 97 36W
nas Ecuador 90 A13 2 15S 80 58W
nas USA 86 B4 36 39N 121 40W
sbury UK 40 F2 51 05N 1 48W
non USA 86 D6 45 11N 113 55W
Finland 48 F3 60 23N 23 10E
Italy 46 D6 45 37N 10 31E
on-de-Provence Fr. 42 G2 43 38N 5 06E
nta Romania 45 K3 46 49N 21 40E
sk Russia 49 F4 46 28N 41 33E
a Argentina 90 D9 24 46S 65 28W
dal Norway 48 E4 67 06N 15 25E
illo Mexico 88 D5 25 30N 101 00W
Lake City USA 86 D5 40 45N 111 55W
o Uruguay 91 F7 31 27S 57 50W
ador Brazil 90 K11 12 58S 38 29W
vah Saudi Arabia 57 M8 24 44N 50 49E
veen r. China/Myanmar 64 B8 20 00N 103 00E
burg Austria 44 F3 47 48N 13 03E
ar i. Philippines 65 G6/H6 12 00N 125 00E
ara Russia 54 H6 53 10N 50 10E
arinda Indonesia 65 F3 0 30S 117 09E
arkand Uzbekistan 54 J4 39 40N 66 57E
arra' Iraq 56 D5 34 13N 43 52E
balpur r. India 59 E4 21 28N 84 04E
bas Indonesia 64 D4 1 22N 109 15E
bor Ukraine 45 L4 49 31N 23 10E
e Tanzania 79 E2 4 04S 37 44E
OA 70 J6
os i. Greece 47 M2 37 45N 26 45E
sun Turkey 49 E3 41 17N 36 22E
ut Prakan Thailand 64 C6 13 38N 100 35E
ut Sakhon Thailand 64 C6 13 31N 100 16E
Mali 76 C4 13 21N 4 57W
Yemen 56 D2 15 23N 44 14E
ndaj Iran 56 E6 35 18N 47 01E
Andrés Tuxtla Mexico 88 E3 18 28N 95 15W
Angelo USA 86 F3 31 28N 100 28W
Antonio Chile 91 C7 33 35S 71 39W
Antonio USA 87 G2 29 25N 98 30W
Bernardino USA 86 C3 34 07N 117 18W
Bernardo Chile 91 C7 33 37S 70 45W
Carlos Philippines 65 G6 10 30N 123 29E
Carlos Philippines 65 G5 11 59N 120 22E
Carlos Venezuela 90 D15 9 39N 68 35W
Cristóbal Mexico 88 F3 16 45N 92 40W
Cristóbal Venezuela 90 C15 7 46N 72 15W
ti Spíritus Cuba 89 J4 21 55N 79 28W
lakan Malaysia 65 F5 5 52N 118 04E
iego USA 86 C3 32 45N 117 10W
loway USA 86 A7 18 28N 94 20E
point tn. USA 86 C4 48 17N 116 33W
elipe Mexico 88 B6 31 03N 114 52W
elipe Venezuela 90 D16 10 25N 68 40W
ernando Mexico 88 A5 29 59N 115 10W
ernando Philippines 65 G7 16 39N 120 19E
ernando Sp. 43 B2 36 28N 6 12W
ord USA 87 K2 28 49N 81 17W
rancisco Argentina 91 E7 31 29S 62 06W
rancisco Dom. Rep. 89 K3 19 19N 70 15W
rancisco USA 86 B4 37 45N 122 27W
i South Korea 63 A3 36 25N 128 08E

Sangli India 58 C3 16 55N 74 37E
Sangmélima Cameroon 76 G2 2 57N 11 56E
Sanjō Japan 62 C3 37 38N 138 19E
San José Costa Rica 89 H1 9 59N 84 04W
San José Uruguay 91 F7 34 27S 56 40W
San José USA 86 B4 37 20N 121 55W
San José del Cabo Mexico 88 C4 23 01N 109 40W
San Juan Argentina 91 D7 31 33S 68 31W
San Juan Peru 90 B10 15 22S 75 07W
San Juan Puerto Rico 89 L3 18 29N 66 08W
San Julián Argentina 91 D4 49 17S 67 45W
Sanliurfa Turkey 49 E2 37 08N 38 45E
Sanlúcar de Barrameda Sp. 43 B2 36 46N 6 21W
San Lucas Mexico 88 C4 22 50N 109 52W
San Luis Argentina 91 D7 33 20S 66 23W
San Luis Obispo USA 86 B4 35 16N 120 40W
San Luis Potosí Mexico 88 D4 22 10N 101 00W
San Marcos USA 87 G2 29 54N 97 57W
SAN MARINO 46 E5 44 00N 12 00E
San Miguel El Salvador 88 G2 13 28N 88 10W
Sanming China 61 L3 26 16N 117 35E
San Pablo Philippines 65 G6 14 03N 121 19E
San Pedro Argentina 90 E9 24 12S 64 55W
San Pedro Dom. Rep. 89 L3 18 30N 69 18W
San Pedro Sula Honduras 88 G3 15 26N 88 01W
San Rafael Argentina 91 D7 34 35S 68 24W
San Rafael USA 86 B4 37 58N 122 30W
San Remo Italy 46 B5 43 48N 7 46E
San Salvador El Salvador 88 G2 13 40N 89 10W
San Sebastián Sp. 43 E5 43 19N 1 59W
San Severo Italy 46 F4 41 41N 15 23E
Santa Ana El Salvador 88 G2 14 00N 89 31W
Santa Ana Mexico 86 D3 30 33N 111 07W
Santa Ana USA 86 C3 33 44N 117 54W
Santa Barbara USA 86 C3 33 29N 119 01W
Santa Clara Cuba 89 J4 22 25N 79 58W
Santa Cruz Bolivia 90 E10 17 50S 63 10W
Santa Cruz Canary Islands 76 A7 28 28N 16 15W
Santa Cruz USA 86 B4 36 58N 122 03W
Santa Fé Argentina 91 E7 31 35S 60 50W
Santa Cruz USA 86 C4 35 41N 105 57W
Santa Maria Brazil 91 G8 29 45S 53 40W
Santa Maria USA 86 B3 34 56N 120 25W
Santa Marta Col. 90 C16 11 18N 74 10W
Santander Col. 90 B14 3 00N 76 25W
Santander Sp. 43 D5 43 28N 3 48W
Sant' Antioco Italy 46 C3 39 04N 8 27E
Santarém Brazil 90 G13 2 26S 54 41W
Santarém Port. 43 A3 39 14N 8 40W
Santa Rosa Argentina 91 D7 36 37S 64 17W
Santa Rosalia Mexico 88 B5 27 20N 112 20W
Santa Teresa Gallura Italy 46 C4 41 14N 9 12E
Santiago Chile 91 C7 33 30S 70 40W
Santiago Dom. Rep. 89 K3 19 27N 70 42W
Santiago Panama 89 H1 8 08N 80 59W
Santiago de Cuba Cuba 89 J4 20 00N 75 49W
Santiago Ixcuintla Mexico 88 C4 21 50N 105 11W
Santipur India 59 K9 23 16N 88 27E
Santo Andre Brazil 90 H9 23 39S 46 29W
Santo Domingo Dom. Rep. 89 L3 18 30N 69 57W
Santoña Sp. 43 D5 43 27N 3 26W
Santos Brazil 90 H9 23 56S 46 22W
San Vicente El Salvador 88 G2 13 38N 88 42W
Sanya China 61 J1 18 25N 109 27E
São Borja Brazil 91 F8 28 35S 56 01W
São José Brazil 91 H9 27 35S 48 40W
São José do Rio Prêto Brazil 90 H9 20 50S 49 20W
São José dos Campos Brazil 90 H9 23 07S 45 52W
São Luís Brazil 90 J13 2 34S 44 16W
São Paulo Brazil 90 H9 23 33S 46 39W
São Tomé i. Gulf of Guinea 76 F2 0 25N 6 35E
SÃO TOMÉ AND PRINCIPE 76 F2
São Vicente Brazil 90 H9 23 57S 46 23W
Sape Indonesia 65 F2 8 35S 118 59E
Sappemeer Neths 41 E6 53 10N 6 47E
Sapporo Japan 62 C4 43 05N 141 21E
Saqqez Iran 56 E6 36 14N 46 15E
Saraburi Thailand 64 C6 14 32N 100 53E
Sarajevo Bosnia-Herzegovina 47 H5 43 52N 18 26E
Saransk Russia 54 G7 54 12N 45 10E
Sarapul Russia 49 H6 56 30N 53 48E
Sarasota USA 87 K2 27 20N 82 32W
Sarata Ukraine 45 P3 46 00N 29 40E
Saratov Russia 54 G7 51 30N 45 55E
Saravan Iran 57 H4 27 25N 62 17E
Sardinia i. Italy 46 C3/C4 40 00N 9 00E
Sargodha Pakistan 58 C6 32 01N 72 40E
Sarh Chad 77 J3 9 08N 18 22E
Sarmiento Argentina 91 D4 45 38S 69 08W
Sarnia Canada 85 U2 42 58N 82 23W
Sarny Ukraine 45 N5 51 21N 26 31E
Sarpsborg Norway 48 D2 59 17N 11 06E
Sarrebourg Fr. 42 H5 48 43N 7 03E
Sarreguemines Fr. 42 H5 49 06N 6 55E
Sartène Corsica 42 J1 41 37N 8 58E
Sasebo Japan 63 A2 33 10N 129 42E
Saskatchewan province Canada 84/85 P5/Q5 53 50N 109 00W
Saskatoon Canada 84 P4 52 10N 106 40W
Sassandra Côte d'Ivoire 76 C2 4 58N 6 08W
Sassari Italy 46 C4 40 43N 8 34E
Sassnitz Germany 44 F7 54 32N 13 40E
Sassuolo Italy 46 D6 44 32N 10 47E
Satna India 58 E4 24 33N 80 50E
Sattahip Thailand 64 C6 12 36N 100 56E
Satu Mare Romania 45 L3 47 48N 22 52E
SAUDI ARABIA 56 D3/F3
Sault Ste. Marie Canada 85 U3 46 31N 84 20W
Saumur Fr. 42 D4 47 16N 0 05W
Saurimo Angola 78 D6 9 39S 20 24E
Savannah USA 87 K3 32 04N 81 07W
Savannakhet Laos 64 C7 16 34N 104 45E
Savanna la Mar Jamaica 89 T14 18 13N 78 08W

Savona Italy 46 C6 44 18N 8 28E
Sawada Japan 62 C3 38 01N 138 19E
Sawahlunto Indonesia 64 C3 0 41S 100 52E
Sawara Japan 63 D3 35 52N 140 31E
Saylac Somalia 77 P4 11 21N 43 30E
Saynshand Mongolia 61 K7 45 00N 111 10E
Scarborough Trinidad & Tobago 89 V15 11 11N 60 44W
Scarborough UK 40 F4 54 17N 0 24W
Schaerbeek Belgium 41 C3 50 52N 4 22E
Schaffhausen Switz. 44 D3 47 42N 8 38E
Schagen Neths 41 C5 52 47N 4 47E
Schefferville Canada 85 X4 54 50N 67 00W
Schenectady USA 87 M5 42 48N 73 57W
Schiedam Neths 41 C4 51 55N 4 25E
Schleswig Germany 44 D7 54 32N 9 34E
Schwaz Austria 44 E3 47 21N 11 44E
Schwechat Austria 45 H4 48 09N 16 27E
Schweinfurt Germany 44 E5 50 03N 10 16E
Schwerin Germany 44 E6 53 38N 11 25E
Schwyz Switz. 44 D3 47 02N 8 34E
Sciacca Italy 46 E2 37 31N 13 05E
Scotland country UK 40 C5/F5 56 10N 4 00W
Scottsbluff USA 86 F5 41 52N 103 40W
Scranton USA 87 L5 41 25N 75 40W
Scunthorpe UK 40 F3 53 35N 0 39W
Seattle USA 86 B6 47 35N 122 20W
Sebeş Romania 45 L2 45 58N 23 34E
Sedalia USA 87 H4 38 42N 93 15W
Sedan Fr. 42 G5 49 42N 4 57E
Segamat Malaysia 64 C4 2 30N 102 49E
Ségou Mali 76 C4 13 28N 6 18W
Segovia Sp. 43 C4 40 57N 4 07W
Seine r. Fr. 42 E5 49 15N 1 15E
Sekondi Takoradi Ghana 76 D2 4 59N 1 43W
Sekudai Malaysia 65 R16 1 31N 103 39E
Seldovia USA 84 E5 59 29N 151 45W
Sélestat Fr. 42 H5 48 16N 7 28E
Seletar Singapore 65 T15 1 23N 103 52E
Selkirk Canada 85 R4 50 10N 96 52W
Selma USA 87 J3 32 24N 87 01W
Semarang Indonesia 64 E2 6 58S 110 29E
Sembawang Singapore 65 S15/T15 1 27N 103 49E
Seminole USA 87 G4 35 15N 96 40W
Semipalatinsk Kazakhstan 54 L7 50 26N 80 16E
Semnān Iran 56 F6 35 30N 53 25E
Sendai Japan 62 D3 38 16N 140 52E
SENEGAL 76 A4/B4
Senhor do Bonfim Brazil 90 J11 10 28S 40 11W
Senibong Malaysia 65 S15/T15 1 29N 103 50E
Senj Croatia 46 F6 45 00N 14 55E
Senlis Fr. 42 F5 49 12N 2 35E
Sennar Sudan 77 M4 13 31N 33 38E
Sens Fr. 42 F5 48 12N 3 18E
Seoul South Korea 63 A3 37 32N 127 00E
Sept-Îles tn. Canada 85 X4 50 10N 66 00W
Seraing Belgium 41 D3 50 37N 5 31E
Seram i. Indonesia 65 H3/J3 3 30S 129 30E
Serangoon Singapore 65 T15 1 22N 103 52E
SERBIA AND MONTENEGRO 47 H6/K6
Seremban Malaysia 64 C4 2 43N 102 57E
Serenje Zambia 78 F5 13 12S 30 15E
Sergino Russia 54 J9 62 30N 65 40E
Sergiyev Posad Russia 54 F8 56 20N 38 10E
Seria Brunei 64 N11 4 39N 114 23E
Serian Malaysia 64 E4 1 10N 110 35E
Serov Russia 54 J8 59 42N 60 32E
Serowe Botswana 78 E3 22 23S 26 43E
Serpukhov Russia 49 E5 54 53N 37 25E
Serra Brazil 90 J10 20 06S 40 16W
Sérres Greece 47 K4 41 03N 23 33E
Sète Fr. 42 F2 43 25N 3 43E
Sete Lagoas Brazil 90 J10 19 29S 44 15W
Sétif Algeria 76 F9 36 11N 5 24E
Seto Japan 63 C3 35 14N 137 06E
Settat Morocco 76 C8 33 04N 7 37W
Setúbal Port. 43 A3 38 31N 8 54W
Sevastopol' Ukraine 54 D3 44 36N 33 31E
Severodvinsk Russia 54 F9 64 35N 39 50E
Seville Sp. 43 C2 37 24N 5 59W
Seward USA 84 F6 60 05N 149 34W
SEYCHELLES 73
Sézanne Fr. 42 F5 48 44N 3 44E
Sfax Tunisia 76 G8 34 45N 10 43E
Shache China 60 C5 38 27N 77 16E
Shah Alam Malaysia 64 C4 3 02N 101 31E
Shahdol India 58 E4 23 19N 81 26E
Shahjahanpur India 58 D5 27 53N 79 55E
Shakhty Russia 49 F4 47 43N 40 16E
Shanghai China 61 M4 31 06N 121 22E
Shangqui China 61 L4 34 27N 115 07E
Shangrao China 61 L3 28 28N 117 54E
Shannon r. Rol 40 B3 52 45N 8 57W
Shantou China 61 L2 23 23N 116 39E
Shaoguan China 61 K2 24 54N 113 33E
Shaoxing China 61 M3 30 02N 120 35E
Shaoyang China 61 K3 27 10N 111 25E
Shaqrā' Saudi Arabia 56 E4 25 18N 45 15E
Shari r. 77 D4 34 56N 144 41E
Sharjah UAE 57 P9 25 20N 55 23E
Sharon USA 86 K5 41 46N 80 30W
Shar'ya Russia 54 G6 58 22N 45 31E
Shashi China 61 K4 30 16N 112 20E
Shawinigan Canada 85 W3 46 33N 72 46W
Sheberghān Afghanistan 57 J6 36 41N 65 45E
Sheboygan USA 87 J5 43 46N 87 44W
Sheffield UK 40 F3 53 23N 1 30W
Shelburne Canada 85 X2 43 37N 65 20W
Shelby USA 86 D6 48 30N 95 22W
Shenandoah USA 87 G5 40 48N 95 22W
Shenyang China 61 M6 41 50N 123 26E
Shenzhen China 61 K2 22 31N 114 05E
Shepetovka Ukraine 45 N5 50 12N 27 01E
Sherbrooke Canada 85 W3 45 24N 71 54W

Sheridan USA 86 E5 44 48N 106 57W
's-Hertogenbosch Neths 41 D4 51 41N 5 19E
Shetland Islands UK 40 F6/F7 60 00N 1 15W
Shibata Japan 62 C3 37 57N 139 20E
Shibecha Japan 62 D4 43 17N 144 34E
Shihezi China 60 E6 44 19N 86 10E
Shijiazhuang China 61 K5 38 04N 114 28E
Shikarpur Pakistan 58 B5 27 58N 68 42E
Shikoku i. Japan 63 B2 33 40N 134 00E
Shiliguri India 59 F5 26 42N 88 30E
Shillong India 59 G5 25 34N 91 53E
Shimada Japan 63 C2 34 50N 138 10E
Shimizu Japan 63 C2 35 01N 138 29E
Shimla India 58 D6 31 07N 77 09E
Shimoga India 58 D2 13 56N 75 31E
Shimonoseki Japan 63 B2 33 59N 130 58E
Shinaş Oman 57 P8 24 46N 56 27E
Shindand Afghanistan 57 H5 33 16N 62 05E
Shingū Japan 63 C2 33 42N 136 00E
Shinjō Japan 62 D3 38 45N 140 18E
Shinyanga Tanzania 79 C3 3 40S 33 26E
Shiogama Japan 62 D3 38 19N 141 00E
Shirakawa Japan 63 D3 37 07N 140 11E
Shiraoi Japan 62 D4 42 34N 141 19E
Shiraz Iran 57 N9 29 38N 52 34E
Shizuishan China 61 J5 39 04N 106 22E
Shizuoka Japan 63 C2 34 59N 138 24E
Shkodër Albania 47 H5 42 03N 19 01E
Shōbara Japan 63 B2 34 52N 133 00E
Shreveport USA 87 H3 32 30N 93 46W
Shrewsbury UK 40 E3 52 43N 2 45W
Shuangliao China 61 M6 43 30N 123 29E
Shuangyashan China 61 N7 46 42N 131 20E
Shumen Bulgaria 47 M5 43 17N 26 55E
Shunde China 61 K2 22 50N 113 16E
Shuqrā Yemen 56 E1 13 23N 45 44E
Shwebo Myanmar 60 G2 22 35N 95 42E
Shymkent Kazakhstan 54 J4 42 16N 69 05E
Sialkot Pakistan 58 C6 32 29N 74 35E
Siauliai Lithuania 48 F2 55 51N 23 20E
Šibenik Croatia 46 F5 43 45N 15 55E
Sibi Pakistan 58 B5 29 31N 67 54E
Sibiti Congo 78 B7 3 40S 13 24E
Sibiu Romania 45 M2 45 46N 24 09E
Sibolga Indonesia 64 B4 1 42N 98 48E
Sibu Malaysia 64 E4 2 19N 111 50E
Sibut CAR 77 J3 5 46N 19 06E
Sicily i. Italy 46 E2/F2 37 00N 14 00E
Sicuani Peru 90 C11 14 21S 71 13W
Siderno Italy 46 G3 38 16N 16 17E
Sidi Barrani Egypt 77 L8 31 38N 25 58E
Sidi Bel Abbès Algeria 76 D9 35 15N 0 39W
Sidi Ifni Morocco 76 B7 29 24N 10 12W
Siedlce Poland 45 L6 52 10N 22 18E
Siegburg Germany 41 F3 50 48N 7 13E
Siegen Germany 44 D5 50 52N 8 02E
Siem Reap Cambodia 64 C6 13 21N 103 50E
Siena Italy 46 D5 43 19N 11 19E
Sierra Blanca tn. USA 86 F3 31 10N 105 22W
SIERRA LEONE 76 B3
Siggiewi Malta 46 P8 35 51N 14 26E
Sighişoara Romania 45 M3 46 12N 24 48E
Sigüenza Sp. 43 D4 41 04N 2 38W
Siguiri Guinea 76 C4 11 28N 9 07W
Sikar India 58 D5 27 33N 75 12E
Sikasso Mali 76 C4 11 18N 5 38W
Sila UAE 57 N8 23 59N 51 50E
Silchar India 59 G4 24 49N 92 47E
Silifke Turkey 49 D2 36 22N 33 57E
Silistra Bulgaria 47 M6 44 06N 27 17E
Silves Port. 43 A2 37 11N 8 26W
Simferopol' Ukraine 49 D3 44 57N 34 05E
Sinai, Mount Egypt 77 M7 28 32N 33 59E
Sincelejo Col. 90 B15 9 17N 75 23W
Sindelfingen Germany 41 G1 48 42N 8 59E
Sines Port. 43 A2 37 58N 8 52W
SINGAPORE 65 R15/U15
Singida Tanzania 79 D2 4 49S 34 45E
Singkawang Indonesia 64 D4 0 57N 108 57E
Sinhyo-ri South Korea 63 A2 33 16N 126 35E
Sinop Turkey 49 E3 42 02N 35 09E
Sintra Port. 43 A3 38 48N 9 22W
Sinuiju North Korea 61 M6 40 04N 124 25E
Sion Switz. 44 C3 46 14N 7 22E
Sioux City USA 87 G5 42 30N 96 28W
Sioux Falls tn. USA 87 G5 43 34N 96 42W
Siping China 61 M6 43 15N 124 25E
Sipiwesk Canada 85 R5 55 27N 97 24W
Siracusa Italy 46 F2 37 04N 15 19E
Sirajganj Bangladesh 59 K10 24 27N 89 42E
Sir Bani Yās UAE 57 N8 24 19N 52 37E
Sirte Libya 77 J8 31 13N 16 35E
Sisak Croatia 46 G6 45 30N 16 22E
Sisophon Cambodia 64 C6 13 37N 102 58E
Sisteron Fr. 42 G3 44 16N 5 56E
Sitka USA 84 J5 57 05N 135 20W
Sittard Netherland 41 D4 51 00N 5 52E
Sittwe Myanmar 60 F2 20 09N 92 55E
Siuri India 59 J9 23 53N 87 32E
Sivas Turkey 49 E2 39 44N 37 01E
Siwa Egypt 77 L7 29 11N 25 31E
Sjaelland i. Denmark 48 D1 55 30N 11 30E
Skagway USA 84 H5 59 23N 135 20W
Skellefteå Sweden 48 F3 64 45N 21 00E
Skierniewice Poland 45 K5 51 58N 20 10E
Skikda Algeria 76 F9 36 53N 6 54E
Skopje FYROM 47 J4 42 00N 21 28E
Skövde Sweden 48 D2 58 24N 13 52E
Skovorodino Russia 55 Q7 54 00N 123 53E
Slatina Romania 47 M6 44 26N 24 22E
Slave Lake tn. Canada 84 N5 55 17N 114 43W
Slavonski Brod Croatia 47 G6 45 09N 18 02E
Sliema Malta 46 Q8 35 55N 14 31E
Sligo Rol 40 B4 54 17N 8 28W
Sliven Bulgaria 47 M5 42 40N 26 19E

Slobozia Romania 45 N2 44 34N 27 23E
Slough UK 40 F2 51 31N 0 36W
SLOVAKIA 45 J4/K4
SLOVENIA 46 F6
Slov'yans'k Ukraine 49 E4 48 51N 37 36E
Słupsk Poland 45 H7 54 28N 17 00E
Slutsk Belarus 45 N6 53 02N 27 31E
Smith Canada 84 N5 55 10N 114 02W
Smithers Canada 84 K5 54 45N 127 10W
Smiths Falls tn. Canada 85 V2 44 45N 76 01W
Smolensk Russia 54 F7 54 49N 32 04E
Sneek Neths 41 D6 53 02N 5 40E
Snow Lake tn. Canada 85 R4 54 56N 100 00W
Snyder USA 86 F3 32 43N 100 54W
Soa-Siu Indonesia 65 H4 0 40N 127 30E
Sobral Brazil 90 J13 3 45S 40 20W
Sochi Russia 54 F5 43 35N 39 46E
Socotra i. Yemen 56 F1 12 05N 54 10E
Sodankylä Finland 48 E3 67 26N 26 35E
Söderhamn Sweden 48 E3 61 19N 17 10E
Sodertälje Sweden 48 E2 59 11N 17 39E
Sodo Ethiopia 77 N3 6 49N 37 41E
Soest Germany 41 G4 51 34N 8 07E
Sofia Bulgaria 47 K5 42 40N 23 18E
Sogamoso Col. 90 C15 5 43N 72 56W
Sohâg Egypt 77 M7 26 33N 31 42E
Soignies Belgium 41 G3 50 35N 4 04E
Soissons Fr. 42 F5 49 23N 3 20E
Sōja Japan 63 B2 34 40N 133 42E
Sokcho South Korea 63 A3 38 13N 128 35E
Sokhumi Georgia 49 F3 43 01N 41 01E
Sokodé Togo 76 E3 8 59N 1 11E
Sokoto Nigeria 76 F4 13 02N 5 15E
Solāpur India 58 D3 17 43N 75 56E
Solihull UK 40 F3 52 25N 1 45W
Sol'-Iletsk Russia 49 H5 51 06N 54 58E
Solingen Germany 41 F4 51 10N 7 05E
Sollefteå Sweden 48 E3 63 09N 17 15E
Sóller Balearic Islands 43 G3 39 46N 2 42E
Solms Germany 41 G3 50 32N 8 24E
SOLOMON ISLANDS 67 L9/M9
Solothurn Switz. 44 C3 47 13N 7 32E
Soltau Germany 44 D6 52 59N 9 50E
SOMALIA 77 Q2/Q3
Sombor SM 47 H6 45 46N 19 09E
Somoto Nicaragua 88 G2 13 29N 86 36W
Sønderborg Denmark 48 C1 54 55N 9 48E
Sondrio Italy 46 C2 46 11N 9 52E
Songea Tanzania 78 G5 10 42S 35 59E
Songkhla Thailand 64 C5 7 12N 100 35E
Songnam South Korea 63 A3 37 29N 127 12E
Sonobe Japan 63 C3 35 09N 135 25E
Sonoita Mexico 88 B6 31 53N 112 52W
Sonsonate El Salvador 88 G2 13 43N 89 44W
Sopot Poland 45 J7 54 27N 18 31E
Sopron Hungary 45 H3 47 40N 16 35E
Sora Italy 46 E4 41 43N 13 37E
Soria Sp. 43 D4 41 46N 2 28W
Sorong Indonesia 65 J3 0 50S 131 17E
Soroti Uganda 79 C5 1 42N 33 37E
Sosan South Korea 63 A3 36 49N 126 26E
Sosnowiec Poland 45 J5 50 16N 19 07E
Souillac Fr. 42 E3 44 53N 1 29E
Souillac Mauritius 73 E2 20 31S 57 31E
Sousse Tunisia 76 G9 35 50N 10 38E
Southampton UK 40 F2 50 55N 1 25W
South Australia state Aust. 66 F4/G5 27 00S 135 00E
South Bend USA 87 J3 41 40N 86 15W
South Carolina state USA 87 K3 34 00N 81 00W
South Dakota state USA 86 F5 45 00N 102 00W
Southend-on-Sea UK 40 G2 51 33N 0 43E
Southern Ocean 71
South Island NZ 69 A2/E4 42 30S 172 00E
SOUTH KOREA 63 A3
South Pole Antarctica 71 90 00S
Southport UK 40 E3 53 39N 3 01W
South Sioux City USA 87 G5 42 28N 96 24W
Sovetsk Russia 48 F2 55 02N 21 50E
Sovetskaya Gavan' Russia 55 S6 48 57N 140 16E
Spa Belgium 41 D3 50 29N 5 52E
SPAIN 43 C3/E3
Spanish Town Jamaica 89 U13 17 59N 76 58W
Sparks USA 86 C4 39 34N 119 46W
Spartanburg USA 87 K3 34 56N 81 57W
Spárti Greece 47 K2 37 05N 22 25E
Spassk-Dal'niy Russia 55 R5 44 37N 132 37E
Speightstown Barbados 88 S11 13 15N 59 39W
Spencer USA 87 G5 43 08N 95 08W
Speyer Germany 41 G4 49 19N 8 24E
Spijkenisse Neths 41 C4 51 52N 4 19E
Spirit River tn. Canada 84 M5 55 46N 118 51W
Spittal an der Drau Austria 44 F3 46 48N 13 30E
Split Croatia 47 G5 43 31N 16 28E
Spokane USA 86 C6 47 40N 117 25W
Spoleto Italy 46 E5 42 44N 12 44E
Springbok RSA 78 C2 29 44S 17 56E
Springdale Canada 85 Z3 49 30N 56 06W
Springfield NZ 69 C3 43 20S 171 56E
Springfield USA 87 J4 39 49N 89 39W
Springfield USA 87 M5 42 07N 72 35W
Springsure Aust. 67 J6 24 09S 148 04E
Squamish Canada 84 L3 49 41N 123 11W
Sri Aman Malaysia 64 E4 1 17N 111 30E
Srikakulam India 59 E3 18 19N 84 00E
SRI LANKA 58 E1
Srinagar Kashmir 58 C6 34 08N 74 50E
Stade Germany 44 H6 53 36N 9 28E
Stafford UK 40 E3 52 48N 2 07W
Stalowa Wola Poland 45 L5 50 34N 22 03E
Stanley Falkland Islands 91 F3 51 45S 57 56W
Stara Zagora Bulgaria 47 L5 42 25N 25 37E
Starogard Gdański Poland 45 J6 53 58N 18 30E
Staryy Oskol Russia 54 F7 51 20N 37 50E
State College USA 87 L5 40 48N 77 52W
Staunton USA 87 L4 38 10N 79 05W

Stavanger Norway 48 C2 58 58N 5 45E
Staveley NZ 69 C3 43 39S 171 26E
Stavropol' Russia 54 G6 45 03N 41 59E
Stebbins USA 84 C6 63 32N 162 20W
Steen River tn. Canada 84 M5 59 40N 117 15W
Steenwijk Neths 41 E5 52 47N 6 07E
Stein Neths 41 D3 50 58N 5 45E
Steinfurt Germany 41 F5 52 09N 7 21E
Stenay Fr. 41 D2 49 29N 5 12E
Stendal Germany 44 E6 52 36N 11 52E
Stephenville Canada 85 Z3 48 33N 58 34W
Sterling USA 86 F5 40 37N 103 13W
Sterlitamak Russia 54 H7 53 40N 55 59E
Steubenville USA 87 K5 40 22N 80 39W
Stewart Crossing Canada 84 H6 60 37N 128 37W
Steyr Austria 44 G3 48 04N 14 25E
Štip FYROM 47 K4 41 44N 22 12E
Stirling Canada 84 N3 49 34N 112 30W
Stirling UK 40 E5 56 07N 3 57W
Stockerau Austria 45 H4 48 24N 16 13E
Stockholm Sweden 48 E2 59 20N 18 05E
Stockport UK 40 E3 53 25N 2 10W
Stockton USA 86 B4 37 59N 121 20W
Stœng Trêng Cambodia 64 D6 13 31N 105 59E
Stordal Norway 48 D3 63 18N 11 48E
Støren Norway 48 D3 63 03N 10 16E
Stornoway UK 40 C6 58 12N 6 23W
Storuman Sweden 48 E4 65 05N 17 10E
Stralsund Germany 44 F7 54 18N 13 06E
Stranraer UK 40 D4 54 55N 5 02W
Strasbourg Fr. 42 H5 48 35N 7 45E
Straubing Germany 44 F4 48 53N 12 35E
Stryy Ukraine 45 L4 49 16N 23 51E
Sturgeon Landing Canada 85 Q4 54 18N 101 49W
Stuttgart Germany 44 D4 48 47N 9 12E
Stykkishólmur Iceland 48 K7 65 05N 22 44W
Suakin Sudan 77 N5 19 08N 37 17E
Subotica SM 47 H7 46 04N 19 41E
Suceava Romania 45 N3 47 37N 26 18E
Sucre Bolivia 90 D10 19 05S 65 15W
SUDAN 77 L4/M4
Sudbury Canada 85 U3 46 30N 81 01W
Suez Egypt 77 M7 29 59N 32 33E
Suez Canal Egypt 77 M8 31 30N 32 20E
Suhâr Oman 57 P8 24 22N 56 44E
Sühbaatar Mongolia 61 J8 50 10N 106 14E
Sukabumi Indonesia 64 D2 6 55S 106 50E
Sukagawa Japan 62 D3 37 15N 140 21E
Sukkur Pakistan 58 B5 27 42N 68 54E
Sukumo Japan 63 B2 32 59N 132 42E
Sulawesi i. Indonesia 65 F3/G3 2 00S 120 00E
Sulingen Germany 41 G5 52 41N 8 48E
Sullana Peru 90 A13 4 52S 80 39W
Sumatera i. Indonesia 64 B4/C3 0 00 100 00E
Sumba i. Indonesia 65 F2/G1 10 00S 120 00E
Sumbawa i. Indonesia 65 F2 8 00S 118 00E
Sumbawa Besar Indonesia 65 F2 8 30S 117 25E
Sumbawanga Tanzania 79 B1 7 58S 31 37E
Sumoto Japan 63 B2 34 20N 134 53E
Sumqayit Azerbaijan 49 G3 40 35N 49 38E
Sumy Ukraine 49 D5 50 55N 34 49E
Sunch'on South Korea 63 A2 34 56N 127 28E
Sunderland UK 40 F4 54 55N 1 23W
Sundsvall Sweden 48 E3 62 22N 17 20E
Sungai Petani Malaysia 64 C5 5 38N 100 28E
Suntar Russia 55 P9 62 10N 117 35E
Sunyani Ghana 76 D3 7 22N 2 18W
Superior USA 87 H6 46 42N 92 05W
Superior, Lake Canada/USA 87 H6/J6 48 00N 88 00W
Suphan Buri Thailand 64 C6 14 28N 100 07E
Sür Oman 57 G3 22 34N 59 32E
Surabaya Indonesia 64 E2 7 14S 112 45E
Surakarta Indonesia 64 E2 7 32S 110 50E
Surat India 58 C4 21 10N 72 54E
Surat Thani Thailand 64 B5 9 09N 99 20E
Surgut Russia 54 K9 61 13N 73 20E
Surigao Philippines 65 H5 9 47N 125 29E
Surin Thailand 64 C6 14 53N 103 29E
SURINAME 90 F14
Susa Japan 63 B2 34 39N 131 36E
Susaki Japan 63 B2 33 22N 133 16E
Susami Japan 63 C2 33 32N 135 29E
Susuman Russia 55 S9 62 46N 148 08E
Suva Fiji 67 Q7 18 08S 178 25E
Suwa Japan 63 C3 36 02N 138 09E
Suwałki Poland 45 L7 54 06N 22 56E
Suwon South Korea 63 A3 37 16N 126 59E
Suzhou China 61 L4 33 38N 117 02E
Suzhou China 61 M4 31 21N 120 40E
Suzuka Japan 63 C2 34 52N 136 37E
Svilengrad Bulgaria 47 M4 41 45N 26 14E
Svobodnyy Russia 55 Q7 51 24N 128 05E
Swansea UK 40 E2 51 38N 3 57W
SWAZILAND 78 F2
SWEDEN 48 D2/E4
Sweetwater tn. USA 86 F3 32 27N 100 25W
Swiebodzin Poland 45 G6 52 15N 15 31E
Swift Current tn. Canada 84 P4 50 17N 107 49W
Swindon UK 40 F2 51 34N 1 47W
Swinoujście Poland 45 G6 53 55N 14 18E
SWITZERLAND 44 C3/D3
Sydney Austr. 67 K4 33 55S 151 10E
Sydney Canada 85 Y3 46 10N 60 10W
Syke Germany 41 G5 52 55N 8 50E
Syktyvkar Russia 54 H9 61 42N 50 45E
Sylhet Bangladesh 59 L10 24 53N 91 51E
Syracuse USA 87 L5 43 03N 76 10W
SYRIA 56 C6
Syzran' Russia 54 G7 53 10N 48 29E
Szczecin Poland 44 G6 53 25N 14 32E
Szczecinek Poland 45 H6 53 42N 16 41E
Szeged Hungary 45 K3 46 15N 20 09E
Székesfehérvár Hungary 45 J3 47 11N 18 22E
Szekszárd Hungary 45 J3 46 20N 18 43E
Szolnok Hungary 45 K3 47 10N 20 10E

Szombathely Hungary 45 H3 47 14N 16 38E

T

Taber Canada 84 N3 49 48N 112 09W
Tábor Czech Rep. 44 G4 49 25N 14 39E
Tabora Tanzania 79 C2 5 01S 32 48E
Tabriz Iran 56 E6 38 04N 46 17E
Tabūk Saudi Arabia 56 C4 28 33N 36 36E
Tacloban Philippines 65 G6 11 15N 125 01E
Tacna Peru 90 C10 18 00S 70 15W
Tacoma USA 86 B6 47 16N 122 30W
Taegu South Korea 63 A3 35 52N 128 36E
Taejon South Korea 63 A3 36 20N 127 26E
Tafalla Sp. 43 E5 42 32N 1 41W
Taganrog Russia 54 F6 47 14N 38 55E
Tagum Philippines 65 H5 7 25N 125 54E
Tahiti i. Pacific Ocean 70 M6 17 30S 148 30W
Tahoua Niger 76 F4 14 57N 5 19E
Tai'an China 61 L5 36 15N 117 10E
Taichung Taiwan 61 M2 24 09N 124 40E
Taihape NZ 69 E3 39 41S 175 48E
Tainan Taiwan 61 M2 23 01N 120 14E
Taipei Taiwan 61 M2 25 05N 121 32E
Taiping Malaysia 64 C4 4 50N 100 43E
TAIWAN 61 M2
Taiyuan China 61 K5 37 50N 112 30E
TAJIKISTAN 54 J4/K4
Tajima Japan 63 C3 37 11N 139 46E
Tak Thailand 64 B7 16 51N 99 08E
Takamatsu Japan 63 B2 34 20N 134 01E
Takanabe Japan 63 B2 32 08N 131 30E
Takaoka Japan 63 C3 36 47N 137 00E
Takapuna NZ 69 E6 36 48S 174 46E
Takasaki Japan 63 C3 36 20N 139 00E
Takatsuki Japan 63 C2 34 50N 135 35E
Takayama Japan 63 C3 36 09N 137 16E
Takefu Japan 63 C3 35 54N 136 10E
Takêv Cambodia 64 C6 11 00N 104 46E
Taki India 59 K9 22 35N 88 56E
Takla Landing Canada 84 K5 55 28N 125 58W
Takua Pa Thailand 64 B5 8 55N 98 20E
Talara Peru 90 A13 4 38S 81 18W
Talavera de la Reina Sp. 43 C3 39 58N 4 50W
Talca Chile 91 C6 35 28S 71 40W
Talcahuano Chile 91 C6 36 40S 73 10W
Taldykorgan Kazakhstan 54 K6 45 02N 78 23E
Tallahassee USA 87 K3 30 26N 84 16W
Tallinn Estonia 48 F2 59 22N 24 48E
Tamale Ghana 76 D3 9 26N 0 49W
Tamanrasset Algeria 76 F6 22 50N 5 28E
Tambov Russia 54 G7 52 44N 41 28E
Tampa USA 87 K2 27 58N 82 38W
Tampere Finland 48 F3 61 32N 23 45E
Tampico Mexico 88 E4 22 18N 97 52W
Tampines Singapore 65 T15 1 21N 103 56E
Tampoi Malaysia 65 S16 1 30N 103 43E
Tamworth Aust. 67 K4 31 07S 150 57E
Tanabe Japan 63 C2 33 43N 135 22E
Tanahgrogot Indonesia 65 F3 1 49S 116 13E
Tanah Pidus Malaysia 64 N9 3 59N 114 25E
Tandil Argentina 91 F6 37 18S 59 10W
Tanga Tanzania 79 F2 5 07S 39 05E
Tangail Bangladesh 59 K10 24 15N 89 55E
Tanganyika, Lake East Africa 79 B1 7 00S 30 00E
Tangier Morocco 76 C9 35 48N 5 45W
Tangshan China 61 L5 39 37N 118 05E
Tanjong Langsat Malaysia 65 T15 1 28N 103 59E
Tanout Niger 76 F5 15 05N 8 50E
TANZANIA 79 B1/D1
Tapa Estonia 48 G2 59 16N 25 50E
Tapachula Mexico 88 F2 14 54N 92 15W
Tarakan Indonesia 65 F4 3 20N 117 38E
Táranto Italy 47 G4 40 28N 17 15E
Tarapoto Peru 90 B12 6 31S 76 23W
Tarauacá Brazil 90 C12 8 06S 70 45W
Tarawera NZ 69 F5 38 15S 176 56E
Tarazona Sp. 43 E4 41 54N 1 44W
Tarbes Fr. 42 E2 43 14N 0 05E
Taree Aust. 67 K4 31 54S 152 26E
Tarfaya Morocco 76 B7 27 58N 12 55W
Târgovişte Romania 45 M2 44 56N 25 27E
Târgu-Jiu Romania 45 L2 45 03N 23 18E
Târgu Mureş Romania 45 M3 46 33N 24 34E
Tarija Bolivia 90 D9 21 33S 65 02W
Tarime Tanzania 79 D4 1 21S 34 22E
Tarko-Sale Russia 54 K9 64 55N 77 50E
Tarkwa Ghana 76 D3 5 16N 1 59W
Tarlac Philippines 65 G7 15 29N 120 35E
Tarnów Poland 45 K5 50 01N 20 59E
Tarom Iran 57 P9 28 10N 55 46E
Taroom Aust. 67 J5 25 40S 149 50E
Tarragona Sp. 43 F4 41 07N 1 15E
Tarrasa Sp. 43 G4 41 34N 2 00E
Tarsus Turkey 49 D2 36 52N 34 52E
Tartu Estonia 48 G2 58 20N 26 44E
Tartūs Syria 56 C5 34 55N 35 52E
Tashkent Uzbekistan 54 J6 41 16N 69 13E
Tasmania state Aust. 67 J2 43 00S 147 00E
Tatabánya Hungary 45 J3 47 31N 18 25E
Tateyama Japan 63 C2 34 59N 139 50E
Taumarunui NZ 69 E5 38 53S 175 16E
Taung-gyi Myanmar 64 B8 20 55N 97 02E
Taunton UK 40 E2 51 01N 3 06W
Taupo NZ 69 F5 38 42S 176 05E
Tauranga NZ 69 F5 37 41S 176 10E
Taveta Kenya 79 E3 3 24S 37 41E
Tawau Malaysia 64 F4 4 16N 117 54E
Taymá' Saudi Arabia 56 C4 27 37N 38 30E
Tay Ninh Vietnam 64 D6 11 21N 106 07E
Tayshet Russia 55 M8 55 56N 98 01E
Taza Morocco 76 D8 34 16N 4 01W

T'bilisi Georgia 49 F3 41 43N 44 4[ ]E
Tczew Poland 45 J7 54 05N 18 4[ ]E
Te Aroha NZ 69 E6 37 32S 175 4[ ]E
Te Awamutu NZ 69 E5 38 01S 175 2[ ]E
Teberau Malaysia 65 S16 1 33N 103 4[ ]E
Tébessa Algeria 76 F9 35 21N 8 0[ ]E
Tecate Mexico 86 C3 32 34N 116 38[ ]
Tecuci Romania 45 N2 45 50N 27 2[ ]E
Tefé Brazil 90 E13 3 24S 64 45[ ]
Tegal Indonesia 64 D2 6 52S 109 0[ ]E
Tegucigalpa Honduras 88 G2 14 05N 87 14[ ]
Tehran Iran 56 F6 35 40N 51 2[ ]E
Tehuacán Mexico 88 E3 18 30N 97 26[ ]
Tehuantepec Mexico 88 E3 16 21N 95 13[ ]
Tekirdağ Turkey 47 M4 40 59N 27 3[ ]E
Te Kuiti NZ 69 E5 38 20S 175 1[ ]E
Tel Aviv-Yafo Israel 56 B5 32 05N 34 4[ ]E
Telford UK 40 E3 52 42N 2 2[ ]W
Telok Jawa Malaysia 65 T15 1 28N 103 5[ ]E
Telok Sengat Malaysia 65 U16 1 34N 104 0[ ]E
Teluk Intan Malaysia 64 C4 4 02N 101 0[ ]E
Tema Ghana 76 E3 5 41N 0 0[ ]E
Tembagapura Indonesia 65 K3 4 10S 137 1[ ]E
Teminabuan Indonesia 65 J3 1 30S 131 5[ ]E
Temirtau Kazakhstan 54 K7 50 05N 72 5[ ]E
Temple USA 87 G3 31 06N 97 2[ ]W
Temuco Chile 91 C6 38 45S 72 4[ ]W
Temuka NZ 69 C2 44 15S 171 1[ ]E
Tenali India 58 E3 16 13N 80 3[ ]E
Tenerife i. Canary Islands 76 A7 28 15N 16 3[ ]W
Tennant Creek tn. Aust. 66 F7 19 31S 134 1[ ]E
Tennessee state USA 87 J4 35 00N 87 0[ ]W
Teófilo Otôni Brazil 90 J10 17 52S 41 3[ ]W
Tepic Mexico 88 D4 21 30N 104 5[ ]W
Teradomari Japan 62 C3 37 38N 138 4[ ]E
Teramo Italy 46 E5 42 40N 13 4[ ]E
Teresina Brazil 90 J12 5 09S 42 4[ ]W
Termez Uzbekistan 54 J4 37 15N 67 1[ ]E
Termini Imerese Italy 46 E2 37 59N 13 4[ ]E
Termoli Italy 46 F4 42 00N 15 0[ ]E
Ternate Indonesia 65 H4 0 48N 127 2[ ]E
Terneuzen Neths 41 B4 51 20N 3 5[ ]E
Terni Italy 46 E5 42 34N 12 3[ ]E
Ternitz Austria 45 G3 47 43N 16 0[ ]E
Ternopil' Ukraine 45 M4 49 35N 25 3[ ]E
Terrace Canada 84 K4 54 31N 128 3[ ]W
Terrace Bay tn. Canada 85 T3 48 47N 87 0[ ]W
Terracina Italy 46 E4 41 17N 13 1[ ]E
Terrasini Italy 46 E3 38 09N 13 0[ ]E
Terre Haute USA 87 J4 39 27N 87 24[ ]W
Teruel Sp. 43 E4 40 21N 1 0[ ]W
Teseney Eritrea 77 N5 15 10N 36 4[ ]E
Teslin Canada 84 J6 60 10N 132 42[ ]W
Tete Mozambique 78 F4 16 10S 33 3[ ]E
Tétouan Morocco 76 C9 35 34N 5 2[ ]W
Tetovo FYROM 47 J5 42 00N 20 5[ ]E
Texarkana USA 87 H3 33 28N 94 02[ ]W
Texas state USA 86/87 B7/C7 31 00N 100 00[ ]W
THAILAND 64 C7
Thakhek Laos 64 C7 17 22N 104 5[ ]E
Thames NZ 69 E6 37 09S 175 3[ ]E
Thames r. UK 40 F2 51 32N 0 5[ ]W
Thane India 58 C4 19 14N 73 0[ ]E
Thanh Hoa Vietnam 64 D7 19 49N 105 4[ ]E
Thanjavur India 58 D2 10 46N 79 0[ ]E
Thaton Myanmar 64 B7 16 56N 97 2[ ]E
Thayetmyo Myanmar 64 B7 19 20N 95 1[ ]E
The Dalles tn. USA 86 B6 45 36N 121 10[ ]W
The Hague Neths 41 C5 52 05N 4 1[ ]E
The Pas Canada 85 Q4 53 49N 101 14[ ]W
Thessaloniki Greece 47 K4 40 38N 22 5[ ]E
The Valley Anguilla 88 P10 18 03N 63 04[ ]W
Thiers Fr. 42 F3 45 51N 3 3[ ]E
Thiès Senegal 76 A4 14 49N 16 5[ ]W
Thika Kenya 79 E4 1 03S 37 0[ ]E
Thimphu Bhutan 59 F5 27 32N 89 4[ ]E
Thionville Fr. 42 H5 49 22N 6 1[ ]E
Thiva Greece 47 K3 38 19N 23 1[ ]E
Thomasville USA 87 K3 30 50N 83 59[ ]W
Thompson Canada 85 R5 55 45N 97 54[ ]W
Thouars Fr. 42 D4 46 59N 0 1[ ]W
Thuin Belgium 41 C3 50 21N 4 1[ ]E
Thun Switz. 44 C3 46 46N 7 3[ ]E
Thunder Bay tn. Canada 85 T3 48 27N 89 12[ ]W
Thurso UK 40 E6 58 35N 3 3[ ]W
Tianjin China 61 L5 39 08N 117 12[ ]
Tianshui China 61 J4 34 25N 105 5[ ]E
Ticul Mexico 88 G4 20 22N 89 31[ ]W
Tiel Neths 41 D4 51 53N 5 2[ ]E
Tienen Belgium 41 C3 50 48N 4 5[ ]E
Tierra Blanca Mexico 88 E3 18 28N 96 21[ ]W
Tighina Moldova 45 P3 46 50N 29 2[ ]E
Tigris r. Iraq 56 E5 32 00N 46 0[ ]E
Tijuana Mexico 88 A6 32 29N 117 10[ ]W
Tikhoretsk Russia 49 F4 45 52N 40 0[ ]E
Tikrit Iraq 56 D5 34 36N 43 42[ ]E
Tilburg Neths 41 D4 51 34N 5 0[ ]E
Timaru NZ 69 C2 44 24S 171 15[ ]E
Timimoun Algeria 76 E7 29 15N 0 1[ ]E
Timişoara Romania 45 K3 45 45N 21 15[ ]E
Timmins Canada 85 U3 48 30N 81 20[ ]W
Timon Brazil 90 J12 5 08S 42 52[ ]W
Timor i. Indonesia 65 G1/G2 9 00S 125 00[ ]E
Tindouf Algeria 76 C7 27 42N 8 10[ ]W
Tinsukia India 58 H5 27 30N 95 22[ ]E
Tiranë Albania 47 H4 41 20N 19 4[ ]E
Tiraspol' Moldova 45 P3 46 51N 29 3[ ]E
Tiruchchirappalli India 58 D2 10 50N 78 41[ ]E
Tirunelveli India 58 D1 8 45N 77 43[ ]E
Tirupati India 58 D2 13 39N 79 25[ ]E
Tiruppur India 58 D2 11 05N 77 2[ ]E
Tisdale Canada 85 Q4 52 51N 104 01[ ]W
Titovo Užice SM 47 H5 43 52N 19 50[ ]E
Titov Veles FYROM 47 J4 41 43N 21 48[ ]E
Titu Romania 45 M2 44 40N 25 32[ ]E

voli Italy 46 E4 41 58N 12 48E
zimin Mexico 88 G4 21 10N 88 09W
zi Ouzou Algeria 76 E9 36 44N 4 05E
znit Morocco 76 C7 29 43N 9 44W
emcen Algeria 76 D8 34 53N 1 21W
amasina Madagascar 78 J4 18 10S 49 23E
a Payoh Singapore 65 T15 1 20N 103 51E
bago i. Trinidad & Tobago 89 V15 11 15N 60 40W
bol'sk Russia 54 J8 58 15N 68 12E
co Trinidad & Tobago 89 V15 10 49N 60 57W
copilla Chile 90 C9 22 05S 70 10W
gi Japan 63 C3 37 08N 136 44E
GO 76 E3
jo 63 B2 34 54N 133 15E
kushima Japan 63 B2 34 03N 134 34E
kuyama Japan 63 B2 34 03N 131 48E
kyo Japan 63 C3 35 40N 139 45E
lanaro Madagascar 78 J2 25 01S 47 00E
ledo Sp. 43 C3 39 52N 4 02W
ledo USA 87 K5 41 40N 83 35W
liara Madagascar 78 H3 23 20S 43 41E
lmezzo Italy 46 E7 46 24N 13 01E
losa Sp. 43 D5 43 09N 2 04W
luca Mexico 88 E3 19 20N 99 40W
makomai Japan 62 D4 42 39N 141 33E
mar Port. 43 A3 39 36N 8 25W
matlán Mexico 88 C3 19 54N 105 18W
mbara Japan 63 B3 35 05N 132 45E
mbouctou Mali 76 D5 16 49N 2 59W
mbua Angola 78 B4 15 49S 11 53E
melloso Sp. 43 D3 39 09N 3 01W
msk Russia 55 L8 56 30N 85 05E
nalá Mexico 88 F3 16 08N 93 41W
NGA 70 J5
ngchuan China 61 J5 35 05N 109 02E
nguchon South Korea 63 A3 37 52N 127 02E
nghae South Korea 63 A3 37 33N 129 07E
nghai China 61 H2 24 07N 104 45E
nghua China 61 N6 41 42N 125 45E
ngling China 61 L4 30 58N 117 48E
nopah USA 86 C4 38 05N 117 15W
nsberg Norway 48 D2 59 16N 10 25E
ele USA 86 D5 40 32N 112 18W
owoomba Aust. 67 K5 27 35S 151 54E
peka USA 87 G4 39 02N 95 41W
rbali Turkey 47 M3 38 07N 27 08E
rdesillas Sp. 43 C4 41 30N 5 00W
hout Belgium 41 B4 51 04N 3 06E
nio Finland 48 F4 65 50N 24 10E
onto Canada 85 V2 43 42N 79 46W
oro Russia 79 D5 0 42N 34 12E
re del Greco Italy 46 F4 40 46N 14 22E
relavega Sp. 43 C5 43 21N 4 03W
remolinos Sp. 43 C2 36 38N 4 30W
rente Sp. 43 E3 39 27N 0 28W
reón Mexico 88 D5 25 34N 103 25W
res Vedras Port. 43 A3 39 05N 9 15W
tosa Sp. 43 F4 40 49N 0 31E
kin Poland 43 J6 53 01N 18 35E
'ma Russia 49 F6 59 59N 42 46E
tori Japan 63 B3 35 32N 134 12E
ggourt Algeria 76 F8 33 08N 6 04E
al Fr. 42 G5 48 41N 5 54E
ulon Fr. 42 G2 43 07N 5 55E
ulouse Fr. 42 E2 43 33N 1 24E
ungoo Myanmar 64 B7 18 57N 96 26E
ircoing Fr. 42 F6 50 44N 3 10E
rnai Belgium 41 B3 50 36N 3 24E
rs Fr. 42 E4 47 23N 0 42E
nsville Aust. 67 J7 19 13S 146 48E
ama Japan 63 C3 36 42N 137 14E
ohama Japan 63 B2 34 04N 133 38E
ohashi Japan 63 C2 34 46N 137 22E
okawa Japan 63 C2 34 50N 137 26E
okoro Japan 62 D4 42 48N 143 31E
ota Japan 63 C3 35 05N 137 09E
eur Tunisia 76 F8 33 55N 8 07E
ozon Turkey 49 E3 41 00N 39 43E
l Canada 84 M3 49 04N 111 39W
ee Rol 40 B3 52 16N 9 42W
ng Thailand 64 B5 7 30N 98 33E
ni Italy 47 G4 41 17N 16 25E
oani Italy 46 E3 38 02N 12 32E
un Austria 44 G4 48 14N 14 15E
verse City USA 87 J5 44 46N 85 38W
nta-y-Tres Uruguay 91 G7 33 16S 54 17W
ew Chile 91 D5 43 13S 65 15W
ncín Slovakia 45 J4 48 53N 18 00E
nto Italy 46 D7 46 04N 11 08E
nton USA 87 M5 40 15N 74 43W
Arroyos Argentina 91 E6 38 26S 60 17W
Lagoas Brazil 90 G9 20 46S 51 43W
viso Italy 46 E6 45 40N 12 15E
hur India 58 D2 10 32N 76 14E
Germany 44 C4 49 45N 6 39E
ste Italy 46 E6 45 39N 13 47E
ala Greece 47 J3 39 33N 21 46E
comalee Sri Lanka 58 E1 8 34N 81 13E
dago i. Trinidad & Tobago 89 V15 11 00N 61 30W
IDAD & TOBAGO 89 M2
oli Mauritius 73 E2 20 04S 57 32E
oli Lebanon 56 C5 34 27N 35 50E
oli Libya 77 G8 32 54N 13 11E
andrum India 58 D1 8 30N 76 57E
va Slovakia 45 H4 48 23N 17 35E
sdorf Germany 44 F3 50 49N 7 09E
s-Rivières tn. Canada 85 W3 46 21N 72 34W
lhätten Sweden 48 D2 58 17N 12 20E
nso Norway 48 E4 69 42N 19 00E
dheim Norway 48 D3 63 36N 10 23E
ville Fr. 42 E5 49 22N 0 05E
llo Peru 90 B12 8 06S 79 00W
llo Sp. 43 C3 39 28N 5 53W

Trujillo Venezuela 90 C15 9 20N 70 38W
Truro Canada 85 Y3 45 24N 63 18W
Trusan Malaysia 64 Q11 4 49N 115 16E
Tshane Botswana 78 D3 24 05S 21 54E
Tsu Japan 63 C2 34 41N 136 30E
Tsuchiura Japan 63 D3 36 05N 140 11E
Tsumeb Namibia 78 C4 19 13S 17 42E
Tsuruga Japan 63 C3 35 40N 136 05E
Tsuruoka Japan 62 C3 38 42N 139 50E
Tsuyama Japan 63 B3 35 04N 134 01E
Tuapse Russia 49 E3 44 06N 39 08E
Tubize Belgium 41 C3 50 42N 4 12E
Tubruq Libya 77 K8 32 05N 23 59E
Tucson USA 86 D3 32 15N 110 57W
Tucumcari USA 86 F4 35 11N 103 44W
Tucupita Venezuela 90 E15 9 02N 62 04W
Tucuruí Brazil 90 H13 3 42S 49 44W
Tudela Sp. 43 E5 42 04N 1 37W
Tufayḩ Saudi Arabia 57 M9 26 54N 49 28E
Tugaske Canada 84 P4 50 54N 106 15W
Tuguegarao Philippines 65 G7 17 36N 121 44E
Tuktoyaktuk Canada 84 J7 69 24N 133 01W
Tukums Latvia 48 F2 56 58N 23 10E
Tula Russia 54 F7 54 11N 37 38E
Tulcán Ecuador 90 B14 0 50N 77 48W
Tulcea Romania 45 P2 45 10N 28 50E
Tulle Fr. 42 E3 45 16N 1 46E
Tullamore Rol 40 C3 53 16N 7 30W
Tulsa USA 87 G4 36 07N 95 58W
Tuluá Col. 90 B14 4 05N 76 12W
Tulun Russia 55 N7 54 32N 100 35E
Tumaco Col. 90 B14 1 51N 78 46W
Tumbes Peru 90 A13 3 37S 80 27W
Tumkur India 58 D2 13 20N 77 06E
Tunduru Tanzania 78 G5 11 08S 27 21E
Tunis Tunisia 76 G9 36 50N 10 13E
TUNISIA 76 F8/G8
Tunja Col. 90 C15 5 33N 73 23W
Tupelo USA 87 J3 34 15N 88 43W
Tupiza Bolivia 90 D9 21 27S 65 45W
Turda Romania 45 L3 46 35N 23 50E
Türgovishte Bulgaria 47 M5 43 14N 26 37E
Turgutlu Turkey 47 M3 38 30N 27 43E
Turin Italy 46 B6 45 04N 7 40E
TURKEY 49 C2/E2
TURKMENISTAN 54 H4/J4
Turks and Caicos Islands W. Indies 89 K4 21 30N 72 00W
Turku Finland 48 F3 60 27N 22 15E
Turnhout Belgium 41 C4 51 19N 4 57E
Turnu Măgurele Romania 45 M1 43 44N 24 53E
Turpan China 60 E6 42 55N 89 06E
Tuscaloosa USA 87 J3 33 12N 87 33W
Tuticorin India 58 D1 8 48N 78 10E
Tutong Brunei 64 P11 4 49N 114 39E
Tuttlingen Germany 44 D3 47 59N 8 49E
TUVALU 70 H7
Tuxtla Gutierrez Mexico 88 F3 16 45N 93 09W
Túy Sp. 43 A5 42 03N 8 39W
Tuzla Bosnia-Herzegovina 47 H6 44 33N 18 41E
Tver' Russia 54 F8 56 49N 35 57E
Tyan-Shan' Kyrgyzstan 54/55 K5/L5 41 00N 76 00E
Tyler USA 87 G3 32 22N 95 18W
Tynda Russia 55 Q8 55 10N 124 35E
Tyumen' Russia 54 J8 57 11N 65 29E

U
Ube Japan 63 B2 33 57N 131 16E
Uberaba Brazil 90 H10 19 47S 47 57W
Uberlândia Brazil 90 H10 18 57S 48 17W
Ubon Ratchathani Thailand 64 C7 15 15N 104 50E
Udaipur India 58 C4 24 36N 73 47E
Uddevalla Sweden 48 D2 58 20N 11 56E
Udine Italy 46 E7 46 04N 13 14E
Udon Thani Thailand 64 C7 17 25N 102 45E
Ueda Japan 63 C3 36 27N 138 13E
Ueki Japan 63 B2 32 54N 130 42E
Uelen Russia 55 W10 66 13N 169 48W
Uelzen Germany 44 E6 52 58N 10 34E
Ufa Russia 54 H7 54 45N 55 58E
UGANDA 79 B6/C6
Uijongbu South Korea 63 A3 37 44N 127 02E
Uitenhage RSA 78 E1 33 46S 25 25E
Uji Japan 63 C2 34 54N 135 48E
Ujjain India 58 D4 23 11N 75 50E
Ujung Pandang Indonesia 65 F2 5 09S 119 28E
Ukhta Russia 54 H9 63 34N 53 44E
Ukiah USA 86 B4 39 09N 123 12W
Ukmerge Lithuania 48 F2 55 14N 24 49E
UKRAINE 49 C4/D4
Ulaangom Mongolia 60 F7 49 59N 92 00E
Ulan Bator Mongolia 61 J7 47 54N 106 52E
Ulan-Ude Russia 55 N7 51 55N 107 40E
Ulchin South Korea 63 A3 37 00N 129 26E
Ulhasnagar India 58 C3 19 15N 73 08E
Uliastay Mongolia 60 G7 47 42N 96 52E
Ullapool UK 40 D5 57 54N 5 10W
Ulm Germany 44 D3 48 24N 10 00E
Ulsan South Korea 63 A3 35 32N 129 21E
Ul'yanovsk Russia 54 G7 54 19N 48 22E
Uman' Ukraine 49 D4 48 45N 30 10E
Umeå Sweden 48 F3 63 50N 20 15E
Umiat USA 84 E7 69 25N 152 20W
Umm al Qaywayn UAE 57 P9 25 34N 55 33E
Umm Qasr Iraq 57 M10 30 02N 47 54E
Umm Ruwaba Sudan 77 M4 12 50N 31 20E
Umtata RSA 78 E1 31 35S 28 47E
Umuarama Brazil 90 G9 23 43S 52 57W
Unalakleet USA 84 D6 63 52N 160 50W
'Unayzah Saudi Arabia 56 D4 26 06N 43 58E
Uniontown USA 87 L4 39 54N 79 44W
UNITED ARAB EMIRATES 56 F3
UNITED KINGDOM 40

UNITED STATES OF AMERICA 86/87
Uozu Japan 63 C3 36 50N 137 25E
Upata Venezuela 90 E15 8 02N 62 25W
Upington RSA 78 D2 28 28S 21 14E
Upper Hutt NZ 69 E4 41 07S 175 04E
Upper Liard Canada 84 K6 60 00N 129 20W
Uppsala Sweden 48 E2 59 55N 17 38E
Urakawa Japan 62 D4 42 10N 142 46E
Urawa Japan 63 C3 35 52N 139 40E
Ural Mountains Russia 54 H7/H9 57 00N 60 00E
Ural'sk Kazakhstan 54 H7 51 19N 51 20E
Uren' Russia 49 G6 57 28N 45 47E
Urengoy Russia 55 K10 65 59N 78 30E
Urgench Uzbekistan 54 J5 41 35N 60 41E
Uroševac SM 47 J5 42 21N 21 09E
Uruapan Mexico 88 D3 19 26N 102 04W
Urubamba Peru 90 C11 13 20S 72 07W
Uruguaiana Brazil 91 F8 29 45S 57 05W
URUGUAY 91 F7
Ürümqi China 60 E6 43 43N 87 38E
Urziceni Romania 45 N2 44 43N 26 39E
Ushuaia Argentina 91 D3 54 48S 68 19W
Üsküdar Turkey 49 C3 41 02N 29 02E
Usol'ye-Sibirskoye Russia 55 N7 52 48N 103 40E
Uspenskiy Kazakhstan 60 B7 48 43N 72 43E
Ussel Fr. 42 F3 45 32N 2 18E
Ussuriysk Russia 55 R5 43 48N 131 59E
Ust'-Ilimsk Russia 55 N8 58 03N 102 39E
Ustí nad Labem Czech Rep. 44 G5 50 40N 14 02E
Ust'-Kamchatsk Russia 55 U8 56 14N 162 28E
Ust'-Kut Russia 55 N8 56 48N 105 42E
Ust'-Maya Russia 55 R9 60 25N 134 28E
Usuki Japan 63 B2 33 07N 131 48E
Usulután Mexico 88 G2 13 20N 88 25W
Utah state USA 86 D4 39 00N 112 00W
Utica USA 87 L5 43 06N 75 15W
Utrecht Neths 41 D5 52 05N 5 07E
Utrera Sp. 43 C2 37 10N 5 47W
Utsunomiya Japan 63 C3 36 33N 139 52E
Uttaradit Thailand 64 C7 17 38N 100 05E
Uummannaq Greenland 85 X9 76 30N 68 58W
Uvalde USA 86 G2 29 14N 99 49W
Uvinza Tanzania 79 B2 5 08S 30 23E
Uvira CDR 79 A3 3 24S 29 08E
Uwajima Japan 63 B2 33 13N 132 32E
Uyuni Bolivia 90 D9 20 28S 66 47W
UZBEKISTAN 54 H5/J5
Uzhgorod Ukraine 45 L4 48 37N 22 17E

V
Vaasa Finland 48 F3 63 06N 21 36E
Vác Hungary 45 J3 47 46N 19 08E
Vacoas Mauritius 73 E2 20 18S 57 29E
Vadodara India 58 C4 22 19N 73 14E
Vaduz Liechtenstein 44 D3 47 08N 9 32E
Valdepeñas Sp. 43 D3 38 46N 3 24W
Valdivia Chile 91 C6 39 46S 73 15W
Val-d'Or Canada 85 V3 48 07N 77 47W
Valdosta USA 87 K3 30 51N 83 51W
Valença Brazil 90 K11 13 22S 39 06W
Valence Fr. 42 G3 44 56N 4 54E
Valencia Sp. 43 E3 39 29N 0 24W
Valencia Venezuela 90 D16 10 14N 67 59W
Valenciennes Fr. 42 F6 50 22N 3 32E
Valera Venezuela 90 C15 9 21N 70 38W
Valga Estonia 48 G2 57 44N 26 00E
Valjevo SM 47 H6 44 16N 19 56E
Valladolid Mexico 88 G4 20 40N 88 11W
Valladolid Sp. 43 C4 41 39N 4 45W
Valledupar Col. 90 C16 10 31N 73 16W
Vallée Jonction Canada 87 M6 46 23N 70 55W
Valle Grande Bolivia 90 E10 18 30S 64 49W
Vallejo USA 86 B4 38 05N 122 14W
Vallenar Chile 91 C8 28 36S 70 45W
Valletta Malta 46 Q8 35 54N 14 32E
Valleyfield Canada 85 W3 45 15N 74 08W
Valmiera Latvia 48 G2 57 32N 25 29E
Valparaíso Chile 91 C7 33 05S 71 40W
Van Turkey 49 F3 38 28N 43 20E
Vanadzor Armenia 49 F3 40 49N 44 30E
Vancouver Canada 84 L3 49 13N 123 06W
Vancouver Island Canada 84 K3 49 30N 126 00W
Vännäs Sweden 48 E3 63 56N 19 50E
Vannes Fr. 42 C4 47 40N 2 44W
Vantaa Finland 48 F3 60 20N 24 50E
Vanua Levu i. Fiji 67 Q7 16 30S 179 00E
VANUATU 67 N7
Varanasi India 58 E4 25 20N 83 00E
Varaždin Croatia 46 G7 46 18N 16 21E
Vardø Norway 48 H5 70 22N 31 06E
Varel Germany 41 G6 53 24N 8 08E
Varese Italy 46 C6 45 49N 8 49E
Varkhaus Finland 48 G3 62 20N 27 50E
Varna Bulgaria 47 M5 43 12N 27 57E
Värnamo Sweden 48 D2 57 11N 14 03E
Várzea Grande Brazil 90 J12 6 32S 42 05W
Västerås Sweden 48 E2 59 36N 16 32E
Västervik Sweden 48 E2 57 45N 16 40E
Vasto Italy 46 F5 42 07N 14 43E
Vatra Dornei Romania 45 M3 47 20N 25 21E
Växjö Sweden 48 D2 56 52N 14 50E
Vechta Germany 41 G5 52 44N 8 18E
Veghel Neths 41 D4 51 37N 5 33E
Vejle Denmark 48 C2 55 43N 9 33E
Veldhoven Neths 41 D4 51 24N 5 24E
Vélez-Málaga Sp. 43 C2 36 47N 4 06W
Vélez Rubio Sp. 43 D2 37 39N 2 04W
Velikiye Luki Russia 54 F8 56 19N 30 31E
Veliko Tǔrnovo Bulgaria 47 L5 43 04N 25 39E
Vel'sk Russia 49 F7 61 03N 42 05E
Vendôme Fr. 42 E4 47 48N 1 04E

VENEZUELA 90 D15
Venice Italy 46 E6 45 26N 12 20E
Vénissieux Fr. 42 G3 45 42N 4 46E
Venlo Neths 41 E4 51 22N 6 10E
Ventspils Latvia 48 F2 57 22N 21 31E
Ventura USA 86 C3 34 16N 119 18W
Vera Sp. 43 E3 37 15N 1 51W
Veracruz Mexico 88 E3 19 11N 96 10W
Veraval India 58 C4 20 53N 70 28E
Vercelli Italy 46 C6 45 19N 8 26E
Verden Germany 41 H5 52 56N 9 15E
Verdun-sur-Meuse Fr. 42 G5 49 10N 5 24E
Vereeniging RSA 78 E2 26 41S 27 56E
Verín Sp. 43 B4 41 55N 7 26W
Verkhoyansk Russia 55 R10 67 35N 133 25E
Vermont state USA 87 M5 44 00N 73 00W
Vernon Canada 84 M4 50 17N 119 19W
Vernon USA 86 G3 34 10N 99 19W
Véroia Greece 47 K4 40 32N 22 11E
Verona Italy 46 D6 45 26N 11 00E
Versailles Fr. 42 F5 48 48N 2 07E
Verviers Belgium 41 D3 50 36N 5 52E
Vesoul Fr. 42 H4 47 38N 6 09E
Vesuvio vol. Italy 46 F4 40 49N 14 26E
Veszprém Hungary 45 H3 47 06N 17 54E
Vetluga Russia 49 G6 57 52N 45 48E
Veurne Belgium 41 A4 51 04N 2 40E
Vevey Switz. 44 C3 46 28N 6 51E
Viana do Castelo Port. 43 A4 41 41N 8 50W
Viareggio Italy 46 D5 43 52N 10 15E
Viborg Denmark 48 C2 56 28N 9 25E
Vibo Valentia Italy 46 G3 38 40N 16 06E
Vicente Guerrero Mexico 88 A6 30 48N 116 00W
Vicenza Italy 46 D6 45 33N 11 32E
Vicksburg USA 87 H3 32 21N 90 51W
Victoria Canada 84 L3 48 26N 123 20W
Victoria Chile 91 C6 38 20S 72 30W
Victoria Malta 46 P9 36 03N 14 14E
Victoria Seychelles 73 B1 4 38S 55 28E
Victoria USA 87 G2 28 49N 97 01W
Victoria state Aust. 67 H3/J3 37 00S 145 00E
Victoria, Lake East Africa 79 C4 2 00S 33 00E
Vidin Bulgaria 47 K5 44 00N 22 50E
Viedma Argentina 91 E5 40 45S 63 00W
Vienna Austria 45 H4 48 13N 16 22E
Vienne Fr. 42 G3 45 32N 4 54E
Vientiane Laos 64 C7 17 59N 102 38E
Viersen Germany 41 E4 51 16N 6 23E
Vierzon Fr. 42 F4 47 14N 2 03E
VIETNAM 64 D7
Vieux Fort St. Lucia 88 R11 13 44N 60 57W
Vigia Brazil 90 H13 0 50S 48 07W
Vigo Sp. 43 A5 42 15N 8 44W
Vijayawada India 58 E3 16 34N 80 40E
Vila Vanuatu 67 N7 17 45S 168 18E
Vila Nova de Gaia Port. 43 A4 41 08N 8 37W
Vila Real Port. 43 B4 41 17N 7 45W
Vila Velha Brazil 90 J9 20 23S 40 18W
Vilhena Brazil 90 E11 12 40S 60 08W
Villach Austria 44 F3 46 37N 13 51E
Villa Constitución Mexico 88 B5 25 05N 111 45W
Villahermosa Mexico 88 F3 18 00N 92 53W
Villalba Sp. 43 B5 43 17N 7 41W
Villa María Argentina 91 E7 32 25S 63 15W
Villa Montes Bolivia 90 E9 21 15S 63 30W
Villanueva Mexico 88 D4 22 24N 102 53W
Villarrica Chile 91 C6 39 15S 72 15W
Villarrobledo Sp. 43 D3 39 16N 2 36W
Villa Unión Mexico 88 C4 23 10N 106 12W
Villavicencio Col. 90 C14 4 09N 73 38W
Villefranche-sur-Saône Fr. 42 G3 46 00N 4 43E
Villena Sp. 43 E3 38 39N 0 52W
Villeneuve-sur-Lot Fr. 42 E3 44 25N 0 43E
Villeurbanne Fr. 42 G3 45 46N 4 54E
Vilnius Lithuania 48 G1 54 40N 25 19E
Vilvoorde Belgium 41 C3 50 56N 4 25E
Vilyuysk Russia 55 Q9 63 46N 121 35E
Viña del Mar Chile 91 C7 33 02S 71 35W
Vinaroz Sp. 43 F4 40 29N 0 28E
Vincennes USA 87 J4 38 42N 87 30W
Vineland USA 87 L4 39 29N 75 02W
Vinh Vietnam 64 D7 18 42N 105 41E
Vinkovci Croatia 47 H6 45 16N 18 49E
Vinnytsya Ukraine 45 P4 49 11N 28 30E
Vipiteno Italy 46 D7 46 54N 11 27E
Virginia USA 87 H6 47 30N 92 28W
Virginia state USA 87 L4 38 00N 77 00W
Virginia Beach tn. USA 87 L4 36 51N 75 59W
Virgin Islands W. Indies 89 M3 18 00N 64 30W
Virovitica Croatia 47 G6 45 50N 17 25E
Visalia USA 86 C4 36 20N 119 18W
Viseu Port. 43 B4 40 40N 7 55W
Vishakhapatnam India 58 E3 17 42N 83 24E
Viterbo Italy 46 E5 42 24N 12 06E
Vitichi Bolivia 90 D9 20 14S 65 22W
Viti Levu i. Fiji 67 Q7 17 30S 178 00E
Vitória Brazil 90 J9 20 20S 40 18W
Vitória da Conquista Brazil 90 J11 14 53S 40 52W
Vitoria Gasteiz Sp. 43 D5 42 51N 2 40W
Vitry-le-François Fr. 42 G5 48 44N 4 36E
Vitsyebsk Belarus 49 D6 55 10N 30 14E
Vittoria Italy 46 F2 36 58N 14 32E
Vizianagaram India 58 E3 18 07N 83 30E
Vlaardingen Neths 41 C4 51 54N 4 20E
Vladikavkaz Russia 49 F3 43 02N 44 43E
Vladimir Russia 54 G8 56 08N 40 25E
Vladivostok Russia 55 R5 43 09N 131 53E
Vlissingen Neths 41 B4 51 27N 3 35E
Vlorë Albania 47 H4 40 28N 19 30E
Voi Kenya 79 F3 3 23S 38 35E
Voitsberg Austria 44 G3 47 04N 15 09E
Volendam Neths 41 D5 52 30N 5 04E
Volgodonsk Russia 54 G6 47 35N 42 08E
Volgograd Russia 54 G6 48 45N 44 30E
Volksrust RSA 78 E2 27 22S 29 54E

Vologda Russia 54 F8 59 10N 39 55E
Vólos Greece 47 K3 39 22N 22 57E
Vol'sk Russia 49 G5 52 04N 47 22E
Volzhskiy Russia 54 G6 48 48N 44 45E
Vopnafjördur Iceland 48 M7 65 46N 14 50W
Vorkuta Russia 54 J10 67 27N 64 00E
Voronezh Russia 54 F7 51 40N 39 13E
Võru Estonia 48 G2 57 46N 26 52E
Voss Norway 48 C3 60 38N 6 25E
Votkinsk Russia 49 H6 57 03N 53 58E
Voxnan Sweden 48 E3 61 21N 15 39E
Vranje SM 47 J5 42 33N 21 54E
Vratsa Bulgaria 47 K5 43 12N 23 32E
Vršac SM 45 K2 45 07N 21 19E
Vryburg RSA 78 D2 26 57S 24 44E
Vught Neths 41 D4 51 40N 5 18E
Vukovar Croatia 47 H6 45 19N 19 01E
Vung Tau Vietnam 64 D6 10 21N 107 04E
Vyaz'ma Russia 49 D6 55 12N 34 17E
Vyborg Russia 54 E9 60 45N 28 41E

W
Wa Ghana 76 D4 10 07N 2 28W
Waalwijk Neths 41 D4 51 42N 5 04E
Wabana Canada 85 AA3 47 40N 52 58W
Wabowden Canada 85 R4 54 57N 98 38W
Wabush Canada 85 X4 52 45N 66 50W
Waco USA 87 G3 31 33N 97 10W
Wada Japan 62 D3 39 39N 140 12E
Wadayama Japan 63 B3 35 22N 134 49E
Wadi Halfa Sudan 77 M6 21 55N 31 20E
Wad Medani Sudan 77 M4 14 24N 33 30E
Wagga Wagga Aust. 67 J3 35 07S 147 24E
Wagin Aust. 66 C4 33 20S 117 15E
Wah Pakistan 58 C6 33 50N 72 44E
Wahpeton USA 87 G6 46 16N 96 36W
Waihi NZ 69 E6 37 57S 175 44E
Waimate NZ 69 C2 44 44S 171 03E
Waingapu Indonesia 65 G2 9 40S 120 16E
Wainwright USA 84 D8 70 39N 160 10W
Waipara NZ 69 D3 43 04S 172 45E
Waipawa NZ 69 F5 39 57S 176 35E
Waipu NZ 69 E7 35 59S 174 27E
Wairoa NZ 69 F5 39 03S 177 25E
Waitara NZ 69 E5 39 00S 174 14E
Wajima Japan 63 C3 37 23N 136 53E
Wajir Kenya 79 G5 1 46N 40 05E
Wakayama Japan 63 C2 34 12N 135 10E
Wakkanai Japan 62 D5 45 26N 141 43E
Wałbrzych Poland 45 H5 50 48N 16 19E
Wałcz Poland 45 H6 53 17N 16 29E
Waldbröl Germany 41 F3 50 52N 7 37E
Wales country UK 40 D3/E3 52 40N 3 30W
Wallaroo Aust. 66 G4 33 57S 137 36E
Walla Walla USA 86 C6 46 05N 118 18W
Wallis and Futuna is. Pacific Ocean 70 J6 13 16S 176 15W
Walsall UK 40 F3 52 35N 1 58W
Walsenburg USA 86 F4 37 36N 104 48W
Walvis Bay tn. Namibia 78 B3 22 59S 14 31E
Wanganui NZ 69 E5 39 56S 175 03E
Wangaratta Aust. 67 J3 36 23S 146 21E
Wanxian China 61 J4 30 54N 108 20E
Warangal India 58 D3 18 00N 79 35E
Warburg Germany 41 H4 51 29N 9 08E
Wardenburg Germany 41 G6 53 04N 8 12E
Waregem Belgium 41 B3 50 53N 3 26E
Waremme Belgium 41 D3 50 42N 5 15E
Warendorf Germany 41 F4 51 57N 7 59E
Warren USA 87 K5 41 15N 80 49W
Warrnambool Aust. 67 H3 38 23S 142 03E
Warsaw Poland 45 K6 52 15N 21 00E
Warwick Aust. 67 K5 28 12S 152 00E
Warwick USA 87 M5 41 42N 71 23W
Washington state USA 86 B6/C6 47 00N 120 00W
Washington D.C. USA 87 L4 38 55N 77 00W
Wassenaar Neths 41 C5 52 07N 4 23E
Watampone Indonesia 65 G3 4 33S 120 20E
Watari Japan 62 D3 38 02N 140 52E
Waterford RoI 40 C3 52 15N 7 06W
Waterloo Belgium 41 C3 50 43N 4 24E
Waterloo USA 87 H5 42 30N 92 20W
Waterville USA 87 N5 44 34N 69 41W
Watford UK 40 F2 51 39N 0 24W
Wau PNG 67 J9 7 22S 146 40E
Wau Sudan 77 L3 7 40N 28 04E
Wavre Belgium 41 C3 50 43N 4 37E
Wawa Canada 85 U3 48 04N 84 49W
Waycross USA 87 K3 31 12N 82 22W
Webuye Kenya 79 D5 0 37N 34 44E
Weert Neths 41 D4 51 15N 5 42E
Weiden Germany 44 F4 49 40N 12 10E
Weifang China 61 L5 36 44N 119 10E
Weimar Germany 44 E5 50 59N 11 20E
Weinheim Germany 41 G2 49 34N 8 40E
Weirton USA 87 K5 40 24N 80 37W
Weissenfels Germany 44 E5 51 12N 11 58E
Wejherowo Poland 45 J7 54 36N 18 12E
Wellington NZ 69 E4 41 17S 174 46E
Wellington USA 87 G4 37 17N 97 25W
Wellsford NZ 69 E6 36 18S 174 31E
Wels Austria 44 F4 48 10N 14 02E
Wenzhou China 61 M3 28 02N 120 40E
Wesel Germany 41 E4 51 40N 6 38E
Western Australia state Aust. 66 B6/E6 25 00S 117 00E
WESTERN SAHARA 76 B6/B7
Westerstede Germany 41 F6 53 16N 7 56E
West Indies is. Caribbean Sea 89 K4/L4 22 00N 69 00W
West Memphis USA 87 H4 35 09N 90 11W
West Palm Beach tn. USA 87 K2 26 42N 80 05W
West Plains tn. USA 87 H4 36 44N 91 51W
Westport NZ 69 C4 41 45S 171 36E

Westport RoI 40 B3 53 48N 9 32W
West Virginia state USA 87 K4 39 00N 81 00W
Wetaskiwin Canada 84 N4 52 57N 113 20W
Wetzlar Germany 44 D5 50 33N 8 30E
Wevelgem Belgium 41 B3 50 48N 3 12E
Wewak PNG 67 H10 3 35S 143 35E
Wexford RoI 40 C3 52 20N 6 27W
Weyburn Canada 85 Q3 49 39N 103 51W
Weymouth UK 40 E2 50 37N 2 25W
Whakatane NZ 69 F6 37 58S 176 59E
Whangarei NZ 69 E7 35 43S 174 19E
Wha Ti Canada 84 M6 63 00N 117 30W
Wheeling USA 87 K5 40 05N 80 43W
Whitecourt Canada 84 M4 54 10N 115 38W
Whitehaven UK 40 E4 54 33N 3 35W
Whitehorse Canada 84 H6 60 41N 135 08W
White River tn. Canada 85 T3 48 35N 85 16W
Whitianga NZ 69 E6 36 49S 175 42E
Whitney, Mount USA 86 C4 36 35N 118 17W
Whyalla Aust. 66 G4 33 04S 137 34E
Wichita USA 87 G4 37 43N 97 20W
Wichita Falls tn. USA 87 G3 33 55N 98 30W
Wick UK 40 E6 58 26N 3 06W
Wiener Neustadt Austria 45 H3 47 49N 16 15E
Wierden Neths 41 E5 52 21N 6 35E
Wiesbaden Germany 44 D5 50 05N 8 15E
Wiesloch Germany 41 G2 49 18N 8 41E
Wigan UK 40 E3 53 33N 2 38W
Wijchen Neths 41 D4 51 48N 5 44E
Wil Switz. 44 D3 47 28N 9 03E
Wildeshausen Germany 41 G5 52 54N 8 26E
Wilhelmshaven Germany 44 D6 53 32N 8 07E
Wilkes-Barre USA 87 L5 41 15N 75 50W
Willebroek Belgium 41 C4 51 04N 4 22E
Willemstad Curaçao 89 L2 12 12N 68 56W
Williams Lake tn. Canada 84 L4 52 08N 122 09W
Williamsport USA 87 L5 41 16N 77 03W
Williston USA 86 F6 48 09N 103 39W
Willmar USA 87 G6 45 06N 95 03W
Willow Springs tn. USA 87 H4 36 59N 91 59W
Wilson USA 87 L4 35 43N 77 56W
Winchester UK 40 F2 51 04N 1 19W
Winchester USA 87 L4 39 11N 78 12W
Windhoek Namibia 78 C3 22 34S 17 06E
Windsor Canada 85 U2 42 18N 83 00W
Windward Islands Lesser Antilles 89 M2 12 30N 62 00W
Winnemucca USA 86 C5 40 58N 117 45W
Winnipeg Canada 85 R3 49 53N 97 10W
Winona USA 87 H5 44 02N 91 37W
Winschoten Neths 41 F6 53 07N 7 02E
Winslow USA 86 D4 35 01N 110 43W
Winston-Salem USA 87 K4 36 05N 80 18W
Winterswijk Neths 41 E4 51 58N 6 44E
Winterthur Switz. 44 D3 47 30N 8 45E
Winton Aust. 67 H6 22 22S 143 00E
Wisconsin state USA 87 H6/J6 45 00N 90 00W
Wismar Germany 44 E6 53 54N 11 28E
Wissembourg Fr. 41 H5 49 02N 7 57E
Witten Germany 41 F4 51 26N 7 20E
Wittenberg Germany 44 F5 51 53N 12 39E
Wittenberge Germany 44 E6 52 59N 11 45E
Wittlich Germany 44 C4 49 59N 6 54E
Włocławek Poland 45 J6 52 39N 19 01E
Włoszczowa Poland 45 J5 50 51N 19 58E
Woerden Neths 41 C5 52 05N 4 53E
Wolfsberg Austria 44 G3 46 50N 14 50E
Wolfsburg Germany 44 E6 52 27N 10 49E
Wollongong Aust. 67 K4 34 25S 150 52E
Wolverhampton UK 40 E3 52 36N 2 08W
Wompah Aust. 67 H5 29 04S 142 05E
Wonju South Korea 63 A3 37 24N 127 52E
Wonsan North Korea 61 N5 39 07N 127 26E
Woodstock Canada 85 X3 46 10N 67 36W
Woodville NZ 69 E4 40 21S 175 52E
Woodward USA 86 G4 36 26N 99 25W
Worcester RSA 78 C1 33 39S 19 26E
Worcester UK 40 E3 52 11N 2 13W
Worcester USA 87 M5 42 17N 71 48W
Workington UK 40 E4 54 39N 3 33W
Worms Germany 44 D4 49 38N 8 23E
Worthing UK 40 F2 50 48N 0 23W
Worthington USA 87 G5 43 37N 95 36W
Wrangell USA 84 J5 56 28N 132 23W
Wrexham UK 40 E3 53 03N 3 00W
Wrocław Poland 45 H5 51 05N 17 00E
Wuhai China 61 J5 39 40N 106 40E
Wuhan China 61 K4 30 35N 114 19E
Wuhu China 61 L4 31 23N 118 25E
Wukari Nigeria 76 F3 7 49N 9 49E
Wuppertal Germany 44 C5 51 15N 7 10E
Würzburg Germany 44 D4 49 48N 9 57E
Wutongqiao China 61 H3 29 21N 103 48E
Wuxi China 61 M4 31 35N 120 19E
Wuzhou China 61 K2 23 30N 111 21E
Wyndham Aust. 66 E7 15 30S 128 09E
Wyoming state USA 86 E5 43 00N 108 00W

X
Xaafuun Somalia 77 R4 10 27N 51 15E
Xaghra Malta 46 P9 36 03N 14 16E
Xánthi Greece 47 L4 41 07N 24 56E
Xewkija Malta 46 P9 36 02N 14 16E
Xiamen China 61 L2 24 28N 118 05E
Xi'an China 61 J4 34 16N 108 54E
Xiangfan China 61 K4 32 05N 112 03E
Xiangkhoang Laos 64 C7 19 21N 102 23E
Xiangtan China 61 K3 27 48N 112 55E
Xianyang China 61 J4 34 22N 108 42E
Xigaze China 60 E3 29 18N 88 50E
Xi Jiang r. China 61 K2 23 30N 111 00E
Xingtai China 61 K5 37 08N 114 29E
Xining China 61 H5 36 35N 101 55E
Xinjin China 61 M5 39 25N 121 58E

Xochimilco Mexico 88 E3 19 08N 99 09W
Xuanhua China 61 L6 40 36N 115 01E
Xuchang China 61 K4 34 03N 113 48E
Xuwen China 61 K2 20 25N 110 08E
Xuzhou China 61 L4 34 17N 117 18E

Y
Yabuhara Japan 63 C3 35 56N 137 45E
Yaizu Japan 63 C2 34 54N 138 20E
Yakima USA 86 B6 46 37N 120 30W
Yakutsk Russia 55 Q9 62 10N 129 50E
Yamagata Japan 62 D3 38 16N 140 16E
Yamagawa Japan 63 B2 31 12N 130 39E
Yamaguchi Japan 63 B2 34 10N 131 28E
Yamanokuchi Japan 63 B2 31 48N 130 52E
Yamasaki Japan 63 B2 35 03N 134 31E
Yambio Sudan 77 L2 4 34N 28 21E
Yambol Bulgaria 47 M5 42 28N 26 30E
Yamethin Myanmar 64 B8 20 24N 96 08E
Yamoussoukro Côte d'Ivoire 76 C3 6 50N 5 20W
Yamunanagar India 58 D6 30 07N 77 17E
Yancheng China 61 M4 33 23N 120 10E
Yangon Myanmar 64 B7 16 47N 96 10E
Yangquan China 61 K5 37 52N 113 29E
Yanji China 61 N6 42 52N 129 32E
Yanjing China 60 G3 29 01N 98 38E
Yantai China 61 M5 37 30N 121 22E
Yaoundé Cameroon 76 G2 3 51N 11 31E
Yarmouth Canada 85 X2 43 50N 66 08W
Yaroslavl' Russia 54 F8 57 34N 39 52E
Yarumal Col. 90 B15 6 59N 75 25W
Yatsushiro Japan 63 B2 32 32N 130 35E
Yawatahama Japan 63 B2 33 27N 132 24E
Yazd Iran 56 F5 31 54N 54 22E
Ye Myanmar 64 B7 15 15N 97 50E
Yekaterinburg Russia 54 J8 56 52N 60 35E
Yelets Russia 49 E5 52 35N 38 30E
Yellowknife Canada 84 N6 62 30N 114 29W
Yellow Sea China 61 M5 35 30N 122 30E
YEMEN REPUBLIC 56 D2/E2
Yenakiyeve Ukraine 49 E4 48 14N 38 15E
Yeniseysk Russia 55 M8 58 27N 92 13E
Yerevan Armenia 49 F3 40 10N 44 31E
Yeu Myanmar 59 H4 22 47N 95 26E
Yevpatoriya Ukraine 49 D4 45 12N 33 20E
Ye Xian China 61 L5 37 10N 119 55E
Yiannitsá Greece 47 K4 40 46N 22 24E
Yibin China 61 H3 28 42N 104 30E
Yichang China 61 K4 30 46N 111 20E
Yinchuan China 61 J5 38 30N 106 19E
Yingkou China 61 M6 40 40N 122 17E
Yining China 60 D6 43 50N 81 28E
Yirga Alem Ethiopia 77 N3 6 48N 38 22E
Yishun Singapore 65 S15/T15 1 25N 103 50E
Yiyang China 61 K3 28 39N 112 10E
Yoakum USA 87 G2 29 18N 97 20W
Yogyakarta Indonesia 64 E2 7 48S 110 24E
Yokadouma Cameroon 77 J2 3 26N 15 06E
Yokkaichi Japan 63 C2 34 58N 136 38E
Yokohama Japan 63 C3 35 27N 139 38E
Yokosuka Japan 63 C3 35 18N 139 38E
Yokote Japan 62 D3 39 20N 140 31E
Yonago Japan 63 B3 35 27N 133 20E
Yonezawa Japan 62 D3 37 56N 140 06E
Yŏngdŏk South Korea 63 A3 36 23N 129 23E
Yonghung North Korea 63 A3 39 31N 127 18E
York UK 40 F3 53 58N 1 05W
York USA 87 L4 39 57N 76 44W
York Factory tn. Canada 85 S5 57 08N 92 25W
Yorkton Canada 85 Q4 51 12N 102 29W
Yoshkar-Ola Russia 49 G6 56 38N 47 52E
Yosu South Korea 63 A2 34 50N 127 30E
Yotsukura Japan 62 D3 37 08N 141 00E
Youghal RoI 40 C2 51 51N 7 50W
Youngstown USA 87 K5 41 05N 80 40W
Ytterhogdal Sweden 48 D3 62 10N 14 16E
Yuba City USA 86 B4 39 09N 121 36W
Yuci China 61 K5 37 40N 112 44E
Yukon r. Canada/USA 84 D6 63 30N 159 40W
Yukon Territory territory Canada 84 H6/J6 64 15N 135 00W
Yuma USA 86 D3 32 40N 114 39W
Yumen China 60 G5 39 54N 97 43E
Yurimaguas Peru 90 B12 5 54S 76 07W
Yuzawa Japan 62 D3 39 11N 140 29E
Yuzhno-Sakhalinsk Russia 55 S6 46 58N 142 45E
Yverdon Switz. 44 C3 46 47N 6 38E
Yvetot Fr. 42 E5 49 37N 0 45E

Z
Zaanstad Neths 41 C5 52 27N 4 49E
Zabbar Malta 46 Q8 35 53N 14 32E
Zabol Iran 57 H5 31 00N 61 32E
Zabrze Poland 45 J5 50 18N 18 47E
Zacapa Guatemala 88 G3 15 00N 89 30W
Zacatecas Mexico 88 D4 22 48N 102 33W
Zacatecoluca El Salvador 88 G2 13 29N 88 51W
Zadar Croatia 46 F6 44 07N 15 14E
Zafra Sp. 43 B3 38 25N 6 25W
Zagań Poland 44 G5 51 37N 15 20E
Zagreb Croatia 44 F6 45 48N 15 58E
Zahedan Iran 57 H4 29 32N 60 54E
Zahlé Lebanon 56 C3 33 50N 35 55E
Zalău Romania 45 L3 47 10N 23 04E
Zambezi r. Zambia/Zimbabwe 78 D4 16 00S 23 00E
ZAMBIA 78 D5/E5
Zamboanga Philippines 65 G5 6 55N 122 05E
Zamora Sp. 43 C4 41 30N 5 45W
Zamość Poland 45 L5 50 43N 23 15E

Zanderij Suriname 90 F15 5 26N 55 14...
Zandvoort Neths 41 C5 52 22N 4 3...
Zanesville USA 87 K4 34 03N 82 02...
Zanjan Iran 56 E6 36 40N 48 3...
Zanthus Aust. 66 D4 31 01S 123 3...
Zanzibar Tanzania 79 F1 6 10S 39 1...
Zaozhuang China 61 L4 34 53N 117 3...
Zaporizhzhya Ukraine 49 E4 47 50N 35 1...
Zaragoza Sp. 43 E4 41 39N 0 54...
Zarand Iran 56 G5 30 50N 56 3...
Zaraza Venezuela 90 D15 9 20N 65 2...
Zaria Nigeria 76 F4 11 01N 7 4...
Zarqa Jordan 56 C5 32 04N 36 0...
Zaysan Kazakhstan 55 L6 47 30N 84 5...
Zduńska Wola Poland 45 J5 51 36N 18 5...
Zeebrugge Belgium 41 B4 51 20N 3 1...
Zeist Neths 41 D5 52 05N 5 1...
Zejtun Malta 46 Q8 35 51N 14 3...
Zell-am-See tn. Austria 44 F3 47 19N 12 4...
Zelzate Belgium 41 B4 51 12N 3 4...
Zenica Bosnia-Herzegovina 47 G6 44 11N 17 5...
Zermatt Switz. 44 C3 46 01N 7 4...
Zeven Germany 41 H6 53 18N 9 1...
Zevenaar Neths 41 E4 51 55N 6 0...
Zgierz Poland 45 J5 51 52N 19 2...
Zgorzelec Poland 44 G5 51 10N 15 0...
Zhambyl Kazakhstan 54 K5 42 50N 71 2...
Zhangjiakou China 61 K6 40 51N 114 8...
Zhangzhou China 61 L2 24 31N 117 4...
Zhanjiang China 61 K2 21 10N 110 2...
Zheleznogorsk Russia 49 E5 52 19N 35 2...
Zhengzhou China 61 K4 34 45N 113 3...
Zhenjiang China 61 L4 32 08N 119 3...
Zhezkazgan Kazakhstan 54 J6 47 44N 67 4...
Zhlobin Belarus 45 P6 52 50N 30 0...
Zhmerynka Ukraine 45 P4 49 00N 28 4...
Zhob Pakistan 58 B6 31 30N 69 3...
Zhoukou China 61 K4 33 35N 114 4...
Zhuzhou China 61 K3 27 53N 113 0...
Zhytomyr Ukraine 45 P5 50 18N 28 4...
Zibo China 61 L5 36 51N 118 0...
Zielona Góra Poland 45 G5 51 57N 15 3...
Zierikzee Neths 41 B4 51 38N 3 5...
Zigong China 61 H3 29 25N 104 4...
Ziguinchor Senegal 76 A4 12 35N 16 2...
Zilina Slovakia 45 J4 49 14N 18 4...
ZIMBABWE 78 E4/F4
Zinder Niger 76 F4 13 46N 8 5...
Ziqudukou China 60 G4 33 03N 95 5...
Zlatoust Russia 54 H8 55 10N 59 3...
Znojmo Czech Rep. 45 H4 48 52N 16 0...
Zoetermeer Neths 41 C5 52 03N 4...
Zolochev Ukraine 45 M4 49 49N 24...
Zomba Malawi 78 G4 15 22S 35 3...
Zonguldak Turkey 49 D3 41 26N 31...
Zouar Chad 77 J6 20 30N 16...
Zouérate Mauritania 76 B6 22 44N 12...
Zubova Polyana Russia 49 F5 54 05N 42...
Zug Switz. 44 D3 47 10N 8...
Zunyi China 61 J3 27 35N 106...
Zürich Switz. 44 D3 47 23N 8...
Zurrieq Malta 46 P8 35 50N 14...
Zutphen Neths 41 E5 52 08N 6...
Zvishavane Zimbabwe 78 F3 20 20S 30...
Zvolen Slovakia 45 J4 48 34N 19...
Zweibrücken Germany 41 F2 49 15N 7...
Zwickau Germany 44 F5 50 43N 12...
Zwijndrecht Neths 41 C4 51 49N 4...
Zwischenahn Germany 41 G6 53 12N 8...
Zwolle Neths 41 E5 52 31N 6...
Zyrardów Poland 45 K6 52 02N 20...
Zyryanovsk Kazakhstan 60 D7 49 46N 84...

Acknowledgements

The publishers would like to thank the following for permission to reproduce photographs:

Corbis, p.17; NASA, p.15, 31, 91; Oxford Scientific Films, p.16, 17; Science Photo Library, p.15, 16; Visual Insights, p.35.

Cover image:
Visible Earth / Rich Irish, Landsat 7 Tea... NASA GSFC; data provided by EROS Data Center. Globes / GEOATLAS.

The page design is by Adrian Smith

The publishers are grateful to Peter Sa... of University of Cambridge International Examinations for his helpful comments and advice during the development stage of this atlas.

The publishers would also like to thar... the many individuals, companies, societies, and institutions who gave assistance in the gathering of data.